CONSUMPTION AND EVERYDAY LIFE

Culture, Media and Identities

The Open University Course Team

Claire Alexander, Critical reader

Maggie Andrews, Tutor panel member, Study Guide author

Melanie Bayley, Editor

Veronica Beechey, Critical reader

Robert Bocock, Author

David Boswell, Critical reader

Peter Braham, Author

David Calderwood, Project controller

Elizabeth Chaplin, Tutor panel member, Study Guide author

Lene Connolly, Print buying controller

Jeremy Cooper, BBC producer

Margaret Dickens, Print buying co-ordinator

Jessica Evans, Critical reader

Martin Ferns, Editor

Paul du Gay, Book 1 Chair, Book 4 Chair, Author

Ruth Finnegan, Author

Stuart Hall, Course Chair, Book 2 Chair, Author

Peter Hamilton, Author

Jonathan Hunt, Copublishing advisor

Linda Janes, Course manager

Siân Lewis, Graphic designer

Hugh Mackay, Book 5 Chair, author

David Morley, Goldsmiths College, University of London, External assessor

Lesley Passey, Cover designer

Clive Pearson, Tutor panel member, Study Guide author

Peter Redman, Tutor panel member, Study Guide author

Graeme Salaman, Author

Paul Smith, Media librarian

Kenneth Thompson, Book 6 Chair, Author

Alison Tucker, BBC series producer

Pauline Turner, Course secretary

Kathryn Woodward, Book 3 Chair, Author

Chris Wooldridge, Editor

Consultant authors

Susan Benson, University of Cambridge

Paul Gilroy, Goldsmiths College, University of London

Christine Gledhill, Staffordshire University

Henrietta Lidchi, Museum of Mankind, London

Daniel Miller, University College, London

Shaun Moores, Queen Margaret College, Edinburgh

Keith Negus, University of Leicester

Sean Nixon, University of Essex

Bhikhu Parekh, University of Hull

Kevin Robins, University of Newcastle upon Tyne

Lynne Segal, Middlesex University

Chris Shilling, University of Portsmouth

Nigel Thrift, University of Bristol

John Tomlinson, Nottingham Trent University

This book is part of the *Culture, Media and Identities* series published by Sage in association with The Open University.

Doing Cultural Studies: The Story of the Sony Walkman by Paul du Gay, Stuart Hall, Linda Janes, Hugh Mackay and Keith Negus

Representation: Cultural Representations and Signifying Practices edited by Stuart Hall

Identity and Difference edited by Kathryn Woodward

Production of Culture/Cultures of Production edited by Paul du Gay

Consumption and Everyday Life edited by Hugh Mackay

Media and Cultural Regulation edited by Kenneth Thompson

The final form of the text is the joint responsibility of chapter authors, book editors and course team commentators.

The books are part of the Open University course D318 *Culture, Media and Identities*. Details of this and other Open University courses can be obtained from the Course Reservations and Sales Centre, PO Box 724, The Open University, Milton Keynes MK7 6ZS. For availability of other course components, including video- and audio-cassette materials, contact Open University Educational Enterprises Ltd, 12 Cofferidge Close, Stony Stratford, Milton Keynes MK11 1BY.

SAGE Publications
London ● Thousand Oaks ● New Delhi

in association with

The Open University

CONSUMPTION AND EVERYDAY LIFE

Edited by HUGH MACKAY

The Open University, Walton Hall, Milton Keynes MK7 6AA

© The Open University 1997

First published in 1997

The opinions expressed are not necessarily those of the Course Team or of The Open University.

SAGE Publications Ltd
6 Bonhill Street
London EC2A 4PU

SAGE Publications Inc.
2455 Teller Road
Thousand Oaks
California 91320

SAGE Publications India Pvt Ltd
32, M-Block Market
Greater Kailash - I
New Delhi 110 048

British Library Cataloguing in Publication data

A catalogue record for this book is available from The British Library.

ISBN 0 7619 5437 6 (cased)

ISBN 0 7619 5438 4 (pbk)

Library of Congress catalog card number 97–065515

Edited, designed and typeset by The Open University.

Printed in Great Britain by Bath Press Colourbooks, Glasgow

CONSUMPTION AND EVERYDAY LIFE

edited by Hugh Mackay

Introduction

Hugh Mackay

This volume is concerned with cultural consumption and the practices of everyday life. Our selection of 'consumption' as a term in the title of the book is a heuristic device for drawing together some interesting work which is characterized by its concern with everyday consumption practices; our focus is very much on how we appropriate and make sense of various cultural forms in our routines in everyday settings. The notion of the cultural circuit (see **du Gay, Hall et al.**, 1997*) is a way of identifying the variety of *loci* at which one can explore cultural processes.

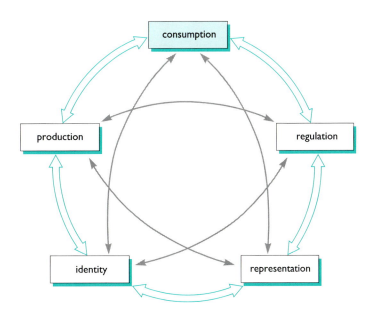

The circuit of culture

So cultural consumption can be conceived as a crucial moment of the cultural circuit. Quite explicitly, the notion of the circuit is *not* intended to suggest that consumption (or any other 'moment' of the circuit) is determined by production, by the economic 'base' – which some characterize as determining the cultural 'superstructure'. On the contrary, work in cultural studies has been at pains to draw out the interrelationships between the various moments, the processes of influence or feedback whereby the various components or stages of the circuit of culture are inextricably linked. Other accounts address cultural production (see **du Gay**, ed. 1997), and, although consistently pointing out the inextricable links between production and consumption, do not focus explicitly on the latter. In discussions of

*A reference in bold indicates another book, or another chapter in another book, in the series.

cultural production there is an *implied* consumer, but in this book our focus is on *active* consumers and their *local* practices, rather than the broader forces and processes by which globalization can be characterized. So, like **du Gay** (ed., 1997), we are concerned with the intersection of the global and the local, but here our focus is more on the practices of everyday life, on the 'local' side of the story.

So what exactly do we mean by consumption? In *The Oxford Dictionary* the term is defined in terms of 'using up; destruction; waste; amount consumed; wasting disease' – a pretty negative set of meanings, one of which refers specifically to the popular name of a disease (pulmonary phthisis). More relevant to our concerns, Raymond Williams tells us in *Keywords* (1988), with the onset of capitalism the word 'consumer' became used in the economic sense, commonly posited as the antithesis of 'producer'. In the twentieth century its usage has increased, with the advent of mass consumption, and as efforts to generate and manipulate markets have developed, with the growth of advertising and marketing. The everyday use of the term nowadays follows the economists' notion that 'consumption' is about 'use', an approach taken up by the consumer movement (and *Which?* magazine). This common-sense approach assumes that we consume what we need, to get something done. However, such a utilitarian approach (like the 'waste' definition) contrasts strongly with recent uses of the term 'consumption' in cultural studies. Here, the 'negative' meanings of 'wasting' or 'using up' have been replaced to a considerable degree by more positive associations. Consumption is seen as an active process and often celebrated as pleasure, and the consumer has even become elevated (by some on both the left and the right) to the status of citizen, the principal means whereby we participate in the polity. In postmodern accounts, cultural consumption is seen as being the very material out of which we construct our identities: we become what we consume.

In this book we shall be engaging with all of these various 'stratified deposits' which lie beneath contemporary meanings of the term. In this introduction, I shall first summarize briefly the key thinkers and schools in the sociology of consumption. I shall then introduce the chapters of the book, and explain how each in its distinctive way offers an approach and case study for understanding cultural consumption. Finally, I shall refer to six themes which are addressed in each of the chapters of this volume.

Within sociology until recently there was a dominant focus on production, with consumption, if addressed at all, accorded a secondary or determined status (Thorstein Veblen, discussed below, is perhaps the most notable exception to this generalization). Clearly, such an emphasis reflects popular conceptions: that consumption is somehow less important than, or subordinate to, the 'real' world of work – of industry, commerce and administration. Whilst work is seen as noble and productive, consumption and leisure are commonly conceived – in the Protestant tradition – as less worthy, frivolous, even wasteful, indulgent or decadent. In addition to a judgement of moral worth, there is a serious gender implication of this orthodoxy: the passivity of consumers is congruent with notions of the passivity of women, and the traditionally male world of work is privileged over the female domestic arena. In political terms, such thinking coincides with much of the rhetoric of both left and right about the centrality of production to generating wealth or income, or to determining the form of social organization.

The traditional view is demonstrated *par excellence* in the perspective often known as the 'mass culture critique', or 'the production of consumption perspective' (discussed in **du Gay, Hall et al.**, 1997). The Frankfurt School and their disciples, writing in the inter-war period, argued that the expansion of mass production in the twentieth century had led to the commodification of culture, with the rise of the culture industries (see **Negus**, 1997). Consumption served the interests of manufacturers seeking greater profits, and citizens became the passive victims of advertisers (see, for example, Packard, 1957). Processes of standardization, they argued, were accompanied by the development of a materialistic culture, in which commodities came to lack authenticity and instead merely met 'false' needs. These needs were generated by marketing and advertising strategies and, it is argued (for example by Hoggart, 1957), increased the capacity for ideological control or domination. In Europe, and in Britain in particular, there was the added notion of 'the spectre of Americanism' – the rather puritan notion of the swamping of authentic, varied, locally distinctive cultural forms and practices by degenerate, inauthentic, homogeneous, North American culture – an argument containing, commonly, a strong undercurrent of moral outrage about change and, especially, about conspicuous and excessive consumption. The rise of leisure and consumption activities increased the capacity for ideological control or domination, and detracted from more 'authentic' experience and from meeting human needs. The shift is often associated with a decline in collective activity and in the public sphere, and the growing privatization (in the home) of our daily lives (discussed in **du Gay, Hall et al.**, 1997, section 6.1). Crucially, this perspective attributed to consumers a profoundly passive role, portraying them as manipulated, mindless dupes, rather than as active and creative beings.

Broadly speaking, consumption today is *not* seen by social scientists as corrupting, nor are consumers seen as the passive victims of capitalism – although arguments about excessive and unnecessary consumption figure with increasing prominence in environmental discourse. In contrast with such traditional approaches to consumption, our focus in this book on consumption practices and everyday life accords to consumers a more important and *creative* role. Our concern is with how cultural texts or artefacts are used in everyday life. In this we are reflecting a crucial recent shift in sociology towards a concern with culture and with consumption – which, increasingly, is seen as worthy of study in its own right. Without it, there would *be* no production. Rather than a passive, secondary, determined activity, consumption (and its focus, the home) is seen increasingly as an activity with its own practices, tempo, significance and determination. Case studies (e.g. **du Gay, Hall et al.**, 1997) demonstrate the *active* role of consumers in shaping technological and cultural artefacts and their meanings; and, of course, they demonstrate the mutually constituted nature of production and consumption.

The sociological analysis of consumption can be traced back to the work of Marx. Marx's theory of capitalism provides a clear and detailed account of the interconnectedness of production and consumption, showing how production is for the market and for profit. But Marx actually writes extremely little about consumption, rooting his analysis of consciousness, or identity, in production and its social relations. The first sustained account of consumption – which in some ways laid the foundation for later work – is Veblen's (1989/1899) research on the conspicuous consumption of the *nouveau riche* in the late-nineteenth-century USA. In this he explores how goods are used as symbolic markers of social status, and how consumption is for the purpose of impressing others with one's good taste and ability to pay for more than most can afford. Veblen found that the *nouveau riche* displayed their status through conspicuous consumption of goods with little or no utility or function.

More recently, Bourdieu (1984) provides a more developed but similar argument (his work on distinction regarding the body (e.g. appearance and posture) is discussed in **Shilling**, 1997). Bourdieu rejects a narrowly economistic definition of social relations, seeing them as *cultural* as well as economic. In capitalist societies, he argues, cultural capital is distributed in such a way that social groups have different capacities to vest cultural value in symbolic goods. Symbolic goods function as signs, and are used to signify prestige, status and social standing. Culture is about the processes of identification and differentiation, with identities produced through practices of distinction: we distinguish ourselves by the taste distinctions we make – for example, between 'cultivated' and 'vulgar'. We bring our cultural capital, our taste, to bear on objects, and consumption involves the consumption of signs and symbols (of meanings) and works like a language in that it is rooted in a system of meaning. But more than such structuralism, Bourdieu points us towards the *active* nature of consumption practices.

Consumption is the articulation of a sense of identity. Our identity is made up by our consumption of goods – and their consumption and display constitutes our expression of taste. So display – to ourselves and to others – is largely for symbolic significance, indicating our membership of a particular culture. As Bourdieu puts it, taste classifies the classifier. Social subjects are classified by their classifications, and distinguish themselves by the distinctions they make, and thus class difference is constructed through consumption. What he calls the 'habitus' is the underlying structured system of classification which is learnt in childhood, and applied in later life – a framework for cultural propriety and personal identity. A habitus is a structured set of dispositions which provides a framework for our exercise of judgement and taste. So, although diverse and varied, consumption practices are socially structured. Thus Bourdieu extends a class analysis to the realm of consumption.

Several criticisms are commonly made of Bourdieu's work. First, he restricts his analysis to class, taking no account of other divisions, notably of gender, 'race', or generation. Secondly, whilst his analysis is rooted in consumption patterns, he ignores the diversity of uses and meanings of artefacts, the richness of everyday life. Thirdly, and crucially, he tends to treat social class as given. In the end, what he is doing is applying to consumption patterns a class analysis which is derived from the realm of production; in this sense he is – despite his focus on consumption – following the conventional wisdom, in which consumption is a largely secondary and determined activity. It is worth noting that, in the past decade or two, those involved in marketing have begun to categorize people by *lifestyle* rather than by class or income level. In their case study of the Sony Walkman, **du Gay, Hall et al.** (1997) show that, from the point of view of producers, consumers are best classified in other than conventional occupational or social class terms. Today, people's sense of identity is bound up with consumption as well as work roles, suggesting a perhaps even greater significance of consumption for contemporary culture than that argued by Bourdieu.

It is the postmodernists who take this line furthest. Broadly, these writers root their analysis in the notions that culture is becoming increasingly fragmented, and the symbolic is of increasing significance – such that any underlying substance is obliterated. Baudrillard (1988) completely rejects and overturns any ideas that consumption is about need, use or utility and that consumers are manipulated by advertisers. Whilst Bourdieu argues that we consume according to who we are, Baudrillard argues that we become what we buy: signs and signifying practices are what is consumed – even if we do not consume the product. Signs have no fixed referent: any object can, in principle, take on any meaning. Rather than representing some signifier, the sign is all that is left. We are left with society as pastiche, a play on signs with no reference beyond the commodity.

Such arguments are probably less fashionable today than in the recent past. Unsurprisingly, they have invoked a range of criticisms: there is little empirical support for the argument; research has often focused on 'youth', the lifestyle stage when experiment with identity is central; identity is less malleable and cannot be so easily changed simply by purchasing goods; and, although goods have a communicational or symbolic value, they also have a materiality.

Empirical, qualitative research on the everyday appropriation of cultural artefacts is precisely the focus of subculture theorists and others who have explored 'the pleasures of consumption'. Subculture theory emerged in the 1970s, largely from the Birmingham Centre for Contemporary Cultural Studies (see, for example, Hall and Jefferson, 1976), and can be seen as a reaction to the 'critique of mass culture' school outlined above.

Subsequently, others have explored the pleasures of consumption from other positions (e.g. see Radway, 1987). These researchers of cultural appropriation found that the reality of mass culture was far more creative than suggested by mass culture critics, and was a means whereby aspirations are expressed creatively. Rather than being passive and easily manipulated, they found that young consumers were active, creative and critical in their appropriation and transformation of material artefacts. In a process of *bricolage*, they appropriated, re-accented, rearticulated or trans-coded the material of mass culture to their own ends, through a range of everyday creative and symbolic practices. Through such processes of appropriation, identities are constructed. For subcultural theorists, these identities are generally born out of conflict with the dominant order. Such consumption writing differs from both Bourdieu's work and the 'critique of mass culture' in its qualitative approach: through ethnographic research methods, 'real' consumers in everyday settings were investigated. This work shows us the value of observational approaches to everyday life. But, more than that, it provides an explanation of the political significance of consumption. Rather than the politics of despair or at least compliance, subcultural theorists found protest and resistance against traditional and elitist cultural forms. Although far from radical, these informal practices constituted tactics of subversion and for 'getting by'.

A more extreme variant of this approach is the 'pleasures of consumption' thesis. Like subcultural work, and congruent with postmodernist approaches, this draws on the work of de Certeau (1984) to celebrate the creativity of consumer practices (e.g. Fiske, 1989a, 1989b). De Certeau is concerned with the production of meaning by consumers. Fiske and other proponents of the 'pleasures of consumption' approach see popular culture as a contested arena which involves a confluence of creative everyday practices and the products of the culture industries. They focus on the creative capacities of consumers, the empowering nature of consumption, and its subversive possibilities – drawing diametrically opposite conclusions from the pessimism of the 'mass culture critique' school.

Like subcultural theory, the 'pleasures of consumption' literature is criticized for its naïvety, romanticism or optimism regarding the significance of subcultural or consumer resistance; and for ignoring the vast numbers to whom shopping is *not* a pleasure. The freedoms and pleasures which are identified are perhaps more relevant to the Thatcherite 1980s than the present day, and are perhaps more applicable to the affluent. For many of us (as Miller argues in Chapter 1 of this book), shopping is an exercise involving thrift, the burden of choice, and something which takes up valuable time – rather than being a pleasure. Like subcultural theory, however, the approach is valuable for foregrounding everyday practices and ethnographic methods of enquiry.

Let us move on to the other term in the book title, 'everyday life'. I have explained that the theoretical approaches and case studies of the book focus our attention on the rich diversity of 'everyday life'. But what do we mean by 'everyday life'? Like 'consumption', it is a complex term and one used with varying meanings. As a starting-point, 'everyday life' can be seen as a concept which lies at the very heart of cultural studies, in that the term expresses the notion that we should conceive of culture, in an anthropological sense, as ordinary. 'Culture' refers to what we all do, what we all take part in – rather than being synonymous with 'high culture', the preserve of an elite. So a focus on 'everyday life' directs our attention to 'the ordinary' – our everyday processes of making meanings and making sense of the world. The focus – carried by the 'life' part of 'everyday life' – means that we are less concerned with the powerful and that which is recorded and codified, and more concerned with the unpredictable, the improvised and with the routine activities and control of ordinary people as they go about their day-to-day lives. I shall refer to three different ways in which the term 'everyday life' is used.

First, used in the anthropological sense, it refers to 'the everyday', the humdrum, the routine, even the drudgery – as distinct from Sunday, the weekend, or the festival. In this sense, it encompasses our taken-for-granted routines, that which we repeat daily – as distinct from the exceptional, or sacred, interludes in these.

Secondly, there is the approach which sees 'everyday life' as productive consumption (de Certeau, 1984). Such an approach sees consumers as almost endlessly creative in the appropriation and manipulation of consumer goods – the complete opposite of the 'mindless dupes', those controlled and manipulated by producers and the production system, discussed by the Frankfurt School and others. Through everyday practices, goods and services are transformed, and identities constituted. This is the approach which has been taken up by John Fiske (1989a, 1989b), referred to above. Consumption is not the *end* of a process, but the beginning of another, and thus itself a form of production (and hence we can refer to the 'work' of consumption).

Thirdly, there are approaches which posit 'everyday life' as the opposite of state bureaucracy and 'the system' (e.g. Gullestad, 1992). 'Everyday life' is characterized by small, local communities, with close and emotional ties, connectedness between people, caring, spontaneity, immediacy, participation and collaboration. So it is a focus which directs us away from the long arm of impersonal bureaucratic and market relations, the state, or other institutions of regulation. In this, of course, it has a spatial dimension, pointing us to the community and the home – very much the focus of this book.

These theoretical perspectives and concepts provide the backdrop for the six chapters of this book. All are concerned with how we read and analyse the ordinary, everyday, popular processes of cultural consumption.

In Chapter 1, Daniel Miller lays out some key elements of debates about consumption, exploring the rich, idiosyncratic and unpredictable nature of local consumption practices. Miller uses several case studies: council flat kitchens in London (the consumption of a state service and of kitchen interiors), soap opera in Trinidad (the consumption of US television broadcasting in another context), soft drinks in Trinidad, and shopping in London. Through these he argues, first, that consumption is not just of utilitarian goods, but is about the construction of identity. Secondly, he argues that culture itself is constructed through the creative 'work' of appropriation, of transforming, customizing and investing meaning in goods as they are domesticated and consumed. The local production of global products and cultural forms demonstrates the continuing salience of the local. Finally, he examines the links between local consumption and the global (production) economy, explaining how places today are interconnected rather than bounded. In this account he rejects completely the notion that it is manufacturers who construct demand and consumers who are duped; on the contrary, he argues that it is retailers and consumers who control the process. His focus on the global interrelations of consumption is an altogether different focus from the 'pleasures of consumption' – which, anyway, he found a far cry from the reality of the 'work' of shopping. An anthropologist, Miller provides rich ethnographic data in relation to each case study – providing an account different from so much of the research on shopping and shopping malls (e.g. Gardner and Sheppard, 1989).

In Chapter 2, Ruth Finnegan outlines and evaluates a complementary perspective and method for understanding local, everyday practices, introducing work on personal narratives and identity. Her focus is on the significance of 'the ordinary' or 'the everyday' in contemporary culture. Personal narratives, she argues, whilst richly idiosyncratic, unpredictable and diverse, are not arbitrary but deeply cultural, in that they are structured in terms of certain conventions, with common themes of time, place and control. Finnegan argues that an autobiography, rather than simply being the sum of events which happen to someone, is a narrative which is used to make sense of life and to construct an identity. Finnegan, like Miller an anthropologist, is concerned to stress the creative and individual nature of personal narratives; she points out the disjunctures between her preference in this respect and approaches in cultural studies which, she argues, are more concerned with the constraints on us as individual actors.

In Chapter 3, Finnegan presents a case study of one particular popular cultural practice. Drawing on Howard Becker's interactionist work on 'art worlds', and on performance-oriented approaches, she stresses the creativity of the full range of local music-making practices in a British new town. Again, Finnegan is concerned with the *active* nature of musical consumption 'work'; and her approach can be seen as that of an anthropologist engaging with some key concerns which are addressed by work in cultural studies on consumption – with a concern with 'art' and 'ritual enactment' rather than more directly with such notions as 'power'. The chapter is interesting for its focus on performance rather than what Finnegan presents as more conventional textual approaches. By focusing on music we are extending our definitions of the media, and by focusing on performance we see that consumption is an *active* practice, not something governed or determined by the strategies of producers. In drawing out the links between production and consumption Finnegan identifies both the creative, active and collaborative work of music producers (who are at the same time consumers of others' music and of cultural, musical conventions) and of music audiences (who 'work' with musicians to 'produce' musical events). Thus, again, we have a case study of the links between production and consumption; and, following the work of subcultural approaches, a concern with the *active* nature of music-making. At the same time, Finnegan avoids using the term 'consumption', arguing that, for her, it carries connotations of passivity and determination.

In Chapter 4, Nigel Thrift explores the significance of place for identity. Our sense of place is not fixed, but is historically specific, culturally constructed and contested. Place is not just location, but is something which is crucial to our identity. A cultural geographer, Thrift argues that places are important, they are becoming commodified, and their meanings are contested. He opens by presenting two arguments about place: that it is fundamentally unchanging; and that its mediation (by the media) means the end of difference. In contrast with these explanations, Thrift is concerned to lay out a 'middle way': as places become media-ted some things are lost, but other things are gained – we have new possibilities for reaching out to others, and for redefining our place. So his argument is for a 'progressive sense of place'. Through a case study of the Sami, Thrift explores ways in which Eurocentric accounts have 'othered' places; in this, he explores notions of 'imagined communities', narratives of the loss of the wild and remote and of exploration and progress, and time–space convergence. Thrift's 'middle way' examines how the Sami are living and telling new stories, through their deployment of new transport and communication technologies, and thus are producing a new sense of place, belonging and identity.

In Chapter 5, Shaun Moores is concerned with the domestic consumption of broadcasting. This is an important instance of the point where symbolic goods encounter the everyday world of life in households. Like other chapters, Moores' examines the inextricable links between production and consumption – between broadcasting as an institution of cultural production and as an institution of everyday life. Regarding the former he explores the industry's orientation to its viewing and listening publics, and, in particular, its communicative styles and modes of address. At the other end he is concerned with the significance of reception – the situated meanings and pleasures which are generated by consumers; this involves consideration of the social relations of power which operate in domestic contexts. We are presented with an analysis which rejects simple notions that meanings are transmitted and passively received. Rather, they are *negotiated*, by *active* audiences, and thus are embedded in a local context. Finally – again like other chapters – he examines the articulation of local cultures and processes of globalization: television and radio link viewers and listeners with distant events; they transform our everyday sense of self and identity; and they are central to social arrangements of time and space, to processes of *time–space compression* or *distanciation*.

In Chapter 6, Hugh Mackay explores domestic information and communication technologies (ICTs) as an example of cultural consumption. Like other chapters, this account of consumption is firmly rooted in an analysis which links consumption with production. In this case, the 'social shaping of technology' is explored – how technology can be understood as a 'text', encoded in its design and decoded in its appropriation. Mackay explores how technologies, like other artefacts, are not merely material or utilitarian, but also symbolic. Rather than being determined by designers and manufacturers and then purchased for what they can do, their meaning, and also their form and function, are shaped by consumers. Applying arguments similar to those of Moores (in Chapter 5), Mackay examines how ICTs are used and made sense of in everyday life. In capturing time and space as they enter the home, new technologies engage with the politics of the households, with gender and family relations. In the process of domestication the technology itself is transformed. Clearly this is an argument for a profoundly active view of the consumer. Mackay concludes by discussing some of the implications for senses of community in the contemporary era. The introduction of ICTs is accompanied by new institutions and regimes of regulation, and this leads in to the theme of the next and final volume of this series, cultural regulation.

In this book we deal with a wide variety of forms of consumption. Each, in its own way, draws on or refers to six themes:

- the balance between creativity and constraint
- the interrelationship between consumption and production
- the situated character of everyday practices
- the broad range of consumption practices
- the value of qualitative, observational and ethnographic research methods
- the spatial dimension of consumption.

First, the volume draws on the theme of *the balance between creativity and constraint* in everyday, local routines and practices. The argument of each chapter is that we are not the passive victims portrayed by the 'critique of mass culture' school; nor are we the liberated consumers discussed by the worst excesses of the 'pleasures of consumption' approach. Somewhere between – and this is the main theme of this book – we find creative, active individuals, working with a range of materials, and, through a range of consumption practices, constructing and making sense of everyday life. You will find that the various chapter authors take different positions on the balance between creativity and constraint, reflecting both their theoretical predilections and the particular consumption processes and practices with which they are concerned. Finnegan's chapters are notable for her preference to emphasize creativity rather than constraint. That there is a huge diversity of possible consumption behaviour is unsurprising given the infinite cultural contexts of consumption 'work'. At the same time, access to material and symbolic resources is patterned, and the chapters identify the various dimensions of these patterns.

Secondly, each chapter acknowledges *the interrelationship of consumption and production*. So our focus on consumption far from precludes giving attention to the two-way links between consumers and producers. We are concerned with the constraints of production processes on consumption practices; but also on how production is informed by the creative 'work' of consumption in everyday life. Given the emphasis on the *active* nature of consumption, chapter authors conceive of consumption as a productive activity, rendering the very terminology of the distinction irrelevant.

Thirdly, our interest in how things are appropriated and transformed by use in everyday life draws our attention to the contexts of consumption, *the situated character of everyday practices*. But, more than that, this involves a focus on the private–public boundary. Each chapter, in its own way, looks at the relationship between the outside world and the private sphere, and is concerned with explaining the mediation of that boundary. Consumption, we find, is crucial to understanding how this boundary operates.

Fourthly, we are working with a broad definition of 'consumption', and address a diversity of areas of consumption and *a broad range of consumption practices*. Crucially, *contra* the 'pleasures of consumption' approach and postmodern work which tends to conflate postmodernism with the consumer society, we are concerned not just (indeed, very little) with shopping – which is the focus of other books (e.g. Gardner and Sheppard, 1989).

Fifthly, our case studies demonstrate *the value of qualitative, observational and ethnographic research methods*. This is because we are interested in *everyday life*, and are concerned with actors' *meanings* – in relation to taste, texts, artefacts and uses. Some of these qualitative methods are discussed in the chapters below; more generally, qualitative data are cited in support of arguments which are presented. So in this book we are dealing with an approach to the study of culture which complements other approaches, such as textual analysis (see **Hall**, ed., 1997).

Finally, a focus on everyday lives and on ethnographic studies points us to the *spatial dimension of consumption:* consumption takes place in space. We have said that a focus on consumption shifts the focus of attention from work to the domestic. In focusing on the domain of the domestic, we must be clear that this is not simply about processes and practices of isolation or individualization. On the contrary, consumption shapes spatial patterns and binds places together; and the rise of mass consumption can be seen as linked to a changing sense of place. Places and communities – commonly seen as largely bounded until the 1960s or 1970s (see Bell and Newby, 1971)

– are now seen as bound together more than ever before, in global interdependency, and as entities to which symbolic meanings are given. Each chapter has a particular concern with place, and with the local articulation of global cultural processes.

References

BAUDRILLARD, J. (1988) *Jean Baudrillard: selected writings* (ed. Poster, M), Cambridge, Polity Press.

BELL, C. and NEWBY, H. (1971) *Community Studies*, London, Allen and Unwin.

BOURDIEU, P. (1984) *Distinction*, London, Routledge & Kegan Paul.

DE CERTEAU, M. (1984) *The Practice of Everyday Life*, Berkeley, CA, University of California Press.

DU GAY, P. (ed.) (1997) *Production of Culture/Cultures of Production*, London, Sage/The Open University (Book 4 in this series).

DU GAY, P., HALL, S., JANES, L., MACKAY, H. and NEGUS, K. (1997) *Doing Cultural Studies: the story of the Sony Walkman*, London, Sage/The Open University (Book 1 in this series).

FISKE, J. (1989a) *Understanding Popular Culture*, Boston, MA, Unwin Hyman.

FISKE, J. (1989b) *Reading the Popular*, Boston, MA, Unwin Hyman.

GARDNER, C. and SHEPPARD, J. (1989) *Consuming Passions: the rise of retail culture*, London, Unwin Hyman.

GULLESTAD, M. (1992) *The Art of Social Relations*, Oslo, Scandinavian University Press.

HALL, S. (ed.) (1997) *Representation: cultural representations and signifying practices*, London, Sage/The Open University (Book 2 in this series).

HALL, S. and JEFFERSON, T. (1976) *Resistance Through Rituals: youth subcultures in post-war Britain*, London, Hutchinson.

HOGGART, R. (1957) *The Uses of Literacy*, Harmondsworth, Penguin.

NEGUS, K. (1997) 'The production of culture' in du Gay, P. (ed.) *Production of Culture/Cultures of Production*, London, Sage/The Open University (Book 4 in this series).

PACKARD, V. (1957) *The Hidden Persuaders*, London, Longmans, Green & Co.

RADWAY, J. (1987) *Reading the Romance: women, patriarchy and popular literature*, London, Verso.

SHILLING, C. (1997) 'The body and difference' in Woodward, K. (ed.) *Identity and Difference*, London, Sage/The Open University (Book 3 in this series).

VEBLEN, T. (1989) *The Theory of the Leisure Class*, New York, Macmillan (first published 1899).

WILLIAMS, R. (1988) *Keywords: a vocabulary of culture and society*, London, Fontana.

CONSUMPTION AND ITS CONSEQUENCES

Daniel Miller

Contents

1   Observations over a cup of tea

'Would you like to come into the kitchen and have a cup of tea, the kettle's just boiled?' It would be difficult to research domestic consumption in London if you weren't fond of tea. This was particularly true for a study which I carried out that was concerned with the kitchen itself (Miller, 1988). The setting was forty flats within a council estate in North London. As with most council estates, the interiors of each flat had been identical to all the other flats when they had been handed over to the tenants some 12–14 years previously. The kitchens had had the same black and white squares of lino on the floor, the same fitted cupboards, the same rather cramped but serviceable facilities. But now, sipping tea in one kitchen after another, it was evident that in many cases a great deal had changed. There was a limit to quite how nosy I could be, but in each case the kitchen was photographed so that the changes could be observed at leisure and then discussed.

To choose to examine changes in council-flat kitchens is itself to challenge the way we think about **consumption**. The term consumption evokes above all the idea of shopping for goods. Here, by contrast, instead of shopping, people are consuming facilities which are provided by the state. Furthermore, these are not immediately consumed but represent long-term changes over more than a decade. Yet, clearly, both the use and changing of these kitchens could be regarded as consumption. By looking at so many kitchens it was also evident that consumption can represent a considerable degree of work. Most households strive to make a 'home' out of their flat – that is, to create something that they may relate to as specifically their own. This is a process that may take many years of gradual transformation.

consumption

To describe this gradual making of one's home, we can use the term '**to appropriate**'. The term suggests that tenants have to work to achieve this goal and do not feel at home simply by living in a property. This was evident in the tenants' own sense of distance from the place they lived in. The research took place at a time when the British government was encouraging the selling-off of council properties. As such there was plenty to support the already clear feeling of many tenants that they were socially stigmatized by their lack of owned property. This need not have been the case. There are other countries, such as Sweden, where tenants do not feel in the slightest degree stigmatized simply by virtue of their housing tenure. There are also many countries where the upper classes traditionally rent rather than own property. This was once the case in Britain, but over this century a particular and local history has resulted in what the tenants saw as a problem in their being council tenants. This feeling is also the legacy of several decades during which tenants were highly restricted in the changes they were allowed to make to their flats, especially the exterior of the flats. This led to a constant sense of powerlessness. One of the first things people who purchased their properties tended to do was to change the exterior precisely to make the point that they were now allowed to make such changes. The

appropriation

FIGURE 1.1   A largely unaltered council kitchen.

FIGURE 1.2   A replacement fitted kitchen purchased by the tenant.

result of all this was that in most cases tenants talked to me about their kitchen fitments as 'council' fitments, representing a kind of alien presence, against which tenants constantly reiterated their complaints.

From this common starting-point, however, the years had created some considerable differences. At one extreme there were those kitchens which looked almost the same as when they had originally been occupied, with the same lino, and the cupboards repainted their original black and white (see Figure 1.1). At the opposite extreme were those which had been radically transformed. Indeed, in a couple of instances the whole interior had been thrown out and a new fitted kitchen purchased (see Figure 1.2), even though the tenants had no intention of buying their flats – in what was not a particularly desirable estate. In others, the fronts of the kitchen units had been taken off and replaced with elaborate wooden ones. In one case, fake aged oak beams had been put along the ceiling and around a low-level cupboard which had been opened up, to give the whole kitchen the aura of a medieval hearth.

After visiting many flats, some patterns seemed to emerge which could be related to what was known about the households concerned. Even kitchens that were relatively unchanged needed explanation, since over a decade they had required considerable repainting and repair, which therefore constituted

FIGURE 1.3
A kitchen aesthetic created with matching decorations.

FIGURE 1.4
A kitchen whose ornaments reflect gifts and memories.

an active decision to remain with the original scheme and not to change it. The one factor that could be largely ruled out was resources. With the exception of the replacement fitted kitchens, the costs involved in changing the kitchens spread over this period were very small, and the degree of change did not relate to household income. Nor, despite the comments of the tenants to the contrary, could these be seen as functional improvements, since the main constraints upon the kitchens were structural and the main changes were decorative.

The changes made in the kitchens appeared to correspond to a number of distinct categories. Most were neither unaltered nor radically transformed or replaced. More common were those where the basic kitchen remained but various decorative changes had taken place. Sometimes this resulted in a clear kitchen aesthetic where each object had been chosen to match the others within the space (e.g. see Figure 1.3 – a colour picture would have revealed that all the plastic items were red). Thus, if the kitchen cupboards had been painted blue, then the wallpaper had been chosen to match and the plastic drainer in the sink was also likely to be blue. In stark

contrast, there were kitchens in which the objects displayed made no sense as a unified aesthetic. Instead, they found their unity in the memories of the householder who knew that this mug was a souvenir from a seaside holiday while that wall clock was a gift from a niece, and so forth (see Figure 1.4). Often these differences corresponded to the circumstance of the woman who used the kitchen. In general, constellations of memories were more likely to be found amongst the elderly. A bright 'designed' kitchen was common amongst a group of housewives, one of whom described herself as a 'kitchen bird', who enjoyed having the company of other housewives and chatting in the kitchen.

Although I noted a number of different factors, the single most important factor quite unexpectedly turned out to be gender. In general, the transformation of kitchens was regarded as a positive move that changed the relationship from one of alienation from 'council things' to one of a sense of belonging within a home created from one's own labour. But many had failed to make this change. The most common failure came from men living on their own, or women who as housewives felt that their domestic labour was unsupported or unrecognized by the males of the household. One often felt that the more depressed the householder, the less the changes that had taken place.

In listening to stories about how transformations had occurred, a common theme arose. In many cases the changes were in the form of a gift or exchange between the woman who mostly used the kitchen and either her husband or her son. Behind this lay a clear and explicit division of labour between the sexes. There was very little evidence that the ideas associated with feminism had taken hold on this estate. Rather, there was a powerful sense that each gender retained specific differences in abilities and concerns. The kitchen was unambiguously a female domain, with most females expressing considerable pleasure at any presence of males in *their* kitchen. Women were expected to have an interest in and knowledge of the aesthetics of the home, such that they might read magazines which discussed interior decoration and opinions about what style of object should fit which position in a room.

Men, by contrast, were associated with manual labour. Traditionally, this has been labour performed outside the home, but in the last two decades there has been a considerable rise in the use of DIY, a form of manual labour devoted to the home itself, which relates to the increased amount of time spent by males in the home. This is a result partly of a decline in employment, partly of a shorter working week, and partly of a decline in public sociality – for example, a decline in pub culture. In a study in south London (Gershuny, 1982), it has been shown that, of all objects in the home, it was the use of the power drill which exhibited the strictest gender segregation.

Given this degree of gender difference, the transformation of the kitchen depended upon an exchange between the two. Women might have strong ideas of how the kitchen should look, but eschewed the use of the tools and

FIGURE 1.5   A DIY kitchen.

instruments for making the physical transformation. Men were interested in making the changes but did not wish to know about, or express themselves through, aesthetic choices. Indeed, the one or two kitchens that had been changed by men on their own were quite distinct. They looked like DIY kitchens, with a hotchpotch of doors, hinges and contraptions that clearly marked a form of labour unsubjected to any aesthetic concern (see Figure 1.5). Similarly, the kitchens that were virtually unchanged from their original state tended to be occupied by single men. In many cases this notion of a gift was quite explicit. A husband or son might offer to 'do up' the kitchen for their wife or mother for a birthday, anniversary or some other gift occasion. They would expect to be informed as to how she wanted the kitchen to be, and they would undertake the work. The detailed decorative elements, such as ornaments and kitchen objects, would then gradually be added to by the women themselves (for further details, see Miller, 1988).

READING A

You should now read Reading A, 'The home as an expressive statement', by the Norwegian anthropologist Marianne Gullestad, which you will find at the end of this chapter. This is a brief description of home-making amongst working-class families in Bergen, Norway. Think about the following questions while you are reading this extract:

1   What are the similarities and differences between British and Norwegian attitudes to home decoration?

2   How might the values expressed in home decoration be related to the social identities of the occupants in terms of gender, class and family structure?

3   What are you, your friends or your relations trying to say by the way in which your home is decorated and objects for it collected and arranged?

In reading Gullestad's work, you are being confronted with evidence that decorating your house is not just a particular individualistic act that expresses your own taste. At another level, an observer can make many generalizations about the kinds of concern that a particular group of people are likely to have when engaged in this task. By contrasting ourselves with the Norwegians, we become ourselves generalized. It will be evident that there are some similarities between the British and the Norwegian concern to make homes personal in contrast with the impersonality of the state. But there are also many differences that relate to the specific concerns of the people of each area. For example, these Norwegians show a stronger concern with sameness of home decoration that relates to dominant representations of Norwegian society as in key ways egalitarian: Norwegians commonly represent their society as amongst the most equal in the world. Within this general difference between Britain and Norway there are countless smaller differences which relate to the particular values which groups wish to express based on class, age, household type and simply individual character or concern.

1.1   The aims of this chapter

This chapter has begun in the private space of people's homes and will end there too – since in many ways it is domestic consumption that has become the pivotal arena of modern life. It provides the foundation for the three main aims of this chapter:

• To change how you think about consumption from being merely the act of buying goods to being a fundamental process by which we create identity.

• To demonstrate that consumption can be a means for creating authentic culture. Our dominant model of culture is one based on the creative artist. A work of art is authentic because it is created by an artist. But in modern society we live almost entirely through goods which we do not make, so that our relationship to such goods is secondary. Does this mean that we have a more superficial or inauthentic relationship to culture? I will argue that consumption is also an act of work through which we create our cultural identity (as is shown in the case study of the Sony Walkman in **du Gay, Hall et al.**, 1997), though that work may be based on choice or forms of appropriation rather than manual labour. This may be as true of nations having to create identity out of imported goods as it is of individuals working with purchased goods.

- To show that our domestic consumption cannot be separated from its consequences for the global economy. By the end of the chapter, I will show that the local consumption of culture has some severe and often destructive consequences for global production, since the goods we try to appropriate are still often the result of the exploitation of the labour of people in other lands. This is a part of a broader aim to examine the inextricable links between production and consumption (see **du Gay**, ed., 1997, especially Chapter 1 by Robins).

Finally, there is a subsidiary aim of this chapter, which is to draw you into a consideration of your own acts of consumption so that you examine the degree to which you exemplify the general points that are being made.

In this chapter, I am addressing a fundamental shift in modern life. A century ago most people saw production as the place in which our identity is rooted – as workers or owners. Two decades ago there was a struggle over identity forged in relation to the means of distribution – whether we identified with state socialism or the free market. Today, however, there is an increasing realization that the key domain is neither production nor distribution, but consumption, because that is the one arena where most of us still feel we have some power left to influence whom we might become. This makes the domestic arena, the main site of consumption, of considerable importance.

Home is where most people in Britain spend most of their time, as time spent in work and alternative social arenas such as the pub has declined. The household remains our primary concern for much of our lives. But consumption, as a process of identity formation, has further consequences, which may make it a key locus of power in the contemporary world. To make that argument we will have to leave the home and look at consumption within a much broader spectrum: first, travelling upwards to areas where nations and not just households make themselves through this process of appropriation; then moving to even broader arenas where key economic institutions – which can truly be called 'global' – structure the relationship between countries, before plunging back down to everyday domestic shopping.

ACTIVITY 1

Before leaving the topic of home, consider a room within your own home. Different people are likely to use home decoration to fulfil different concerns. If you are a younger member of a household, for example, you might concentrate upon your bedroom. Do you use this to assert your separation from family control? Are there systematic differences between this room and other rooms in the house? Why does tidying so often become a key area of contention between parents and children? If, by contrast, you are a more senior member of a household, you might consider your chosen room in a less isolated way, seeing it more as part of a broader household project of taste. Where do you choose to place your books and music? Are the titles conspicuous? What kind of 'atmosphere' do you wish to express? Do you ever have fantasies about who might see these furnishings and the comments they might pass? Do you feel they express better the way you see yourself at present, or your aspirations for the future? You may emphasize relationships that are established in gifts. Examine your ornaments and wall decorations for the particular room you have chosen. How have they come to be where they are? Did this involve any 'negotiations' between different members of a household? What has been the role of DIY in family relations? Do different rooms express similar facets of family life, or perhaps complementary or even opposed sets of values?

2   The dominant model of modern life

Before launching ourselves into the broader arena of consumption, we need to consider the generalizations that are commonly made about the relationship between persons and objects and about consumption in our society. There exists a model of modern life, commonly expressed both by academics and in everyday conversation, which views the present time as a kind of fall from grace when compared with the past. According to this view, humanity once lived in real communities, in which the individual was subservient to group norms and religious sanctions. The primary mechanism for the classification of people was kinship, and people acted mainly according to the normative expectations of, say, a mother's brother or a sister's son. They formed particular and local communities which were gradually swamped by larger forces that tore up their roots and replaced them, first with class, and then with forces, such as the state, that increasingly favoured homogenized and global institutions to which each individual related as an independent unit. There are many forces which are credited with destroying these earlier forms of community. Most of the major founding figures of the social sciences, such as Marx, Weber, Durkheim and Simmel, made a contribution to this model of modern life, partly through providing their respective candidates as to what produced this 'fall'. These included the rise of capitalism, state bureaucracy, nationalism, secularization, or the abstract and quantitative view of the world objectified in money.

One of the main disciplines that contributed to this image of lost community was anthropology. It has often been held that contemporary non-industrial societies are in some ways equivalents of the historical if not social evolutionary origins of present industrial societies. Within anthropology, this distinction between modern and traditional communities is probably most fully developed in the opposition between **the gift** and **the commodity**. The origin of the anthropological use of this distinction lies in the book *The Gift* (1970), by Marcel Mauss, first published in France in 1925. In brief, he argued that in primitive societies the gift is an object given which imposes upon its recipient an obligation to give something in return. In some societies the obligation to reciprocate was seen as a spiritual force inherent in the gift. Mauss interprets this belief by explaining that, when one gives a gift, one in effect gives something of oneself. Since this human aspect is inalienable (i.e. something that cannot really be given away), it becomes the force which necessitates a return. This often sets up a continual cycle of exchange between individuals, or more often between societies, in which at any given time one side is in debt to the other. It might thus be seen as the basic bond from which social life could be developed securely.

the gift and the commodity

By contrast, when an individual buys a commodity in a shop there is no similar implication. The identity of the shopkeeper is of no concern to the buyer, nor the buyer to the shopkeeper (see Gregory, 1982, for the theory of the gift–commodity distinction; and Carrier, 1994, for a history of commodity development). Commodities do not involve the construction of social relations. It is therefore much easier to develop individual freedoms within commodity-based societies, but at the expense of the breakdown of social relations. In addition, Simmel argued that the rise of abstract exchange symbolized by money and the quantitative rise of commodities destroyed the particularity of persons and communities. In this century, terms such as 'Americanization' and 'globalization' are seen as having gone still further in the direction of forcing the end of specific communities.

This focus upon the commodity has culminated in a flood of recent writings – associated with influential authors such as Baudrillard and Jameson – which proclaim in a variety of different forms the death of society and community and of any real sense of attachment either between people or between people and things. Indeed, one of the most common arguments is that, in this modern materialistic and capitalist world, an orientation towards objects has so replaced an orientation towards persons that, instead of objects symbolizing people, we have now become merely 'lifestyles' – that is, the passive carriers of meanings which are created for us in capitalist business. In most of these models, consumption appears as merely a continuation of the forces of capitalism and bureaucracy which destroy local difference in the name of global homogeneity, or, more recently, foster a diversity which sells goods but has no real depth or contribution to make to cultural development (for a summary of such views, see Featherstone, 1991; for a critique, see Miller, 1987, pp. 163–77).

Evidently, then, the relationship between people and things occupies a central place in the story of how modern society fell from true community. For example, Karl Marx saw the issue of fetishism, where workers could not recognize their own labour objectified in the commodities they produced, as a core mechanism which sustained the social relations of capitalism. The problem with many of the more recent versions of these critiques is that they have very much the same faults as they imply for modern society generally. They are vastly abstract generalities about the modern 'global' world, and they rarely return to the kinds of population they are supposed to be about in order to see whether these descriptions really apply. In this chapter, we shall examine two regions, London and Trinidad, each of which is an ideal case study for this model of modern life, and we shall show just how much is missing from the grand theoretical schemes that have been proposed to account for modern consumption.

The first main site will be some streets in North London. This highly urbanized environment, which includes large council estates and a mass of suburban housing, seems to fit most people's image of the de-socialized urban world. The second main site, the island of Trinidad (within the nation of Trinidad and Tobago), fits the image of modernity for a slightly different reason. With the destruction of the original population, Trinidad was repopulated largely with slaves from Africa, and then indentured labourers mainly from South Asia, but also from China, Madeira and elsewhere, to produce a hotchpotch of people systematically torn from their original societies and thrown together. In a sense then, if the model of the end of community and the death of society should apply anywhere, these two regions should fit the bill.

I will not argue that dominant theories of modernity are completely wrong, nor deny that secularization, the rise of new media and communications, and shifts in family life have occurred. Rather, I want to argue that the populations of these regions are themselves just as concerned as are academics with the negative consequences of such changes. We cannot assume that their consumption of goods is merely an expression of capitalism or the state, or that these are the forces which create and distribute these goods. Indeed, consumption often represents people's attempt to negate these larger forces. On the other hand, consumption is rarely simply either a struggle or some pure act of resistance against a sense or experience of oppression. As we shall see, in our complex and contradictory world it is often the actions we intend as liberating ourselves that come back as consequences which we find oppressive. We need to go beyond any simple attempt to characterize consumption as 'good' or 'evil' within some grand myth about modernity. Instead, we need to return to the detailed understanding of what consumption actually does and to recognize that its consequences may be very far from those intended by the groups and forces involved.

How does the example of kitchens in North London relate to these grand theories about the consumer society? According to those who condemn consumption as an expression of a materialist obsession with goods, it is assumed that there is an opposition between a concern with social relations and with material goods. In the kitchen study, exactly the opposite conclusion arose. Doing up the kitchen was not the work of isolated housewives who had lost their social contacts. Such housewives were much more likely to be living in kitchens they disliked and yet felt unable to change. It was those who were socially most involved and supported by families and friends who had the confidence and support to transform their environment and to create their own aesthetic.

Instead of a simple opposition between a 'commodity' society and a 'gift' society, we find something rather more complex. Curiously, what was found in North London is very similar to the concept of gender which has recently been proposed for societies in New Guinea, the region which provided the key models for anthropological studies of gift exchange. Recent work in New Guinea has reflected upon debates deriving from feminist concerns in Europe. For example, there was a new emphasis upon what women exchanged and a debate about whether their work to produce fat pigs used by men in exchange was a form of exploitation. Marilyn Strathern, an anthropologist, in a book called *The Gender of the Gift* (1988), has challenged all these debates as imposing concepts of gender developed in Europe upon a region which has a different way of conceptualizing such things. Instead of starting with two different genders and then focusing upon what work they do, Strathern notes that gender is simply one of many expressions of cultural difference, and we have to see how differences are created and sustained. She argues that at different stages people are seen as more or less gendered, and sometimes it is aspects of the person, rather than the person as a whole, that are gendered. Above all, people are separated as different in order to create the basis for exchange through which social relations are constituted.

I have already noted, in reviewing the study of kitchens in North London, that there were several instances of males explicitly changing the kitchen as a direct 'gift' to a wife or mother, as a birthday or anniversary present. If we follow the theories of gender that derive from these studies of New Guinea, we should not simply see this as something that 'men' or 'women' do. Strathern (1988) has argued that in New Guinea it is better to see gender itself as a dynamic sense of difference applied in a variety of ways to people and things. If we apply this to the British case, it is reasonable to suppose that the core definition of male labour and female domesticity, established in the nineteenth century and re-established after the Second World War in the 1950s, was under threat from the changes in employment – a decline in male work and an increase in female, part-time work. The reduction of gender inequalities and of other differences between the genders has been welcomed by feminists. There remained, however, large sections of the population that instead sought new modes by which gender differences could be reconstructed. In this case, the rise of DIY was not simply a function of economic considerations but rather a way of creating a specifically male regime within the home, resulting from a decline in time spent at work or in pubs. Through such changes, gender definitions have both remained consistent with longer-term structures of difference and yet shown their dynamic ability to change to reflect changing conditions. DIY does shift a little the way we evoke images of maleness and of femininity. Thus, in research on shopping in North London (discussed at greater length in section 7 of this chapter), it was often found that women would remark forcefully about their partners' lack of interest in or intolerance towards shopping, but then add as an aside that they did, however, like browsing in DIY stores.

I am not trying to suggest that such distinctions are either good or bad. Rather, I am arguing that we are not so different from Melanesia as we have been led to believe. Despite living in a capitalist, self-consciously modern society, we still evolve new and complex forms of exchange and difference that employ objects to construct a changing but widely held sense of how people should act and of the kinds of relationship they should have with each other. As in Melanesia, our choice of goods is most often dominated by a focus upon relationships in the family – that is, kinship. These processes of consumption help to shift our conception of what women and men are, by shifting to a small degree what we see as appropriate for each gender to do. We cannot simply read off what is happening in our society from a knowledge of business or politics, or even the more overt and explicit discussions of social change, as in feminism.

There is a further lesson from this study, relating more clearly to the field of politics. We have been brought up to believe that the most important political distinctions are between what we commonly call left- and right-wing politics. The former favours state distribution of goods, the second would leave this to the market. In practice, if we look around the world we find problems with both systems. The market has constantly shown itself to be more concerned with its own profits and uninterested in the welfare of populations, unless forced to develop such an interest by non-market political forces. But, similarly, in socialist societies we find that goods have been produced according to the interests of producers and industrial forces with little concern as to whether the products are those that are wanted or can be appropriated by the consumer.

READING B

At this point, turn to Reading B, 'Make-up and other crucial questions', by the Croatian journalist Slavenka Drakulic, which recalls the problems of living in Eastern Europe under the Soviet system. When reading this account, you need first to try to empathize with the situation of the writer by imagining life under similar restrictions. As you read, consider the following questions:

1   Would it be possible to have been less dissatisfied if one identified with the larger goals of the state or ideology?

2   Where do you think the desires that remained unfulfilled arose from in the first place?

3   We often feel we have too much choice, much of it unnecessary, in our society. How does one determine what the correct balance might be between choice and constraint?

A further question that arises from reading Drakulic is whether there may not be a direct link between the decision of Karl Marx to ground the construction of social being in production rather than consumption and what Drakulic sees as the failure to produce a good quality sanitary napkin. Whatever the reason why communist regimes neglected consumption, this reading suggests that it may have been a primary cause for popular dissatisfaction and their final overthrow despite some enlightened concerns with equality.

The political implications of this case are of immense significance. The triumph of the market as an economic institution has come about in large measure because it did indeed address the concerns of consumers – unlike state socialism. Critics of the market have replied that it gives an illusion of consumer choice, but only to those who have the money to buy, and that its orientation to profit can be as much at the expense of consumers as to their benefit. Under the Soviet system, politicians often claimed to be acting in the interests of workers; under the capitalist system, they more often claim to be acting in the interests of consumers. Both of these claims are often treated with scepticism, since in the first case it may be the state and in the second case it may be company profits that are the interests really being served. What might a political system that was genuinely concerned with consumers look like?

So far, I have used the case study of some kitchens in London to demonstrate that consumption is not simply the final resting place of goods and actions that start with production and which come to us through distribution. I have suggested that consumption should be understood as a social activity, which has increasingly become more important than either production or distribution as the site through which we change and develop our social relations. I have also implied that both academic and political debates have yet to grasp some of the implications of these changes and still have difficulty coming to terms with the importance of consumption – which they tend to dismiss as trivial or superficial. **Consumption**, then, is more than just purchasing, it is better understood as a struggle which begins with the problem that in the modern world we increasingly live with institutions and objects that we do not see ourselves as having created. We start then with a kind of second-hand relationship to the cultural world. We may not, however, accept this passively; our aim is often to **appropriate** and use these forms for our own purposes. To follow my argument, just consider the implications of reading this text as a student. If you just passively 'buy' the argument I am presenting to you, you may have difficulty obtaining a good degree. The aim is that you should take these ideas and indeed appropriate them, struggle with them, criticize them, apply your own experience to them and make out of your consumption of them something that becomes your active contribution, an argument which you can identify with as your own.

consumption

appropriation

Production and consumption are better understood as linked in a circuit (as shown using the example of the Sony Walkman in **du Gay, Hall et al.**, 1997). As an anthropologist, I tend to work more with larger social groups than just individuals. So at this point I want to draw you away from your own individual identity as a consumer and to consider how much larger entities such as islands and nations may also be seen as creating themselves through acts of consumption.

3   Trinidad

When in Britain we think of more distant regions, we most often see the rise of mass consumption as transforming places which we regard as being naturally 'green' and having 'real' communities into homogenized and characterless versions of our own consumer society. As tourists, we desire to travel ever further in our search for a vision of some surviving remnant of authenticity. We talk as through these distant lands are today becoming afflicted by some curse from which we can no longer escape. Many people in such regions do indeed have issues of authenticity with which they are concerned, but these may take a rather different turn from those we project on to them, and are more likely to be mediated by the desire to escape from poverty and to gain opportunities which we now take for granted.

Because of these differences, one cannot hope merely to replicate work done in London in a place such as Trinidad. With a different historical trajectory, goods and facilities have different connotations. State provision does not carry the same sense of stigma, and there is virtually no sense of resistance to the market as symbolic of capitalism.

What then is the equivalent set of issues for a country such as Trinidad? While in Britain the sense of alienation is most likely to be expressed against either the state or the market, in Trinidad the issue that constantly arises is more likely to be the problem of having a Trinidadian identity that had some kind of authenticity. There are good reasons for this. Trinidad at first glance stands little prospect of authenticity, given the assumptions made in the conventional view of culture. Its history is one of rupture and barbarism: an extinction of the native population which no longer exists as a discrete group, followed by the slave trade and the practice of slave owners in systematically separating peoples who came from the same area in order to try to minimize any cultural continuity with Africa. Slave owners often worked their slaves to death, as long as the slave trade made them expendable, after which they imported other groups such as East Indians under only slightly less horrific conditions. The population today is best described as Creole, since it includes the descendants of African slaves, East Indian indentured labourers, but also free Africans, demobilized black American soldiers, large numbers of immigrants from Spanish South

America, French planters, Middle Eastern traders, Chinese indentured labourers, Portuguese retailers and others (Brereton, 1981).

Under Creole conditions, any claim to regional roots is immediately under attack from a majority who would not share places of origin. To compound the problem, no sooner does immigration end than emigration begins. So many Trinidadians have moved to countries such as Canada, England and the United States that perhaps the majority of families are literally transnational. A mother may fly off this week to help her sick daughter in London and then a month later to be present at the birth of a grandson in New York.

If this were not enough, one has to look at the economy. The Caribbean was developed as a systematic periphery to the world economy – what Mintz has called the world's first agro-industrial complex, devoted to the growing, processing and exporting of sugar (1985, pp. 47–52). In this century, sugar has been replaced in Trinidad by oil, making it for a short time in the late 1970s, during and oil boom, one of the wealthiest countries in the Americas. Trinidad exports oil but imports nearly everything else, from its basic grains – wheat and rice – through even to tropical fruits. There is hardly a category of manufactured goods where the bulk of them are not imported, at best the materials are packaged locally, and even the souvenirs for tourists are mainly made in the Far East. This is reflected in the media, where television is clearly dominated by a mixture of American, Australian and British soap operas (for further details see Miller, 1994, 1997a).

It may then not be surprising to learn that it is a Trinidadian writer – V.S. Naipaul – who has provided amongst the most eloquent renditions of a culture of alienation and negativity. In books with titles such as *The Mimic Men*, he argues that Trinidadians never have and never could produce anything which could possibly be considered authentic culture, precisely because they are in the deepest sense a consumer society, based around other people's history, culture and products.

There are some obvious grounds for challenging Naipaul. He is, after all, one of a galaxy of creative Trinidadian writers and artists, and comes from an island which, through steel band, calypso and carnival, has had a vastly disproportionate influence upon global arts. But rather than taking such straightforward images of the possibilities of consumption, we shall here explore precisely the areas in which it has been argued that Trinidad has collapsed into the kind of inauthenticity bemoaned by Naipaul. In particular, we shall focus upon American soap opera and Coca-Cola – the sorts of consumption most likely to be dismissed as mere capitulation to external forces.

4   The young and the restless

(For further details of the case study of the consumption of soap opera in Trinidad discussed in this section, see Miller, 1992.)

Commercial surveys of media consumption in Trinidad in both 1988 and 1990 show clearly that by far the most popular television programme was a soap opera imported from the United States and called *The Young and the Restless*. The programme had become a part of common culture, satirized in calypso, its title a stock phrase. A newspaper that started printing the story-lines in advance, cribbed direct from the United States where the programme was shown earlier, quickly became the bestselling paper in the country. One retailer, commenting on its influence, suggested that Trinidadian fashion and *The Young and the Restless* were synonymous.

There are many soap operas shown in Trinidad, and when *The Young and the Restless* was introduced as a daily lunch-hour soap, it was not expected to have the same importance as established serials such as *Dynasty* and *Dallas*. But Trinidadians have shown considerable ingenuity in arranging to see the show. There is a big trade in imported miniature televisions which can be set up in shops and offices. In a squatting community which I studied, people without water or electricity supplies would have a car battery recharged weekly to power the television in their home.

My study of the consumption of soap opera was based upon the way *The Young and the Restless* was referred to and used in daily conversation. The first clear finding was the sense of its relevance to contemporary conditions in Trinidad and the lessons to be learnt from it. Typical comments would be: '... the same thing you see on the show will happen here, you see the wife blackmailing the husband or the other way around, I was telling my sister-in-law, Liana in the picture, just like some bacchanal woman'; 'I believe marriage should be 50–50 not 30–70 the woman have to be strong she have to believe in her vows no matter what ... that make me remember *The Young and the Restless*, Nicky want her marriage to work but Victor is in love with somebody else, but she still holding on'; and, referring to a current story-line, 'You always go back to the first person you loved, in my own family my elder sister went with a Moslem boy, and so was married off by parents to a Hindu man, but she left her husband, gone back to the first man and had a child by him.'

A calypsonian contender gave the reasons for the soap opera's success in the chorus of a calypso with the same title, whose content was largely a summary of the plot. One version of the chorus:

> 'You talk of commess[*]
> check the young and restless,
> commess at its best
> check the young and restless.'

[*]'Commess' means confusion, usually caused by scandal.

alternated with the version:

'They like the bacchanal

they like the confusion.'

The key term here is 'bacchanal'. If one asks a Trinidadian to summarize their country in one word, the likelihood is the response will be 'bacchanal'. The term has a specific meaning in Trinidad, although, as elsewhere, it evokes the values celebrated in carnival; that is, the general heightening of excitement, disorder and expressive sexuality. At the centre of carnival is an inversion ritual called 'Jouvert' which stresses the emergence into the light of things which normally inhabit the dark. Bands dressed in mud and ashes assemble before the dawn to reveal themselves in the first light as the 'truth' by their satirical exposures of the pretensions of the established order.

Similarly, the calypsos indicate that the chief connotation of the term bacchanal is clearly 'scandal', with lyrics such as 'Bacchanal Woman, sweet scandal where she walks', or 'We people like scandal. We people like bacchanal'. Scandal again implies the bringing into light of that which others want to remain hidden. The second clear connotation of the term bacchanal is confusion or disorder, and in this case the stress is on 'commess' as expressing the idea of confusion which is directly caused by scandal.

These ideas are central to a conflict between two opposing ideals which lies at the heart of Trinidadian culture. On the one hand, there is the desire for respectability and what may be termed 'transcendence', based in long-term concerns for one's roots and the future of the family and the subsumption of the individual in larger moral projects such as religious, ethnic or political identity. Against this, on the other hand, there is the attraction of what may be called 'transience', which is a more egalitarian and individualistic conception of the self, orientated to the expressive project of being stylish and the cultivation of freedom from being defined institutionally.

From the perspective of the values of 'transience' which are celebrated at carnival, the term 'bacchanal' is largely benign. It is scandal and exposure to light which constantly demonstrate that the pretensions of establishment figures and institutions are nothing but façades, beneath which lies a hollowness, rather than the substance which is claimed. Whether through the prim schoolteacher's sexual indiscretions or the politician's uncontrollable self-interest, a truth will inevitably emerge as to the reality of a world whose claims beyond transience are false. Scandal and confusion have highly ambiguous moral overtones, at once undermining patiently constructed systems of order and stability but also bringing us closer to the true nature of social being. Many in the squatting community identified with bacchanal. It is here that gossip flows freely through the walls of houses built from the boxes in which car parts are imported. Friendship in bacchanal is seen as spontaneous and genuine.

From the perspective of respectability or 'transcendence', bacchanal has negative overtones. For Trinidadians, the current government – which was called the National Alliance for Reconstruction, but which was in practice falling apart into warring factions – was a clear case of bacchanal. The previous government's insistence, through fairly heavy-handed control, on keeping its internal divisions from public view was seen as a much more 'serious' form of rule. When, as often happens, an apparently stable and close family is broken asunder into disordered fragments following a dispute over inheritance, the appellation of bacchanal has nothing good about it.

A major preoccupation in the soap opera has been the manner by which individuals are, as it were, thrown off course or driven to extreme actions by sexual desire. So a person writing a critical biography, almost against her will, starts an affair with the object of her work. A female working hard to integrate within the respectable family of her child's father is seduced from these efforts by a good-looking male recruited for the purpose. Here, as in the Trinidadian ideology of the domestic, it is often the women who assert one morality but find themselves inexorably drawn through sexual attraction into overturning these same principles.

The popularity of the soap opera makes sense in its context. People commonly report that life in Trinidad seems to be like a speeded-up soap opera. The oil boom gave a tremendous impetus to the growth of the middle class – to the extent that it emerged at the peak of the boom as dominant both numerically and culturally. With the recession, however, many of the more fragile pretensions of the *nouveau* element within this class have become exposed. There is a continual discourse about the financial plight that exists behind closed domestic doors, which is only brought to light by events such as cutting off the phone through unpaid bills. Even in the suburban community which I studied, there were frequent rumours about how many properties were back in the hands of the banks or deserted by migrants to Canada.

Many writings on soap opera and serials tend to assume that these lend some reassurance, stability and so forth as part of their power. Much of this may stem from the legacy of the mass culture critique originally associated with the Frankfurt School (see **du Gay, Hall et al.**, 1997, section 5). Some of the early critics treated soap opera as a kind of visual Valium that stupefies its audience in the interest of some dominant will. In certain cases this may well be the impact, but not in Trinidad. Here, far from patching up a wound or 'functioning' in the interests of social cohesion, the attraction of *The Young and the Restless* is that it has forced its point into the key fissure which manifests the basic contradiction of Trinidadian culture, at a time when this is especially sensitive.

This is precisely why Trinidadian television cannot produce a programme of this kind. Constantly watched over as a local product, it has to produce the respectable and serious discussions of things like the problems of ministerial planning. It is left to the imported programmes to deal with these highly sensitive and difficult problems as faced in daily life. The soap opera may not look like Trinidad, but it has the realism of an open-ended daily narrative, and out of all the imports it is the one which bears closest on local problems. It may be made in the United States by people who have barely heard of Trinidad, but in its consumption it becomes more genuinely Trinidadian than anything which is locally made.

The point that emerges from this study of soap opera is that even items that are seen as the worst aspects of foreign domination can, through the process of consumption, be turned into instruments for exploring highly localized questions – in this case the concept of bacchanal. Trinidad provides an even more poignant example of consumption as local appropriation in the case of the steel band. The steel drum has become one of the international symbols of Trinidad, which is now familiar in Britain, partly through the influence of Notting Hill Gate carnival. On reflection, there could hardly be a more apt symbol of Trinidadian dependency. Trinidad imports virtually everything – not just media but around 80 per cent of its foodstuffs. It pays for these imports through its export of oil, upon which Trinidad is entirely dependent. Trinidad has experienced wealth and poverty, not because of anything Trinidadians have done, but because the price of oil happens to go up and down. Yet from this symbol of dependency Trinidadians had the idea of creating a musical form. Cutting up and then moulding what might seem quite intractable metal results in a range of musical instruments which can be played individually, or can form orchestras of sixty or more players. Through the appropriation of the detritus of global dependency, Trinidadians have literally forged an instrument by which they create local identity, a key sign of what it means to be Trinidadian (the claims of other Caribbean islands with respect to the development of steel bands are wilfully ignored!). This is as profound an example of consumption as creative appropriation as one could wish for.

5   Linking production and consumption: the case of Coca-Cola

(For further details of the case study of the consumption of Coca-Cola in Trinidad discussed in this section, see Miller, 1997b.)

So far, the story told has been of households in London, and then of the island identity of Trinidad being created through consumption as appropriation. The arena of production has, however, been almost entirely absent. The people who made the soap opera *The Young and the Restless* may never have heard of Trinidad and may have had little interest in the consequences of their actions for Trinidadians. For one thing, Trinidad was not a significant market for them. A problem with this approach is that we might start to be led into the belief that all the complex and important action happens during consumption, and production becomes almost irrelevant. Clearly this would be nonsense and would swing the pendulum too far from the time when it was believed that only relations of production were of significance. We can now start to reintegrate issues of production and consumption in order to investigate their articulation.

The issue of the relationship between consumption and production will be explored using another of those commodities that are frequently used by academics and others as a kind of clichéd shorthand for global homogenization – Coca-Cola. Even prior to examining the evidence within Trinidad, there are grounds for challenging the assumption that this drink merely represents the power of the transnational corporation that makes it, or that it is simply the classic case of globalization. In a recent comprehensive history of the Coca-Cola company, Pendergrast (1993) describes what he calls the greatest marketing blunder of the century (see also Oliver, 1986). His account shows clearly that the company had absolutely no idea of what the response might be to their decision to change the composition of the drink in the 1980s in response to the increasing popularity of Pepsi. The enforced restitution of classic Coke was surely one of the most explicit examples of consumer resistance to the will of a giant corporation we have on record. After all, the company had behaved impeccably with respect to the goal of profitability. The new taste scored well in blind tests, it responded to a change in the market shown in the increasing market share of Pepsi, and it seemed to be a sensitive response which acknowledged the authority of the consumer. Despite this, when the company tried to change the formula, in marketing terms all hell broke loose, and it was publicly humiliated. The huge upsurge of protest showed clearly that many consumers felt betrayed by the company, and in effect insisted that the flavour of the drink was not in fact the possession of the company, which could thereby change it at will, but was a complex historical artefact which by now belonged as much to the global population of consumers.

In Trinidad, as in the United States, Coca-Cola is saturated in history. Coke's arrival in Trinidad coincided with that of the American troops based on the island during the Second World War. The Americans are remembered as having brought a new affluence and relative egalitarianism compared with the colonial authority of the British. This was mediated, however, by a memory of sexual and other forms of exploitation of Trinidadian people. The contradictory relationship was portrayed in calypsos and in novels with titles such as *Rum and Coca-Cola*.

Coke was established through a franchise agreement with a local company called Cannings, which had been bottling drinks since 1912. As a result, the local significance of Coke comes partly through the association with this particular firm, as against the other firms which produced soft drinks in competition with it. Coke by no means dominated Cannings which also runs the largest chain of grocery stores on the island, and has refused to allow Coke to develop Fanta in competition with its own orange soft drink. In 1975, Cannings was taken over by another Trinidadian firm, Neil and Massey, which claims to be the largest grocery-related firm in the entire

Caribbean. In this case, the Trinidadian transnational, with over 7,000 employees and subsidiary companies in sixteen countries, has grown even larger locally than much better known rivals such as Lever Brothers, Nestlé and Nabisco.

Cannings, and in turn Neil and Massey, do not, however, represent localization in any simple sense, since both derive from old colonial firms. While they may therefore be seen as representing national interests as against foreign interests, they may also be seen as representing white elite interests as against those of the dominant populations in the country. There are six main bottlers of soft drinks in Trinidad. Each has a specific reputation which bears on the drinks it produces. Solo is owned by an Indian family, but has been identified with opposition to the government for many decades. Jaleel, also associated with the Indian population, has at times had closer links with the government, but is also most closely linked with the south where the Indian population is concentrated. L.J. Williams, by contrast, is associated with Chinese Trinidadians. Coke has around 35 per cent of the market compared to around 20 per cent for Solo and 10 per cent each for Jaleel and Cannings own brand.

We might expect that soft drinks would be regarded as a luxury item which a country suffering acute recession in the 1980s could ill afford, and also as a mark of foreign domination. Neither the government nor the people of Trinidad regard soft drinks in this way. First, soft drinks are seen as earning foreign currency rather than taking it away. Indeed, about the only part of the drink that is imported is the concentrate. Trinidad has a large, modern, glass-producing factory which makes all the glass bottles and more recently has been making plastic containers also. The gas used in the drinks is a by-product of a local industry, and sugar has always been a major product of the Island. Given that Trinidad exports soft drinks to a number of other Caribbean islands, the claim that this benefits the local exchequer is probably a reasonable one. Secondly, for many years the government put the industry under price control, much to the horror of the business interests involved, on the grounds that it is a basic necessity, used by everyone from schoolchildren for their lunchboxes to families for their meals and workers for their breaks. It was therefore categorized alongside products such as rice. I suspect few Trinidadians would dissent from the idea that soft drinks are a basic need rather than a superfluous luxury, and I estimate a per capita consumption of around 170 bottles per annum.

If, then, the production of soft drinks can be understood as localized both economically and by the government, the same is true of the process of consumption, where consumption is regarded as more than just a lone individual buying a product. There are two main ways in which the consumption of Coke has become localized – one as a mixer and the other as a drink in its own right. The national drink of Trinidad is undoubtedly rum. It is the drink which most fully expresses a sense of a local product whose history is inextricably linked with the sugar cane fields from which modern

Trinidad developed. Trinidadians never drink spirits neat or even with ice; they are always consumed with a mixer, and in the case of rum the preferred mixer is overwhelmingly Coke. Coke is thereby an integral part of the drink which is most fully associated with the sense of being Trinidadian. Its only rivals would be a few relatively rare drinks for special occasions such as Christmas, and possibly the beer brand 'Carib'.

Even without this link, Coke may still be appropriated as a specifically Trinidadian beverage. In a community of squatters, soft drinks were hardly ever called by brand names. Rather, people tended to ask for either a 'red' or a 'black'. Both of these drinks have historically developed complex connotations. The red drink is generally regarded as particularly sweet and is associated with the cane fields and with diabetes, its best known association being with roti, the main food of the East Indian population. The black sweet drink has more urban and sophisticated connotations, and, partly through rum and Coca-Cola, is more associated with the African or white populations. These associations do not accurately reflect the popularity of the drinks with given populations. In many respects, the 'Indian' connoted by the red drink today is in some ways the African's more nostalgic image of how Indians either used to be or perhaps still should be. So it may well be that the appeal of the phrase 'a red and a roti' is actually more to African Trinidadians, who are today avid consumers of roti. Meanwhile, segments of the Indian population have sometimes used foreign education and local commercial success to overtrump the African population in their search for images of modernity, and thus readily claim an affinity with Coke. Indeed, to be Trinidadian is to incorporate a range of ethnicities. In a sense, then, the Africans who take 'a red and a roti' are completing their sense of being Trinidadian by ingesting what for them is a highly acceptable version of 'Indian-ness'.

It is not that soft drinks simply stand for different populations as a symbolic code. Nor have Coke or its advertising been the producers of the ethnic stereotypes involved here. In this region, much of the specific stereotyping came from the British colonial regime's concern to utilize different populations for different purposes (Williams, 1991). It may be that desires for particular commodities are often – like myth (following Lévi-Strauss rather than Roland Barthes) – an attempt to resolve contradictions in society and identity. Where once societies might have used a story about their origins, now they use longstanding commodities with which they have grown up and been socialized. The point for our purposes is simply that such drinks cannot be dismissed as superficial emblems of business or capitalism, just because they are commodities. They may evolve complex and highly local connotations. At this level, Coke has become simply the most expensive and high-profile manifestation of a 'black' soft drink with all its particular evocations and meanings.

None of this negates the obvious point that Coke remains a global commodity. The point is that the global is always experienced within a given

locality. In Britain, being global may evoke world music and the green
movement's notion of responsibility to the earth. In another region, being
global may be about the universality of Islam's message or about having a
Rolex wrist-watch. Indeed, Coke and McDonalds probably do not represent
trends to greater global identity. Coke has been around for quite some time,
and very few other brands have been able to develop successfully with
European, let alone global, images. Rather, they work as one emblem of the
global held against counter-tendencies such as the Campaign for Real Ale,
which work to develop highly localized reference points, or the promotion of
European lagers which are in between. For this reason, to know what Coke
means, it is not enough simply to turn to its business or American
associations. We would need, in each region, to see how this image of the
global is itself appropriated within the complex interplay of local culture.

READING C

At this point, read Reading C, 'You can't beat the feeling: Coca-Cola and
utopia', by Marie Gillespie, about the consumption of adverts for Coke in
Southall, London. Consider the following points as you read this article:

1   Note the considerable differences between the example of Trinidad,
     where the drink has been localized, and Southall, where the focus is
     upon global images.

2   How far do you think these differences have arisen from the focus
     upon the drink in Trinidad as against the adverts in Southall?

3   What other factors might account for these differences? Consider, for
     example, the length of time the populations have been present in each
     area, and the age of the respondents.

Gillespie is concerned about the meaning of Coca-Cola within a particular
local context. This extract is taken from a broader ethnographic study of
young Asians in Southall, with an emphasis upon media consumption. In
this case there are some similarities with my observations concerning
Trinidad but also some important differences. First, you will have noted that
in Southall there is much more concern with the adverts *per se* rather than
the drink. Also, there is a much greater emphasis on the American identity
of the drink. There have been many studies which suggest that groups which
see themselves as minorities within their own society find an appeal in
larger transnational identities that make that society in turn appear limited
and parochial. Another example is the way in which the Turkish minority in
Germany, who found running *döner kebap* (doner kebab) businesses to be
successful but low status, have tended to develop names such as 'McKebap'
in emulation of McDonalds in order to change their image in Germany from
backward to modern (Caglar, 1995). The situation is very different from
Trinidad, where America is incorporated within the sense of being
Trinidadian. These differences are important, because they demonstrate that,
although Coke may be a global drink, glib generalizations about its global
impact are usually false.

ACTIVITY 2

Consider the implications of the drinks you buy in public, first from the point of view of the producers and advertisers, and secondly from your point of view as a consumer. Consider the drinks you might order in a pub, or at a restaurant, or in other public contexts. What images are you affected by in making your choice? The place they come from – for example, a local bitter, or a cosmopolitan lager? The effects of alcohol? How sophisticated they make you look? Fashion? Cool? Tradition? Then try to work out what images you see as being conveyed by the drinks being consumed by some of your close friends. Do you feel you have been influenced by advertising? Do you feel the image you wish to portray is the same as that promoted by the company which produces the drink? Is the 'meaning' of the drink that which it is given by the company which produces it; that which the drinker intends to convey by drinking it; or that which is conveyed to a third party in making judgements about the person who they see drinking it?

There are a number of important differences between the case studies of Coke and soap opera in Trinidad and the original example of kitchen units in London. First, I have moved from individuals trying to overcome their sense of stigma in relation to the state to a highly generalized society trying to forge a sense of identity and authenticity despite complex and difficult historical origins. Secondly, in the case of Coke, I have returned to consider the place of production and commerce in direct association with consumption rather than treating the two as entirely separate. Certain key conclusions apply to all these cases, however. Instead of assuming we know the meaning and consequences of goods and images, we have tried to find out the way a particular population of consumers creates meanings and finds uses which are often very different from those we might have predicted. We would not have predicted the degree of localization in either Coke or soap opera. An analysis that had not bothered with the close listening-in to how Trinidadians are using these forms would most likely simply have dismissed such things as bound to be forms of Americanization, rather than as part of what makes Trinidad specific and 'local'.

We might try to conclude with a simple formula: the state and commerce try to universalize and oppose localization, while consumption is always the mechanism that promotes localization. Once again, such a simple conclusion can quickly be challenged. First, take the idea that companies always oppose localization. The biggest advertising agency in Trinidad is part of a huge transnational company. But as with most businesses in Trinidad, most of the local personnel are Trinidadian with a keen interest in expanding local business. A problem arises in that there are basically two possibilities for the local branch of an advertising agency. It can merely arrange for international adverts to be shown locally, in which case it will be a small branch of the global corporation. Alternatively, it can make its own adverts, in which case it will be a large enterprise with many local employees and with local influence.

From the point of view of the global corporation as a whole, profits are best generated by making one set of adverts and showing it in as many countries as possible. From the point of the view of the local office of that same company, however, its own size and interests are best developed by persuading the international group that such adverts won't work locally and that the local office should be commissioned to produce local adverts with local themes. In the case of the Trinidadian advertising agency, to do this it has to argue that Trinidad is somehow different and special. Ironically, then, I found (Miller, 1997a) that the people who were most vigorous at promulgating the idea that Trinidad is indeed authentic and different were transnational companies in the form of their local offices. Indeed, they were very successful in this argument, and most advertising shown on Trinidadian television is made in Trinidad and constantly features specifically Trinidadian themes. So transnational companies are not always globalizing.

The second generalization – that consumption is always localizing – is equally problematic. Apart from the clear evidence that consumers balance such localizing with attempts to show how cosmopolitan they are in their consumption of global commodities, the very idea of local as against global may be too simple.

READING D

You should now read Reading D, 'Learning to be local in Belize: global systems of common difference', by the anthropologist Richard Wilk. Wilk provides a fascinating account of how the new global cultural system promotes *difference* rather than homogeneity. Bear in mind the following points and questions while you are reading:

1   Note how Belizean culture has grown, even emerged, coincidentally with the arrival of global media and tourism.

2   Can you think of other examples that would fit Wilk's model?

3   Can competition between nation-states over topics ranging from popular songs to agricultural policy be reduced to this kind of model?

4   If we agree to differ along common lines, does that make us more similar or more different?

5   You might think Wilk's approach makes differences more superficial, but, alternatively, it might be that with more transnational communication we simply need a common language to express our particularity in such a way that others can understand it.

structures of common difference

The idea of **structures of common difference** came to Wilk through a study of beauty contests, though the extract in Reading D is mainly about food within the small state of Belize situated in Central America. In beauty contests, as in so many competitions, people are using a person or team to represent themselves as a separate locality but doing so using a structure that has become a global medium for comparing all such localities. Wilk helps us to avoid any simple labelling of things as either 'local' or 'global', and also makes clear the importance of commodities for affirming and structuring identity. There are many obvious parallels. In Britain, we may increasingly demand a 'real ale' brewed near to the place of consumption, but if the pun may be excused, so does everyone else's 'local'. In other words, even the idea of being local can be a sign of our involvement in increasingly global relations. We may do this at many different levels at once. In the local pub, we can decide that, instead of a 'real ale', we will have a European wine or lager, or something as international as Coca-Cola or spirits.

6   In the name of consumers

The various case studies described so far show how we have to monitor constantly the actions of consumers and not merely assume that we know the consequences of commodities by studying their production and distribution. We would be quite wrong, however, to assume that this active role of consumers is always something to be positively regarded and welcomed. Indeed, as we shall now see, some of the most disastrous and disempowering movements in the contemporary world are being promulgated precisely in the name of the active consumer and the notion of free consumer choice. Trinidadians may be able to localize Coca-Cola, but at present they are clearly being overwhelmed and indeed homogenized by a force of such power that even the Coca-Cola Corporation pales by comparison. This section will continue the move to higher levels, from the domestic kitchen up through national identity, by focusing upon this force – the World Bank – which may be regarded as the archetypical *global* institution. This does not mean you have to lose sight of the domestic consumption you started with. As you are about to find out, the most global institutions justify their work most often in the name of the individual consumer.

Alongside many, if not most, countries, Trinidad was encouraged to borrow money and attempt to expand in the 1970s. In this case, as an oil producer, it was supported by a huge increase in resources that came with the oil boom. In the 1980s, however, when the oil price declined, Trinidad, like most other countries, found itself with debts it could not repay. As a result, in 1989, the government of Trinidad and Tobago decided to request financial guarantees from the International Monetary Fund (IMF). This was followed in 1990 by a request for further standby credit, and then the development of a programme within the World Bank. This was a reluctant move – in 1987, the government had declared this to be the worst option available to them. But by 1989 they had come to the conclusion that the worst option was the only option open to them.

In effect, countries such as Trinidad and Tobago declare themselves bankrupt and go to these international bodies which, acting like receivers, strip down the national economy to what they regard as economically sound policies and then in return grant them a credit rating so that they can secure further funds to repay their debts. The programme is known as **structural adjustment**. The pretence is that the local government constructs the package, but in practice only one kind of package is accepted by the IMF and the World Bank. This consists of almost total adherence to the policies created by academic economists, of whom the elite work for organizations such as the World Bank.

structural
adjustment

There is considerable consensus as to the effects of these policies, to which other Caribbean regimes such as Jamaica have been subject for many years. In almost every instance this seems to have been a disastrous encounter which in and of itself has been a significant factor in the increase of poverty, social conflict and general suffering in the Caribbean and other regions. Structural adjustment is based on the economists' vision of a pure global market, in which all goods are produced at their cheapest possible rate in order to provide the cheapest possible goods to the consumer. So, if the Philippines can produce a particular fruit or chair more cheaply than Mexico, then it should be encouraged to do so. The idea was that such global competition would favour countries with cheap labour and thus provide work for the poor. In practice, it is countries such as Germany or the United States, with highly developed technologies that can produce goods through industrial processes involving very little labour, which are outcompeting even the cheapest and poorest countries, with the result that the developing world is highly unlikely to develop.

In structural adjustment programmes, economists attempt to force the country receiving aid to abolish policies which interfere with pure market principles. They favour the privatization of companies, the reduction of state involvement, and the abolition of currency exchange controls and of all duties paid on imported goods to protect local industry. They also push countries to abolish welfare policies that in effect subsidize the labour force. In many respects, they embody to perfection what are free-market, liberal economic policies, commonly right-wing but promulgated under the guise of necessity demonstrated by the science of economics. It is these changes which result in the suffering and impoverishment that are the typical results of structural adjustment (see Mosley et al., 1991). In practice, such conditions can more easily be imposed upon small countries such as Trinidad and Tobago than upon the United States or Europe. So, while Trinidad has already abolished its subsidies and protectionist policies, its sugar industry is devastated because Europe continues to subsidize sugar beet which otherwise would cost more than Trinidadian sugar cane, and the

United States prevents the importation of Trinidadian steel rods while
Trinidad cannot prevent any imports from the United States.

READING E

At this point, read Reading E, 'Structural salvation', about the World
Bank, by Susan George and Fabrizio Sabelli. You should follow their
argument that the World Bank represents in it purest form the strict
academic logic of a certain form of economics that takes virtually no
notice of any differences between the contexts in which it operates.
Consider the following questions while you are reading this extract:

1   How is it that economists seem to have developed such a powerful
    position in the modern world?

2   Should one's response be simply to reject these models of economic
    development, or do we need first to construct some positive, feasible
    alternatives? In the case of the latter, how would a better under-
    standing of consumption help?

In that it takes no notice of any differences between national contexts, the
World Bank is an example of a genuine form of globalization. Unlike the
other institutions we have looked at, it cannot be appropriated locally
because it has the power to change the local and remake it in the image of
academic economics. Where it gains power, each country has to reformulate
its political and economic policies to fit with economists' models. In this
respect, it is more genuinely 'global' than even Coca-Cola or soap opera.

But why should we be reading about the relationship between the World
Bank and the non-developing world in the middle of a discussion about
consumption and identity? The reason is that all of this is justified by an
economic theory of the consumer and consumer choice. Most of the elements
of this economists' model of the consumer and consumer choice are quite
nonsensical. According to this theory (usually called the neo-classical
theory), each consumer chooses to act, not only entirely independently of
each other, but making choices unaffected by their other choices. Each
consumer works with a pure rationality in order to maximize the utility of
each aspect of the commodity they choose. These ideas do not equate with
any study of real consumers or the imperatives behind their choices. They
bear no relation to how Londoners transform kitchens or why Trinidadians
drink Coca-Cola. This point will be clarified when I return, in the next
section, to first world consumption, and consider the case of Londoners
shopping.

The reasons why neo-classical economics continues to survive as a model
are twofold. First, it relies on a highly theoretical 'science' that is more
concerned as to whether a social behaviour can be modelled with a
mathematical algorithm than whether this algorithm actually describes
anything in the world outside. Secondly, there is one element of consumer
choice which, when considered at the level of the aggregate (or collective)

impact of consumers, does serve to support the economists' model – this is the concern for low prices. The idea of supporting the cheapest producer is to create the cheapest goods for the consumer. With the collapse of Marxist regimes, the concept of consumer choice and value has become the criterion by which the global economy and increasingly the global polity now operates.

It would be relatively simple to depict countries such as Trinidad as the victims of this grand neo-imperialist plot which favours first world countries at the expense of the developing world, but while this is quite clearly the effect of current economic changes, the causes are, as usual, more complex. Most Trinidadians would wish to preserve political autonomy for their government, and resent the degree to which their government is today unable to exercise any serious form of independent policy making as the result of being forced to follow the dictates of structural adjustment. At the level of the political vote they would be against these changes. As consumers, however, they act very differently. To favour their political aspirations they would have to buy more expensive goods – either because they were made in Trinidad, or because they were produced by paying a fair wage to local workers – in order to subsidize the survival of traditional activities. As consumers, however, Trinidadians 'vote' by systematically favouring goods that are often the result of the kind of cheap and exploited global labour that economists have in practice preferred. Furthermore, they favour foreign goods over local goods, and goods that come in through structural adjustment rather than goods that might have been protected by previous governments. In short, as consumers, they consistently act against their own interests as producers. In practice, Trinidadian consumers are of little consequence: there are too few of them and their resources are too limited. The reason for noting their preferences is simply to show that they are not merely honourable victims who would, if given the choice, follow a more enlightened or moral strategy than any other population of consumers. Meanwhile, because they are being hit by these changes as workers, and their economy may well go into decline, they will become still less important as consumers.

The current beneficiaries of these transformations in the global political economy are undoubtedly the consumers in the first world (in other words, you and I). For this group, it must be conceded that modern capitalism does to a degree deliver its goods in the form of ever lower prices for a growing and higher quality range of goods. A number of social scientists influenced by Marxism (e.g. Ewen and Ewen, 1982; Haug, 1986) have tried to claim that capitalism tended to produce goods of ever poorer quality and value. They were supported by philosophers (e.g. Baudrillard, 1981; Marcuse, 1964) who claimed that consumer culture is one in which we have all lost our humanity or authenticity through the spread of mass commodities. This is surely wrong. The last few decades have brought an impressive spread of wealth to most (though certainly not to all) of the first world. The working classes of the metropolitan regions have emerged from a tradition of considerable poverty and deprivation to a world in which they can shop in hypermarkets that provide them with greater value for their wages, and in which 'luxuries' such as holidays abroad and electronic communications have become commonplace basic goods. The amount of labour required to pay for particular goods has constantly declined over the century (although recently this has gone into reverse). There are few grounds for asserting that lives of poverty with few opportunities were more authentic or meaningful. A more pressing issue would seem to be the significant minority who at present are denied access to the affluence that surrounds them. The reasons for this increase in wealth in the first world lie partly in the growth of intensive industrialization that produces value through technology rather than labour, and partly in putting out production in a kind of international division of labour to the cheapest labour source – be this Latvia or Peru.

There is, then, a direct link between ourselves as the consumers in the first world and the massive changes that are being dictated to workers in developing countries such as Trinidad. This is based, however, less on the actual nature of consumer demand than on the theoretical models of consumption used by extremely powerful economists. According to these economists, structural adjustment is required in order to serve the attempt by consumers to optimize rationally the utility function of goods. It is worth returning now to the first world consumers to see if this is actually what they are doing, and to consider the consequences. In other words, having reached the most abstract and global institutions, we find that their actions are constantly justified with reference to the very domestic scene from where we began.

7   The London shopper

The argument has brought us full circle to the people who inhabit kitchens with which this chapter started, though this may be expanded to include the middle-class London consumer. The increasing importance of the consumer is evident. If we go to any high street in London (or in any provincial city), we are likely to find a series of key retail outlets such as Tesco, Sainsbury, Marks and Spencer, BHS and W.H. Smith. With the development of their point of sale information and own brand labels, it is evident that they are increasingly not the end-point of a chain that starts with manufacture but rather the controlling bodies that determine the shifts in demand and order manufacturers to design, create and supply what they require. Where once manufacturers determined what should be made, and then used advertising and retailing to sell it, today an advertising agency is more likely to be involved with manufacturers in creating a commodity that relates to a demand found in retail. It is retail which will tell manufacturers that consumers want a meat pâté that is also low in fat. This is a chain of power which feeds back eventually to the host of countries which supply raw materials that may end up in typical supermarket foodstuffs, cosmetics or items of clothing. (See **du Gay, Hall et al.**, 1997, for an illustration of the importance of these links between manufacture, retail and consumption, in the case of the Sony Walkman.)

To the inhabitant of the developing world, the first world consumer may appear to be the ultimate materialist and hedonist, concerned only to amass vast quantities of superfluous goods which are then wasted in profligate use. Many academic theories of consumption seem to portray a similar mindless superficiality, and the green movement confirms the notion of profligacy and waste as features of modern consumer societies. However, very few such opinions are based on any kind of direct encounter with shoppers or take account of their imperatives and demands. To the first world consumer, these ideas look just as far from reality as the ideas of the theoretical economists with their rational individuals and optimizing functions.

To gain a better understanding of the grounds for at least one arena of first world consumption, I spent one year, 1994–5, studying the occupants of one fairly nondescript street in North London (Miller, forthcoming). The street was chosen because it appeared to represent households a bit above and a bit below national average incomes, judged in the first instance by the housing stock. The street included two small council estates, which were not particularly run-down, a large number of purpose-built maisonettes, and some larger houses. The middle-class sample was expanded by including some of the more affluent streets that lead into the main road studied. During this year, time was spent chatting with a large variety of different households ranging from mothers with young children through to households consisting of single elderly persons. The householders ranged from a core of the locally born, to those with a wide diversity of origins from Jewish to Hindu, from West Indian to West African. The chats covered not only shopping but also other means whereby people obtain goods – such as catalogues, car-boot sales, gifts and making things for themselves. In many cases, I accompanied households on shopping expeditions or to events such as Tupperware parties.

The richness of detail and diversity of experience cannot possibly be fully condensed into a few paragraphs, but one observation may be made that demonstrates how absurd the usual theories and models of modern consumption are in relation to consumer concerns. The dominant picture of self-seeking hedonists might be reasonable for a few teenagers who are obsessed with a concern about how they appear to others. Most shopping is, however, a highly routinized activity. At its core is a regular, usually weekly, visit to a large supermarket for purchasing food and household materials. Most clothes purchasing is based on the notion of replacement of items or on the needs of a particular occasion, such as a job, wedding, or school uniform for a child. Most household purchasing is again seen as related to the provisioning of the home, based around what are now experienced as basic functional items such as washing machines and sofas. Many of the decorative items come in the form of gifts, or mementos of people or social occasions.

In almost every case the concern is not with maximizing individual utilities but with expressing responsibility to others, of which by far the most important 'others' are members of one's family. The most common consumer is a female who sees herself as bearing this responsibility of housewifery, irrespective as to whether she is also engaged in paid work. These North London housewives (with a few exceptions) do not fit well into the ideas about hedonism and materialism or 'lifestyles' that have been developed to account for modern consumption and are constantly encountered both in academic texts and in popular magazines. In practice, most people don't feel they have enough time to develop anything that might be called 'a lifestyle'. On the contrary, they regard themselves with much justification as largely self-sacrificial, and with a high moral sense of their responsibilities as expressed through the provisioning of families (for further evidence of this point, see Devault, 1991). As noted in the case of the kitchen units study, consumption not only expresses relationships: it also becomes a primary form through which our very understanding of what it means to be, say, female and male is created.

Indeed, the degree to which the role of shopping is not based on indulgent individualism is clearly demonstrated in the development of a special category, normally known as a 'treat', which is designated to fulfil such a function. A treat may consist of anything from a bar of chocolate, consumed by the shopper before returning home, to a leisurely browse through clothing stores which may sometimes include a purchase that has no reason behind it other than the desire to possess the item. Treats represent a very small proportion of actual shopping and, in a sense, by being understood as personal indulgence, they help to define the rest of shopping as based around sacrifice and need. Even treats are commonly understood as a kind of reward that the shopper deserves for having gone through the task of the weekly supermarket shop. Even more common as a treat is a trip to McDonalds as a reward to an accompanying child for having been good while the parent undertook the main part of the shopping.

How is the North London household based on money and commodity transactions able to become more like a peasant household than a capitalist firm? One of the main ways in which the North London household is able to see their shopping as quite unrelated to materialism and hedonism is by turning the act of spending into an act of saving. When shoppers describe their shopping, the subject most dwelt upon is their skill and ability to save money by finding cheap goods. Different groups have different ideals. Middle-class shoppers will conspicuously parade clothing from charity shops or second-hand baby equipment obtained through a National Childbirth Trust jumble sale. Working-class households tend to stress their patronage of shops, such as Kwiksave and Iceland, which they associate with low prices. Both groups may stress their use of sales and, above all, the 'specials' and 'savers' which are now a constant feature of supermarket shelves. Indeed, it was quickly evident that, in explaining discrepancies between what shoppers intended to buy or wrote on lists and what they actually bought while out shopping, it was not advertising that was important but these specials and savers which constantly persuaded shoppers to alter their intentions. The effectiveness of this policy is evident enough in the desire of the shops to capitalize upon it. In the local major supermarket, up to a fifth of all goods were given special labels that showed they were either reduced that day, or implied that they were especially good value. This is probably about the maximum concentration a shop can achieve without devaluing the whole concept of the 'reduced item'. As a result of this emphasis, many shoppers could return from their shopping with the view that they had not so much spent out the resources of their household as acted to save money and stored resources for their household. Apart from the very occasional treat, very little shopping was based on a sense of personal indulgence or hedonism.

This portrait of shopping bears no relation to the more fashionable theories of consumption as mindless and superficial materialism, nor to the emphasis placed by academic economists upon individualized rational choice. Real shopping is usually experienced as a moral project based on expressing one's concerns for others rather than oneself. The desire to save is not based on the rationalizing of budgets but on an essentially moral project of self-sacrifice. Amongst the most avid savers are pensioners, who may live at a level of consumption which causes suffering and shortage for themselves in order to give a very large present to a descendant whom they hardly ever see, and may little appreciate the gift, but who manages to represent the concept of family continuity for that pensioner. The middle class is often offended by the way working-class shoppers save money on what they would regard as proper priorities, such as healthy food, in order to spend large sums on what they regard as improper purchases, such as Sega and Nintendo games for their children. In this and in most other cases, the details are best understood not as a rationality based on objective need, but as a series of moral debates about the kinds of relationships we ought to have. In general, there is no relation between income and a concern for savings – such a concern is expressed as fully by households that might be regarded as wealthy as by those who would be deemed poor.

8 Conclusion

The story of this chapter has been more like a helter-skelter ride than a smooth set of transitions. We started with the relative peace and quiet of North Londoners doing up their kitchens, then passed through a variety of turbulent and sometimes bizarre 'theories' of consumption, none of which seemed to bear any relation to actual consumption. At one point the story shot off to the highly contrastive situation of consumers in Trinidad, and then took an enormous sweep from domestic or national concerns up to the highest and most general conditions of the modern political economy exemplified by the World Bank, before finally coming to rest back home at the doors of Tesco and similar high street shops. At this stage you are entitled to feel confused and perhaps even somewhat queasy.

Unfortunately, such tortuous explorations are quite essential if we are to struggle to understand modern consumption and not simply rest complacently with some simplistic explanation or some dismissive attitude whereby everyone else is a consumer but not us. One of the most unfortunate findings has been that we are constantly beset by paradox. On the one hand, shopping turns out to be much more of a moral project than is generally thought. On the other hand, these same moral concerns, as expressed in thrift and searching for good value goods, have devastating consequences upon the workforce of the developing world, since the money saved may turn out to be their wages. To understand modern consumption, we have to make these gigantic leaps from the private lives of ordinary households, where it seems intrusive to enquire too closely into what lies behind demand, right up to massive international bodies such as the World Bank and the IMF. This is because each exists partly in terms of a model, often a quite mistaken model, of the other. In private consumption, we see ourselves as rescuing a little domestic world of family against the huge alienating forces of business and the state which threaten to overwhelm us. These same institutions justify themselves with reference to what they claim are quite different determinants of demand theorized in their models of consumers.

At present, the massive scale of the modern political economy separates consumers from any sense of the consequences of their actions. They are left with a vague sense of an even larger or global economy. We can see one response in the green movement, as people try to see themselves as responsible citizens of 'the globe' and believe they can take steps to protect it. Again and again what we see is a desire on the part of consumers to reconstruct small moral worlds that tame these vast forces. Faced by global commodities, we find ways of reducing these to instruments that relate closely to local dilemmas and to questions of identity. Faced by a growing state and by capitalist markets, we bargain-hunt and save money in the name of a small moral economy that is above all centred around a nuclear or subnuclear family to which we return and dedicate our lives after experiencing the wilder freedoms of teenage life.

The world of the consumer is not, then, merely a continuation of these massive changes to abstraction and globalization. Rather, consumers are concerned to negate these changes and to retain the small-scale, the moral and the sensitive. Because consumers are acting with deeply held values and are not mindless hedonists, it does not, however, follow that the consequences of what they do are good for others. On the contrary, the more consumers try to save money on behalf of their families, the more they enable global economic agencies to justify the reduction of labour costs and to end welfare to people who produce these goods. Indeed, increasingly in the complex modern economy, the same people may, in their role as workers, be the people hurt by the actions they take as consumers. This conclusion does not lead to any simple politics either. Rather, it leads to a politics of compromise and pluralism which respects difference and opposes economists' attempts to homogenize us, both in theory and in practice.

ACTIVITY 3

As well as reading further about shopping, you could do worse than reflect upon your own experiences. Consider your trolley or basket of produce the next time you go shopping at a supermarket. How much do you know about the origins of the goods which you buy? How much do you know about the 'green' or environmental consequences of these particular products? How much do you know about the conditions of work or possible exploitation which might have been part of the creation of the products? Of the amount you pay, how much do you think goes to the producers? How could you find this out? Should we all become 'ethical' consumers, scanning the environmental and political consequences of each thing we buy, or should we have governments and international bodies that take from us some of this burden or responsibility by ensuring that goods are produced according to values to which we would wish to subscribe? If such ethical goods cost more, would you buy them (you might want to think twice about that), and if not, who then is responsible for the unethical consequences of your shopping?

As pointed out in the introduction to this chapter, consumption is much more than just shopping. How do you relate to the services that come from the government, such as education and health, as against the things you buy? The terms 'consumer' and 'consumer choice' are increasingly being used for your relationship to state services, but are there problems with these terms? With regard to our larger relationship to goods, how is it that everyone else seems to embrace mindless materialism but not us personally? What are the goods which have become over time inalienable – that is, goods we would never wish to part from – and what qualities do they have that make them so important to us?

In a world that is so full of contradictions, perhaps we expect too much of ourselves in assuming that we would make consistent consumers. Most shoppers are more concerned to create a balance between conflicting demands. You might buy something that represents your ability to deal with the sophisticated outside world, such as a Mexican or Singaporean beer, right next to a purchase of some highly localized regional British beer. You might buy fat-free milk in order to compensate for the fact that you are also buying a cream dessert. Most of us do not want to be local or global, we want to be both. Equally, as shown in the case study of the kitchen units, the individual's consumption is often only meaningful when taken within a larger context – men's passion for DIY can only be understood in terms of a domestic context traditionally dominated by women.

Reflection upon the complexity of your own decision making in the area of consumption may help you avoid oversimplistic or over-dismissive accounts of other people's consumption. This chapter has led you to examine the diversity of relationships which may develop between consumers and goods, and has encouraged you to face up to their complexity. Understanding such relationships depends upon patience and sensitive listening and observing, but it also depends upon bearing in mind the global institutions that sometimes mean that these small local acts of consumption can have major consequences.

References

BAUDRILLARD, J. (1981) *For a Critique of the Political Economy of the Sign*, St Louis, MO, Telos Press.

BRERETON, B. (1981) *A History of Modern Trinidad 1783–1962*, Oxford, Heinemann.

CAGLAR, A. (1995) '*McDöner: Döner kebap* and the social positioning of German Turks' in Costa, J. and Bamossy, G. (eds) *Marketing in a Multicultural World*, London, Sage.

CARRIER, J. (1994) *Gifts and Commodities: exchange and western capitalism since 1700*, London, Routledge.

DEVAULT, M. (1991) *Feeding the Family*, Chicago, IL, University of Chicago Press.

DRAKULIC, S. (1992) *How We Survived Communism and Even Laughed*, Vintage, London.

DU GAY, P. (ed.) (1997) *Production of Culture/Cultures of Production*, London, Sage/The Open University (Volume 4 in this series).

DU GAY, P., HALL, S., JANES, L., MACKAY, H. and NEGUS, K. (1997) *Doing Cultural Studies: the story of the Sony Walkman*, London, Sage/The Open University (Volume 1 in this series).

EWEN, S. and EWEN, E. (1982) *Channels of Desire*, New York, McGraw-Hill.

FEATHERSTONE, M. (1991) *Consumer Culture and Postmodernism*, London, Sage.

GEORGE, S. and SABELLI, F. (1994) *Faith and Credit*, Harmondsworth, Penguin.

GERSHUNY, J. (1982) 'Livelihood IV: household tasks and the use of time' in Wallman, S. (ed.) *Living in South London*, Aldershot, Gower.

GILLESPIE, M. (1995) *Television, Ethnicity and Cultural Change*, London, Routledge.

GREGORY, C. (1982) *Gifts and Commodities*, Cambridge, Cambridge University Press.

GULLESTAD, M. (1992) 'Home decoration as popular culture' in Gullestad, M. *The Art of Social Relations*, Oslo, Scandinavian University Press.

HAUG, W. (1986) *Critique of Commodity Aesthetics*, Oxford, Polity Press.

MARCUSE, H. (1964) *One Dimensional Man*, London, Routledge and Kegan Paul.

MAUSS, M. (1970) *The Gift*, London, Routledge (first published 1925).

MILLER, D. (1987) *Material Culture and Mass Consumption*. Oxford, Blackwell.

MILLER, D. (1988) 'Appropriating the state on the council estate', *Man*, Vol. 23, pp. 353–72.

MILLER, D. (1992) 'The young and the restless in Trinidad: a case of the local and the global in mass consumption' in Silverstone, R. and Hirsch, E. (eds) *Consuming Technology*, London, Routledge.

MILLER, D. (1994) *Modernity: an ethnographic approach*, Oxford, Berg.

MILLER, D. (1997a) *Capitalism: an ethnographic approach*, Oxford, Berg.

MILLER, D. (1997b) 'Coca-Cola: a black sweet drink from Trinidad' in Miller, D. (ed.) *Material Cultures*, London, University College London Press.

MILLER, D. (forthcoming) *A Theory of Shopping*, Cambridge, Polity.

MINTZ, S. (1985) *Sweetness and Power*, New York, Viking Penguin.

MOSLEY, P., HARRIGAN, J. and TOYE, J. (1991) *Aid and Power: the World Bank and policy based lending*, London, Routledge.

OLIVER, T. (1986) *The Real Coke, The Real Story,* London, Elm Tree Books.

PENDERGRAST, M. (1993) *For God, Country and Coca-Cola*, London, Weidenfeld and Nicolson.

STRATHERN, M. (1988) *The Gender of the Gift*, Berkeley, CA, University of California Press.

WILK, R. (1995) 'Learning to be local in Belize: global systems of common difference' in Miller, D. (ed.) *Worlds Apart: modernity through the prism of the local*, London, Routledge.

WILLIAMS, B. (1991) *Stains on my Name, War in my Veins*, Durham, NC, Duke University Press.

READING A:
Marianne Gullestad, 'The home as an expressive statement'

What values and ideas are made manifest through the home? One answer is that people create themselves as individuals and as families through the processes of objectification involved in creating a home. The home is a rich, flexible, and ambiguous symbol; it can simultaneously signify individual identity, family solidarity, and a whole range of other values. The following lists some elements in the symbolic value of a home: personal identity; the identity of the family; marital, filial and parental love; closeness (*nærhet*), sharing and togetherness (*deling og fellesskap*); a sense of wholeness (*helhet*), integration and unity in life; independence and self-sufficiency; safety, security (*trygghet*), control, order, 'peace and quiet', coziness (*kos*) and comfort (*hygge*), decency (*være skikkelig*); practical sense and a realistic outlook; control and mastering; direction in life; social reference groups.

The connotations of the expression 'a good home' (*et godt hjem*) are moral, while the connotations of the expression 'a nice home' (*et pent hjem*) are of an aesthetic kind. However, it is through aesthetics that a vision of a moral order is created and expressed. One of the worst things one can say about somebody's home is that it is impersonal (*upersonlig*) and without ambiance (*uten atmosfære*). Impersonal interiors give off the connotations of institutions or public waiting rooms, and do not really qualify as homes. The centrality of the home in Norwegian culture is thus complemented by a fear of institutions. A nice home should literally and figuratively be warm. The figurative meanings of warmth (*varme, lunhet, hygge, kos*) are, among other things, achieved through the arrangement of and care for objects. A home should be decorated (*pyntet, utsmykket*) in order not to give off an impression of impersonal emptiness. In addition, a nice home should, of course, be relatively clean and tidy, and thus bear witness that the inhabitants are decent (*skikkelige, ordens*) people.

A home is a setting for relaxation (*å slappe av*) as well as for feelings of security (*trygghet*) and 'peace and quiet'. Two other important notions are *hygge*

and *kos*, both used as substantives, verbs, and adjectives. The word *hygge* is almost impossible to translate: only some of its connotations are captured in the English word 'comfort'. The connotations of the adjective form of *kos*, *koselig*, is close to but not quite the same as the English words with the same root, 'cozy'. Both notions imply ideas of beauty, warmth, emotional closeness, feelings of solidarity, and relaxation from work. If we keep to the furnishings, a cozy home has a wealth of textiles, potted plants, souvenirs, paintings, and photographs.

When interviewing people about their house, one quickly discovers that talking about houses often involves telling a life story. The individual's life cycle and the family's development cycle are closely connected to moving house or forming and reforming a house. Improving the home is a lifetime project which gives meaning to life. It also expresses what social categories one belongs to, i.e. whom one would prefer to be compared to. For most categories, and especially the elderly and the young, living alone is an important sign of independence. Being able to 'manage by oneself' (*rå seg sjøl*), is highly valued. It is important to be 'the master of the house' (*herre i eget hus*), and to preferably 'not need to take heed of others' (*ikke behøve å ta hensyn til andre*). In addition, using money on the home goes hand in hand with the Norwegian ideals of diligence, simplicity, and having a realistic outlook. Norwegians generally emphasize all those things that are practical and useful and place little direct and explicit emphasis on aesthetics and playful creativity.

This emphasis on practicality is illustrated by some of the particular reasons that people usually give for redecorating their house or apartment. Most often, practical and functional reasons are given, even if the work of installing the improvements exceeds by far the time and work saved over a subsequent period of time. Economic reasons are also often given, for example, that the improvements will increase the value of the apartment or the house if it were to be sold in the future. Such reasons, which of course can be real enough, allow Norwegians to pursue contradictory values. On the one hand, they want their homes to be considered 'tasteful', 'personal', and unique, but, on the other hand, they do not want to be accused of lavishness and status hunting. As mentioned earlier, equality is defined as sameness, and sameness is emphasized in social interaction through a code of modesty [...]. Emphasizing practicalities allows each person the opportunity to appear both modest and creative. Thus home improvement gives Norwegian men and women the opportunity to carry out creative and playful activities camouflaged as serious useful things which 'must' be done. Norwegians often play not out in the open but under the cover of doing something practical and reasonable.

Source: Gullestad, 1992, pp. 79–81.

READING B:
Slavenka Drakulik, 'Make-up and other crucial questions'

Once when I was in Warsaw, a friend told me about a spate of red-haired women: suddenly it seemed that half of the women in the city had red hair, a phenomenon that couldn't pass unnoticed. It might have been a fashion caprice. More likely, it had to do with the failure of the chemical industry to produce or deliver other kinds of dye. Imagine those women confronted by the fact that there is no other color in the store where they buy their dye and knowing that if there isn't any in one store, it's generally useless to search others. There is only the one shade of red. (I've seen it; it's a burgundy-red that gives hair a peculiarly artificial look, like a wig.) They have no choice – they either appear untidy, with bleached ends and unbleached roots sticking out, or they dye their hair whatever colour they can find, so they dye it, hoping that other women won't come to this same conclusion. They don't exactly choose.

Standing in front of a drugstore on Václavské Náme'stí in Prague last winter, I felt as if I were perhaps thirteen years old and my mother had sent me to buy something for her – soap, perhaps, shampoo. The window of that drugstore was a time machine for me: instantly, I was transported into years of scarcity long past, years of the aesthetics of poverty. Even though I'm not an American, it seemed there was absolutely nothing to buy. In front of that shop window I understood just how ironic the advice in today's *Cosmopolitan* or any other women's magazine in the West is, advice about so-called 'natural' cosmetics, like olive and almond oil, lemon, egg, lavender, camomile, cucumbers, or yoghurt. I can still recall my mother's yearning to buy a 'real' cream in a tiny glass jar with a golden cap and a fancy French name, something she would have paid dearly for on the black market.

If Western women return to the old recipes, they do so by choice; it is one of many possibilities. Not so for Czech or Bulgarian or Polish women. I can see them arriving in Yugoslavia after days and nights in a train or car. They go to the market, put a plastic sheet on the street at the very edge of the market (afraid that the police might come any moment) and sell the things they've brought. Among them are professional black market vendors, women who make a fortune by buying foreign currency and then selling it back home for five or six times as much. But I also saw a young Polish woman, a student maybe, selling a yellow rubber Teddy bear, deodorant, and a green nylon blouse (the kind you can find only in a communist country or a second-hand vintage clothing store in Greenwich Village). I couldn't help thinking that she was selling her own things. But why would anybody in the world travel 1,500 miles just to sell a plastic toy? And what if she sells it, what is it that she wants to buy with the money? Perhaps a hair dye that is not red ... However, she is young, and there is hope that her life will be different. For my mother and women of her generation, it is already too late. If only they had had cosmetics, it might have changed their lives. On the other hand, it might not. But shouldn't they have had the right to find that out for themselves?

Once, when we used to play a childish adolescent guessing game, we would try to guess which of the women on the beach in Split were Polish and which Czech. It was easy to tell by their old-fashioned bathing suits, by their make-up, hairdo, and yes – the color of their hair. Somehow, everything in their appearance was wrong. Today I realize that women in Poland like green and blue eye shadow about as much as they like artificial red hair – but they wear it. There is nothing else to wear. It is the same with the spike-heeled white boots that seemed to be so popular in Prague last winter. It is the same with pullovers, coats, shoes: everyone is wearing the same thing, not because they want to, but because there is nothing else to buy. This is how the state creates fashion – by a lack of products and a lack of choice.

To avoid uniformity, you have to work very hard: you have to bribe a salesgirl, wait in line for some imported product, buy bluejeans on the black market and pay your whole month's salary for them; you have to hoard cloth and sew it, imitating the pictures in glamorous foreign magazines. What makes these enormous efforts touching is the way women wear it all, so you can tell they went to the trouble. Nothing is casual about them. They are over-dressed, they put on too much make-up, they match colors and textures badly, revealing their provincial attempt to imitate Western fashion. But

where could they learn anything about a self-image, a style? In the party-controlled magazines for women, where they are instructed to be good workers and party members first, then mothers, housewives, and sex objects next, – never themselves? To be yourself, to cultivate individualism, to perceive yourself as an individual in a mass society is dangerous. You might become living proof that the system is failing. Make-up and fashion are crucial because they are political. In Francine du Plessix Gray's book *Soviet Women*, the women say that they dress up not for men, but to cheer themselves up in a grim everyday life or to prove their status to other women. In fact, they are doing it to show difference; there are not many other ways to differentiate oneself. Even the beginnings of consumerism in the 1960s didn't help much; there were still no choices, no variety. In fact, in spite of the new propaganda, real consumerism was impossible – except as an idea – because there was little to consume. Trying to be beautiful was always difficult; it involved an extra effort, devotion perhaps. But most women didn't have time or imagination enough even to try.

Living under such conditions and holding *Vogue* magazine in your hands is a very particular experience – it's almost like holding a pebble from Mars or a piece of a meteor that accidentally fell into your yard. 'I hate it,' says Agnes, an editor at a scientific journal in Budapest, pointing to *Vogue*. 'It makes me feel so miserable I could almost cry. Just look at this paper – glossy, shiny, like silk. You can't find anything like this around here. Once you've seen it, it immediately sets not only new standards, but a visible boundary. Sometimes I think that the real Iron Curtain is made of silky, shiny images of pretty women dressed in wonderful clothes, of pictures from women's magazines.' Fed up with advertising, a Western woman only browses through such magazines superficially, even with boredom. She has seen so much of it, has been bombarded by ads every single day of her life, on TV, in magazines, on huge billboards, at the movies. For us, the pictures in a magazine like *Vogue* were much more important; we studied their every detail with the interest of those who had no other source of information about the outside world. We tried to decode them, to read their message. And because we were inexperienced enough to read them literally, the message that we absorbed was that the other world was a paradise. Our reading was wrong and naïve, nevertheless, it stayed in the back of our minds as a powerful force, an inner motivation, a dormant desire for change, an opportunity to awaken. The producers of these advertisements, Vance Packard's 'hidden persuaders', should sleep peacefully because here, in communist countries, their dream is coming true; people still believe them, women especially. What do we care about the manipulation inherent in the fashion and cosmetic industries? To tell us they are making a profit by exploiting our needs is like warning a Bangladeshi about cholesterol. I guess that the average Western woman – if such a creature exists at all – still feels a slight mixture of envy, frustration, jealousy, and desire while watching this world of images. This is its aim anyway; this is how a consumer society works. But tomorrow she can at least go buy what she saw. Or she can dream about it, but in a way different from us, because the ideology of her country tells her that, one day, by hard work or by pure chance, she can be rich. Here, you can't. Here, the images make you hate the reality you live in, because not only can you not buy any of the things pictured (even if you had enough money, which you don't), but the paper itself, the quality of print, is unreachable. The images that cross the borders in magazines, movies, or videos are therefore more dangerous than any secret weapon, because they make one desire that 'otherness' badly enough to risk one's life by trying to escape. Many did.

In our house there was an old closet where my mother would stockpile cloth, yards and yards of anything she could get hold of – flannel, cotton, pique, silk, tweed, cashmere, wool, lace, elastic bands, even buttons. Sometimes she would let us play with this cache, but it was her 'boutique'. She would copy a blouse or a skirt from pattern sheets from *Svijet (World)*, the only magazine for women, and sew it on Grandma's Singer sewing machine. Every woman in my childhood knew how to sew, and my mother insisted that I learn too. By the age of five I knitted my first shawl and embroidered a duck with ducklings that she still keeps. Later on, she let me use a sewing machine under her supervision, and by the age of fifteen I was making my own dresses, not because it was a woman's duty, but because it was the only way to be dressed nicely. When, for the first time, she went to Italy to

visit a relative there, she came back dressed in a white organdy blouse, a black pleated skirt, and high-heeled black patent leather shoes. She brought back a mohair pullover, a raincoat made of a thin, rustling plastic (it was called suskavac and everybody wanted to have one, since it was a sign of prestige), an evening dress made of tulle, covered with sequins that glittered in the night. What fascinated me most was her new pink silk nightgown and matching silk overjacket with lace lapels. So light, almost sheer, hanging down to her ankles, with two tiny straps that would leave her shoulders bare, it was the finest negligée I'd every seen. I used to tell her that she ought to wear it to the theater, not to bed. Mother's nightgown was for me the very essence of femininity. This was the first time, in 1959, that I'd seen that 'otherness' with my own eyes.

My mother brought something special for me too: three dozen sanitary napkins made of terrycloth and a belt. The napkins had buttonholes at each end to fasten them to the belt, so they wouldn't slip. She would hand-wash them, then hang them on a clothesline in the bathroom to dry overnight. More than thirty years later, in Sofia, my friend Katarina saw my package of tampons in her bathroom and asked if I could leave it for her. I am going on to Zagreb and she needs them when she has a performance in the theater. 'We don't have sanitary napkins and sometimes not even cotton batting. I have to hoard it when I find it, or borrow it,' she said. For a moment, I didn't know whether I should laugh or cry. I sprinkled Eastern Europe with tampons on my travels: I had already left one package of tampons and some napkins, ironically called 'New Freedom', in Warsaw (plus Bayer aspirin and antibiotics), another package in Prague (plus Anaïs perfume), and now here in Sofia ... After all these years, communism has not been able to produce a simple sanitary napkin, a bare necessity for women. So much for its economy and its so-called emancipation, too.

Rumiana is a Bulgarian movie director and a member of the international organization of women in the film industry known as KIWI. In Bulgaria, KIWI operates like a kind of feminist organization, helping women in different ways, for example, by taking care of the children of women prisoners, helping out girls in reform schools and orphanages, and so on. Rumiana told me that she is 'in charge' of a reform school near Sofia. Every time she goes for a visit, girls there ask her to bring cotton batting. So she goes to a cotton factory, loads up her car, and then visits them. 'They are so grateful,' says Rumiana, 'even when it is something that they have a right to.' Today, when I think that my mother's silk nightdress doesn't necessarily have much to do with femininity, I still ask myself, what is the minimum you must have so you don't feel humiliated as a woman? It makes me understand a complaint I heard repeatedly from women in Warsaw, Budapest, Prague, Sofia, East Berlin: 'Look at us – we don't even look like women. There are no deodorants, perfumes, sometimes even no soap or toothpaste. There is no fine underwear, no pantyhose, no nice lingerie. Worst of all, there are no sanitary napkins. What can one say except that it is humiliating?'

Source: Drakulic, 1992, pp. 24–31.

READING C:
Marie Gillespie, 'You can't beat the feeling: Coca-Cola and utopia'

Coca-Cola ads have sustained an unparalleled popularity among the youth of Southall over the last decade or so. Over the years, the ads and their accompanying jingles and songs – which have repeatedly been major chart hits – have entered every young person's repertoire of media knowledge. Coca-Cola songs and slogans are familiar to all, and few would be unable to recite them upon request. They are seen to convey a 'feeling' which is captured in the slogan:

> DALVINDER : I love the Coca-Cola ads, I don't know why, there's just something about them, they're just good, more lively, teenagers jumping around and having a laugh […], I don't know [laughs] you just can't beat the feeling.

This slogan is a catch-phrase among local youth. Its very ambiguity (the reference to 'feeling' as both an emotional state and a physical experience), is the source of many a *double entendre*, especially in exchanges between boys and girls. The tensions inherent in that ambiguity seem to capture something of the nature of the emotional and sensual experience of adolescence.

Discussions of Coca-Cola ads also refer to the 'feeling' that they convey in terms of the representation of a teenage world and lifestyle to which many young people aspire. It is an imagined or projected feeling of participating, albeit vicariously, in an idealised lifestyle where young people sing, dance, have fun, socialise, fall in love, and easily gain friends, status and popularity. The following exchange took place during a taped discussion between two 16-year-old vocational students about why they like their favourite advertisements. It captures the ads' utopian quality:

> SAMEERA: My favourite ads are the Coca-Cola ads, they're American ads, I prefer American ads, I don't know why but I could watch them over and over again without getting bored […]. I like them cos I just love drinking Coca-Cola […]. I enjoy listening to the music […]. I think the characters are fantastic. Every time I see the ad I

always feel tempted to go out and buy it, even when I go out shopping, I always buy Coke cos, well, I love the ad [...].

SUKHI: Yeah, they're really happy and active cos they mix pop songs with kids in America, you know, the sun's always shining and everyone is smiling and it gives the impression of being free. The music and song puts more energy into it and like each line of the song is backed up with dancing, sports and fun [...]. 'You just can't beat the feeling!'

SAMEERA: Yeah, and all races seem to get on well, their roles aren't changed around because of the colour of their skin. There are no signs of people being angry [...].

SUKHI: They have a very tempting way of selling Coke [...], you know the one where the guy is sweating, he's thirsty as anything but he drinks it very slowly, taking his time as if it is something precious.

SAMEERA: Yeah, it's like after a hard day's work he's rewarded with a refreshing Coke. The little droplets of water on the bottle glisten and sort of add to the temptation.

SUKHI: After watching the ad you think, 'Oh yeah, next time I need a cool drink, I'll have a Coke'.

SAMEERA: [...] then there's a boy and a girl about to kiss but then, just as their lips are about to meet another shot comes [...].

The preference for American advertisements is stated without any explicit reasons being offered, but the chain of associations in the exchange implies that it is based on the attractiveness of the American teenage lifestyle portrayed. The feelings ascribed to the young people are conflated with the advertisement and the product. Coke-drinkers are seen to be 'happy', 'active' 'kids in America' where 'the sun is always shining', everyone is 'happy' and 'free', 'all races get on' and there are 'no signs of anger'.

'TV ad talk' is clearly influenced by the discourse of advertising itself which relates products to

myths and dreams, fantasies and emotions, rewards and promises in order to sell products. Advertisements are the most condensed of all TV narratives and viewers have to make symbolic associations in order to read them. These associations become evident in ad talk, which can take on some of the persuasive rhetoric of the ads themselves. The repeated use of the word 'temptation' in several different contexts highlights an awareness of the persuasive techniques used. Sameera claims that when she sees the ad she is tempted to go out and buy a Coke both because she loves the ad and because she loves drinking Coke. Sukhi adds that the way 'they' sell Coke is tempting. The glistening droplets on the bottle in the ad 'add to the temptation'. Then Sameera introduces the idea of being rewarded with a Coke after a hard day's work, making the connection with Coke-drinking and leisure. Finally, the temptation of a kiss appears, only to disappear at the very end of the advertisement. In this account, thirst and desire are connected: thirst is satisfied by a Coke but desire, as represented by the promise of a kiss, is left to the imaginative fulfilment. By placing the product within an idealised world of teenagers, free from parental and other constraints, a utopian vision of a teenage lifestyle is represented. The plausibility of the idyllic lifestyle and utopian relationships depicted by the ad is not questioned.

The following exchange between two 16-year-old vocational students further highlights the way in which the Coke ads lead some young people to engage in talk that would otherwise appear foolish or utopian:

GURVINDER: It makes you think if you drink Coke that you will be popular and loved by people you didn't even know existed.

GITA: Innit, it's like everyone cares about each other, their relationships are simple, they all get on, life is peaceful and full of fun so enjoy it while you can.

GURVINDER: They all socialise together, boys and girls, everyone loves each other and if you buy Coke it makes you feel that you could be happy and free like them.

GITA: But I don't think the ads influence us to buy it, most of us buy it anyway.

GURVINDER: And old people won't be influenced because they think that soft drinks are bad for you anyway.

GITA: But I think you are supposed to value the feeling that you get after drinking it, you know [sings] 'you can't beat the feeling', and for such a small cost.

GURVINDER: The music is great as well and goes with the feeling.

Thus the consumption of Coke promises happiness, love, friendship, freedom and popularity. In the world promised by the ads, relationships are uncomplicated (unlike in real life); young people simply care for each other, everyone loves one another and socialises together (unlike in the peer culture where group boundaries are strong); life is fun and free (a teenage dream). If they do not feel themselves to be influenced by the ads, it is evidently only because they already have been: the girls buy Coke in any case. Finally, teenage tastes are distinguished from those of older people who think Coke is unhealthy.

Discussions of Coke ads invariably lead to a consideration of what it is like to be a teenager in America, articulated in contrast to what it is to be a teenager in Southall. The word most consistently used to describe American teenagers is 'free'. They are seen to have much greater freedom to do what they want, to participate in 'fun' activities; freedom from parental constraint; and especially, freedom to have boyfriends and girlfriends. The emphasis on freedom appears to be exaggerated, but when considered against the background of social constraints under which girls especially live, it becomes easier to appreciate.

Perceptions of American 'kids' obviously derive from a variety of media sources, but the Coke ads have undoubtedly played a formative influence in shaping perceptions of an idealised teenage lifestyle. The following exchange again highlights the rosy image of American 'kids' which is presented in the ads, as well as in the popular American 'college films' and 'vacation films' (such

as *Dirty Dancing*), and TV series such as *Beverly Hills 90210* which revolves around the recreational pursuits of high-school teenagers:

GURINDER: American kids ... they're ideal ...

BALJIT: ... they're really good-looking ...

PERMINDER: ... they all drink Coke and drive fast cars, like in *Beverly Hills 90210*, the girls are so pretty ...

AMRITA: ... Brandon is so cute ...

GURINDER: ... so's Dylan he's r-e-a-l-l-y nice ...

BALJIT:... they're free ...

PERMINDER: ... all rich, they've got massive huge houses and all dress smart and they've got wicked cars ...

GURINDER: ... they've got more things to do as well ...

AMRITA: ... they're all sunbaked aren't they ...

BALJIT: ... they're always going to pool parties ...

PERMINDER: ... they're all healthy ...

BALJIT: ... like the Coke ads make you think they're free and have lots of fun and they have ...

GURINDER: ... boyfriends! [All laugh]

The idealisation of American youth in the Coke ads is recognized by Baljit to be a constructed image, but the others talk about the representation as if it were 'the real thing' (another Coke slogan). This representation of American kids as rich and above all free (to have boyfriends) contrasts sharply with the lives of these girls who consider themselves neither rich nor free to have boyfriends. Thus the Coke ads and other media sources encourage girls to fantasize about what life might feel like as an attractive teenager in Beverly Hills.

Whilst the ideal of teenage freedom is a recurrent theme when Coke ads are discussed, some young people are also aware of the darker side of the 'American way of life':

> KARIM (19): American kids have more freedom [...], freedom to rebel AND WIN, you know, like in films like *Dirty Dancing* [...] they rebel AND the family stays together but, over here, if you rebel against your family, you're out on your own, parents won't tolerate certain things [...]. They have more freedom, they also have more of a drug problem, more violence and there's more of a colour problem there as well [...], the Hispanics and blacks are stuck in ghettos and slums [...], even though they're American they're not integrated.

The impression of 'racial harmony' produced by the Coke ads is seen to be contradicted by other available images, of 'ghetto' life and 'racial conflict'. Nevertheless, Coke – and Pepsi – are favourite drinks among young people locally, strongly associated with a 'cool', 'safe' image. In one of the local Punjabi cafés, 'Rita's' in old Southall – a 'hang-out' for local youth in the lunch-hour – red cans of Coke stand on almost every table. Often, that is all there is on the table, because eating 'out' is expensive (compared to school dinners or home lunches) and most youngsters can only afford a kebab roll or a samosa and a can of Coke.

No other drink has quite the 'cool image' of Coke. The Pepsi ads are considered to be very attractive because they use famous stars like Michael Jackson, Tina Turner and Madonna, but most prefer the taste of Coke and claim to find Pepsi sweeter: 'I think they spend more money on the Pepsi ads but Coke ads are more for the common people and cos they're young people, you can sort of relate to them'. This idea that Coke is for the 'common people' relates to a perception of Coke being a drink consumed by young people in all parts of the world; it is testimony to the success of Coke's 'multi-local' global marketing strategy [...]. The 'cool' image of Coke evidently 'rubs off' on its consumers; and this creates problems for other drinks manufacturers.

For example, a company called Rubicon, producing 'exotic', 'tropical' canned drinks, based on flavours such as mango juice or passion-fruit, organised a vigorous TV advertising campaign specifically targeting ethnic-minority consumers, broadcasting on Channel 4 over several months during the period of fieldwork. In discussions of this campaign, the consensus seemed to be that the major problem was that the can lacked style:

> I've tried it and I like the taste of the mango juice but the can is so awful I wouldn't be seen dead with it, it's so badly designed [...]. I hate it, it's so uncool'. And not only is the can 'uncool', but the ad itself is seen by many to portray 'Asian' families as 'stupid':

> GURINDER: I hate that Rubicon ad, you know the one where there's this Indian family, the mum, dad and the two kids – the kids are so cute! I think they're *gore* [whites] – and they're all in the kitchen watching a Hindi film and the husband goes to his wife, 'Have you got any mango juice dear?' and they're all really engrossed in the film so they ignore him. Then he goes dancing round the kitchen to the fridge and gets out the mango juice and starts singing [...]. They're watching the bit in the film where Rajesh Kanna takes her to a hut [...] and the tune to the ad is the same as in the actual film, you know, it goes 'Rubicon must have some' [all laugh and sing it]. They're so stupid though, I hate the way they do that, it makes Indian people look really stupid.

However good it tastes, if a drink does not have the right kind of 'cool' image, the terms of which are pre-established by the dominant advertising media, many will not buy it. And such attempts to construct an 'ethnic' image are particularly unlikely to find favour among Southall youth. No 'Indian' ads were mentioned in the survey, but they were brought up in every group discussion and interview and critically or humorously juxtaposed to 'more sophisticated' British or American ads. The consistent denigration of 'Indian' ads – including both those for 'Indian' products appearing in 'Indian' media, and those targeting 'British Asians' in 'western' media – stands in sharp contrast to the high regard for 'western' ads targeted at teenagers.

In their ad talk about soft drinks young people establish hierarchies of consumer taste and style in sharp contrast to those which exist in the parental culture. The stylistic qualities and persuasive techniques of ads targeted at the parental generation are seen to be 'unsophisticated'. The representation of the 'Asian' family in the above example is considered to be demeaning. The father, dancing and singing around the kitchen, is perceived as 'stupid'. Many young people who discussed this ad showed concern that it would just reinforce negative stereotypes of 'Asians'. They argue that, because there are so few representations of 'Asian' families on British TV, those that do appear have greater representational power. Yet implicit in this ad talk are a series of un-answered questions: How should an Indian father behave and act? What should an 'Asian' family look like? Why are the children found to be cute because *gore* ('white')? Gurinder's detailed and accurate recall of an ad she hates – including recognition of the intertextual reference to a Hindi movie – may be likened to the detail in which *pendu* style was elaborated, as a means of underlining the contrast between 'classy', 'cool' style and its antithesis.

In juxtaposing Rubicon and Coke in discussions about soft drinks advertisements young people are drawing connections between texts which are incomparable in certain crucial ways; they seem to be unaware that the Rubicon advertisements are targeted at 'British Asian' families, and mothers as shoppers, whereas those for Coca-Cola are aimed specifically at teenagers. However, they feel themselves to be implicated in these ads as young 'British Asians', and are highly critical of the way adult 'Asians' are invariably portrayed as having Indian accents. As young people born and brought up in Britain, without Indian accents for the most part, they often express aspirations toward a greater participation in mainstream British society, from which they feel cut off by Southall's 'island' status. Representations which emphasise the 'foreignness' of 'Asians' are seen to further alienate them from society. Such concerns override the fact that the depiction of a family watching a popular Hindi movie and the playful behaviour of the father are features of the ad which make it attractive to many local adults. For young people, it is a further unwelcome marker of their difference.

Their comments reveal a sense of the excessive 'burden of representation' which affects those few images of 'Asians' which appear in mainstream media, especially on British TV. As Williamson points out, this is a question of collective cultural power: 'the more power any group has to create

and wield representations, the less [any one image] is required to be representative' (1993, p. 116). Young people are faced with what they believe are inappropriate representations of 'Asians' in the very few British TV ads in which they are portrayed. Ads in 'Indian' media fare no better, but are treated as objects of ridicule in the peer group. In criticising both so vociferously, they are demarcating distinctions in taste and style between the parental and peer cultures, and also, at least implicitly and sometimes explicitly, expressing a desire for alternative images. Again, the politics of ethnicity are involved: Who represents us? Who speaks for us, or to us? Since the spaces available for public representation of what they see as their generational culture are so limited, and since neither British nor Indian media offer representations which they view as acceptable or appropriate, it is perhaps no wonder that they turn to a third, alternative space of fantasy identification: they draw on utopian images of America to construct a position of 'world teenagers' which transcends those available in British or Indian cultures.

References

WILLIAMSON, J. (1993) 'A world of difference. The passion of remembrance' in Williamson, J. *Deadline at Dawn. Film Criticism 1980–90*, London, Marion Boyars. First published in *New Statesman*, 5 December 1986.

Source: Gillespie, 1995, pp. 191–7.

READING D:
Richard Wilk, 'Learning to be local in Belize: global systems of common difference'

The local in the global in Belize

Belize, independent from Britain since 1981, has a tiny but diverse population – less than 200,000 people who speak more than six languages. Today the country is increasingly cosmopolitan. The economy is open to foreign capital, the stores full of imports. Belizeans themselves are transnational – their families scattered across the United States and the Caribbean, with most of the young expecting to spend parts of their lives abroad. Those at home are bombarded by foreign media – there are nine stations broadcasting a steady diet of American and Mexican satellite TV, and one can hook up to full-service cable systems in every town with more than a thousand people. When Belizeans turn off the TV they can look out of the window at a parade of foreign tourists, resident expatriates, and students in search of authentic local experience, traditional medicine, untouched rainforests and ancient ruins.

The paradox is that amidst all this transnational influence, Belize's national and ethnic cultures have never been so strong or so distinct. In fact, until foreign cultural influence became so pervasive, most people denied that such a thing as 'Belizean culture' existed at all. When I began to work in Belize in the early 1970s, people carefully explained to me that the numerically dominant African-European group, the descendants of slaves and their masters collectively labelled 'Creoles,' had no culture of their own. They were 'really' British or Caribbean. The predominantly Spanish-speaking rural communities were 'just Mestizos', the same people as neighbouring Guatemalans or Mexicans. The only people in the country who were generally acknowledged to have culture were marginalised minority immigrants – Mayans, Hindus, Lebanese, Chinese, Garifuna and Mennonites.

When I asked about 'Belizean food', I was met with blank stares or nervous laughter, or a patient explanation that there was no such thing. 'Creole food' was a term of embarrassment; like the local English-Creole dialect, it was considered a 'broken' and imperfect version of the metropolitan English standard. By definition, cooking was the preparation of European and American dishes with imported ingredients, a skill that required sophistication and training. As an honoured guest from the north, I was usually treated to something from a can (Wilk, 1992).

In those days when I looked for Belizean gifts for my friends in the US, there were simply no distinctive or emblematic objects one could take home to prove that one had been to a place called 'Belize'. Only stamps, coins and bottles of 'local' Belikin beer (brewed next to the Belize City airport by an American, in a Canadian brewery using Dutch malt concentrate and English bottles). Belize was an ethnographic blank. While *I* found something there quite special and distinctive, there were no public symbols, no public discussions about that distinction.

About the only other people who seemed to believe in something called 'Belizean culture' were politicians, especially in the nationalist Peoples United Party, which had engaged in some fitful cultural decolonisation projects after achieving internal self-government in 1964. Black woollen coats and ties were banned as official garb, and a plain Guayabera dubbed a 'Belize Jack', or a neutral safari suit were briefly in vogue. The party leader and first Prime Minister George Price gave speeches about the need to develop a Belizean culture that would bring together the country's diverse ethnic groups, sometimes hinting at American-style syncretism, but more recently favouring the pluralist metaphor of the stewpot over the blender (Judd, 1989).

But the content of this national culture was never specified, beyond that it was to be a unique blend of the best of the Caribbean and Latin American. Starting in 1975, local intellectuals and public servants tried to fill the void by staging an annual cultural festival, modelled explicitly on the Jamaican 'Carifesta'. But through the 1970s and early 1980s, 'Belizean culture' was still the project of a small minority – in the countryside it was still an oxymoron.

Today all of this has dramatically changed. Belize is awash with emblematic local goods – woodcrafts, hot pepper sauces, dolls and dresses. There is a literally booming local music industry, boasting its own 'Punta Rock', now internationally marketed. A Belizean cuisine has appeared, first in expatriate Belizean restaurants in new York and Los Angeles, then in the form of a 'Belizean Dish of the Day' at tourist hotels. Belizean cookbooks were produced by the Peace Corps, and today almost every eatery which isn't Chinese is advertising 'authentic Belizean food'. There is a touring national dance troupe, a national theatre movement, a new historical society that is designating landmarks and choosing national heroes. Art galleries feature oils of village life by Belizean artists, Belizean poetry flourishes.

This furious rate of cultural production is not just a preoccupation of an educated or economic elite. When I conducted a large-scale survey in 1990, reproducing the format of Bourdieu's *Distinction*, I found that a majority in all ethnic, occupational and income groups believe there is a national culture, and are proud of it. In ranking their favourite music, food, home decorations and entertainment, they consistently placed local products above foreign imports. Even as actual consumption of imports of all kinds has increased dramatically, as frozen and packaged foods from the United States have entered every home, pride in emblematic local products has risen too (Wilk, 1990, 1991).

This is not to say that Belizeans in any way agree about the content or meaning of their national culture. Controversy and political contest over the cultural content and effects of local and foreign television, sports, music, arts, dance, food, money, drugs and migration are intense. But 'culture' has emerged as a legitimate topic, as an objectified matter of debate and dispute in everything from political campaigns to the wildly popular radio call-in programmes. There is now a daily programme of 'cultural music' on Radio Belize, 'cultural dance' graces most public events, and shops feature cabinets of 'cultural goods'.

The emergence of a public national culture in Belize provides an interesting contrast with the similar process documented on the Caribbean island of Nevis by Olwig (1993). In both Belize and Nevis national identity has emerged through an interaction between local cultural politics and the cultural processes of diaspora. In Nevis the island economic base is weak, and the rate of emigration is enormous. Nevisian national identity is now largely a performance for the benefit of returning expatriates, for whom the island provides a 'cultural homeland'. In Belize the expatriate community has a much smaller role, and contestation of identity is played mostly by local actors for a local audience. As the size of the Belizean expatriate community increases, this may well change in the direction that Nevis has taken.

[...]

I would argue [...] that the nature of cultural hegemony may be changing, but it is hardly disappearing, and the consequence is not de-homogenisation or global fragmentation. The new global cultural system *promotes difference* instead of suppressing it, but difference of a particular kind. Its hegemony is not of content, but of form. Global structures organise diversity, rather than replicating uniformity (to paraphrase Hannerz, 1990, and Appadurai, 1990). Another way to say this is that while different cultures continue to be quite distinct and varied, they are becoming different in very uniform ways. The *dimensions* across which they vary are becoming more limited, and therefore more mutually intelligible. In this way the societies competing for global economic and cultural dominance build their hegemony not through direct imposition, but by presenting universal categories and standards by which all cultural differences can be defined.

In other words, we are not all becoming the same, but we are portraying, dramatising and communicating our differences to each other in ways that are more widely intelligible. The globalising hegemony is to be found in *structures of common difference*, which celebrate particular kinds of diversity while submerging, deflating or suppressing others. The global system is a common code, but its purpose is not common identification; it is the expression of distinctions, boundaries and disjunctures. The 'local', 'ethnic' and the 'national' cannot therefore be seen as opposed to or resisting global culture, but instead, insofar as they can be domesticated and categorised, they are essential constitutive *parts* of global culture. As Fusco (1990) points out, recent intellectual discourse about 'the other' functions inside this system, rather than constituting an external critique.

I want to emphasise that my argument for the expression of locality through a system of common difference is not an attack on the *authenticity* of those differences. The typical postmodern critique of commoditisation of culture on the global stage argues that all local cultures are becoming equally inauthentic, distanced and incoherent, as images become disconnected from experience (see Featherstone, 1991, pp. 122–8). In sharp contrast, I see a world where very real and 'authentic' differences in experience and culture continue to exist, but are being expressed and communicated in a limited and narrow range of images, channels and contests. Furthermore, people have very good reasons to want to express themselves in this way.

References

APPADURAI, A. (1990) 'Disjuncture and difference in the global cultural economy', *Theory, Culture and Society*, Vol. 7, pp. 295–310.

FEATHERSTONE, M. (1991) *Consumer Culture and Postmodernism*, London, Sage.

FUSCO, C. (1990) 'Managing the other (A gestao do outro)', *Lusitania*, Vol. 1, No. 3, pp. 77–83.

HANNERZ, U. (1990) 'Cosmopolitans and locals in world culture', *Theory, Culture and Society*, Vol. 7, pp. 237–51.

JUDD, K. (1989) 'Who will define us? Creole history and identity in Belize', paper presented at the Annual Meeting of the American Anthropological Association, Washington, DC.

OLWIG, K.F. (1993) *Global Culture, Island Identity*, Chur, Switzerland, Harwood.

WILK, R. (1990) 'Consumer goods as dialogue about development: research in progress in Belize', *Culture and History*, Vol. 7, pp. 79–100.

WILK, R. (1991) 'Consumer goods, cultural imperialism and underdevelopment in Belize' in Third Annual Studies on Belize Conference, Spear Report No. 6, Belize City.

WILK, R. (1992) 'I would be proud to be a Belizean – if I could figure out what a Belizean is', paper presented at conference 'Defining the National', Lund, April 1992.

Source: Wilk, 1995, pp. 111–13; 118.

READING E:
Susan George and Fabrizio Sabelli, 'Structural salvation'

Between its independence in 1980 and 1987 Zimbabwe received nine Bank loans plus four IDA credits totalling $646 million. The country was not subjected to structural adjustment because it was not in arrears to any of its creditors and had never had to ask for debt rescheduling.

In the course of the 1980s Zimbabwe was hard-hit by many factors beyond its control, including drought and South-African-sponsored violence that nearly destroyed the tourist industry and forced the government to increase defence spending. In spite of all this, Zimbabwe was doing remarkably well among African countries, applying policies which were if not socialist as the authorities often claimed, at least nationalist.

Here was a non-adjusting country measurably more successful than the adjusters. How embarrassing that a country which protected its infant industries and local suppliers, which was self-sufficient in food, which had even managed to diversify into manufactured exports should prosper! Zimbabwe even contrived to sell wine to Europe. It was growing at two or three times the average rate elsewhere in Africa, while at the same time employing policy measures like trade controls, subsidies and high government spending on health and education.

By 1987 people at lower levels of the Bank who were genuinely committed to the country's success had almost completed arrangements for a loan to promote the export of manufactured goods. It would follow a previous, similar loan which Zimbabwe had used to extremely good effect. Then,

> after a long delay in Washington, without any technical problems being raised, nor any doubts being cast on the potential of Zimbabwe to benefit from the loan, it was finally vetoed for ideological reasons at the highest levels of the Bank. The last thing the Bank wanted to happen was for Zimbabwe to succeed with 'the wrong policies'.

(Stoneman, 1993)

Stoneman has been following the Bank's activities in Zimbabwe since independence. He sees it as an institution

> whose overall intention, and increasingly effect, is to promote the construction of a single world market, *substantially on the basis of the present world division of labour* ... [a] role mediated through an ideology that is claimed to be value-free science (emphasis added).

(Stoneman, 1989)

[...]

The economists who were the Bank's eyes and ears in Zimbabwe produced various reports and recommendations. Stoneman remarks fatalistically that, 'All World Bank or IMF reports in the end turn what evidence they have to recommending the standard free market package' (1989), which invariably includes currency devaluation, removal of foreign exchange controls and import restrictions, cutbacks or removal of subsidies, adaptation of relative price structures to the world market, and reduction of the state's role in the economy.

[...]

Another Bank report on Zimbabwe analysed by Stoneman provides recommendations which 'are in all respects exactly those which someone with no knowledge of Zimbabwe, but familiarity with the World Bank, would have predicted' (1989). This report does acknowledge – the evidence is too strong not to – that so far, Zimbabwe has made progress by using precisely those policies the Bank wants to abolish. The Bank's author reacts by saying that this is surprising. (The Bank is always surprised, too, by the failure of those who apply its policies to the letter.)

[...]

The Bank's project can also be analysed, however, as a religious utopia. Structural adjustment does not *set out* to make countries fail. But nor can these countries be allowed to succeed with the 'wrong' policies as the case of Zimbabwe shows. The Bank must, again and again, affirm the rightness of its teachings, in the teeth of all the evidence.

The Bank did not invent neo-classical economics, liberalism, free market orthodoxy, or whatever one cares to call this doctrine. It did not even invent the notion that the doctrine works in all places and at all times, regardless of the historical and social context and the relationships and inequalities between nations. The formalist school of economic anthropology has claimed the same thing for half a century. The Bank was, however, the first (along with the IMF) to put this doctrine into practice and to convince most of its contemporaries that the greatest good for the greatest number will necessarily emerge from its adoption, voluntarily if possible; if not, then under duress.

The salvation of the people and of the nations shall come about through binding them ever more tightly to the international market, equated with the world community. There, the poor shall partake of the same substance as the rich. Like any universal truth, adjustment is a purely abstract notion even if its application causes concrete pain. The available choices are reduced to one, There Is No Alternative; we are all bound by a single, compulsory, truth which shall be recognized. Then shall the wayward nations be freed from their errors.

References

STONEMAN, C. (1989) 'The World Bank and the IMF in Zimbabwe' in Campbell, B.K. and Loxley, J. (eds) *Structural Adjustment in Africa*, New York, St Martin's Press.

STONEMAN, C. (1993) 'The World Bank, income distribution and employment: some lessons for South Africa', proceedings of a conference at the University of East Anglia, 25 March 1993.

Source: George and Sabelli, 1994, pp. 61–2; 64, 65, 72.

CHAPTER TWO

'STORYING THE SELF': PERSONAL NARRATIVES AND IDENTITY

Ruth Finnegan

Contents

1   Introduction: who are you?

Shirley Lambert is in her early thirties and living in a council house in
Milton Keynes. She talks about her life:

> Our family personally, we had a lot of trouble with our family because
> we had a violent father, and my mother was actually mentally ill. We
> didn't do well at school at all because we had so much trouble with the
> family, it was more had we survived the day, you know, than actual
> getting down to it. My father would wake us up at 3 o'clock in the
> morning because there was dust on the stairs, so we would all have to
> sweep the whole house, you know what I mean, and so you didn't get a
> lot of sleep and then by the time you got to school you felt too tired and
> things like this and we didn't learn a lot. My teacher just thought I was
> disruptive and I ended up going into a children's home.
>
> I actually left home by the time I went in the children's home, because it
> was a residential place in Aylesbury, what we did was come home for
> the weekends, but I had actually been kicked out of home, so they didn't
> realize that I wasn't going home. So what we would do was, we would
> go to the children's home during the week, come home and just walk the
> streets for the whole weekend. There was a lot to walk, and because
> there were fields and things like that you could hide in Milton Keynes
> quite easily. And then when my assessment was over we actually went
> to college and everything, they decided that yes, you can now go back to
> your family, but what they didn't know was I couldn't go back to the
> family, because everything was like through the courts, and as soon as I
> walked in the door and all the abuse would start up again, the fighting,
> so coming up to 14 I left home, and I actually lived with a lady who I
> looked after her children, and that was the only home life I knew.
>
> Job wise it was very difficult because I was so young I couldn't get a job
> in Milton Keynes, I couldn't claim, because I didn't have the sense to
> claim, you know for help, I knew I was far too young, so I didn't even go
> and check out or try and bang on anybody's door to beg for it, you know,
> so you just made do, you know. When I was about 15 I got a small job in
> a little clothes store, but I got in awful trouble there because it is like all
> that glitters is gold to me, and because I had worked there for a pittance
> and couldn't have the things that were in the store I decided to help
> myself! And that was that, and I remember that was my first ever job and
> looking back now I think to myself if only I had the sense to not see
> everything as glittering and you can just do that, it would have been
> quite good, it would have been a good memory but it is a bad memory for
> me to know that I had messed it up quite horribly.
>
> After that, coming up sixteen round here was quite fun. 16/17 I worked
> for McDonalds until I was about 19, but it was great I was earning
> money, them days you could get a flat if you were earning money, I got a
> little flat and everything and I was on like sky-high, this is brilliant you
> know my life is coming together ...

That went very well, by this time I had lost contact with my family because I couldn't go back to the house, and with all the turmoil it was easier not going back ... One day I saw my little sisters outside a shop, and they were terrified of me, and I couldn't get why they were terrified of me, and I thought oh talk to me, and they said we are not allowed to talk to you, and you have got to go because their father was in the shop, and I said this is ridiculous you know, I thought what is happening, and so it was apparently he had left my mother, and taken all the kids and furniture and left her in the house with nothing, you know. ... and in the conversation they kind of told me she was ill.

So me, worry, worry, worry, backed up courage and a couple of friends and we went down there, and she actually had turned mad, and she was like living off cat food and things like that, you know. In big Milton Keynes, nobody realized, no neighbours realized, how awful it was, and actually I had to commit her at 18 to the mental hospital.

She continues with her story (for its background, see pages 79–80 below). She tells how she helped her sisters, coped with other hard experiences, continued to 'back up courage', and started to feel established in the local community. She concludes:

I mean like I said ending the story, I went all to the ripe age of 14 like and I couldn't even spell my own name, and I had to learn, and now like I'm the most magazine queen now, it is like I am always reading, and anybody can do it. I might not be a professional, I can't do a degree, my concentration span right doesn't – you know I can't sit still that long, I couldn't do something like that. But then you can always do something else, I can be special somewhere else, and that is basically my life.

personal narrative

When we read a **personal narrative** of this kind we are, it seems, brought right to a most personal point in contemporary culture: individual experience. This 'individual experience' will turn out to be more complex than it may seem at first sight. But it should be clear at least that, in personal stories, we are not focusing on formal structure, mass media or large-scale institutions and industries, but the everyday experience of ordinary individuals as they formulate it in their own words.

identity

The story here (abridged as it is) also raises the issue of personal **identity**: 'Who am I?' is the question which, in one sense, Shirley Lambert's narrative is grappling with. This is a serious question, which you have no doubt considered at various points in your life, and certainly in tackling this volume.

ACTIVITY 1

Who are you? If you *had* to answer that question in a couple of sentences, and after only a moment's reflection, how would you start to reply?

Your answer to that question could have drawn on a range of concepts which have been developed in sociology and cultural studies (see **du Gay, Hall et al.**, 1997; **Hall**, ed., 1997; and **Woodward**, ed., 1997). Alternatively, it could have reproduced the kind of thing you might say to an enquirer in some everyday situation (the two are not necessarily mutually exclusive!). Either way, you might be interested to see whether and how far your own response overlapped with any of the following categories.

One response would be to build on ideas about *similarity and difference* (see **Hall**, ed., 1997 and **Woodward**, ed., 1997). You could describe your identity by referring to the *social categories* in terms of which you (or Shirley Lambert) distinguish yourself from other people and are so distinguished by them. Classification by your work, for example, is one common response, both 'everyday' and theoretical; or similarly by your age, gender, class, status, 'race', ethnicity, family role, religion, etc. This might be combined with a view of identity as a *site of struggle* where relations of power are produced and reproduced.

Or the emphasis might be on a *situational* sense of identity, differentially developed according to the context you found yourself in or wished to highlight at a particular moment in time. Occupation might be the relevant factor in some situations; family or national origin in others; or a particular age category, place or family relationship (changing over the years); and so on: a *multifaceted and relative* sense of identity.

Or you might extend the reply in the previous paragraph by drawing on an approach which stresses the *historically contingent* nature of identity and the sense of self. Your own (or Shirley Lambert's) identity might then be understood by relating it to the *contemporary cultural concept* of identity or personhood (perhaps the fragmented, de-centred self said by some to be typical of late-modernity).

A contrasting approach might focus on a sustained *subjective sense of self*. This could draw particularly on the kind of reflective self-consciousness and 'inner life' which seems to make you as you are – a view which tends to accord with the idea of identity as essentially self-generated rather than determined by cultural factors (and one evident theme in Shirley Lambert's story).

You could also have drawn on a *multi-part model of the person* (familiar from Freudian analyses, as discussed in **Woodward**, 1997, though also with a long earlier history). Or, again, it could have been the idea of *the self as actively performed*, expressed through the performed activities and rituals in which you take a bodily part and collaborate with other people, rather than a matter of intellect or self-consciousness (as in the discussion of 'the body' in **Benson**, 1997, and further elaborated in the next chapter of this volume).

Or your response could simply be to start *telling the story of your life*.

All these answers represent acceptable approaches to the analysis of identity. You will doubtless recognize them either from the widely shared conventional wisdom of our culture or from your reading in this or comparable volumes. Between them they reflect major theoretical traditions – partly contrasting, partly overlapping – that have influenced our thinking about the nature of the self through the centuries.

What this chapter does is to expand on the final answer above: the idea of the self as *story*. This has direct implications for the study of identity, as well as linking into discussion about the significance of narrative in human affairs more generally.

The idea of 'self as story' both overlaps and contrasts with other models of identity. It also extends the idea of 'culture' and 'media' beyond the organizational structures of, say, the culture industries, broadcasting or the published media, into the everyday modes in which we express and construct our lives in personal terms, telling our own stories. It makes the assumption that it is valuable to look not just at the products of professionals and specialists but also at the practices of ordinary people in their everyday lives.

1.1   Preview and aims

the self is 'storied'

This chapter proceeds, first, to set the concept of 'story' in a more general perspective through the discussion of some recent work on narrative, and then moves on to explain a view of **the self as** essentially **'storied'** – formulated and experienced through self-narratives. In the examples of personal stories at the everyday level and also in the more general discussion, you will find that personal stories are being analysed less as the reflection of some irreducible 'inner experience' or 'external reality' than as both culturally constructed and actively *enstoried* by their tellers. In this story-based view of the self, the individual story-tellers are viewed as at once drawing on narrative conventions – a kind of art form – to realize their stories of the self, and as being creative and artistic actors themselves in the production of culture.

The approach in this chapter thus draws on a model of the self as 'storied' and of culture as both moulded and moulding through the personal stories of individuals. This is an increasingly popular viewpoint on the self, and you may well find it an illuminating perspective on the study of culture and of identity. But since any perspective will have limitations as well as insights, the chapter concludes with some brief reflections on the assumptions behind this approach, and some criticisms you might wish to consider. The concluding section also comments on ways in which this approach both overlaps and contrasts with other perspectives on culture and identity. As you will notice, the focus in this (and the following) chapter is on the 'everyday life' element of the volume's title – but in the last section we come back to debates about how this also relates to debates around 'consumption'.

Ultimately you will wish to reach your own informed judgement about which perspective (or blend of perspectives) you find most illuminating for your own work.

The main objectives of this chapter are thus to equip you to:

- Engage in general with the approaches of narrative analysts and, in particular, with the idea of 'life as a story' in the context of personal narratives in an everyday setting – thus gaining a further perspective on the self and the opportunity to reach the most 'personal' dimension of all (or is it?) in your analysis of culture, media and identity.

- Recognize and assess a narrative perspective which envisages personal story-telling as a medium through which people creatively produce 'stories of the self', both shaping and shaped by cultural conventions of narrative and identity – a further context for this book's focus on the balance between creativity and constraint.

- Reach your own evaluation of this narrative perspective as compared and contrasted with other approaches to culture and identity, and apply it to examples from your own observation and experience.

2   Narrative and humanity

One response, then, to the question 'Who are you?' is to tell a story of your life.

This may seem a trivial reply to a serious question – simplistic and 'merely' personal. Certainly it seems at first sight to have little of the grandeur of other ways of theorizing **the self**: in terms, say, of Freudian or Foucauldian theory, or of sociological approaches which illuminate the complex social factors and interactions which can influence – or arguably determine – our lives.

the self

But the concept of 'story' or 'narrative' is becoming another recognized approach to identity. It links, also, to an increasing stress by some scholars on the profound significance of narrative in the shaping and interpretation of human culture more generally. Despite all the controversies that this approach involves, it has none the less emerged as a powerful tool for analysing cultural products and processes.

Given its current influence, let me start with a short diversion to give some background to this general idea of **narrative** before moving on to specific cases.

narrative

In spite of the many controversies involved in studying narrative, one essential theme recurs. This is – to put it at its simplest – the view that human beings are story-telling animals. Whether explicitly or silently, we join together and make sense of our experiences in a more, or less, coherent narrative:

... only animals live entirely in the Here and Now. Only nature knows neither memory nor history. But man – let me offer you a definition – is the story-telling animal. Wherever he goes he wants to leave behind not a chaotic wake, not an empty space, but the comforting marker-buoys and trail-signs of stories, he has to go on telling stories, he has to keep on making them up.

(Swift, 1992, pp. 62–3)

The quotation above comes from an imaginative novel, Graham Swift's *Waterland*. But (provided you bypass the distraction of what today might be regarded as sexist terminology) he is aptly summarizing what has become a central theme in recent analysis.

Salaman (1997) provides some interesting examples of this use of narrative in his discussion of the 'narratives of corporate culture and of enterprise', and the tale of the manager as epic hero/ine. According to Deal and Kennedy, 'The company has explicit values and beliefs which its employees share. It has heroes. It has storytellers and stories' (1989, p. 12; see also Jeffcutt, 1994; Clark and Salaman, 1996). One formative element in the culture of production, it emerges, is the process by which both managers and employees construct reality by 'telling stories'.

This concept of story is increasingly applied to people's definitions in all spheres of life. In the context of analysing cultural processes, it illuminates how people's ideologies and theories are all the more influential and evocative when they chime in with familiar narrative motifs, themes and hero figures.

But it is not just the 'subjects' of academic study who recount stories. Academics and intellectuals too tell their own tales. The grand paradigms of social science, for example, have been described as forms of narrative – the 'good story' told by Marx, Durkheim, Weber or Simmel for instance (Clegg, 1993, p. 15). Similarly, the many interpretations posited within sociology and cultural studies are nowadays often referred to as 'stories'. This has become one dominant theme in cultural studies, where 'narratives and their interwoven textures are the stuff of life' (Inglis, 1993, p. 244). Historians' accounts too, it has been pointed out, are *stories* about what happened. The term can be applied not just to their straight chronological narratives but also to their varying assumptions about the causes or results of lengthy processes over time. Some of their accounts, for example, are rooted in stories highlighting the deeds of individual actors, others in very different stories depicting (for example) class-based causes, revolutionary changes or evolution from (say) 'traditional' to 'modern' or to 'postmodern' epochs (White, 1973; Cronon, 1992). The same 'story' theme is evident in psychology, as in Sarbin's *Narrative Psychology: the storied nature of human conduct* (Sarbin, 1986; see also Schafer, 1992), and in Freudian therapy. The natural sciences are no exception, with the 'narratives of human evolution' interpreted as versions of the widespread hero tale (Landau, 1991). And if you look through this volume or other volumes in the *Culture, Media and Identities* series you will find many examples of theoretical interpretations being referred to as 'stories'.

As you may have noticed, this use of 'story' is by now pretty much taken for granted as an analytic term across a range of social sciences and humanities (for further examples, see Plummer, 1995, especially p. 181). Indeed, whether due to sceptical postmodernist critiques or just an increasing interest in narrative, it seems to have become a widely accepted convention in much social scientific writing to refer to academic theories and interpretations as 'stories'.

But just what is implied by the term 'story' in such contexts? What difference does such a label make? It has to be admitted that precisely what is meant by calling something a 'story' is not always totally clear. Sometimes 'story' seems to be more a bit of fashionable terminology than a thought-out analytic term! Or it may be used as just a decorative if somewhat faded metaphor. But where the term is applied in a more considered way its minimum features are reasonably agreed. Referring to something as a **'story'**   story (or 'narrative' – the two terms are used synonymously for present purposes) normally conveys both some idea of *time/sequence* and an element of explanation or coherence – some kind of *plot* that makes sense to the teller and audience. You can see both of these in even the sketchy extracts from Shirley Lambert's story. Further, a story usually manifests some accepted *conventions about form and content*. In other words it constitutes a culturally recognized **genre** (for further discussion of definitional and related   genre issues, see Bauman, 1986; Linde, 1993; Mumby, 1993; Plummer, 1995; Prince, 1989; Riessman, 1993; Rosenwald and Ochberg, 1992).

Applying the term 'story' to either academic interpretations or (insofar as this is different) to the actors' assumptions thus implies that these can be treated *as* stories: that is, that we can analyse them in terms of temporal/ sequential framework, intelligible plot, and culturally constructed conventions about what makes up an accepted piece of story-telling. Certain kinds of protagonists may be expected: the hero for example – as in the tales of corporate culture – or the victim, villain or trickster. There may be recurrent recognizable plots too. We can recognize, for example, the hero going on a quest; the success or otherwise of evil; a change over time from deprivation/suffering/immaturity to riches/happiness/maturity, or from modernity to postmodernity; or, alternatively, the fall from grace, from the golden age of true community and harmony to the woes of the present.

One common implication is that, as summed up in Graham Swift's view of human beings as 'story-telling animals', a narrative framework is a characteristically human way for formulating and conveying experience. As Barbara Hardy put it: 'We dream in narrative, day-dream in narrative, remember, anticipate, hope, despair, believe, doubt, plan, revise, criticize, construct, gossip, learn, hate, and love by narrative' (1968, p. 5; quoted in MacIntyre, 1985, p. 197). Equally relevant is the implication that, insofar as they are labelled 'stories', such formulations can be analysed less as simple reflections of 'reality' than as texts mediated through the cultural conventions by which they are shaped and told.

For some analysts, applying the concept of 'story' to academic interpretations has a further implication. It gives a vantage-point on academic writing, enabling a critique of *its* culturally recognized conventions. In this view, rather than being 'objective', 'neutral' or 'scientific' accounts of reality, academic theories too have their own 'rhetoric' and 'poetics': they are as much 'art' as 'science', being shaped by current narrative conventions in the same way as other stories (e.g. Clifford and Marcus, 1986; Van Maanen, 1988). Non-written texts can be treated similarly. It becomes possible to analyse the 'poetics' of the story conveyed through a particular juxtaposition of photographs, or constructed in an exhibition like the Museum of Mankind's *Paradise* (see **Lidchi**, 1997). The ideas of 'poetics' and of 'story' hint that what is constructed is more akin to fiction or poetry, artfully crafted, than to the disinterested and neutral recording of reality which was once assumed to be the model for scientific enquiry.

Sometimes the label 'story' implies the more extreme claim that the theories put forward by academics are no more authoritative than stories told in any other voices. Far from being the final word, the interpretations of scholars – who are often in a position of power – should not in this view be taken as *the* authoritative and 'above-the-battle' account. Above all, this argument might go on, the academics' versions should not obscure the definitions of reality in the stories of those they study: the colonized, the 'hidden', the minority groups or, indeed, anyone that 'research' is conducted *on* – the subjects of the scholars' story-making.

You may or may not wish to go along with all the viewpoints implied in some of these usages of the term 'story' (though it is useful to be able to recognize them if you encounter them). However, that final position of pointing out that there is a multiplicity of voices, not just those of the dominant scholars, appropriately leads us back to the central focus of this chapter: the voices of ordinary people speaking about their lives in the context of everyday activities.

3 Stories as the individual voice of the self – or not?

3.1 Personal narratives

If we want to know about people's experience and how they interpret it, there is something to be said for looking not to broader generalizations but to the stories of the participants themselves, and, better still, to stories told not in others' words but as the tellers themselves express them.

For example, we can certainly read informative general accounts of the Industrial Revolution. But how much more vivid is the insight we get from a narration of how this was actually experienced in an individual case. Take Thomas Wood's life story, to be found in Burnett's *Useful Toil: autobiographies of working people from the 1820s to the 1920s* (1974, pp. 304–12).

Thomas Wood was born in Yorkshire in 1822, the son of a handloom weaver. He started at the local woollen mill at the age of 8, working the regular hours of 6 a.m. to 7.30 p.m. But he longed to be delivered from 'the bondage of factory life', and, at the age of 14, persuaded his parents to apprentice him to a local engineer manufacturing powerlooms:

> So I was to be a mechanic and have my heart's desire. As will be seen my parents paid dearly for it. Our food was of the plainest, the quantity seldom sufficient. I seldom satisfied my appetite unless I called at Aunt Nancy's after dinner to pick up what she had to spare. As to the luxury of pocket money, it was unknown. ...
>
> There was a ['Mechanics'] Institute at Wilsden, perhaps the best in the country then. It was only three miles off, so I resolved to enter that. ... The terms were 1½d per week ... more than I could raise. I therefore got bundles of rotten sticks in the wood and sold them for firewood. Turnip tops and nettles when in season with mushrooms I collected, and whatever would sell. Well pleased was I when I had 3d to meet my fortnight's contributions. Then, as to reading, in winter I had to read by firelight excepting when I could afford a ½d candle, which I used to save to read with in bed. I have read perhaps scores of times till 12 or 1 o'clock. There were no curtains to fire. There were no interruptions. A house with seven or eight children on one floor is a fine opportunity for the display of patience on the part of a student or an earnest reader. Get into bed for the warmth and then the luxury of an unbroken reading was a treat that compensated for any privations, and lifted me, for the time being, into another world.
>
> (Burnett, 1974, pp. 307–8)

Autobiographical accounts of this kind perhaps once seemed too 'trivial' or, alternatively, too 'personal' for serious academic study. They neither comprised the products of elite writers nor fitted with the 'collective' focus of much social science. But there is now greater interest in such personal accounts. Historians and others now make a point of collecting and analysing working-class autobiographies (e.g. Burnett, 1974, 1982; Burnett et al., 1984–9; Vincent, 1981) and those of women as well as of men (e.g. Stanley, 1984, 1992; Personal Narratives Group, 1989). This trend has been further supported by recent interests in 'history from below' and the turn towards social rather than just political history.

An interest in the life stories of 'ordinary' people has long been one strand in the social sciences, although often rather submerged compared to more generalized or macro studies. But a specific focus on personal lives has been emerging strongly in recent years (e.g. Plummer, 1995; Stanley and Morgan, 1993), balancing the still-powerful stress of much sociology on the collective by reviving earlier interests in life stories and the creative role of individual actors (Plummer, 1983). This has been reinforced by the growing influence of oral history, giving access to ordinary people's subjective experience and their spoken life stories, and by the family history movement which has, among other things, encouraged older people to tell the story of their lives. There is also the general interest in documenting the experiences of hitherto 'invisible' and 'unsung' groups and individuals.

As a result, the study of personal narratives is currently the focus of extensive interdisciplinary collaboration, involving – among others – anthropologists, psychologists, folklorists, historians, therapists and literary scholars as well as sociologists. And there are now many studies of personal narratives, not just from the past but of living people, young as well as old, in the present.

3.2   'Life as narrative' and the 'storied' self

personal narrative

Our interest in **personal narratives** here, however, is not primarily in the factual evidence that these stories can provide about the past or present (critically analysed and interpreted with due care, needless to say). This is one valid approach, of course, although not without its epistemological problems. But more significant for present purposes is the role such narratives play in formulating and shaping their tellers' experience. Put another way, personal narratives can be regarded not as a *reflection* of life but rather as a way of *constructing* it (for further discussion, see **Hall**, 1997a).

life as narrative

This view is eloquently stated in Jerome Bruner's image of '**life as narrative**'. Though coming from a background in psychology, Bruner draws on wide interdisciplinary insights and his influential writings have also been much read by sociologists. He puts forward a 'constructivist view of narrative', building on the philosophical position that 'world making' is a function of *mind* rather than of external reality. In a parallel way, he argues, autobiography should be viewed as 'a set of procedures for "life making"' (Reading A, p. 105).

> READING A
>
> You should now read Reading A, 'Life as narrative', by Jerome Bruner, which you will find at the end of this chapter. Bruner starts by explaining his 'constructivist view' of self-narrative in general terms before moving on to his discussion of 'four self-narratives'.
>
> As you come to the end of the article try to summarize:
>
> 1   What you consider to be Bruner's main conclusion.
>
> 2   How far you agree with it.

Bruner gives a clear exposition of his view of 'life as narrative'. The telling of life stories represents not a mere expression of either outward reality or inner state but an active form of organizing personal experience: 'A life as led is inseparable from a life as told ... a life is not "how it was" but how it is interpreted and reinterpreted, told and retold' (Reading A, p. 111).

Bruner states his position in blunt terms. But his basic point is broadly shared by other analysts of narrative (including those he cites). It is by now a familiar assumption in the comparative literature within social and humanistic studies that narrative does not just reflect or report experience but also shapes it (e.g. Neisser and Fivush, 1994; Personal Narratives Group, 1989; Rosenwald and Ochberg, 1992; Stromberg, 1993; see also **Hall**, 1997a, 1997b, on constructing the world in and through language). We formulate our experience through our knowledge of the stories of others and by telling our own stories, whether aloud or to ourselves. It is through storying that we *experience* – and recognize that experience – in the first place.

> ACTIVITY 2
>
> Can you think of any examples of this role of story-telling from your own observation and experience?

This 'meaning-ful' role of narrative is particularly apparent when older people write or recount their life stories. The very fact of storying their life gives it validity, an enhanced sense of 'reality'. It is also constructively utilized in therapeutic and gerontological contexts, and in the 'reminiscence' movement (Bornat, 1989). But the basic point is equally applicable to all ages. **'The self' is** inevitably **'storied'** and identity lies in the narratives *the self is 'storied'* constructed by the storying self. Structuring experience in narrative terms creates order out of chaos and gives meaning to what otherwise would be experienced as anarchic or fragmented (Bruner, 1987; Abrahams, 1985; Shotter and Gergen, 1989).

The general significance of narrative for constructing and ordering human experience has already been alluded to in section 2. But the telling of *personal* stories above all, it seems, can formulate, justify and express personal experience through narrating the identity and self-understanding of the individual self.

3.3   Personal creation – cultural convention

With self-narratives, then, it could be argued that we have reached the irreducibly personal and individual. The representation is not that of external observers or theorizers, but in the authentic voice and words of the creative and thinking self-narrator.

ACTIVITY 3

How far would you accept the view that self-narratives are irreducibly personal and individual? And, returning to Reading A, do you consider that Bruner would agree with that way of putting it?

Certainly there is much to be said for such a formulation. Seeing the self as 'storied' does indeed give insight into subjective experience and personal interpretation in ways not provided for in more generalizing, deterministic and, as it were, 'outside' perspectives. Thus, it is not just to such dimensions as the mass media, the political economy or even the conceptualizations of academics that we should look to see how culture is created or identities formed. Self-narratives are a medium through which individuals at every level play a creative role in formulating both their own identities and, by extension, the culture in which they are participants.

So much would probably be widely agreed (if not always sufficiently emphasized). But taking the further step of suggesting the 'authenticity' or total 'freedom' of the narrator would be to overstate the case. Narrative scholars themselves – including Bruner – have been among the first to point to the culturally constructed conventions that emerge in personal narratives.

genre

Self-narratives may at first sight seem too personal to contain recurrent stylistic or thematic patterns. But life stories or personal narratives do seem to form a recognized **genre** in our culture. It is an 'informal' and often unwritten one, it is true. But the existence and – as it were – artistry of generic conventions are not confined to examples which have been visibly written down or formally published (a point nicely made in the title of Bakhtin's influential *Speech Genres,* 1986). As with the narrators in Bruner's research, so too more widely: people understand what is meant by telling a life story. Whether or not they have done so in that particular format before, they are ready and able to come up with intelligible versions of relevant narratives in culturally appropriate situations (you could test out this assessment from your own observation; for further discussion see Langellier, 1989; Linde, 1993; Abrahams, 1985; Finnegan, 1992).

A genre is culturally defined – an art form rather than 'a fact of nature'. Thus we can identify the conventions which broadly make up the genre of soap opera (as in **Gledhill**, 1977). Similarly, different genres of music each have their own conventions about their style, performance, audience, etc. (see Chapter 3 in this volume). In the same way, approaching self-narrations from this viewpoint means that we can try to investigate the culturally defined

conventions

conventions – their art as it were – which narrators utilize to formulate their stories.

So, although life stories and self-narrations are indeed personal, they also turn out manifest a range of recurrent, culturally expected features. There are the structuring frameworks of the hero tale, the battle of good and evil, or the various protagonists and plot elements mentioned in Bruner's paper. Others are evident in particular historical periods or cultural situations. The short extract from Thomas Wood's life story reproduced in section 3.1 above is one example. It looks highly personal and transparent. However, David Vincent's study of nineteenth-century working-class autobiographies, *Bread, Knowledge and Freedom* (1981), shows how, amidst the personal variety of the stories, a series of stock themes come up time and again, notably the struggle toward self-improvement and success through self-education. One way of experiencing and making sense of one's story in that social and historical context was to utilize this familiar plot.

Other recurrent themes pertain to specific groups, perhaps quite small ones. Luisa Passerini looked at the stories of imprisoned women members of terrorist organizations like the Red Brigade in Italy in the 1970s and early 1980s, identifying 'the world of the imaginary' in their life stories. She is not by this implying that the stories were 'false' or hallucinatory – as opponents of these women claimed – but describing how the women related their lives to recurrent images:

> ... heroic stories of revolutionaries in other countries and other times; the legend of the hero or heroine who leaves home to help the oppressed ...; the ideal of a small community united against the world, united beyond death; fables of the loyalty of mothers who do not abandon their defeated daughters, but are ready to give their lives for them.
>
> (Passerini, 1990, p. 54)

These women had been imprisoned and defeated. Nevertheless, their otherwise very diverse life stories showed how the tellers could define their reality by drawing on common mythic themes, 'a shared imaginary' (ibid., p. 54).

We could track other culturally constructed features in personal stories. But perhaps enough has been said to suggest that we cannot just take life stories as the 'natural' and unmediated effusions of asocial individuals. They remain uniquely personal, it is true – but they also deploy recognized cultural conventions.

The point is partly that other things are involved in personal narratives than just the individual teller. In other words, an 'intentional' analysis focusing *only* on the individual author is not sufficient (see **Hall**, 1997a). Equally important, personal stories are not just creations of a 'free' autonomous individual – one model of the self – but also of the cultural conventions he or she makes use of. The stories are themselves constructed cultural forms as well as constructing the life and experiences of their tellers.

The perspective here, then, involves viewing self-narratives neither as uncreative reflections of social attitudes nor as adjustments to external forces. Rather, they are culturally developed resources which – like language – people can draw on, manipulate and enact in the creation and experience of their storied lives.

4   Some contemporary stories

The same narrative perspective can be extended to contemporary lives around us, including those that have not hitherto been written down. Among the many possible cases, let me give some illustrations from the stories of people living in my own town (the examples of personal narratives drawn on in this section are reported more fully in Finnegan, forthcoming).

The tales are interesting in their own right. But at the same time as considering these personal narratives and their narrative analysis, you can also relate them to the wider theories about the nature of the self. The activity below lists three questions you could ask as you read through this case study.

ACTIVITY 4

As you go through the examples of life stories that follow, consider how you would respond to the following questions:

1   Do the personal narratives below take us directly into individuals' personal experience of identity and the self (a similar question to that in Activity 3 in the previous section)?

2   How far do one or more of the various approaches to the self (e.g. those summarized in section 1) seem to be applicable or illuminating for these personal narratives?

3   Can analysing personal narratives contribute in any way to the book's theme of the balance between creativity and constraint?

How, if at all, then, do the personal narratives below and their analysis illuminate these questions – and vice versa?

4.1   Stories of a city

For this section we must travel to Milton Keynes, that famous (or notorious) 'new city' planned in the late 1960s as part of the British 'new towns' policy of the time. We shall be considering the stories of individuals in one of its housing estates.

Fishermead was one of the first 'grid squares' to be built in the new city, having been started in the mid-1970s. By the 1990s, the estate had a poor reputation among other city-dwellers – a view not totally shared by its residents. One of these Fishermead residents was Shirley Lambert, whose story opened this chapter. But she was not the sole narrator, and widening the analysis to the personal tales of others who were also living in Fishermead at the time of their narrations (in 1994) can set her story in perspective.

FIGURE 2.1   A street in Fishermead.

Before turning to the stories themselves I should briefly comment on how they were recorded. As in Bruner's study, the speakers were invited to talk about their lives in short narrations only – a recording session of about an hour – and the sessions were generally undirective. Narrators were found largely by 'snowball' methods: that is, they were not selected as a statistically representative 'sample' – not in any case an appropriate method for qualitative narrative analysis where the individuality of the speakers is as significant as any supposed 'typicality'. There was however some attempt to include a range of ages, backgrounds and educational experience. The narrators varied in fluency, with some more eager or available than others to talk about their experiences, perhaps explaining why women's narratives outnumbered those of men. Most seemed not to find it strange to produce a relatively sustained account of their lives, even if it was the first time they had presented accounts in this form.

All the narrators included here were interested in telling their stories and were prepared to have them quoted (under pseudonyms). It is on this basis that they are referred to and quoted here, but on the understanding that these tales belong ultimately to their tellers and not to the researcher (for further background, see Finnegan, 1996, and forthcoming).

A notable characteristic of the 35 self-narratives featured in this study was their diversity. The stories depicted strikingly contrasting backgrounds, outlooks, experiences and speaking styles. The narrators had come to the area at different times, had different backgrounds, were more – or less – reflective, held contrary assessments of the locality, and had spent differing proportions of their lives in Milton Keynes. These highly individual stories make it difficult to reach definitive *generalized* conclusions about their 'identity'.

The overwhelming impression was of the richness of the individual and differing personalities and of their formulation in narrative. Shirley Lambert's was perhaps a particularly memorable tale. But *each* story in its way presented its own personality and unique experience. It conveyed the voice of a thinking individual who, through personal memories and verbal articulation at one point in time, conveyed some sense of expressing meaning, of creating coherence, of somehow controlling and enunciating a distinctive place in the universe (points that you will recall from Bruner's analysis in Reading A, and which are also made in similar narrative studies).

But beyond this personal diversity, some recurrent themes began to emerge. They were used in different ways in different tales, and no story contained all of them. But there did indeed seem to be a range of stock topics, motifs, protagonists and plot structures.

Let me illustrate a few of these narrative patterns. I will focus especially on the devices used to produce tales which, despite their rapid and compressed telling, conveyed some sense of a *coherent and intelligible story*.

The motif of *continuity from the past* was one accepted rationale for the plot. Narrators often took it for granted that it would make sense both for themselves and their listeners if they linked important features of their lives with one or other of their parents or recounted their 'roots' and 'family tradition'. Stories commonly opened with the teller's family origins and their inheritance from the past. The family and/or the place was presented as the ground from which the individual grew, in some sense explaining their life. Brenda Dawson's story started with her 'firmly working class roots' in Southall, portraying her family's background and her grandmother's tales: 'She was fascinating, and I used to listen to stories of her childhood, and how she had to walk four miles to school and back in all weathers, and what they used to get up to. It was wonderful, it was like living history.' (All quotations here are taken from transcripts of the recordings made in Fishermead in 1994 and pseudonyms are used, as described above.)

The thread running through another story was the teller's father who 'for me is still alive and guiding me'; 'I still thank him for all the things he did that made me the person that I am today'. Similar values came out in one narrator's 'Dorset pride', another's identity as a Londoner, or a third's view of himself as 'proud to be a Somerset man'.

The continuities were sometimes presented as a kind of cyclical progression from the past to the future. Dennis Travers told how his son had inherited his interest in art 'from me', while Alison Stanley explained: 'We are a family of readers. ... All of us, my grandchildren are the same, and my children are the same, every house you go into in my family there are books.' On a lighter note perhaps, but personally important to the teller, Sally

Vincent set her rotundity in longer perspective by her family inheritance: 'We are all little and round!'

This structuring from the past was usually presented as benign but some stories narrated individuals' determination *not* to perpetuate some parental trait – an equally effective plot device. Agnes Farley's story told how her early life made her a 'rebel':

> Well I was born in Devon in 1917 and I lived on a farm until I was 23. ... And although I lived in an idyllic spot and really I didn't have anything to complain about, but on reflection I think I had a very lonely childhood because my brothers being that much older, and there were not a lot of children around, but also a very strong class distinction in that part of the world, and my mother was very aware of this and she insisted that I played only with the right children and this made life very difficult.
>
> The prospects were in those days that one would live at home until one married, and most of my friends did just that. ... I think I was a bit cheesed in my teens and always wishing I was somewhere else, very much so. I was restricted, and I became so deceitful. I think if you live that existence you either become like a dummy or a rebel and I became a rebel.

Whether positive or negative in tone, narrators were taking for granted that an intelligible narrative structure, one shared with their listeners, was to set their experiences in the perspective of successive generations, framing their lives within a longer cycle of family continuity or discontinuity. The precise content of this was unique to each teller. But the underlying framework was to convey the story not of a meaningless isolated individual from nowhere, but of someone with a just base for their own identity and place in history.

ACTIVITY 5

If you were telling your own story, is continuity from the past a theme that you might employ?

Another integrating device invoked some *personal avocation or principle* as a continuing thread through the story. This could be a consuming interest held throughout life, like music, sport or religious adherence – recognized and value-laden pathways in our culture – as a kind of signature tune with a meaning over and above specific events. Experiences around this continuing theme somehow conveyed a quasi-mythic flavour and were recounted with particular fluency and conviction.

An enthusiasm for music was one such theme. 72-year-old Andrew Cunningham was recovering from a stroke, but became fluent once he started talking about music. His passion as a child was to learn drumming:

I couldn't afford it, a pound an hour for lessons. Well, my dad said 'Well there you are, I can't pay for it, it's too much money'. I thought well blow it, I'll find my own way.

So he taught himself:

– by sound, and a record player, you used to put the HMV records on it. Seventy-eights. ... The thing I have never learned to do properly is a roll. Yeh, I couldn't do it now, cos of the hands you see, but I could do it slowly with a good drum kit. ... Course I had a drum kit and a great big bass drum like you see in The Salvation Army up there. ... And when the war came and I went to Wales and that was when I got in the band with the *Hotshots*. ... It was good it was.

His musical interests continued throughout his life.

Jonathan Tyler, too, spoke enthusiastically about music. The pride of his life was his huge and well-used tape collection of some 120 composers. The same theme sets him in the longer scheme of family continuity:

My love of music, well my mother used to play the piano very well, she was a good amateur pianist, and difficult things mostly Beethoven, and Schumann and that is probably what ignited it, and that probably put it in my brother's mind, because he played jazz all his life.

Music was an evocative metaphor for his own experience: 'I do like Milton Keynes now and I appreciate it, but it took time, it's like learning a new composer.'

Adherence to a particular religion and its discourse is another familiar framework for personal experience. The 100-year-old Timothy Hopkins was clear about its structuring significance in his life story. He started with his church upbringing, several times emphasizing his long membership of the local church choir in Dorset: 'I almost lived in the church, I loved it.' As a young man he lost an early job through loyalty to his own church's football team when he declined to play for the firm's team. The same theme appeared in his vivid account of his godfather's voice saving him from death when his troop ship was torpedoed in the First World War. He couldn't swim much, and stood on deck wondering what to do:

And it may seem strange to you, but when I was born ... and my mother had sent for the minister to baptise me in my living room which he did, and she said we haven't got a godfather, vicar, and he said that's alright I'll be godfather and look after him all his life. That's the point I'm getting at, I stood on this deck, not knowing, alone, a voice suddenly said to me 'Jump', and I turned around and there was nobody around, and it said 'Jump' and I ran to the side and I jumped over and down. The boat was going down the side and I jumped into this boat full of men and that saved my life, because we were only about twenty yards away, rowing, when the [ship] went down.

He later spent time in a Cairo hospital where what he recounted was not his illness but his church involvement, for, as he put it, 'The church has been my life'. He struggled out to a service, held in a marquee:

> The minister spoke to me when the service was over, like they do at the door. He said 'Have you always attended church?', and I said 'Yes I almost live in the church'. He said, 'Well I wonder if you would help me with communion next Sunday, as my server?' ... I did that and I wasn't very old and it was a great thing to me to serve communion in a marquee church.

Religious terminology continued throughout his story, and he finally reflected: 'People say oh you are fond of flowers, and I say I am, I love flowers, to me they are one of God's gifts, from tiny little seeds you get wonderful flowers like that.'

Music and religion are intelligible and familiar frameworks for a life story. Other preoccupations are less widely recognized and so need more elaboration to convey their centrality for the teller. Peter Sutton's story, for example, was one of great upsets, but bound together by one lifelong passion. He linked this to his family roots:

> My mother was a great film fan, we never had a television until I was 13, she adored the cinema, and in London it was a – what is the word I am looking for? – a paradise. Film goers' delight. There were cinemas everywhere, so consequently I spent a lot of time going to the theatres, she loved live shows as well, my father was just not interested at all. That was where I started to get a great interest before I was even 8 or 9, I was totally in love with the movies ... I have got to do these things called movies.

His plans to go to college were upset by his father's sudden death, so he took a factory job. But his love affair with film continued. The turning-point came one Friday afternoon:

> I watched a chap of 64, 65 coming up, he was planing a piece of wood [at the factory], a carpenter, and doing it at a fairly slow pace, and going backwards and forwards, and I was holding the broom, and I looked at him and I said to myself that man has been doing that for forty years. I am not going to do that for forty years, and I went into the office to Mr M – and I said I am so sorry but I don't think this is for me. ...
>
> I was out of work. I went to the Youth Unemployment and ... they said we don't know [how to get into the movies], the only way to do it is you will have to knock on a few doors, and go up to that place called Wardour Street, Soho, very nasty. And that is just what I did, got an underground train, a bus, underground train, down to Wardour Street, started at the bottom and ended up at the top at Oxford Circus, and

half-way down someone said they wanted a teaboy, a rewind boy, rewinding the films, and I said, 'Great terrific', £3. 17s. 6d. in those days, and I had a job. And that is how I started as a teenager.

His story continued about how he 'went on from there', his professional pride in film-editing and the pressures of the job – 'beautiful, phenomenal'. Sad as he was over many disappointments, his devotion to film integrated – and justified – his narrated life.

The most prominent theme of all centred on the idea of the *individual narrator* and the narrator's *sense of identity and control.* In one sense this is too obvious to need stating. Speakers were invited to recount their personal experiences and the subject of many sentences was predictably 'I'. This indeed is the cultural convention we expect and exploit when we use the recognized autobiographical form of expression, one accepted framework for organizing individual experience. But was there perhaps more to it than that? It was certainly striking how forcibly the concept of the individual emerged as a key structuring theme in the life stories.

This was conveyed in several ways. Some tales centred on the individual's *character*, one common mode for structuring a life story (see Linde, 1993). This was sometimes related to the complementary theme of family background but also figured as a trait developed independently and individually.

Sally Vincent's story for example was notable for her confrontations, sticking up vociferously for her rights against neighbours, partners, relations, officials. Her narration was punctuated by explanatory asides: 'I am not a very patient person', 'I have never had patience, I ain't got none', 'You couldn't change me, not after all this time'. Similar – if less confrontational – was Brenda Dawson's assessment of herself as 'never very good at sort of lying quietly down like a doormat'. Though she stressed the frustrations of her life as an army wife, her story was structured round how she did indeed 'complain about things' and finally, by *not* being a 'doormat', won back an identity that she had 'kind of lost': 'It was very good because you know, I was sort of earning some money. It was just getting things sort of back for me – a life which wasn't just totally involved with children and looking after husband. ... It has been worthwhile.'

Another related theme in which individual identity and control were conveyed by narrators centred on the individual teller's *positive action and enterprise* – something more than just their enduring character. Shirley Lambert's story, already quoted in section 1, is one example. As she told it, despite her early (and partly continuing) misfortunes, she created her own life, exerted herself and step by step 'backed up courage' to help others and control events. Her initial foray into fostering 'made me feel proud that I could do something for somebody else what I couldn't do for my own family', and gradually her actions enabled her to avoid her violent father and help her younger sisters and mentally ill mother, as well as gaining the confidence to advise others about the courage needed when 'it's hard'. Her philosophy was 'to be my own boss, right, and try and earn money and help everybody around me'.

Rachel Jacobs's narrative was in its way similar. It presented some horrific personal experiences but also her enterprise in dealing with them. This concluded in a relatively happy ending as she met her successive problems by – in turn – founding her own firm, leaving the partner she felt had let her down (and consequently being left totally destitute), working as a cabbie to make ends meet, sacrificing that job to uphold the morals she wanted her children to observe, and exploring new ways of maintaining herself. Finally, she had now found a group of congenial friends.

Not all examples were as explicitly articulated as these. Also, it has to be said that the patterns in these otherwise very individual stories were emergent rather than elicited through quantitative or experimental analysis. Nevertheless, I was surprised by the prevalence of the emphasis on personal enterprise and action. The stories regularly narrated active decisions and follow-through: from choosing to leave home for Milton Keynes at the age of 16, or teenage persistence in finding a job, to insisting on respect from others (like the bakery shopkeeper who forbade swearing in her shop), supporting one's own children against those of others, or sticking up for a principle whatever the consequences.

This might not have been so. Given the social constraints we all labour under, not least these narrators, the integrating narrative artistry might equally have deployed themes about powerlessness or the determining force of external events. There was something of this, but surprisingly little. The individual teller – in the role of hero – was presented as the essential reality of the story and took the central motivating role in its plot.

Stories involve other people and, particularly at certain life stages, the subject was sometimes 'we'. Nevertheless, the active mover in these personal narratives was mostly 'I'. Stories recounted how this active 'I' detached itself to gain personal independence or achieve a particular aim. Leaving the parental home was one common turning-point. Joy Osborne recounted her hesitations about leaving her foster-home when she was 18 but her satisfaction when she managed it:

> It took me three months for me to actually tell [my foster mother] that I had got this flat ... because she had been so good to me, and I felt like I was letting her down by leaving in a way. In the end I told her and she was over the moon for me and she came over and saw it and so I moved in. But although I moved in, I spent most of the time out sleeping at other people's houses because Christ, I was frightened really.
>
> Eventually I remember being round a friend's house and I said I think I'll go home tonight, I am not going to stay, I'm going to go home, and that was the beginning of me getting into the homely type thing, and wanting

to decorate and getting me stuff together. I was eighteen then, I got it just after I was eighteen, and I really enjoyed it, it was like you know this is my own pad.

ACTIVITY 6

Have you noticed any instances of this theme of positive action and enterprise in your own experience of other people's stories (whether stories of their life generally or short anecdotes about particular experiences)?

Individual action and control were expressed even in tales recounting external constraints or disappointments, things 'happening' rather than consciously planned. Brenda Dawson's tale of forced and reluctant moves as an army wife also told how she dealt with them, while another narrator immediately amplified her 'not so much a decision as something that happened' by 'and making the most of what happened'. Shirley Lambert's tale ended with the reflective commentary on her scarcely-easy life: 'Everybody is allowed a chance, and I didn't have the chance and I gave myself the chance though and I think if I can do it anybody can.'

Lesley Lambert (Shirley's younger sister) was one of very few who directly referred to her *lack* of power:

> I feel like I should try and do something [for Milton Keynes], but what can you do, when you have an idea and you go somewhere with it, they beat you down, because they are like oh you are just small fry, once you try you just get kicked down, and you can't win, unless you have got money.

But she then followed this by a long episode depicting her effectiveness in another context – 'trivial' to some readers, perhaps, but notably one of the liveliest and most fluent episodes in the narration (also reminiscent of the discussion of attitudes towards home decoration in the previous chapter):

> It was a really big house, three bedrooms and it was a three-storey house, the wallpaper was dire and it was really really bad it was half pink and half blue, and I used to think who in their right mind would paint their wallpaper half pink and half blue, it was like a nightmare, and so we got to painting it straight away, and there is so many good memories in that house. ...

> We had this brainwave that we were going to decorate the little toilet, and we wanted to do something really different and Paula is really arty and I said why don't we print handprints going up the wall, we can have a little border and then they could go up the wall, and she said that is a good idea we could do it in the middle of the wall and go up and then she said no, I think we should paint our hand and stick handprints on the wall, so we got this paint and painted our hands and stuck our hands up the wall, and we got our friend's little brother and we painted his feet

and stuck his footprints up the wall, and we signed it and it was really like, we were proud of our toilet, and everybody that came round we would say come and see our toilet ... and they said wow. We were really proud of that toilet. ... The things we used to do, the memories are really good in that house, excellent. ... We were proud of our little house, it was nice.

That story ended with the narrator's confident plans for the future: '... it has all worked out really well.'

An account of struggles or problems can be used to convey a sharp sense of individual control. Andrew Cunningham's recollections of his battle, as an 11-year-old boy, to learn drumming was one example. Other stories elaborated their narrator's 'struggle', 'hard work', or 'hard times'. Individual determination was emphasized in the vivid accounts of divisive quarrels, often between partners, with their 'I said'/'(s)he said' interchanges, or of parents sticking up for their own children against others: 'I am a mum and will protect them to the end ... .' Jill Blackwell, when asked whether 'It has made a difference to your life, being in Milton Keynes?', responded in words recalling a motif evident in many stories: 'Yeh it has made a difference, well, I have made the difference, I have gone out and made the difference.'

This sense of personal control was partly conveyed through the personal motivation and interventions depicted in the story's events. Partly too, it came from the control that, as evidenced in other research on narrative, lies in the personally activated processes of memory and narration themselves playing a part in shaping the world, and from the coherence that perhaps emerges through the very process of creative retrospection. It was the self-reflective way stories were told and their small throw-away comments as much as the actions themselves that conveyed this personal determination and energy. 'It's a tough world', commented one narrator, while Shirley Lambert reflected that, 'If people don't help themselves ... they will go under'. Bessie Wyatt summed up her story about getting her foot on the ladder, progressing upwards, loving her job and divorcing her husband in difficult circumstances with the words, 'If you want something you've got to work for it'.

This individual action and control was sometimes formulated through well-known plots. One was that of a *hero's progress* upwards, re-enacted in the narrator's life. The 'final' ending might not yet be revealed but the successes of the present moment represented a kind of closure. Lucy Dale struggled for – and achieved – her educational qualifications, Agnes Farley her independence, Brenda Dawson her 'identity'. Several narrators told of beginning from almost nothing in material, educational or personal terms, and gradually winning through. One recalled moving into her present house:

> There was a cardboard box. I'll never forget it. All my dishes in a cardboard box! We set the telly on it. We had the cheek to go and buy a tablecloth to sit on top of it. Oh God. Oh, I used to be really embarrassed to open the door to somebody and say 'Oh, come in'. It was all right if you went upstairs for there was a carpet though we were all sleeping on the floor. It took me years to get where I am.

Fishermead may have been classed as a city sink by outsiders. But the tellers living there could – and did – also experience their lives as exemplifying the narrative themes of progress and personal control. They were creatively drawing on the narrative resources developed in our culture as they told and experienced the story of their lives.

Life was also sometimes presented as a kind of *adventure tale.* Some tellers recounted pioneering days in the early development of Milton Keynes, of coping with mud, new friends, and the absence of shops or a hospital. Others related childhood adventures, the 'enjoyment' and challenges of parenthood, a job, or a particular house or area. Accounts of excitement and enjoyment marked out particular stages of life – and thus of the plot – and again foregrounded the self-conscious reflecting individual.

Life imaged as a *journey of self-discovery* came into several stories, with the narrator looking back on the stages of a personal voyage. Stories progress through episodes of making mistakes and learning from them, of gathering strength – 'becoming stronger and more resolved than carrying on the wishy washy existence I was beforehand' – or of changing views at different stages: 'What was so important isn't quite so important when you get older and you have different values.' One narrative was shot through with 'learning about myself as a person', and concluded that a recent visit to America 'really helped me to grow as a person', quoting a friend's comment that she was: '... almost like this little flickering light and you have just come brighter. ... I am really chuffed with myself, and I have been back eight months now, and I have done everything I said I was going to do.' Rachel Jacobs reflected on her own story, one with many trials:

> It is now really that I feel good about Milton Keynes, I feel like I am home. ... It has actually been a personal journey, not just a financial one. ... And I suspect that in five years time I suppose I will see where I am now as just another stage along the way.

ACTIVITY 7

Can any of the themes discussed in this section be recognized in stories you know (e.g. in the story of your own life, in that of an older person recalling his/her life, or in written autobiographies you have come across)?

There is not space here to follow up further issues about 'time' in the stories or the conventions for starting and ending. However, it is worth noting that, unlike many written or fictional stories, these personal stories were not closed – in one sense the end had yet to come, for the living teller continued. Tales stopped rather than ended. But some tellers did introduce explicit closing comments or conclusion-like reflections, especially older people, whose narratives often convey a greater sense of a 'completed' story than those of young and middle-aged narrators (Abrahams in Myerhoff, 1980, p. 31). Emma Hardy concluded, '… it's not a very exciting life, but when we look back on it we have such great memories, it's so lovely … It wasn't a wasted life', while Frank Dyer reflected, 'I have lived through a period of life [with many changes] … I think I have lived through sixty years of the greatest advancement in all respects, and I treasure it'. 100-year-old Timothy Hopkins concluded, 'Well that's my story… and as I say I went through life, and that is exactly my life story'. But some younger people's stories too conveyed something of the same quality, as in the conclusion to Shirley Lambert's tale quoted earlier in this section. Several narratives conveyed a quiet end as the narrators expressed themselves to be content with their present state, others rounded off by looking to the future.

For their tellers, these narrations did indeed seem to fulfil the role identified in the comparative literature of shaping, not just reflecting, experience. Both at the time of the recording and from follow-up discussion later it was evident that they found the experience of telling their stories satisfying, sometimes surprising. It provided a proof of the reality and significance of their lives, and their capacity to control and make them meaningful through the creative process of verbalized self-reflection.

The conventions for telling life stories also carry some measure of implicit generalization – this is what makes them intelligible to both tellers and listeners. The personal tales may tell of unique individuals and their experiences, but the overtones of their recurrent themes draw the tale beyond the immediate situation. The shared familiarity of their recognized plots and figures takes them beyond just the deeds of single individuals – even as at the same time they communicate precisely *because* they present the accepted general motif of individuals' deeds. It is striking how between them these personal stories so clearly project a theoretical model which, in contrast to many traditional sociological accounts, emphasizes the significance of the self-conscious, creative self.

4.2   Stories, tellings … and more stories

Before leaving these personal narratives, I want briefly to draw attention to two other of their features: their ambiguous nature as 'texts' and/or 'performances', and their relation to other forms of stories in and about Milton Keynes.

The concept of talking about their own life and memories was not an unfamiliar notion to the tellers recorded here. But few if any had actively narrated their lives in the concentrated forum of a one-hour session (although Timothy Hopkins had previously written the story of his life).

When it came to the occasion of recording – essentially a *dialogue* situation, in which the teller interacted with another interlocutor, rather than a single-line monologue text – some tellers formulated a relatively sustained and fluent story with little prompting. They had doubtless told parts of it before in other situations. Some had perhaps formed the habit – or the need – of articulate justification of their lives, or reached a stage in life (old age and grandparenthood in particular) when reflecting upon their lives was an expected activity. Others were less fluent overall, though sometimes very articulate on particular episodes. Some tellers invoked more interaction with the interviewer than those who had in one sense 'rehearsed' aspects of their tales before. Many were surprised and pleased by their capacity to tell their story, commenting that they had never done it in that way before. But all had the resources to do so. All responded to the occasion by formulating the story in a form which – fluent or not – both told of their lives and was unique to that specific occasion.

performance

The stories here were thus each delivered on one particular occasion, and with the **performance** attributes typical of an interactive process rather than a fixed text. They were not carefully meditated or sustained narratives, nor were they worked up and 'improved' between recording sessions. They drew on a combination of personal experience and accepted conventions for such tellings, but had probably not been told in *that* particular form before, nor perhaps would be again.

Such oral narrations thus need to be pictured less on the model of a fixed written text than as a kind of store of accepted resources for personal story-telling. Speakers drew variously on these resources in interaction with their own experiences and perspectives to formulate a story – long or short – with varying emphases and selection depending on the audience and the occasion. The recurrent themes, plots and protagonists of the stories are no less significant for being activated in performance rather than in closed textual form. Indeed, oral delivery lays all the more onus on the individual teller's creativity in deploying both conventional store and personal originality on the live occasion of performance.

There is also a second issue. So far, the focus has been on the personal stories themselves. However, there were also, of course, *other* concurrent stories with which these self-narratives interacted – and interacted within the context of the specificities of time and place.

The stories told in our culture are multiple, and – as emerged in section 2 – are of many different kinds and are told at many levels. We can think not only of the unending series of personal tales, but also of the overarching myths shaping and expressing both widespread human assumptions (perhaps) and the contingent viewpoints of specific cultures on, say, the nature of human society or of personhood. Added to these are the interpretations of contrasting groups and sections, both general and in relation to specific events or situations, and – not to be forgotten among the manifold stories which influence our views – the diverse storied interpretations of academics.

Relevant too for these personal narratives were other stories specific to Milton Keynes. These stories took a variety of forms. One powerful – but not universally accepted – story was the upbeat success tale told by and about the planners of the new city, led by the heroic Milton Keynes Development Corporation to its happy conclusion. Then there was the alternative version of the new city as a routinized, cultureless, over-bureaucratized wasteland, bereft equally of human artistry or community roots, a tale often symbolized through the image of the artificial 'concrete cows' in one of the city's parks. This, above all, was the popular story in the mass media. It also fitted well with the pessimistic stories of much urban sociology and the deeply-engrained English myth of the battle between rural 'natural' community and intrusive 'artificial' town. Or again – and less widely known outside Milton Keynes – there was the emergent narrative being constructed by local historians and artists eager to create a storied history for Milton Keynes, a story which could celebrate not only its part in the historical diversities of Buckinghamshire over the centuries, but also the personal deeds and adventures of its inhabitants. All these many tales contributed to the store of cultural resources on which personal narrators could draw in formulating their personal self-narrations.

FIGURE 2.2   The Concrete Cows of Milton Keynes.

One surprising feature about the personal narratives I studied was how unpredictably and variously – indeed how little – they drew directly on the more general Milton Keynes stories. Certainly there were the recurrent themes discussed above, and some others too. But in the end the most striking feature about these personal stories remained their diversity rather than their sameness.

The overall impression was of individual narrators moulding their own stories – deploying accepted narrative conventions, it is true, but putting their own individual stamp on their stories rather than merely reproducing other (arguably more 'powerful') stories in the culture. And insofar as they did draw on more widespread cultural stories – the varying *different* theories about the nature of the self, for example – they did so differentially and selectively among a plurality of differing tales.

It is clear that these stories were both personal and yet not *purely* personal. In that they were cultural constructs, not 'natural' phenomena, their tellers were able to draw from a store of themes and generic conventions which gave them a culturally-recognized art form to organize personal experience and the development of a life – a store which in principle included all the multiple stories in diverse voices to be encountered in Milton Keynes and beyond. But this did not stop them from also being individual. These storied formulations were essentially generated and realized by their tellers rather than being the results of control by others or the products of outside forces. Influenced and shaped they certainly were by the emergent store of generic conventions and narratives in the culture which these personal stories in turn helped to generate. But they also represented an intensely personal creation, not just an automatic reflection, of the cultural resources which both moulded and were moulded by the personal tellings.

5   Conclusion: revisiting identity, culture and the self

There are many approaches to the study of culture and of identity. As always, the different perspectives have their strengths and weaknesses, largely depending on what you want to use them for. This last section will look back briefly to consider how the perspective used in this chapter both complements and contrasts with others.

> ACTIVITY 8
>
> Why not anticipate (and improve) this conclusion by considering how you feel the narrative perspective in this chapter resembles and differs from other approaches to identity and culture, whether in this volume or elsewhere? And which approaches most appeal to you personally (and why)?

Approaching the study of culture and identity through personal stories both overlaps and in some ways differs from other approaches. I will go on shortly to sketch some possible comparisons. But let me start, in section 5.1

with a quick run-down of some *problems* about a narrative approach as used in this chapter. These will also emerge from the comparisons in section 5.2 (for what look like strengths from one viewpoint will be precisely what will seem like weaknesses from another). You will doubtless think of further possible critiques, perhaps from trying out its application yourself, perhaps from preferring alternative approaches.

5.1 Some critical questions about the narrative approach of this chapter

One question that could be asked about the research reported here or about comparable investigations is just how 'typical' the stories are of story-telling in our culture more generally. Would the stories necessarily have remained the same when told on different occasions or to a different listener (if not, would this matter)? And how far can the elucidation of the 'themes' in the stories be a fair one without more rigorous quantification or experiment?

More far-reaching but equally pertinent is the general question of the relation of these personal stories to the wider culture and institutions in which their tellers conduct their lives. What about the possible argument that by focusing on the creativities of personal narratives we have given insufficient attention to broader constraints (those posed by global economic forces, for example, or governmental regulation)? Is it naïve to describe narrative conventions through terms like the 'store of cultural resources' or the 'recognized arts of story-telling' which narrators can 'draw on creatively' to formulate and experience their individual lives – rather than in terms of the fetters or power which constrain them? And if some other approaches could be criticized for overemphasizing constraint or implying a passive model of human beings, does a focus on personal storying overvalue agency and voluntarism?

There is also the related issue of how we think of truth and falsity. The general approach to 'story' and to the 'cultural construction of reality', used not just in this analysis of personal narratives but in many recent uses of 'story' in social theory, tends to draw broadly on a *coherence* theory of truth: the view that truth is ultimately what makes sense and is culturally accepted, rather than defined by its *correspondence* to, or *reflection* of, some objective 'reality'. Certainly that coherence theory of truth would generally fit with the approach to the personal stories here. It also tends to be followed by many analysts of personal narrative. (There is an illuminating parallel here to the discussion in section 3.3 above – the model of experience as culturally formulated rather than reflecting something 'natural' or unmediated.) The reality of the stories is thus seen to lie in the way they are told and experienced by their tellers, and not in their reflection of some external world or of meanings imposed from outside. In one sense the concepts of 'truth' and 'falsity' become irrelevant.

But does this 'coherence' approach go too far? Do we really want to give up any idea of either empirical evidence or the forces of the 'real world'? Indeed, even those studies of personal narratives which explicitly avoid correspondence or reflection theories of truth are now raising this issue (e.g. Mumby, 1993). Rosenwald and Ochberg argue broadly for non-realist interpretations of life stories, but continue:

> As its limit, however, this line of reasoning can be taken to support the notion that social life counts for nothing outside of discourse. On this tack the improvement of life can be accomplished if one tells a better story about it. But life is not merely talk; inequalities of opportunity, for example, are not redressed if individuals, or even whole classes, tell more 'agentic', optimistic autobiographies.
>
> (1992, p. 7)

There are no easy ways to cope with such issues (long the focus of philosophical argument). They also, of course, crop up in other areas of sociological and cultural analysis, not just in the personal stories discussed here (remember, for instance, the more general application of 'story' discussed in section 2 above, and see also discussions of the issues of 'meaning' and 'construction' in **Hall**, 1997a, 1997b). But it is worth bearing them in mind as continuing debates (see, for example, recent discussions in Layder, 1996; Neisser and Fivush, 1994). A focus on personal story indeed has its strengths. But it can no more give us an uncontestable and problem-free final answer to all our questions than can any other approach.

5.2   Comparisons and contrasts

Despite the (justified) qualifications above, a focus on personal stories along the lines illustrated in this chapter can bring its own insights, giving a possible jumping-off ground for further application to cases from your own observation and experience. Some of these insights are shared with other well-known approaches, others present a contrast.

The narrative perspective on the self overlaps with several of the approaches to identity referred to in section 1 above – at least in the sense that they themselves form part of the store of themes and ideas on which narrators can potentially draw to formulate their own life experiences (a point to which we will return). Those approaches do not coincide exactly with the perspective here however. A *purely* self-generated and subjective theory of the self, for example, does not, as we have seen, accord with a narrative perspective which emphasizes that, although active narrators certainly generate their own narratives and create and build on a sense of continuity, they do not do so in a cultural vacuum. Similarly, narrators may indeed variously draw on socially recognized categories – class, 'race', gender, religion or whatever – in their narratives; but none of these collective categories seems to give a full account of the creative process by which individuals produce their variegated and individual tales.

Two themes will however be familiar. One is the idea of treating the self as in a sense 'actively performed'. It is true that a narrative perspective perhaps lays particular stress on the processes of *verbalization*. But the basic idea of engaging in active personal story-ing – production drawing on generic conventions – draws the expression beyond a mere verbal text, in the narrow sense of that term, into a form of lived and embodied personal enactment.

The second familiar theme is that treating the self – or, to use Bruner's language, one's 'life' – in terms of narrative implies rejecting the idea of identity as founded on 'nature' rather than culture. This position is consonant with a rejection of both simple 'reflection' theories of reality (or of experience) and 'essentialist' concepts of the self (see **Hall**, ed., 1997; **Woodward**, ed. 1997). The particular narrative perspective in most of this chapter represents a specific twist on social constructionist approaches which not all theorists would accept – but it is still a variant around the same basic theme. Its extension to the sphere of the active formulation of personal experience and identity through narrative is a topic the more worth highlighting in that this has in the past often been neglected in traditional sociology.

The narrative perspective here also goes along with the rejection of the so-called 'productionist' theory of culture (for example, see **du Gay**, 1997) and challenges the feasibility of making a sharp division between 'production' and 'consumption'. In self-narratives, as in some other spheres, the two processes – insofar as they are distinct at all – are overlapping rather than separate, both conceptually and in practice. Personal narrative could equally be seen as itself a type of production (personal intellectual/artistic production if you like) rather than consumption. And if the 'cultural circuit' idea is to be drawn on, the process of personal story-telling might be regarded as itself comprising an internalized personal circuit – one enacted and reproduced in the tellings – rather than as something to be placed in a sector labelled 'consumption'.

However, some of the other connotations of the term 'consumption' chime less well with the view of the self as story. Insofar as the connotations of that term in popular usage suggest consuming and using up what is produced by others rather than created by oneself, it is not the most obvious term for describing these personal stories. The somewhat derogatory overtones sometimes carried by the term also sit uneasily with the creative art of producing vivid individual narrative of the kind illustrated here. Such overtones sometimes seem to spill over into more theoretical formulations, whether those suggesting a near-deterministic model of identity (like the personal identity created and marketed by others, as one author, Tomlinson (1990, p. 13), puts it) or, at the other extreme, the picture of consumers picking and choosing among the cafeteria of identities on offer. The present discussion draws less on the vocabulary of 'consumption' than on the 'constructivist' view of personally created narrative – to recall Bruner's term – and its active role in the complex interactive processes of cultural convention and personal formulation.

One influential strand in the analysis of culture emphasizes the concept of struggle, whether diffused throughout society (including in the struggles over identity), or in the more extreme form of an essentially dualistic model of culture: a struggle between the stories of those in power as against those of the powerless. The latter engage in resistance or accommodation, sometimes contesting the dominant versions or telling their own 'counter-stories': for example, women against men, black against white, or employees against management.

Conflictual models of culture are not in themselves necessarily opposed to narrative analysis – indeed they can be one effective arena for its application. But the particular perspective on personal narrative in this chapter, you will have noticed, is little concerned with questions of power (diffused or otherwise), still less with the essentially dualistic model of traditional Marxism. It also tends to emphasize plurality (rather than two-sided antagonisms): the huge number of alternative stories in a culture. Far from being explicable by hierarchies of power relations, personal narratives can and do both deploy and develop a rich multiplicity of diverse themes.

Finally, the emphasis here tilts the balance towards the creative narrator, the individual story-teller. This is partly a matter of the level at which the analysis has been conducted. Keith Negus makes a contrast between:

> ... a *macro* perspective which stresses social and organizational *structures* and *economic* relationships [and] a more *micro* approach which focuses on everyday human *agency* and the making of *cultural* meanings. The first approach foregrounds the issue of control over production and constraint on creative practices; the second emphasizes human autonomy and the active ability to engage in creative activities despite such constraints.
>
> (**Negus**, 1997, p. 69)

Clearly, both emphases are valuable. But the spotlight in this chapter is more on the second of the approaches identified by Negus – the micro perspective. It is all the more important to take account of the role and artistry of personal narratives, since it is precisely this aspect that has often been played down in macro analyses which place large-scale structures and institutions at the centre of the picture.

But it is of course more complex than a straight alternative between a view of the self as formed by *either* (1) the external constraints of 'society' *or* (2) one's own inner and autonomous being – a dichotomy that tends to build on the old, but arguably misleading, opposition between 'individual' and 'society' (or indeed between 'base' and 'superstructure'). As Stanley and

Morgan put it in describing their 'auto/biographical' approach, a preferable perspective is: 'The rejection of the older dichotomy between "structure" and "action" ... [so as to] steer a course between the over-determinism of some varieties of socialization theory, and the opposite extreme of seeing selves as entirely unique individuals' (Stanley and Morgan, 1993, p. 2; see also Worthington, 1996). For, as will now be clear, personal stories are both fully individual – an actively formulated narration of someone's unique life – *and* formulated through recurrent cultural conventions and interactions with other storying in the culture. These are drawn on by the narrator to create what is at once an intensely personal and an intensely 'cultured' story. And this personal formulation in its turn plays its individual creative role in formulating and shaping the emergent conventions – the culture.

5.3   Identity, cultural relativity and plurality

One last topic needs to be revisited before concluding. This chapter broadly accepts the view that our concept of the self is not a 'fact of nature' but rather is historically and culturally contingent (see **du Gay**, 1997; also Carrithers et al., 1985; Morris, 1994). Indeed, it seems clear from comparative research in the social sciences that concepts of personhood vary cross-culturally.

The cultural relativity of concepts of the self is by now widely recognized among sociologists. Beyond this, however, there are different theories about just *what* concept of personhood is indeed characteristic of different eras and/or cultures. And when we move to theories about precisely what the 'contemporary' or 'western' (or, alternatively, the 'modern' or 'postmodern') sense of self/identity essentially comprises, it starts getting highly controversial.

One such theory envisages non-western and non-industrial cultures as essentially holistic or collective, contrasting with the rational and individualistic concept of the self in the modern industrial West, a view enunciated by Mauss (1938/1985) among many others. This has long been an influential model. It is, however, now under challenge. First, it is held to invoke outdated evolutionary and ethnocentric views of human history (a criticism I would strongly endorse). In addition, there is the argument that some concept of individual personhood is in fact found very widely rather than confined to the West (Carrithers et al., 1985; Cohen, 1994; Spencer, forthcoming).

An alternative, partly overlapping, theory has proposed that there is a particular sense of fragmentation of the self in western countries in the 1990s. The suggestion is that people are nowadays especially concerned to make and remake identities, which are the more fleeting, fragile and perhaps illusory because of the fragmentation of contemporary ideas and institutions. Some theorists, notably Giddens (1991), develop this further. Giddens builds on his view of 'late modernity' as characterized by risk, uncertainty and rupture to suggest that a parallel characteristic is the development of the self as a 'reflexive project' with revisable narratives of self-identity as individuals negotiate their lifestyles among a diversity of individual options: 'A self-identity has to be created and more or less continually reordered against the backdrop of shifting experiences of day-to-day life and the fragmenting tendencies of modern institutions' (ibid., pp. 185–6).

This is a currently influential cluster of ideas (see, for example, the discussions and further references in Hall, 1992; Sarup, 1996; Warde, 1994; and also the discussion of Giddens in Chapter 5 of this volume). One could, however, invoke the same argument against it as against Mauss – focusing upon its intimations of an outdated evolutionist framework as well as of that familiar, golden-age, mythic story of the loss of once-harmonious community. Other writers (such as Friedman, 1994) query it as resting on questionable evidence for the kind of divide between 'traditional' and modern exchange that could justify the claim that 'consumer culture' is a distinctive feature of recent western societies. Again, others criticize Giddens's view of human agency as, in the last analysis (and despite the promises of his more open concept of 'structuration'), adjusting *to* society rather than playing a part in its creation so that the power of individuals is, ultimately, merely that of 'reflexivity, but not of motivation: they seem doomed to be perpetrators rather than architects of action' (Cohen, 1994, p. 21; see also Layder, 1996). There is also the view that these 'postmodernist conceptions of the fragmented individual' are in practice rejected by 'ordinary folk going about their daily lives' (Silverstone, 1994, p. 1001) – a position which might well be supported by the Milton Keynes narrators.

These recent theories have thus proved both illuminating and controversial. But it is also worth pointing to a further point – one that will return us again to the Milton Keynes stories. It is obviously right to try to relate ideas of identity to their locale in a specific culture. But we also need to exercise some caution about over-literal applications of the theory that concepts of the self are historically contingent. Tying them inextricably to particular eras or types of society risks giving an unhelpfully monolithic, even deterministic, impression of 'the' concept of the self in a particular culture. However (as argued in Spencer, forthcoming), there are likely to be several *concurrent* ideas about the nature of personal identity – and not just in the 'modern' or 'postmodern' West either. It can be misleading to state definitive conclusions about *the* typical 'modern' or 'western' or 'Chinese' concept of the self; or indeed that of Japan (see **du Gay, Hall et al.**, 1997, section 3). Certainly, in the Milton Keynes narratives, *several* different perspectives came through about the nature of personhood.

A narrative perspective encourages us instead to take a more pluralist approach to the nature of culture and the concepts of the self. In practice, the models that we use to tell our personal tales present a *range* of different stories about the self. Some come from conventional wisdom, some (overlappingly) from among the many analyses of the self in intellectuals' formulations, which in turn mutually interact with theoretical models developed by individuals in their personal narratives.

Recall Activity 1 on page 67 of this chapter. If you hesitated between your personal 'everyday reactions' and more abstract theories in answering the question of 'Who are you?', you had a point. The two interpenetrate. And we are now more sensitive to the existence of theoretical formulations at every level – including personal stories – for which intellectuals can act as interpreters rather than legislators (Bauman, 1987). It is not only self-styled academics that are, ultimately, the theorists and intellectuals of our culture. The many different viewpoints on the self in personal stories are themselves part of the complex plurality of theories by which we live our lives. The situation is more complex – and more interesting – than having just *one* type of identity 'typical' of our culture.

The personal identities narrated in the Fishermead dwellers' stories can be seen as playing variously on potentially contrasting ideas about identity. They too are theorizing. Their personal tales are producing and re-enacting theoretical models of identity. While it is true that each tale had its own personal uniqueness – part of the rich multiple mix of our culture – there were also the recurrent themes. We encountered images of the enterprising self; of things 'happening'; of success and control; of an inner reflective self; of a struggle to cope with pulls both within and outside oneself; of the significance or otherwise of family, of work, of religion, of special interests; of a variety of values through which the self was in part defined.

It remains tempting to look for *one* interpretation of identity which is 'characteristic' of – or determined by – a particular socio-cultural context. But this may be a misleading quest. Perhaps we need to start from a model of multiplicity rather than of uniformity. This multiplicity may be found and expressed not only through the series of culturally recognized stories and recurrent narrative motifs, but also by the many diverse and overlapping voices – themselves theorizing as they story their lives – which are represented in individuals' personal formulations.

5.4   Finally ...

You will want to make up your own mind about the strengths and limitations of the various perspectives on identity and the self. The ultimate test must be how far you can *apply* them to the analysis of everyday life around you, perhaps at the same time relating them to the issues of human creativity and constraint raised in this book. In doing so, you will by now be aware that one of the possible approaches you can follow is to take some serious account of those important verbalized narrative conventions through which, as described in this chapter, we have the cultural resources to 'story' our lives through personal narrative.

References

ABRAHAMS, R.D. (1985) 'Our native notions of story', *New York Folklore*, Vol. 11, No. 1/4, pp. 37–47.

BAKHTIN, M.M. (1986) *Speech Genres and Other Late Essays,* Austin, TX, University of Texas Press.

BAUMAN, R. (1986) *Story, Performance, and Event: contextual studies of oral narrative*, Cambridge, Cambridge University Press.

BAUMAN, Z. (1987) *Legislators and Interpreters: on modernity, post-modernity and intellectuals*, Cambridge, Polity.

BENSON, S. (1997) 'The body, health and eating disorders' in Woodward, K. (ed.) (1997).

BORNAT, J. (1989) 'Oral history as a social movement: reminiscence and older people', *Oral History*, Vol. 17, pp. 16–24.

BRUNER, J. (1987) 'Life as narrative', *Social Research*, Vol. 51, pp. 11–32.

BURNETT, J. (ed.) (1974) *Useful Toil: autobiographies of working people from the 1820s to the 1920s*, London, Allen Lane.

BURNETT, J. (ed.) (1982) *Destiny Obscure: autobiographies of childhood, education and family from the 1820s to the 1920s*, London, Allen Lane.

BURNETT, J., VINCENT, D., and MAYAL, D. (eds) (1984–9) *The Autobiography of the Working Class: an annotated critical bibliography*, 3 vols, Hassocks, Harvester Press.

CARRITHERS, M., COLLINS, S. and LUKES, S. (eds) (1985) *The Category of the Person: anthropology, philosophy, history*, Cambridge, Cambridge University Press.

CLARK, T. and SALAMAN, J.G. (1996) 'The management guru as organizational witch doctor', *Organization,* Vol. 3, No. 1, pp. 85–107.

CLEGG, S.R. (1993) 'Narrative, power, and social theory', in Mumby, D.K. (ed.) (1993).

CLIFFORD, J. and MARCUS, G.E. (eds) (1986) *Writing Culture: the poetics and politics of ethnography*, Berkeley, CA, University of California Press.

COHEN, A.P. (1994) *Self Consciousness: an alternative anthropology of identity*, London and New York, Routledge.

CRONON, W. (1992) 'A place for stories: nature, history, and narrative', *The Journal of American History,* Vol. 78, pp. 1347–76.

DEAL, T.E. and KENNEDY, A.A. (1989) *Corporate Cultures: the rites and rituals of corporate life,* Harmondsworth, Penguin.

DU GAY, P. (1997) 'Organizing identity: making up people at work' in du Gay, P. (ed.) *Production of Culture/Cultures of Production*, London, Sage/The Open University (Book 4 in this series).

DU GAY, P., HALL, S., JANES, L., MACKAY, H. and NEGUS, K. (1997) *Doing Cultural Studies: the story of the Sony Walkman*, London, Sage/The Open University (Book 1 in this series).

FINNEGAN, R. (1992) *Oral Traditions and the Verbal Arts*, London, Routledge.

FINNEGAN, R. (1996) 'Personal narratives and urban theory in Milton Keynes', *Auto/Biography*, Vol. 4, No. 2/3, pp. 13–25.

FINNEGAN, R. (forthcoming) *Tales of the City*, Cambridge, Cambridge University Press.

FRIEDMAN, J. (1994) *Consumption and Identity*, Switzerland, Harwood Academic Publishers.

GIDDENS, A. (1991) *Modernity and Self-identity: self and society in the late modern age,* Cambridge, Polity.

GLEDHILL, C. (1997) 'Genre and gender: the case of soap opera' in Hall, S. (ed.) (1997).

HALL, S. (1992) 'The question of cultural identity' in Hall, S., Held, D. and McGrew, A. (eds) *Modernity and Its Futures,* Cambridge, Polity.

HALL, S. (1997a) 'The work of representation' in Hall, S. (ed.) (1997).

HALL, S. (1997b) 'Introduction' in Hall, S. (ed.) (1997).

HALL, S. (ed.) (1997) *Representation: cultural representations and signifying practices*, London, Sage/The Open University (Book 2 in this series).

HARDY, B. (1968) 'Towards a poetics of fiction: an approach through narrative', *Novel*, Vol. 2, pp. 5–14.

INGLIS, F. (1993) *Cultural Studies*, Oxford and Cambridge, MA, Blackwell.

JEFFCUTT, P. (1994) 'The interpretation of organization: a contemporary analysis and critique', *Journal of Management Studies*, Vol. 31, No. 2, pp. 225–50.

LANDAU, M. (1991) *Narratives of Human Evolution*, New Haven, CT, and London, Yale University Press.

LANGELLIER, K.M. (1989) 'Personal narratives: perspectives on theory and research', *Text and Performance Quarterly*, Vol. 9, No. 4, pp. 243–76.

LAYDER, D. (1996) 'Contemporary sociological theory', *Sociology*, Vol. 30, pp. 601–8.

LIDCHI, H. (1997) 'The poetics and the politics of exhibiting other cultures' in Hall, S. (ed.) (1997).

LINDE, C. (1993) *Life Stories: the creation of coherence*, New York and London, Oxford University Press.

MACINTYRE, A. (1985) *After Virtue*, London, Duckworth.

MAUSS, H. (1938) 'A category of the human mind: the notion of person; the notion of self' in Carrithers et al. (eds) (1985).

MORRIS, B. (1994) *Anthropology of the Self: the individual in cultural perspective*, London and Boulder, CO, Pluto Press.

MUMBY, D.K. (ed.) (1993) *Narrative and Social Control: critical perspectives*, London, Sage (Sage Annual Reviews of Communication Research, Volume 21).

MYERHOFF, B. (1980) 'Telling one's story', *The Center Magazine*, Vol. 13, No. 2, March, pp. 22–40.

NEGUS, K. (1997) 'The production of culture' in du Gay, P. (ed.) *Production of Culture/Cultures of Production*, London, Sage/The Open University (Book 4 in this series).

NEISSER, U. and FIVUSH, R. (eds) (1994) *The Remembering Self: construction and accuracy in the self-narrative*, Cambridge, Cambridge University Press.

PASSERINI, L. (1990) 'Mythbiography in oral history' in Samuel, R. and Thompson, P. (eds) *The Myths We Live By*, London, Routledge.

PERSONAL NARRATIVES GROUP (ed.) (1989) *Interpreting Women's Lives*, Bloomington, IN, Indiana University Press.

PLUMMER, K. (1983) *Documents of Life: an introduction to the literature of a humanistic method*, London, Allen and Unwin.

PLUMMER, K. (1995) *Telling Sexual Stories: power, change and social worlds*, London and New York, Routledge.

PRINCE, G. (1989) 'Narrative' in Barnouw, E. (ed.) *International Encyclopedia of Communications*, New York and Oxford, Oxford University Press.

RIESSMAN, C.K. (1993) *Narrative Analysis,* London, Sage (Qualitative Research Methods Series, Volume 30).

ROSENWALD, G.C. and OCHBERG, R.L. (eds) (1992) *Storied Lives: the cultural politics of self-understanding*, New Haven, CO, and London, Yale University Press.

SALAMAN, G. (1997) 'Culturing production' in du Gay, P. (ed.) *Production of Culture/Cultures of Production*, London, Sage/The Open University (Book 4 in this series).

SARBIN, T.R. (ed.) (1986) *Narrative Psychology: the storied nature of human conduct*, New York, Praeger.

SARUP, M. (1996) *Identity, Culture and the Postmodern World*, Edinburgh, Edinburgh University Press.

SCHAFER, R. (1992) *Retelling a Life: narration and dialogue in psychoanalysis*, New York, Basic Books.

SHOTTER, J. and GERGEN, K.J. (eds) (1989) *Texts of Identity*, London, Sage.

SILVERSTONE, R. (1994) 'The power of the ordinary: on cultural studies and the sociology of culture', *Sociology*, Vol. 28, No. 4, pp. 991–1001.

SPENCER, J. (forthcoming) 'Fatima and the enchanted toffees: an essay on contingency, narrative and therapy'.

STANLEY, L. (ed.) (1984) *The Diaries of Hannah Cullwick, Victorian Maidservant*, London, Virago.

STANLEY, L. (1992) *The Auto/biographical I: theory and practice of feminist auto/biography*, Manchester, Manchester University Press.

STANLEY, L. and MORGAN, D. (eds) (1993) *Auto/biography in Sociology*, special issue, *Sociology*, Vol. 27, No. 1.

STROMBERG, P.G. (1993) *Language and Self-transformation: a study of the Christian conversion narrative*, Cambridge, Cambridge University Press.

SWIFT, G. (1992) *Waterland*, London, Heinemann.

TOMLINSON, A. (ed.) (1990) *Consumption, Identity, and Style: marketing, meanings and the packaging of pleasure*, London and New York, Routledge.

VAN MAANEN, J. (1988) *Tales of the Field: on writing ethnography*, Chicago, IL, and London, University of Chicago Press.

VINCENT, D. (1981) *Bread, Knowledge and Freedom: a study of nineteenth-century working class autobiography*, London, Europa Publications.

WARDE, A. (1994) 'Consumption, identity-formation and uncertainty', *Sociology*, Vol. 28, pp. 877–98.

WHITE, H. (1973) *Metahistory*, Baltimore, MD, Johns Hopkins University Press.

WORTHINGTON, K.L. (1996) *Self as Narrative*, Oxford, Clarendon Press.

WOODWARD, K. (1997) 'Concepts of identity and difference' in Woodward, K. (ed.) *Identity and Difference*, London, Sage/The Open University (Book 3 in this series).

WOODWARD, K. (ed.) (1997) *Identity and Difference*, London, Sage/The Open University (Book 3 in this series).

READING A:
Jerome Bruner, 'Life as narrative'

I would like to try out an idea that may not be quite ready, indeed may not be quite possible. But I have no doubt it is worth a try. It has to do with the nature of thought and with one of its uses. It has been traditional to treat thought, so to speak, as an instrument of reason. Good thought is right reason, and its efficacy is measured against the laws of logic or induction. Indeed, in its most recent computational form, it is a view of thought that has sped some of its enthusiasts to the belief that all thought is reducible to machine computability.

But logical thought is not the only or even the most ubiquitous mode of thought. For the last several years, I have been looking at another kind of thought [see, for example, Bruner, 1986], one that is quite different in form from reasoning: the form of thought that goes into the constructing not of logical or inductive arguments but of stories or narratives. What I want to do now is to extend these ideas about narrative to the analysis of the stories we tell about our lives: our 'autobiographies'.

Philosophically speaking, the approach I shall take to narrative is a constructivist one – a view that takes as its central premise that 'world making' is the principal function of mind, whether in the sciences or in the arts. But the moment one applies a constructivist view of narrative to the self-narrative, to the autobiography, one is faced with dilemmas. Take, for example, the constructivist view that 'stories' do not 'happen' in the real world but, rather, are constructed in people's heads. Or as Henry James once put it, stories happen to people who know how to tell them. Does that mean that our autobiograpies are constructed, that they had better be viewed not as a record of what happened (which is in any case a nonexistent record) but rather as a continuing interpretation and reinterpretation of our experience? Just as the philosopher Nelson Goodman argues that physics or painting or history are 'ways of worldmaking' [Goodman, 1978], so autobiography (formal or informal) should be viewed as a set of procedures for 'life making'. And just as it is worthwhile examining in minute detail how physics or history go about their world making, might we not be well advised to explore in equal detail what we do when we construct ourselves autobiographically? Even if the exercise should produce some obdurate dilemmas, it might nonetheless cast some light on what we might mean by such expressions as 'a life'.

Culture and autobiography

Let me begin by sketching out the general shape of the argument that I wish to explore. The first thesis is this: We seem to have no other way of describing 'lived time' save in the form of a narrative. Which is not to say that there are not other temporal forms that can be imposed on the experience of time, but none of them succeeds in capturing the sense of *lived* time: not clock or calendrical time forms, not serial or cyclical orders, not any of these. It is a thesis that will be familiar to many of you, for it has been most recently and powerfully argued by Paul Ricoeur [1984]. Even if we set down *annales* in the bare form of events [see White, 1984], they will be seen to be events chosen with a view to their place in an implicit narrative.

My second thesis is that the mimesis between life so-called and narrative is a two-way affair: that is to say, just as art imitates life in Aristotle's sense, so, in Oscar Wilde's, life imitates art. Narrative imitates life, life imitates narrative. 'Life' in this sense is the same kind of construction of the human imagination as 'a narrative' is. It is constructed by human beings through active ratiocination, by the same kind of ratiocination through which we construct narratives. When somebody tells you his life – and that is principally what we shall be talking about – it is always a cognitive achievement rather than a through-the-clear-crystal recital of something univocally given. In the end, it is a narrative achievement. There is no such thing psychologically as 'life itself'. At very least, it is a selective achievement of memory recall; beyond that, recounting one's life is an interpretive feat. Philosophically speaking, it is hard to imagine being a naive realist about 'life itself'.

The story of one's own life is, of course, a privileged but troubled narrative in the sense that it is reflexive: the narrator and the central figure in the narrative are the same. This [...] reflexivity of self-narrative poses problems of a deep and serious order – problems beyond those of verification, beyond the issue of indeterminacy (that the very telling of the self-story distorts what we have in mind to tell), beyond 'rationalization'. The whole enterprise seems a most shaky one [...].

Yet for all the shakiness of the form, it is perfectly plain that not just any autobiography will do – either for its teller or for his listener, for that matter. One imposes criteria of rightness on the self-report of a life just as one imposes them on the account of a football game or the report of an event in nature. And they are by no means all external criteria as to whether, for example, one did or did not visit Santander in 1956. Besides, it may have been Salamanca in 1953 and by certain criteria of narrative or of psychological adequacy even be 'right' if untrue. There are also internal criteria relating to how one felt or what one intended, and these are just as demanding, even if they are not subject to verification. Otherwise, we would not be able to say that certain self-narratives are 'shallow' and others 'deep'. One criterion, of course, is whether a life story 'covers' the events of a life. But what is coverage? Are not omissions also important? And we have all read or heard painfully detailed autobiographies of which it can be said that the whole is drastically less than the sum of the parts. They lack interpretation or 'meaning', we say. As Peter Winch reminded us a long time ago, it is not so evident in the human sciences or human affairs how to specify criteria by which to judge the rightness of any theory or model, especially a folk theory like an account of 'my life' [Winch, 1958]. All verificationist criteria turn slippery, and we surely cannot judge rightness by narrative adequacy alone. A rousing tale of a life is not necessarily a 'right' account.

All of which creates special problems, as we shall see, and makes autobiographical accounts (even the ones we tell ourselves) notably unstable. On the other hand, this very instability makes life stories highly susceptible to cultural, interpersonal, and linguistic influences. This susceptibility to influence may, in fact, be the reason why 'talking cures', religious instruction, and other interventions in a life may often have such profound effects in changing a person's life narrative.

Given their constructed nature and their dependence upon the cultural conventions and language usage, life narratives obviously reflect the prevailing theories about 'possible lives' that are

part of one's culture. Indeed, one important way of characterizing a culture is by the narrative models it makes available for describing the course of a life. And the tool kit of any culture is replete not only with a stock of canonical life narratives (heroes, Marthas, tricksters, etc.), but with combinable formal constituents from which its members can construct their own life narratives: canonical stances and circumstances, as it were.

But the issue I wish to address is not just about the 'telling' of life narratives. The heart of my argument is this: eventually the culturally shaped cognitive and linguistic processes that guide the self-telling of life narratives achieve the power to structure perceptual experience, to organize memory, to segment and purpose-build the very 'events' of a life. In the end, we *become* the autobiographical narratives by which we 'tell about' our lives. And given the cultural shaping to which I referred, we also become variants of the culture's canonical forms. I cannot imagine a more important psychological research project than one that addresses itself to the 'development of autobiography' – how our way of telling about ourselves changes, and how these accounts come to take control of our ways of life. Yet I know of not a single comprehensive study on this subject.

How a culture transmits itself in this way is an anthropological topic and need not concern us directly. Yet a general remark is in order. I want to address the question of how self-narratives as a *literary* form, as autobiography, might have developed. For the issue may throw some light on how more modest, less formulated modes of self-telling have emerged as well. [...]

[...]

While the act of *writing* autobiography is new under the sun – like writing itself – the self-told life narrative is, by all accounts, ancient and universal. People anywhere can tell you some intelligible account of their lives. What varies is the cultural and linguistic perspective or narrative *form* in which it is formulated and expressed. And that too will be found to spring from historical circumstances as these have been incorporated in the culture and language of a people. I suspect that it will be as important to study *historical* developments in forms of self-telling as it is to study their ontogenesis. I have used the expression 'forms of self-telling', for I believe it is form rather than content that matters. We must be clear, then, about what we mean by narrative form. Vladimir Propp's classic analysis of folktales [1968] reveals, for example, that the *form* of a folktale may remain unchanged even though its content changes. So too self-told life narratives may reveal a common formal structure across a wide variety of content. [...]

Four self-narratives

Let me turn now the business of how a psychologist goes about studying issues of the kind that we have been discussing. Along with my colleagues Susan Weisser and Carol Staszewski, I have been engaged in a curious study. While it is far from done (whatever that may mean), I would like to tell you enough about it to make what I have been saying a little more concrete.

We were interested in how people tell the stories of their lives and, perhaps simplemindedly, we asked them to do so – telling them to keep it to about half an hour, even if it were an impossible task. We told them that we were not interested in judging them or curing them but that we were very interested in how people saw their lives. After they were done – and most had little trouble in sticking to the time limits or, for that matter, in filling up the time – we asked questions for another half hour or so, questions designed to get a better picture of how their stories had been put together. Had we followed a different procedure, we doubtless would have obtained different accounts. [...] But such variations will get their innings later. Many people have now sat for their portraits, ranging in age from ten to seventy, and their stories yield rich texts. But I want to talk on only four of them now: a family – a father, a mother, and their grown son and grown daughter, each of their accounts collected independently. There are two more grown children in the family, a son and daughter, both of whom have also told their stories, but four are enough to handle as a start.

We have chosen a family as our target because it constitutes a miniature culture, and provides an opportunity to explore how life stories are made to mesh with each other in Sartre's sense. Beyond that, of course, the individual autobiographies provide us the opportunity to explore the issues of

form and structure to which I have already alluded.

If you should now ask how we propose to test whether these four lives 'imitated' the narratives each person told, your question would be proper enough, though a bit impatient. The position I have avowed, indeed, leaves entirely moot what could be meant by 'lives' altogether, beyond what is contained in the narrative. We shall not even be able to check [...] whether particular memories were veridical or distorted in some characteristic way. But our aim is different. We are asking, rather, whether there is in each account a set of selective narrative rules that lead the narrator to structure experience in a particular way, structure it in a manner that gives form to the content and the continuity of the life. And we are interested, as well, in how the family itself formulates certain common rules for doing these things. I hope this will be less abstract as we proceed.

Our family is headed by George Goodhertz, a hard-working heating contractor in his early sixties, a self-made man of moral principles, converted to Catholicism in childhood and mindful of his obligations, though not devout. Though plainly intelligent and well informed, he never finished high school: 'had to go to work'. His father was, by Mr Goodhertz's sparse characterization, 'a drinker' and a poor provider. Mr Goodhertz is neither. Mrs Goodhertz, Rose, is a housewife of immediate Italian descent: family oriented, imbedded in the urban neighborhood where she has lived for nearly thirty years, connected with old friends who still live nearby. Her father was, in her words, 'of the old school' – arrogant, a drinker, a poor provider, and unfaithful to her mother. In the opening paragraph of her autobiography she says, 'I would have preferred a better childhood, a happier one, but with God's influence, I prayed hard enough for a good husband, and she [*sic*] answered me'.

Daughter Debby, in her mid-twenties, is (in her own words) 'still unmarried'. She graduated a few years ago from a local college that she never liked much and now studies acting. Outgoing, she enjoys friends, old and new, but is determined not to get 'stuck' in the old neighborhood with the old friends of her past and their old attitudes. Yet she is not ambitious, but caught, rather, between ideals of local kindliness and of broader adventure, the latter more in the existential form of a desire for experience than by any wish to achieve. She lives at home – in Brooklyn with her parents in the old neighborhood. Her thirty-year-old brother, Carl, who is about to finish his doctorate in neurophysiology at one of the solid, if not distinguished Boston-area universities, is aware of how far beyond family expectations his studies have taken him, but is neither deferential nor aggressive about his leap in status. Like his sister Debby, he remains attached to and in easy contact with his parents though he lives on his own even when he is in New York working at a local university laboratory. At school Carl always felt 'special' and different – both in the Catholic high school and then in the Catholic college he attended. The graduate school he chose is secular, and a complete break with his past. He is ambitious to get ahead, but he is not one to take the conventional 'up' stairway. Both in his own eyes and, indeed, by conventional standards, he is a bit eccentric and a risk taker. Where his sister Debby (and his mother) welcomes intimacy and closeness, Carl (like his father) keeps people more at arm's length. Experience for its own sake is not his thing. He is as concerned as his sister about not being 'tied down'.

And that, I now want to assure you, is the end of the omniscient auctorial voice. For our task now is to sample the texts, the narratives of these four lives – father's, mother's, son's, and daughter's – to see not what they are *about* but how the narrators *construct* themselves. Their texts are all we have – though we may seem to have, so to speak, the hermeneutical advantage of four narratives that spring from a common landscape. But as you will see, the advantage that it yields is in narrative power and possibility, not in the ontology of verification. For one view of the world cannot confirm another, though, in Clifford Geertz's evocative phrase, it can 'thicken' it.

Let me begin the analysis with Kenneth Burke's pentad, his skeleton of dramatism, and particularly with the setting or Scene of these life stories [Burke, 1945]. Most psychological theories of personality, alas, have no place for place. They would not do well with Stephen Daedalus in Joyce's *Portrait of the Artist as a Young Man*, for he is inexplicable without the Dublin that he carries in his head. In these four life narratives too, place is

crucial and it shapes and constrains the stories that are told or, indeed, that could be told. Place is not simply a piece of geography, an established Italian neighborhood in Brooklyn, though it helps to know its 'culture' too. It is an intricate construct, whose language dominates the thought of our four narrators. For each, its central axis is 'home', which is placed in sharp contrast to what they all refer to as 'the real world'. They were, by all their own accounts, a 'close' family, and their language seals that closeness.

Consider the psychic geography. For each of our narrators, 'home' is a place that is inside, private, forgiving, intimate, predictably safe. 'The real world' is outside, demanding, anonymous, open, unpredictable, and consequently dangerous. But home and real world are also contrastive in another way, explicitly for the two children, implicitly and covertly for the parents: home is to be 'cooped up', restricted by duties, and bored; real world is excitement and opportunity. Early on, the mother says of the children, 'We spoiled them for the real world', and the father speaks of 'getting them ready for the real world'. The son speaks of its hypocrisies that need to be confronted and overcome to achieve one's goals. It is a worthwhile but treacherous battlefield. The daughter idealizes it for the new experience to be harvested there. Each, in their way, creates a different ontological landscape out of 'the real world' to give it an appropriate force as the Scene in the narratives they are constructing.

One thing that is striking about all four narratives is the extent to which the spatial distinction home–real world concentrates all four of them on spatial and locative terms in their autobiographical accounts. Take Carl. His account is laden with spatial metaphors: *in/out, here/there, coming from/ going to, place/special place*. The movement forward in his story is not so much temporal as spatial: a sequential outward movement from home to neighborhood to Catholic school to the library alone to college to the Catholic peace movement to graduate school and then triumphantly back to New York. In his *Bildungsroman* of a life story, the challenge is to find a place, the right place, and then a special place in each of these concentric outgoings. For Carl, you get involved *in* things, or you feel '*out* of place'. You 'go to' Boston or to a course or a lab, and fellow students 'come from' prestigious schools. Or 'I started gaining a fairly special place in the Department', and later 'I ended up getting a fairly privileged place in the Department'. The 'special places' *allow, permit, make possible*. 'After about six months I really started settling in and enjoying the program and enjoying the opportunities it gave me.' And later, about the students who get a special place, 'The faculty are committed to shielding their graduate students from negative repercussions of failure'.

Two things are both surprising and revealing about Carl's language. One is the extent to which his sentences take self as object, and the other is the high frequency of the passive voice. With respect to the latter, some 11 per cent of his sentences are in the passive voice, which is surprisingly high for such an action-oriented text. But they both are of a piece and tell something interesting about his world making. Recall the importance for Carl of 'place' and particularly of the 'special place'. Whenever he recounts something connected with these places, the places 'happen' and then he acts accordingly. His sentences then begin with either a passive or with self-as-object, and then move to the active voice. At a particular colloquium where he knew his stuff, 'It allowed me to deal with the faculty on an equal footing'. Or of his debating team experience, 'It taught me how to handle myself'. Occasions in these 'special places' are seen as if they had homelike privileges: allowing and permitting and teaching. It is as if Carl manages the 'real world' by colonizing it with 'special places' that provide some of the privileges of home.

With Debby, thirty-seven of the first hundred sentences in her life narrative contain spatial metaphors or locatives. The principal clusters are about her place in the family (the *gap* or *span* in ages); the life layout ('the house I was brought home to is the house I live in now'; or 'I travelled, my relatives are all over the country'; or 'I've been coming to the city by myself ever since I was fourteen'); the coming-back theme ('everybody except me has gone out and come back at one time or another').

So much for Scene, at least for the moment. Come now to the agentive, to Burke's Actor. Rorty's typology turns out to be enormously useful, for in all four self-portraits the tale moves from Actor as figure, figure becoming a person, person becoming a self, self becoming an individual [Rorty, 1976]. Well into her fifties, even Mrs Goodhertz has finally taken a job for pay, albeit working as secretary for her husband's heating-contracting business, motivated by the desire for some independence and the wish not to get 'stuck' raising her eldest daughter's child. She remarks that it is 'her' job and that she now 'works'. The transformation of her language as she runs through the chronology of her life is striking. When speaking of her childhood, self is often an object in such sentences as: 'everything was thrown at us'. But finally, by the time she takes her first job as a young woman, 'I decided to take things in my own hands'. Throughout her account, she 'owns her own experience', to use Rorty's phrase. More than eight in ten of her sentences contain a stative verb, a verb dealing with thinking, feeling, intending, believing, praying. (This contrasts with five in ten for her more action-oriented husband.) One is easily deceived, reading Mrs Goodhertz's self-portrait, into thinking that she is accepting of fate, perhaps passive. Instead, she believes in fate, but she also believes that fate can be nudged by her own efforts. And we rather suspect that the style is cultivated. For a closer analysis of her language reveals a very high 'subjectivity level' as carried in those stative verbs.

We must return again to Scene, or perhaps to what might better be called mise-en-scène. Both the elder Goodhertzes – unlike their children – construct their lives as if they constituted two sides of a deep divide. That divide is marked by an escape from childhood, an old life, indeed, an old *secret* life of suffering and shame as figures in unbearably capricious family settings. Personhood is on the other side of the divide. Mrs Goodhertz gets to the other side, to personhood, by 'praying for the right husband' and getting him, of which more in a moment. Mr Goodhertz crosses the divide by work, hard work, and by the grace of 'the owner [who] took me under his wing'. To him, achieving mastery of your work and, as we shall see, helping others help themselves are the two dominant ideals. For her, it is somewhat more complex. The linguistic vehicle is the '*but ...*' construction. She uses it repeatedly, and in several telltale ways, the most crucial being to distinguish what *is* from what *might have been,* as in talking about teenage drug taking, '... but I am blessed *my* kids didn't start in on it', or 'I would have been stricter, but they turned out with less problems than others'. The construction is her reminder of what *might* have been and, at the same time, a string on her finger to remind her that she is the agent who produces the better event on the other side of the ... *but* ... Her courtship and marriage are a case in point. Yes, she was waiting for God to bring the right man, *but* in fact she decided the moment her eyes fell on Mr Goodhertz that *he* was the man and knew not an instant's remorse in throwing over her then fiancé.

Their secret childhoods provide a unique source of consciousness for the elder Goodhertzes. It is a concealed secret that they share and that provides the contrast to what they have established as the organizing concept of 'home'. Mrs Goodhertz's knowledge of her macho father as a bad provider, a drinker, and a philanderer is secret knowledge, quickly and hintingly told in her narrative in a way that brooked no probing. It was there only to let us know why she prayed for a good husband and a better life for her children. Mr Goodhertz goes into even less detail. But note the two following quotations, both about hopes for the children, each said independently of the other. Mr Goodhertz: 'I wanted to give them all the things I didn't get as a kid.' And Mrs Goodhertz: 'To a point, I think, we try not to make our children have too much of what we had.'

So Debby and Carl start on the other side of the divide. Each of them tells a tale that is animated by a contrast between a kindly but inert, entrenched, or 'given' world and a 'new' one that is their own. Carl is a young Werther. His tale begins with the episode when, as an aspiring young football player, he and his teammates are told by the coach to knock out the opposing team's star quarterback. He keeps his own counsel, quits football, and starts on his own road. For Debby the tale is more like the young Stephen Hero in the discarded early version of *Portrait*. She exposes herself to experience as it may come, 'trying' in the sense of 'trying on' rather than of striving. Her involvement in acting is in the spirit of trying on new roles. Of life she says, 'I don't like doing one thing, ... the same thing all my life, ... shoved into a house and cooped up with four kids all day'. If Carl's autobiography is a *Bildungsroman*, Debby's is an existential novel. His account is linear, from start to end, but it is replete with what literary linguists call *prolepsis*. That is to

say, it is full of those odd flash-forwards that implicate the present for the future, like 'if I had know then what I know now' and 'learning to debate would stand me in good stead later'. His narrative is progressive and sequential, the story tracks 'real time'. It 'accounts' for things, and things are mentioned because *they* account for things. Privileged opportunities 'happen to' him, as we have seen, and he turns them into ventures.

The exception to this pattern is the dilemma of moral issues – as with the coach's murderous instructions or his becoming a conscientious objector in the Vietnam war, inspired by the Berrigans. Then his language (and his thought) becomes subjunctive rather than instrumental, playing on possibilities and inwardness. In this respect, he is his father's son, for Mr Goodhertz too is principally oriented to action (recall that half his sentences contain nonstative verbs) save when he encounters issues he defines as matters of morality. Don't condemn, he would say, 'you never know the whole story'. And in the same spirit, Mr Goodhertz's self-portrait is laced with literally dozens of instances of the intransitive verb *to seem*, as if he were forever mindful of a feather edge separating appearance from reality. When Carl decided he would become a conscientious objector against the Vietnam draft, his father stood by him on grounds that Carl's convictions, honestly arrived at, were worthy of respect even though he did not agree with them. Carl unwittingly even describes his intellectual quest in the same instrumental terms that his father uses in describing his ducting work. Both emphasize skills and 'know-how', both reject received ways of doing things. Theirs is 'instrumental' language and thought, as well suited to talking about heat ducting as to Carl's strikingly procedural approach to visual physiology. The father confesses to having missed intimacy in his life. So, probably, will Carl one day. Their instrumental language leaves little room for it in their discourse.

Debby's highly stative language is specialized for the reception of experience and for exploring the affect that it creates. It is richly adjectival, and the adjectives cluster around inner states. Her own acts are almost elided from her account. The past exists in its own right rather than as a guide to the present or future. In recounting the present there are vivid analeptic flashbacks – as in an unbid memory of an injured chicken on the Long Island Expressway, the traffic too thick for rescue. Like so many of her images, this one was dense with plight and affect. It evoked her tenderness for helpless animals, she told us, then veering off to that topic. And so her order of telling is dominated not by real time sequences but by a going back and forth between what happens and what she feels and believes, and what she felt and believed. In this, and in her heavy use of stative verbs, she is her mother's daughter – and, I suspect, both are locked in the same gender language. Finally, in Debby's self-story 'themes and variations' are as recursive as her brother's is progressive, and hers is as lacking in efforts to give causes as his are replete with causative expressions.

Recipes for structuring experience

You will ask whether the narrative forms and the language that goes with them in our four subjects are not simply expressions of their inner states, ways of talk that are required by the nature of those internal states. Perhaps so. But I have been proposing a more radical hypothesis than that. I believe that the ways of telling and the ways of conceptualizing that go with them become so habitual that they finally become recipes for structuring experience itself, for laying down routes into memory, for not only guiding the life narrative up to the present but directing it into the future. I have argued that a life as led is inseparable from a life as told – or more bluntly, a life is not 'how it was' but how it is interpreted and reinterpreted, told and retold: Freud's *psychic reality*. Certain basic formal properties of the life narrative do not change easily. Our excursion into experimental autobiography suggests that these formal structures may get laid down early in the discourse of family life and persist stubbornly in spite of changed conditions. Just as Georges Gusdorf argued that a special, historically conditioned, metaphysical condition was needed to bring autobiography into existence as a literary form, so perhaps a metaphysical change is required to alter the narratives that we have settled upon as 'being' our lives.

References

BRUNER, J.S. (1986) *Actual Minds, Possible Worlds*, Cambridge, MA, Harvard University Press.

BURKE, K. (1945) *The Grammar of Motives*, New York, Prentice-Hall.

GOODMAN, N. (1978) *Ways of Worldmaking*, Indianapolis, IN, Hackett.

PROPP, V. (1968) *The Morphology of the Folktale*, Austin, TX, University of Texas Press.

RICOEUR, P. (1984) *Time and Narrative*, Chicago, IL, University of Chicago Press.

RORTY, A. (1976) 'A literary postscript: characters, persons, selves, individuals' in Rorty, A.O. (ed.) *The Identity of Persons*, Berkeley, CA, University of California Press.

WHITE, H. (1984) 'The value of narrativity in the representation of reality' in Mitchell, W.J.T. (ed.) *On Narrative*, Chicago, IL, University of Chicago Press.

WINCH, P. (1958) *The Idea of a Social Science*, London, Routledge and Kegan Paul.

Source: Bruner, 1987, pp. 11–17; 21–31.

MUSIC, PERFORMANCE AND ENACTMENT

Ruth Finnegan

CHAPTER THREE

Contents

1   Introduction: how do we study the 'ordinary'?

The Amateur Operatic Society had been started off by a local businessman in 1952. He got some of his business and church friends together and told them how much he loved the music of *Lilac Time*, urging them to take it on. That became their first performance. Next they did *The Maid of the Mountains*, then *Quaker Girl*. From then on the society snowballed, drawing in not only local businessmen but enthusiastic participants from all sorts of backgrounds: teachers, bricklayers, electricians, secretaries, a self-employed plumber, housewives, and professionals of various kinds. It had close links with local churches, financial and moral support from the local business community, and local notables among its 'patrons'. The founder continued as Musical Director for many years and the society became one of the most flourishing in the area with around a hundred active members, backed up by large numbers of supporters and regular audiences.

Preparations and rehearsals went on most of the year, starting off with the enrolment and AGM in the autumn, then the start of the cycle of regular rehearsals. Even during earlier stages 'it took over my life', as one member put it – sometimes with practices two nights a week for acting, one for singing and another for dancing. Rehearsals became every weekday evening, and weekends too as the main annual performance approached – and there were major productions (over the years) of such operas as *My Fair Lady, The Student Prince, The Sound of Music*, and *The Merry Widow*. Each year saw a run of five, six or seven nights in a local hall in the early summer. The society also put on less elaborate 'variety concerts' and musical evenings, while their light-hearted week-long Christmas pantomimes, filled with topical references as well as age-old themes, were extremely popular with local audiences. Having celebrated their 'Silver Jubilee' in 1977, they were looking forward to their golden celebration in 2003.

This example can remind us of the richness of local usage and the practices of 'everyday life'. Although the latter phrase is not entirely transparent, at least it indicates that, as with the previous chapter, the main focus is not on the cultural industries, production processes or large-scale formal institutions. Here we are closer to home, dealing with cases more likely to be within direct personal experience.

The case above is one instance of the kinds of practices considered in this chapter: carried out at a local level by active participants, mainly outside the sphere of formal employment. It might equally have been a local group for sport, dance, model railways, film, or poetry; a choir or popular band; or a less organized activity like flower-arranging, constructing photograph albums, embroidery, reading, or DIY (remember the kitchen alterations discussed in Chapter 1). (Similar examples are noted in Hoggett and Bishop, 1986; Hutchinson and Feist, 1991; Cricher et al., 1995; for definitional issues about 'ordinary' and 'everyday', see the Introduction to this book, and also de Certeau, 1984; Lefebvre, 1991; Silverstone, 1994a, 1994b).

Local examples like these might at first sight seem 'simpler' to study than those pitched at a national or international level. As in the study of personal narratives in the last chapter, we ourselves, you might feel, rather than the generalizing theorists, are the experts and actors. But as this book is illustrating, just how to 'see', let alone analyse, the familiar – the 'ordinary' – is no more self-evident than it is for other cultural topics. It may be equally interesting – but it is also no less elusive and controversial.

ACTIVITY 1

Going back to the Amateur Operatic Society example that started this chapter, what are your off-the-cuff reactions to this case? In what ways might it be relevant in the context of a series of volumes entitled 'Culture, media and identities'?

Local amateur operatic activities may at first seem somewhat marginal, at least to the middle term in our series title. They are not drawn from the mass media which, whether in broadcast, recorded or printed form, are often the first referent when people speak of 'the media', as well as forming one major focus in this series.

But 'media' in a wider sense is also understood to include *all* the channels we use for communication and expression: not just the broadcast or recorded media but also the channel of live performance and interpersonal communication. From that perspective, the Amateur Operatic Society participants certainly utilized the media of language, of material and auditory display, and of music (even if the latter, as we shall see, is somewhat elusive to analyse). Their activities have visual and bodily facets too – familiar themes in this series of volumes.

The other terms in our 'culture, media, identities' triad are not so unrelated either. The practices of an operatic society certainly fall within the domain of culture, almost whichever sense of 'culture' you use. And though their precise relevance for identity may remain as yet an open question, it is certainly a reasonable issue to investigate.

Appropriate approaches for *analysing* such examples, however, are less immediately clear. Some ideas may already occur to you, drawn, say, from the place of such cases on the 'cultural circuit' (see the Introduction to this book), or in 'the local production of culture' as discussed in Chapter 1 of this volume. But at this stage I merely want to remind you that in this book we are not only considering 'ordinary' local practices but also grappling with how to analyse them.

Here is a second case to consider. Taken from an anthropologist's study of rock bands in Liverpool in the late 1980s, it describes her observations of how the band called The Jactars set about composing a song:

Dave has come up with an idea for a new song and plays it to the others on his bass. It comprises a short sequence of notes (a 'riff') which he plays over and over to enable the others to get the feel of it. Trav tries out a few chords on his guitar before playing along with Dave. Gary begins to beat out the rhythm on the rim of his snare drum and then joins in on the whole drum kit followed by Tog on keyboards. Dave repeats the riff while the other experiment with different chords and beats. They stop for Trav to check over some chords with Dave and identify which notes he has been playing. Dave suggests that Tog plays some 'deep' notes on keyboards to complement Trav's chords. Again they begin this process of repetition and experimentation using the same short riff as their base. Dave thinks the sound might be too 'dirty' and decides to drop one note of his riff in order to fit in better with what Trav is doing. He and Trav confer, watched by Gary, while Tog continues playing keyboards. They begin again, stopping for Trav to retune his guitar.

Later, Dave demonstrates a second riff he has devised to accompany the first to Trav, who watches with intense concentration. There is a thoughtful pause. For several minutes they then try out various notes and riffs to accompany the second riff before returning again to the first and the process of experimentation/improvisation based around it. ... By now Trav has developed his guitar part into something completely different from that which he started off playing. Dave, echoed by Trav and Gary, compliments Tog on the new keyboard sound and he and Trav agree that the composition has potential. Dave points out that because the second riff is 'harsher' it will complement the first, more 'melodic' riff. Tog wonders what would happen if they speeded it up a little. They try it for a long time before beginning to work on the second riff.

(Cohen, 1991, pp. 136–7)

By the next rehearsal they try lyrics that Dave has written in the meantime, but Trav suggests that the 'pattern' (the music) needs to be developed first. Again there is a long session of thinking, practice and consultation. The process continues over many rehearsals, all marked by 'concentration, discussion, and demonstration' (ibid., p. 137) until the band are reasonably satisfied:

A song or instrumental piece could be judged complete once it became part of the band's 'set' of songs to be performed in front of an audience. There was little intentional improvisation during performances. But the song was never totally finished since later on one band member might, for example, devise an alternative ending which they would try and perhaps substitute for the original. In addition, sequences of chords and notes from old or incomplete songs might be revised and adapted to form a new one. Thus older songs were continually changed and developed, sometimes dropped from the set or brought back into it.

(ibid., p. 142)

ACTIVITY 2

Spend a few moments considering which approaches to 'culture, media and identities' might be useful for analysing this second (or a similar) example, and how it relates to the 'cultural circuit' (for discussion of the circuit of culture, see the Introduction to this book).

Alternatively, if examples from music seem far from your own experience, why not substitute one of your own interests/hobbies, whether sport, cooking, photography, fishing, allotments, train-spotting, going to concerts/gigs/films/plays, private reading, pigeon-fancying – or whatever?

How to set such examples into a wider framework may not be immediately obvious. But there is in fact a range of possible approaches. We could, for example, draw on the 'mass culture' theories developed by Adorno and others, with their view of cultural production as producing 'undemanding cultural commodities which in turn resulted in a type of consumption that was also standardized, distracted and passive' (**Negus**, 1997, p. 70). We could thus ask how far the cases sketched above fit with either that view or its critique (for which also see **Negus**, 1997). Our examples could also be addressed by applying the concepts of consumption or appropriation (as developed, for example, in Chapter 1 of this volume), or the concept of representation (as developed in **Hall**, 1997a). Or we could proceed in terms of the perspective on local/global interactions illustrated in Chapter 1 of this volume, or audience and reception theories (see Chapter 5 of this book). Similarly, the examples here might be related to the 'cultural circuit' exemplified in the story of the Sony Walkman (see **du Gay, Hall et al.**, 1997).

You will doubtless find some of these approaches more appealing than others. All are possible, however, and they offer a variety of perspectives on the 'ordinary'. In this chapter they form the backdrop to the discussion, and we shall complement them by exploring a further approach to everyday practices, especially to the practice of music and performance.

1.1   Aims and preview

In the rest of this chapter, then, you will be taking up some of the issues of studying the everyday and 'ordinary', above all with a performance art like music. Can this be studied in the same way as other cultural forms or processes? Is it yet another 'text'?

The chapter explores in particular Howard Becker's view of *art as collective action* to suggest a perspective on music and other forms of performance which focuses on the collaborative networks that make up an 'art world' whose practitioners jointly recognize and deploy shared artistic conventions. This then leads into a *performance- and ritual-based view of cultural activity*, which can be extended not only to music but to other cultural activities. As you will see, the focus is less on concepts of consumption or power, and more on those of art and performance.

As with other perspectives, this approach has both strengths and weaknesses, so the chapter concludes with some queries and comparisons for you to consider. The final evaluation must be left to you.

The main objectives of this chapter are to help you to:

- Build on a case study of local music-making to engage with a perspective drawing on interactionist and performance-oriented approaches – approaches which you could apply both to examples in this volume or your wider reading, and to analysing cases from your own experience and observation.

- Evaluate the strengths and weaknesses of this perspective as compared with other conceptual tools for analysing cultural activities, including activities you may be involved in yourself.

- Consider how you might apply more widely the insights derived from discussing examples drawn from the important medium of music.

- Relate the book's theme of constraint versus creativity both to the approaches and examples presented here and to everyday and 'ordinary' cases from your own experience.

2   Studying local music-making in an English town

Sections 2 and 3 complement approaches to cultural processes and products (discussed in other volumes of the *Culture, Media and Identities* series) by using an extended example to introduce some additional perspectives – or at the least, further slants on familiar approaches. Here we encounter, first, the concept of 'art worlds' and of 'art as collective action' formulated by the interactionist scholar Howard Becker, and secondly (in section 3), certain related ideas about performance and communicative enactment developed by recent 'performance-oriented' writers.

2.1   A musical ethnography

For our extended example we return to the town of Milton Keynes, discussed in the previous chapter. This time the focus is on the local musical activities.

The Amateur Operatic Society who were first on the stage in this chapter formed just one of many musical groups and practices in the city. These spanned manifold musical traditions – classical, jazz, folk, brass band, country-and-western, and rock/pop. Their activities took place in many different settings – home, school, church, local halls, shops, pubs, clubs,

TABLE 3.1 Musical groups and activities in Milton Keynes in the early 1980s.

Classical	Orchestras: 3–4 leading orchestras Several dozen youth and school orchestras Choirs: 9–10 independent 4-part choirs Many small independent groups Choirs attached to most schools and churches: about 100 in all.
Brass bands	5–8 main brass bands Various smaller bands (e.g. Boys' Brigade, Salvation Army).
Operatic and musical drama	2 Gilbert and Sullivan societies About 4 other amateur operatic or musical drama groups.
Jazz	12 + jazz bands 5 or 6 established jazz venues in local pubs and clubs at any one time.
Folk music	5–6 folk clubs meeting on regular cyclical basis About 12 folk groups/bands 4 'ceilidh' dance bands.
Country-and-western	2 leading bands (performing locally and nationally) 3 or 4 smaller bands Milton Keynes Divided Country and Western Club (very popular locally and regionally) plus some smaller short-lived attempts.
Rock and pop	Several hundred named groups over the period of the research (1980–4); at any one time, approximately 100.
Miscellaneous	Many other groups and individual performers not fitting easily into the above categories (e.g. Milton Keynes and District Pipe Band; dragon dancers for the Chinese New Year; Hindu Youth Organization's musical events; Milton Keynes Organ Society).
Settings and venues for local music	Almost anywhere! Public halls, schools, churches, public streets and greens, people's homes, social clubs (from the Conservative Association or Working Men's Clubs, to local youth clubs or firms' clubs), and – very important – the pubs.
Numbers	Impossible to calculate precisely (groups formed and re-formed over the 4 years' research, probably not all were discovered, and *exactly* what to count as 'Milton Keynes' was disputable) – but there were certainly several hundred functioning musical groups based and performing in and around Milton Keynes in the early 1980s, and many hundreds of live performances each year.

Source: The information above is based on ethnographic study in Milton Keynes (including Bletchley), chiefly undertaken in 1980–4 (methodology and findings elaborated in Finnegan, 1989).

garden sheds, garages, and streets (to mention just some) – and engaged large numbers of active participants.

As I discovered in my ethnographic research into local music in Milton Keynes in the early 1980s (see Finnegan, 1989), the extent and range of local music-making was striking, going well beyond what most people had expected – and that included not only myself and other academics, but also the musicians themselves. Milton Keynes of course has its own unique features and the specific details will certainly not be exactly the same elsewhere. However, the general patterns have many parallels. The widespread notion that 'there is nothing going on locally nowadays, unlike in the past' may be yet another modern myth which cannot stand up to empirical scrutiny (a suggestion you may wish to test for your own locality).

The musical groups and practices summarized in Table 3.1 took many different forms. Some attracted large numbers of committed adherents over long periods on well-trodden pathways, others struggled, others still depended on the enthusiasm of just a few participants or were pushing at the established boundaries, with greater or lesser success. Some were organized through the voluntary-association structure, with committees, officers, AGMs, and formal accounts. Others – like small bands or home music-making – were less formalized but still, as with the rock band described in section 1 above, observed shared conventions about expected social and musical procedures. Musical assumptions varied too, as did the ages, backgrounds and aspirations of the musicians themselves. Their means of support drew variously on governmental help, private patronage, commercial enterprise, parental backing and – not least – their own pockets and the commitment of their own time and energies.

Amidst the variety these musical practices broadly shared two characteristics. First, they depended on the *active and shared participation* of a range of people – and they needed to be 'active' to engage in music. Secondly, their participants were enabled to engage in these joint activities through the existence of a set of *socially accepted conventions*. They were not just the one-off actions of independent individuals.

The activities of musicians within what could be called the 'classical musical world' in Milton Keynes illustrate these cultural practices.

Among the several orchestras in the locality (see Table 3.1) the leading amateur group in the early 1980s was the Sherwood Sinfonia (later retitled the Milton Keynes Sinfonia – see Figure 3.1). This was founded in 1973 as a high-standard amateur orchestra for the area and by the 1980s was playing regularly under a professional conductor. Many of its fifty or so players – both male and female – were music teachers but they also recruited their advanced pupils together with other experienced players from the locality. The criteria for entry normally included advanced grades in the nationally organized music examinations, which emphasized not only performance but also theory and skill in reading notated music – a very different system, it will emerge, from that in the rock world. Their activities followed a predictable annual cycle, with four concerts a year, in local halls, of works from the accepted classical repertoire, and a light-hearted, family, pre-Christmas concert. The weekly evening practices intensified as each concert date approached; and a concert date regularly started with a long afternoon rehearsal, followed by an evening performance to an audience partly made up of players' friends and relations.

The Wolverton Light Orchestra had a longer history. Founded as the Frank Brooks Orchestra by a local bandmaster just after the First World War, it was later renamed the Wolverton Orchestral Society, and gave regular winter concerts in local cinemas, playing light music with a First War flavour. It was revived after the Second War and for many years was conducted by a well-known local musician who had worked most of his life in the local Wolverton railway works where his father was a foreman. As with many others, his musical interests had started from singing in a local church choir. By the 1980s, it had become the Wolverton Light Orchestra, and though lower down the informal local ranking than the Sherwood Sinfonia it still expected to recruit players of good standard in classical music terms. There was a similar cycle of weekly rehearsals and the orchestra regularly gave six to seven concerts of light classical music a year in the smaller halls and churches in the area, often performing in aid of local churches and charities, and playing with formally-taught proficiency and commitment.

FIGURE 3.1 Members of Milton Keynes Sinfonia at a weekly rehearsal.

Classical music at the local level was performed not only by these two orchestras but also by more fluid instrumental groups and home-based ensembles, as well as by youth orchestras, chamber groups, and 25 to 30 school orchestras. There were also the many choirs practising and performing throughout the city, all likely to follow a similar cycle of at least weekly evening rehearsals interspersed with public performances.

Not all music was of the classical variety. A dozen jazz bands also played regularly in and around Milton Keynes in the early 1980s, some short-lived but others with many years' experience of performing in local pubs and clubs to a healthy local following. Each band had its individual characteristics, and players varied greatly in occupational and educational background. All, however, took themselves seriously as *jazz* musicians – as one player put it, 'It's a blood thing, it's in your veins' – and followed the accepted jazz conventions about instrumentation and improvisation. (Quotations in this section are taken from interviews with band members in Milton Keynes carried out during my research in the early 1980s; for further details, see Finnegan, 1989.)

The Fenny Stompers six-member band, to take just one instance, was formed from a nucleus of two brothers in 1978 and their smart white and red uniforms were well-known in the area. Mostly self-taught as musicians and with little formal school education, they continued as amateurs in the sense that they were employed in non-musical (mainly blue-collar) jobs. But they also performed gigs two or three times a week in local pubs and clubs (occasionally further afield) as well as playing for fund-raising events and charitable occasions. Like other jazz players they liked being the 'resident' band on a monthly or fortnightly cycle in one or other of the local 'jazz pubs', where their typical jazz facility for improvisation within the jazz conventions meant they could produce fresh performances time after time. Their Dixieland New Orleans jazz was for people 'to sing along to and have a good time' and drew local audiences of 70–100 people.

Rock music formed another prominent set of activities. At any one time there were around a hundred rock or pop bands playing in the area. Each had its own carefully chosen name, often expressing the band's philosophy, but sometimes ironic or humorous, or just chosen because it sounded attractive. Dancing Counterparts, Solstice, Static Blue, The Memories, Bitza ('a little bit of this, a little bit of that'), Seditious Impulse, Spud and the Fabs, Streets Ahead, Mithras, Figures of Speech, Under the Carpet (the bad things about the social order are swept under the carpet), Scream and the Fits, Urban Cows (ironic reference to the notorious concrete cows of Milton Keynes), Basically Brian, and Bottom of the Bill Band – these are only a few of the many colourful examples. Their members were mostly, though not exclusively, male, but otherwise they varied greatly in musical and educational background, occupation, and age: not all were young, unskilled or rebellious! What they did all share was a musical tradition in which the ability to 'read music' in the classical sense was simply not relevant. Self-teaching was the typical pattern – not an 'easy option' (as pictured by classical musicians), but, for dedicated practitioners, involving huge commitments of time and self-discipline over weeks, months and years.

The bands varied in 'success', measured chiefly by how many performances they could mount. Some bands had as yet seldom or never played in public though were aspiring to get gigs in local pubs or youth clubs – unpaid if necessary – whereas others were performing every week, not only locally but also further afield. A few were considering going professional. Live performance was mostly their prime interest, but the proliferation of small local recording studies also gave them the chance to make their own recordings for demos or for sale to audiences.

FIGURE 3.2 Milton Keynes rock band, Villain, performing.

Bands were organized on a personal and informal basis and frequently split after a time, their players re-forming as another group. Nevertheless, there were emergent conventions for behaviour, leadership, getting a name, seeking gigs, even for breaking up. And despite the cultivated musical individuality of each band, there were also accepted conventions about musical genre, processes of performance, instrumentation and composition. It meant something predictable in terms of playing, performing and practising when someone said 'Let's form a band' or inserted a small advert in a local paper asking for a drummer or bass player for an existing group. Another striking characteristic – and to me a surprise – was that, like The Jactars, practically all these Milton Keynes bands composed their own music. Far from merely 'consuming' or reproducing others' music, they were themselves producers and composers. Composition was a lengthy and complex undertaking and bands typically met to develop their compositions collaboratively on two, three or more occasions a week.

These activities also draw us back to the issues of identity. All those individuals in Milton Keynes (or elsewhere) who were putting in the regular collaborative rehearsing typical of local musicians doubtless found their musical commitments not irrelevant to their personal sense of identity and worth: an investment of the self. But for rock bands there was this extra dimension – they were creating their own original music, expressing something uniquely personal to themselves and their group. The situation was the precise opposite of that pictured by many detractors of rock music or implied in the 'critique of mass culture' approach (see **Negus**, 1997, and the Introduction to this volume). For, rather than passively reproducing works from the mass media, the players invested huge amounts of their own personal expertise, time and collective effort in developing something they regarded as truly their own. The band enabled them 'to work things out for yourself'. In the words of one player, their songs and performances provided a way to 'live our own lives and control our own destiny'.

2.2   Music as collective action

How are we to analyse examples like those sketched out in section 2.1?

This was a question that, like others, I had to tussle with in my own ethnographic research. Which theoretical perspective would be effective was far from self-evident. I went through various possibilities. Certainly individuals and their creativity were relevant – but, no more than with the personal stories considered in the last chapter was it *purely* a matter of individuals. The 'mass culture' approach was a well-established one – but, as indicated at the end of section 2.1 above, it seemed to obscure rather than illuminate certain aspects of local musical practice. Again, these local practices *could* be fitted into a cultural circuit – but was the vocabulary of 'consumption' or of 'pleasure' the most illuminating approach? Would concentrating either on the 'effects' on particular 'audiences' or just on the 'good' musicians be sufficient? And while I could *admire* talented musicians or 'musical works', surely social scientists need more than just admiration (or, indeed, condemnation) as an analytic handle to interpret what they see and experience?

The work of Howard Becker provided a different option. His analysis of '**art worlds**' suggested a framework that many researchers have found helpful for interpreting such activities and extending their understanding.

art worlds

Becker is a well-known sociologist in the interactionist tradition. He has researched and published in a variety of fields including deviance, occupations, music, art, genres of writing, and photography. Equally relevant, he was a jazz player. This was the background to his earlier analysis of the occupation of a jazz musician and the interactions between performers and audience (Becker, 1951, 1963). As he says in the Preface to his influential *Art Worlds*:

> Maybe the years I spent playing the piano in taverns in Chicago and elsewhere led me to believe that the people who did that mundane work were as important to an understanding of art as the better-known players

who produced the recognized classics of jazz ... that the craftsmen who help make art works are as important as the people who conceive them.

(Becker, 1982, p. ix)

collaborative work

He goes on to underline a simple, but crucial, message: that the **collaborative work** of a whole series of people – not just of the few labelled as the 'creators' – is needed for the production of works of art.

READING A

Now read Reading A, 'Art worlds and collective activity', by Howard S. Becker, which you will find at the end of this chapter, in the light of the following questions:

1   Could Becker's analysis be applied to the Milton Keynes musicians?

2   In what ways (if at all) does he seem to you to be presenting a distinctive approach?

Becker's contribution partly lies in reminding us of the *social* nature of musical activity (music, in his view, being one example of 'art'). He is turning us away from the image of music as something 'high' and mystical, network and towards the **network** of ordinary people interacting in their everyday practices – the 'bad' as well as the 'good' musicians. For Becker, 'a network of cooperation [is] central to the analysis of art as a social phenomenon' (1982, p. xi). Far from being the autonomous products of asocial individuals, music, like other art and craft practices – and indeed any kind of work – depends on a system of interlocking institutions and activities which, whether we are conscious of it or not, form a recognized part of our social world.

This gives a handle for analysing examples like those of the Milton Keynes musical groups. Understanding the musical work of the Sherwood Sinfonia, for example, is enhanced when we recognize that it is supported not only by the performers we see before us at a concert, but also by a network of further collaboration. This includes, for example, the instrument manufacturers (producing and marketing their instruments to culturally agreed specifications); the music shops (selling not only instruments but the essential sheet music); music schools and teachers; the music examinations system; publicity and printing; coffee-making (essential, of course, for that halfway break during rehearsals!); local halls, churches or schools for concerts and rehearsals; fund-raising and financial support; committee members and officers; audiences for performances (not always easily achieved!); and, not least, a culturally established system of notation and tuning to allow for musical cooperation.

ACTIVITY 3

Do you know of any similar cases of collaborative networks underlying local art or craft activities in your own experience or observation? Try to list some of the people, organizations or activities that are involved.

Becker's approach need not be confined just to a local dimension. **Negus** (1997) has clearly illustrated the complex network of activities within the British music industry and its recognized division of labour, including the role of the artist and repertoire staff. The same approach can be applied to non-musical activities too, whether professional or amateur: all those practices which in *someone's* definition are regarded as 'art' (a term in which Becker includes what others might call 'crafts' or just 'hobbies'). From embroidery to dancing, model-building to poetry reading, photography to cooking, we can enquire about the cooperative network and activities which make them possible (for further examples, see Hoggett and Bishop, 1986; Hutchinson and Feist, 1991; Silverstone, 1994b). We can explore the division of labour (not just the immediate practitioners and creators, but also the suppliers, marketers, supporters, and audiences); the medium of expression or circulation which both facilitates and constrains production or performance; and the accepted conventions through which these are shaped.

In one way Becker's account might just seem another way of going round the 'cultural circuit' (see the Introduction to this volume). Both frameworks rightly alert us to the complex cultural nature of any practice or product. Because of the many links to other institutions and practices, it cannot be fully understood in isolation, far less by looking at just one individual creator. Such a theme is a familiar one in analyses by social scientists (for instance, see Wolff, 1983).

Becker's terminology and orientation are also distinctive, however, in focusing more on the network of collaborative activities than on the moments named in our 'cultural circuit'. He also stresses examples which make his analysis as applicable to local everyday practices as to products circulated through the mass media. And though he is far from presenting 'art' as something mystical, or the province only of 'the great individual', you may still feel that his vocabulary of 'art' and 'artistic conventions' carries different connotations from some other analyses of everyday life in this volume and elsewhere.

2.3   Conventions

Becker pays particular attention to the **conventions** by which artists coordinate their activities (a concept which will be familiar from Chapter 2). He again traces his interest partly to his own experience. When playing for seven or eight hours a night as a jazz pianist in Chicago nightclubs he found that he could still perform even when more than half asleep:

conventions

> I must have made use of my knowledge that all the phrases of the song were eight bars long, that they used only a few chords from the many possibilities available, and that those were arranged in a few standardized ways. ... These understandings get built into the performer's physical reactions as well as his cognitive equipment, so that playing while asleep becomes understandable and unremarkable.

(Becker, 1982, p. 58)

Becker is not suggesting that all conventions are as tight as in those particular jazz performances. As he illustrates, many are more general and may be social as well as musical. But his example brings home vividly how artistic practice rests on culturally established rather than 'natural' conventions. What is taken as given in one 'world' may be unacceptable in another. In Becker's account, the conventions within any given art world both guide the participants and give that world its definition.

Once the question is raised, it becomes clear that the contrasting musical worlds in Milton Keynes are indeed marked by differing conventions (one does have to *raise* the question however: for the nature of conventions is often precisely that they are so taken for granted as to be hidden even from their participants). These conventions encompassed musical training, composition, performance and audience behaviour, even concepts about what 'music' really was.

A shared assumption within the classical music world, for example, was that music was composed prior to performance and encapsulated in notated scores, themselves written in the conventional western classical format. Classical musicians were normally expected to specialize in recognized instrument(s) and to be *formally* taught over many years. This system was enshrined in the officially recognized graded examinations which stressed the ability to read and reproduce written music. It was in these written scores that 'musical works' in some sense essentially existed. The players transmitted these works in their performances, directing them to an audience who received their renditions in a duly hushed and serious atmosphere.

The conventions were very different in the jazz world. Certainly there was, again, an accepted range of instruments (both overlapping and different from those of classical music) and similar commitment and enthusiasm. Some players had formal musical training but most had taught themselves, and an ability to read music was if anything regarded as a hindrance. For them, music was essentially a *performed* art, developed through performance rather than prior composition: composition *in* performance. Thus it was the ability to exploit the jazz conventions in improvising that was prized, not passively 'reading the dots'. Many jazz musicians were thoroughly contemptuous of the classical music practice of clinging to the written notes – like copy-typing, they said, going in one ear and out the other with no creativity in between. In keeping with their view of music as essentially consisting in performance not in a written score, each performance was different and creative. The audience too were a prominent part of the musical event, usually acquainted with jazz conventions themselves, and often taking an active part, dancing, singing along or even taking a turn in the playing.

FIGURE 3.3   Members of the Milton Keynes Sinfonia reading musical scores while playing their instruments at a weekly rehearsal.

FIGURE 3.4   Members of the jazz sextet Momentum performing, without written musical scores, in a Milton Keynes pub.

The rock conventions partly resembled those of the jazz world. Players were typically self-taught (even more so than in jazz) and had little time for written forms. The essence of music lay in performance not writing, and revolved round timbre, colour, rhythmic realization or mood rather than notated texts. As in the jazz world, the audience often entered actively into the occasion. Typically regarded by classical musicians as not really playing 'music', rock players in turn often despised classical music as just a tedious sequence of notes with no go or creativity about them.

Rock conventions also differed from those of jazz. These partly related to the accepted instruments but also, more significantly, to the mode of composition. The Jactars were a good example of a widespread pattern: prior composition developed through collective practice rather than (as with jazz) improvisation during performance. Unlike jazz players they needed intensive work beforehand, but once their 'set' was developed there was relatively little variation during performance.

The conventions in the contrasting musical worlds were not unchangeable. One or more musicians could work to introduce changes, and, as Becker points out, innovation was possible, if at a cost. But the broad observance of these or similar conventions was essential for the collaborative practices of each of these musical traditions. They gave their participants – audience members as well as musicians – recognized pathways on which to play an active role in a particular art (or musical) world. Becker's concept of 'art world' has successfully drawn attention to the interacting elements that enable the continuance of specific musical traditions, and to the recognized, if often unconscious, conventions which differentiate distinctive musical worlds.

Note too the vocabulary and metaphors in his analysis. These cluster round terms like cooperating network, collective processes, and culturally agreed conventions – social practices rather than individual artists. But at the same time the terminology is more about active collaboration than about concepts of consumption or struggle. As with the analysis of personal narrative in the previous chapter, such a perspective turns the searchlight more on ideas of creativity and artistic expression than on, say, mass culture, the cultural industries or local/global interactions; we hear more of 'art' than of 'power'. The conventions shaping cultural practice are seen less as constraints (though this is certainly one aspect) than as culturally developed channels which – like language – make people's artistic expression and performance possible.

Essentially, Becker's picture of people engaging in artistic activity – in the wide sense of the term 'art' – steers a line between an externally determined and a purely voluntaristic model of human beings. Artistic practices are not totally constrained, for there is both the opportunity for fulfilment and creativity through using the established conventions, and sometimes room – though at a cost – to innovate and change them. At the same time they are not just the products of autonomous and anarchically free individuals. Like the personal story-telling described in the last chapter, it is only through the cooperative observance of agreed conventions and collaborative networks that individuals actively participate whether in musical activity or in other everyday cultural practices.

3   Is analysing music a problem? The example continued

Becker's concepts of art worlds and of art as collaborative action have proved adaptable to a range of everyday activities, including those of the local musicians of Milton Keynes. However, I now want to take you a step further, stimulated in part by his illuminating comments not just on the creation of art but also on its *performance*.

This is not so easy to do. Music-as-performance is harder to capture in intellectual analysis, it seems, than are verbal or visual texts. So we need first to take a short detour among the issues raised in studying specifically *musical* practices.

3.1   Music is like any other cultural activity – and so is its study

It is not hard to argue that there is something distinctive about music. It represents a medium in its own right, characterized above all by its performance quality and its non-linguistic basis. This is a line we must follow up shortly.

But let us first remind ourselves of ways in which musical activity also *resembles* other cultural practices. So too, therefore, do the approaches to analysing it. Thus, many of the same issues arise as in debates about other cultural practices, whether everyday processes or more formal structures.

For example, one well-entrenched approach in traditional studies of music has been to regard the *composer* (or, for other art forms, the *author* or *artist*) as the prior and, in some sense, self-sufficient agent. But as will already be clear from Becker's argument in Reading A, this approach finds less favour in social scientific analyses. These are unlikely to view music and art (or indeed any other cultural products) as essentially defined by the intentions of individual authors/composers. Focusing on single individuals as independent and autonomous agents is obviously a drastically oversimplified analysis of social reality. Similarly, an appreciation of the many interlocking elements in social life, such as is encapsulated in the 'cultural circuit' image (see the Introduction to this volume), must necessarily takes us beyond isolated individual creators.

The social scientist's interest in patterns rather than atomistic individuals is as applicable to music as to any other social sphere. This can be tested by running through theoretical perspectives drawn on in this and similar volumes. We could focus, say, on the social organization of production; for example, through a consideration of recorded music within the context of the 'music industry' and/or 'world music'. Alternatively, the music's marketing or circulation could be foregrounded, or the social background of those involved. Listeners and buyers of music could be explored: are they the standardized cultural dopes implied in some mass culture ideas put forward by Adorno and similar writers (discussed in **Negus**, 1997)? Those ideas are generally criticized as elitist, loaded and perhaps speculative. But they also lead into questions about the degree of social constraint as against individual creativity in the practice of music. Such issues could be explored for cases like the operatic society, the rock bands or the other musical activities described so far in this chapter.

A focus on power and struggle could also lead to illuminating debates, applicable to music as to other facets of cultural life. Musical practice offers a rich field here, open to a wide range of analyses – from cruder Marxist approaches, to more sophisticated Gramscian notions of hegemony, or to questions about the global political economy (as in Chapter 1 above), or about power, ideology or appropriation inspired by such writers as Foucault or Hall (see **Hall**, ed., 1997). Such issues could certainly be raised in a study of the musical practices of local groups such as the Milton Keynes performers.

Music can also be analysed in terms of reception theories and the study of audiences. Who were the audiences of the Amateur Operatic Society, of the

Sherwood Sinfonia, the Fenny Stompers or the Milton Keynes rock bands, and how did they react to their (varied) performances? Admittedly, there are controversies within such studies (see Chapter 5 in this volume). There are also differing perspectives on the 'impact' on audience, or on resistance, appropriation, mediation, 'reception', or questions of active and passive audiences (see Morley, 1993; Silverstone, 1994a, Chapter 6; Stevenson, 1995, Chapter 3). But here again we have well-developed approaches to the study of culture which can be applied as well to music as to other media.

And then there are the concepts of 'art worlds' and 'art as collective action', illustrated in the last section. Becker developed this approach partly through applying to music ideas drawn from the sociology of occupations.

Depending on your own interests, you will probably think of other perspectives which could be drawn on for the study of local music: the theory of 'genre', for example (compare the study of soap operas in **Gledhill**, 1997); or traditional functionalist and Durkheimian perspectives on music's role in upholding the status quo; or approaches which illuminate its relation to sociability, to social mobility, or to ethnic differentiation (see **Gilroy**, 1997, section 5.4, for an example). Questions about social distinctions are also worth investigating (in my own work I found that, somewhat unexpectedly, local musical activities in Milton Keynes turned out, with relatively few exceptions, broadly to transcend class and (often) age divisions; however, gender and stage in the domestic life-cycle did play a significant role).

Thus there *are* established theoretical approaches through which music can be analysed like any other cultural practice. Admittedly, none is without controversy. Just as the overarching traditions of social thought (Marxist, liberal, social reformist, or conservative, to accept Coates's terminology (1990)) can both illuminate and obscure elements in the social world, so too with the social scientific approaches to music which to an extent link to these traditions. Though none is self-evidently the *only* way to approach music, for all are debatable, they are all certainly possible approaches to music.

There is, then, no need to mystify music and its practice. We can make a critical application of the usual theoretical tools of social science, whether to the music products of the mass media or to the ordinary musical practices close to home.

3.2   Or ... *should* music be approached differently?

I hope you will consider following earlier theorists in using some of those perspectives in your own analyses. But you may still have ended up feeling a little uncomfortable, not so much with the specific theories as with the implication that such approaches exhaust our understanding of the medium of music. If so, you are not alone. For music has also been seen as presenting some unique issues.

The central problem is the apparently 'non-representational' nature of music. In contrast to language or visual representation, there is no easy sense in which we can speak of music 'imitating' the world. Even when we move away from a simple imitative or 'mimetic' theory of the media to a more 'constructionist' approach (see **Hall**, 1997a, 1997b) we are still left with the problem of *what* it is that music, or a particular piece of music, could be said to 'signify' or 'represent'.

Meaning may indeed lie in usage and, as has frequently been argued, be culturally constructed rather than given. But for music, we have the additional problem of what kind of thing this 'meaning' might be. This is the more so in that the concept of 'meaning' commonly carries strong linguistic connotations, expressed in metaphors which employ terms like 'text', 'reading', 'linguistic codes', 'decoding', 'encoding', 'signifying'. It is hard to see just how such understandings of meaning can apply in the case of music. It is true that the 'meaning' of verbal texts or visual representations can also be controversial and elusive; they too raise issues about what they 'stand for' or where their 'referents' might lie. But for those media the concept of 'meaning' and of 'reading' their texts does – we can now see – make some kind of sense, and this can up to a point be verbally conveyed. But how can we apply such concepts of meaning to a musical score, let alone performance? And if we enlarge the concepts 'meaning' or 'text' so they can be made to apply, do we risk losing the essential core, the *music* itself?

All this is a long-running argument to which we shall return (in section 3.4 below). But first let us explore an interim solution which both takes music with some seriousness and yet keeps in touch with the social scientific analysis of musical practice, taking us beyond simply the idiosyncratic actions of individuals.

3.3   One way in: studying song texts

Some music has words. An obvious point! – but one that usefully provides the analyst with a hold on at least one element in music, enabling its analysis like other textual forms. Song words can be treated as essentially a form of poetry (lyric poetry). And there is the further advantage that we can examine the lyrics' effect on their hearers, drawing on established approaches in audience studies.

Such analyses can be conducted in various ways. A helpful overview is given by Simon Frith, one of the leading British sociological analysts of music (especially popular music) and himself a practitioner.

READING B

You should now read Reading B, 'Why do songs have words?', by Simon Frith, in the light of the following questions:

1   Might you find any of the approaches Frith describes helpful for analysing examples from your own experience or observation?

2   Do any of them link to approaches discussed elsewhere in this or similar volumes?

Frith helpfully takes us through a series of approaches to the analysis of song words. These overlap with approaches to the media that are familiar in debates in cultural and media studies (some are also taken up in the discussion of audiences in Chapter 5 in this book). He moves from somewhat simplistic to more subtle theories as he goes on.

Frith starts by commenting critically on earlier forms of 'content analysis', in terms which recall arguments against simplified reflection and 'mimetic' approaches to the media (see **Hall**, 1997a, 1997b). The parallel 'realist' approaches are open to similar criticisms for analysing a lyric as a *direct* expression of 'the social or emotional condition it describes and represents' (see Reading B, p. 154). Here, as before, there are revealing debates over what cases are to count. Frith draws attention to what he labels the 'sentimental socialist-realist' assumption that the 'authenticity' of 'folk songs' and 'working-class views' can be contrasted to the banal and imposed escapism of pop music, as well as the complicating possibility that songs symbolize and politicize suffering rather than just reflect or accept it.

Analyses based on Adorno and other mass-cultural critiques are also mentioned by Frith (compare the discussion of these approaches in **Negus**, 1997). These in turn are linked to analyses of songs as propaganda for bourgeois ideology, the 'class function' of pop, and the use of song by musicians or audiences to fight back against powerful social constraints. Frith's account also refers to important trends in audience reception approaches (further discussed in Chapter 5 in this volume). He points to the *differential* effects related to different audiences and identities (a familiar if still sometimes neglected point), and to contrasting audience conventions in different musical genres.

Frith is right to direct us to song texts. Certainly, in the Milton Keynes context this was one way of gaining an insight into local musical practices. His doubts about the validity of simplified 'reflection' approaches are reinforced by the findings about local musicians, for the relation between the words of their songs and their own lives and/or local conditions was complex and elusive rather than direct.

The significance of sung words varied in the different musical worlds in Milton Keynes. In the classical musical world of local choirs, singers could recognize the musical settings in the choral tradition as framing words that had rung down the ages: not just all those Latin Requiems, Masses and Glorias but English words too, like Christmas carols or the sung words in the *Messiah* or the (translated) *St Matthew Passion*. This continuity was also *visible* in the handed-down and borrowed vocal scores which regularly contained pencilled annotations by singers from several generations. Their 'meaning' may seldom be verbally articulated but at a deeper level it is hard not to read into this experience some element of identification with the cultural continuities of the West and its long Christian tradition.

Among rock musicians, the words and their meaning were perhaps more direct. The carefully composed sung lyrics – plus music – had strong emotive significance in having been personally composed, the original creation of the band members themselves. Their value for people's sense of identity and self-expression seemed clear. This lay not only in the musicians' actions and the pride with which they talked about their compositions. It was also at times verbalized explicitly as they explained how their songs gave them a way to control and create the world around them.

Among Milton Keynes rock bands, original compositions were the rule not the exception, developed through similar processes to those used by The Jactars (see section 1 above). This was grounded in a great commitment of not only the self but, at a more mundane level, of time, application and both individual and joint creativity. The extent and range of their compositions were impressive. Among the hundred or more song titles I listed in the course of my research were, for example, such varied and idiosyncratic titles as 'The robot', 'Midnight stroll', 'Pressure on our lives', 'Untold truth', 'I have no gun but I can spit', 'Thoughts of distortion', 'Peace for a new age', 'Morning light', 'Broken hero', 'Treading on thin ice', 'First love', 'Infants of infinity', and 'Into the void'. However hard to pin down precisely, far less to 'prove', there was clearly some relevance here to the musicians' sense of identity, to their meaning and worth both as individuals and as members of a group into whose productions they had jointly invested so much.

But beyond this, the precise meanings attached to the words by either creators or audiences could not be read off in advance. They varied. Bands sometimes did use their lyrics to formulate and convey their views of the world. One group told how their music helped them to 'get a message across to people' in their own right, 'making a stand against the way things are and the way people live. We're all pacifists ... vegetarian, into animals' rights', and they added, 'It's good fun – a good thing'. Another band aimed at lyrics, 'important to the lives of people, to make people hear what young people think about certain issues ... peace and feminism'. A few wanted to compose 'protest' or anti-authority songs – or at any rate to deploy motifs along these lines in their songs (I add this proviso since in other aspects of their lives these band members scarcely fitted the stereotypes of 'youth protest' or of 'working-class' rebels, any more than the uplifting sentiments of other bands' songs reflected every aspect of their behaviour). Other songs used fantasy or humour or irony, or followed and embellished the beauties of the music as much as carrying a semantic message. The conclusion I had to reach was that there was no single interpretation of the lyrics. Insofar as one could attach verbalized meanings, they varied, even with different members and songs within the same band. The complexity of both words and contexts made it difficult to apply either a simplified reflection model or a generalized theoretical perspective for 'reading off' some general meaning from the lyrics.

Frith comments, following his critique of 'reflection' approaches, that another way to look at the genre of pop love songs is to say that they give people the terms in which 'to articulate and so experience their emotions' (see Reading B, p. 158), an insight that will recall the role of personal narratives in formulating people's experience (see previous chapter). A parallel point might be made about the lyrics composed by the Milton Keynes rock musicians and – if in a less direct sense – about the resonant words performed in the classical choirs.

Near the end of his article, Frith starts to move us towards a rather different approach, one oriented towards the *performance* of the music:

> A song is always a performance and song words are always spoken out, heard in someone's accent. Songs are more like plays than poems; song words ... [bear] meaning not just semantically, but also as structures of sound ... . It is not just what they sing, but the way they sing it, that determines what singers mean to us.
>
> (Reading B, pp. 156–7)

Looking only at the verbal texts, it seems, may not after all be enough.

3.4 Performance, ritual and identity

Frith's point is well put, though not a new one. It has already emerged (in section 2.3) that the definition of music in terms of notated text, while at first sight applicable to classical music, simply does not fit the conventions of performed forms like jazz and rock. It now appears, in addition, that it can be misleading to assume that the crucial element in songs – let alone other music – must necessarily be the *verbal* component.

This was evident in The Jactars example (see section 1 above). It was the-music-as-played not the words that was their prime interest. In his article, 'Theodor Adorno meets the Cadillacs', Gendron (1986) similarly pointed out the problem of evaluating popular music from the text-based viewpoint of western classical music. Rather, it should be viewed in terms of its own conventions, emphasizing performance qualities like timbre and connotation rather than musical text.

performance   A thoroughgoing **performance** focus can even challenge our deeply-ingrained assumptions about classical music itself. Our cultural reverence for the written musical text conceals from us the very real performance qualities of classical music as actually practised – all those features *not* conveyed in our written notation. We could also question whether the classical-music audience conventions are as 'natural' as its participants assume. Thus, the ostensibly passive 'reception' of classical music audiences in Milton Keynes can, like other audience conventions, be seen as *learned* and structured rather than 'natural' behaviour. It is only by carrying out these solemn-looking actions that participants in the performance ritual successfully perform their role in the event as a whole.

A performance focus offers one way of getting round the problem of the non-representational and non-linguistic nature of music. Of course, it is *possible* both to define music as a text and to attribute verbalized meanings to music. Many such 'meanings' have been posited, ranging from explications of the emotions it may stir in players and listeners (McClellan, 1995), to the supposed uplifting or, alternatively, degrading messages it conveys, or the sexist or oppressive meanings that the music itself apparently communicates to some analysts. I could certainly have asked Milton Keynes players and listeners to describe in words what they saw in the music, and up to a point I did that. But the drawback in sticking with verbalized accounts is that they somehow lose the *music*. A logocentric (word-based) approach to music bypasses the music itself by a parallel, perhaps interesting, but *different* form of discourse, for verbal representations are not an essential part of music. As the anthropologist-cum-musician Steven Feld puts it:

> Music communication is a primary modelling system, to use John Blacking's (1981) phrase, with unique and irreducible symbolic properties. These must be experienced and approached in their own right and ... freed from any notion that they simply translate or copy the speech mode.
>
> (Keil and Feld, 1994, p. 94)

Approaching music in terms of performance rather than decodable text may not solve all problems. But it does bypass the misleading logocentric – and, as we shall see, possibly ethnocentric – model endemic in some analyses of culture. It directs attention to the conventions not of verbal texts but of performances, to what participants *do* in performance and how they do it, not just what they say.

Highlighting performance means turning away from the assumption that the 'reality' of cultural practices lies essentially in the 'texts' or in the cognitive 'messages' that are conveyed: the 'products'. Rather, people are *performing* – an active *process* – so we also need to appreciate the multifaceted expression of their performances in the round. We have to see the text more broadly than merely in the terms of the *verbal*.

This fits the increasing attention being paid to 'the body' not only by ethnomusicologists (such as Blacking, 1973) but by analysts of the 'performed' and presented element of cultural practices more generally (for example, see **Benson**, 1997). Recent work on performance by scholars such as Bauman (1989, 1992), Schechner (1988, 1990) and Turner (1986) similarly challenges the traditional divide between 'performers' or 'producers' on the one side and audiences on the other as conveying a simplified view of what goes on in a performance. In live performances above all, the audience too must actively observe the recognized conventions for the performance to work. In this sense the audience in a live musical event are themselves part of the performance, playing the role (or range of roles) expected of audience participants in the appropriate music world – or, perhaps, disrupting the event by refusing to follow the conventions. Musical and other performances can be analysed as 'communicative events' in which *all* participants play essential parts rather than just as transmission from performers to recipient audiences/spectators. It draws such events nearer to the vocabulary and definition of ritual.

ritual

Looking at local music-making in Milton Keynes – or elsewhere – from this viewpoint uncovers parallels between musical performance and **ritual**. We can observe how music – like other rituals – helps to mark out the rolling cycle of the year or of the week, or dignifies the public ceremonies of the local community. It plays a crucial part in helping to frame the transition rites that lead individuals through their changing and emergent identities throughout life (think of the importance attached to music in weddings or funerals). As in other rituals, personal involvement in performed music can represent a deep, but not necessarily verbalized, investment and validation of the self. This is the more so when it accords not only with active commitment over time and space but also with shared and ritually enacted values about self-expression, creativity and performance.

As is so often the case, it is hard indeed to locate, let alone 'prove', the arenas in which people develop their sense of identity. But certainly music and its active performance form one sphere in which we can look. Not only is there the investment of the self undoubtedly involved for those people who choose to commit so much of their time, energy and creative abilities to their music-making. There is also the opportunity for identification with specific named groups, offering yet another vehicle for a sense of *personal* expression and control, especially perhaps for the small bands that are so obviously a creation of their players. Music provides ways, furthermore, to shape and present new forms of emerging identity, as in the melting-pot of a new urban environment, whether Milton Keynes or Lagos (Waterman, 1988), or to reinforce the old. Collective performance, finally, gives a potentially deeply experienced medium through which people can not only experience, but display and validate, their own emergent 'reality' in multifaceted bodily ways that go beyond the narrower channel of language.

Let me end this section by suggesting a more radical implication of this emphasis on performance (a postscript to the above, rather than essential to the approach in this chapter, so you may wish to ignore it). You may have noticed that academics tend to privilege linguistic meaning and cognitive content – elements that can readily be encapsulated in visible textual form. The interesting thing is that this perspective may be an essentially western-based and ethnocentric story. Gendron (1986) made a similar point when he spoke of the 'ethnocentrism and elitism' of using a western, text-based model of music to make derogatory judgements about African music and the popular music that it influenced. Instead, he suggested, the elements of music which western conventions capture into textual form are 'simply less important in African music than are rhythm, vocal expressivity, and participation' (ibid., p. 31).

Logocentric models of communication downplay the importance of these performance arts. But a high valuing of *non*-linguistic communication/performance processes is found in many cultures of the world: Pacific dance-songs, Mesoamerican pictorial communication systems, African drumming, Indian dance dramas. O'Hanlon (1983) and others have similarly described the ceremonial display of dancers and the art of body decoration as significant aspects of self-identity and presentation in New Guinea (see Plates 3.I–3.XV in **Lidchi**, 1997): 'When we reduce these other [nonverbal] ways to inconsequence, we unthinkingly reproduce and impose on the people we study the Western valuation of verbal communication' (Carrier, 1995, pp. 196–7; see also Lash and Friedman, 1992, especially Chapter 7; Boone and Mignolo, 1994; Cassen, 1993).

So we may have something more here than just an argument that a linguistic model does not work easily for performance. There is also the possibility that the prioritizing of linguistic text and cognitive message so characteristic of recent centuries of western civilization – or at any rate of intellectuals' powerful definitions of the world – may be at best a limited view of reality, at worst a narrow and self-interested ethnocentrism. Taking performance and bodily enactment more seriously may be one way to redress the balance.

4   Commentary: similarities and differences

It is worth pausing to note some of the implications of the general emphasis on performance and art worlds, if only to set it in a wider theoretical perspective. How is it distinct from other approaches?

ACTIVITY 4

What would your own reaction be on this question?

One possible answer would be that the perspective here partly coincides with recent approaches in sociology and cultural studies. For one thing, it steers away from the model of autonomous, asocial individuals acting in a cultural vacuum. As will be clear in Becker's analysis and elsewhere in this chapter, musicians are seen as drawing on accepted generic conventions as they deploy their art. The focus, furthermore, is not on single artists ('great' or otherwise) nor on an 'intentional' model of culture, but rather – in this case – on the wider art world and its collaborating practitioners.

But there are also points where the approach here is somewhat different (e.g. from that in **Hall**, 1997a, 1997b). One main difference is in its downplaying of the significance of linguistically-based cognitive meaning, of 'text', and of semiotic interpretations. Instead, it turns the spotlight on to issues to do with performance, collaborative activity and bodily enactment.

Consonant with this perspective, it sidesteps the commonly-held model of communication as essentially *information*-based, with messages coming *from* one side *to* another, the latter consisting of the 'audience' or the 'spectators'. As you will see in Chapter 5 of this book, recent work in cultural studies has queried the older model of passive audience reception, pointing to the ways in which audiences engage actively with what they see or hear. But some recent studies still arguably imply a dual model of communication, with the performers and producers of the message on the one side, the audience (however 'active') as essentially its 'decoders' and 'receivers' on the other. This double-sided model may of course be more illuminating for the study of broadcast than of live performance (see also the analysis of emergent interactive information and communication technologies in Chapter 6 of this volume). However that may be, the performance-based picture here is of a complex and multiple – rather than two-sided – communicative event in which participants may be playing many roles, jointly collaborating to carry out the recognized conventions within a shared ritual. In this sense, all are in some degree or another performers, all able in principle to fulfil a formative and an initiating role, not just a dependent secondary one.

The approach in this chapter also implies a certain perspective on the various positions about the relationship of cultural consumption to cultural production.

ACTIVITY 5

Thinking back over the various viewpoints on consumption you have encountered, whether in this volume (e.g. the Introduction) or in your reading elsewhere (e.g. see **du Gay, Hall et al.**, 1997, section 5), where would you locate the perspective of this chapter?

The perspective here, as in the last chapter, rejects the so-called *'productionist' view of consumption* associated with the theories of mass culture analysts like Adorno: a model of consumption as determined by production and thus essentially standardized and passive, with little role for human agency (e.g. Adorno, 1976, 1991, Adorno and Horkheimer, 1979, discussed in **Negus**, 1997; see also **du Gay, Hall et al.**, 1997, section 5.2.1 and the Introduction to this volume). A second approach to consumption, in terms of a definitive link to patterns of inequality and *social differentiation*, with consumers ultimately reproducing their class positions (e.g. Bourdieu, 1984; further discussed in **du Gay, Hall et al.**, 1997, section 5.2.3), similarly turned out to have only a limited payoff when it came to the varied backgrounds and practices of Milton Keynes musicians.

It is also clear – as has been argued both in this volume and in **du Gay** (ed., 1997) – that the traditional *division between production and consumption* often breaks down in practice, a point certainly reinforced by the examples here (even if partly reincarnated in the title of this book). The challenge to the traditional distinction between production and consumption is of course particularly striking in the case of musical performance where the local practitioners are themselves the active producers of the cultural forms they enjoy (see also Laing, 1990). Either for analytic purposes or from the viewpoint of their own assessment of what they are doing, to regard their activities as 'consumption' in the sense in which this term is *opposed* to 'production' seems a strained interpretation.

In similar vein, local musical activities have not been analysed here through the terminology of 'consumption', either in the narrow sense of shopping or its extended meanings of, for example, appropriating state-provided facilities (as in the kitchen alterations example of Chapter 1 above). Local musicians and their supporters do, of course, need to use music shops and to exploit local facilities, both governmental and private, for a whole range of purposes. But within the perspective here this has been pictured less as a matter of 'consumption' than as an involvement in a network which includes both the musicians themselves and their links into wider cultural processes and collaborators – the 'art world' as a whole.

There is another possible viewpoint. This uses the model of consumption as *appropriation* and *resistance* (sometimes identified as the third main approach to consumption; see, for example, **du Gay, Hall et al.**, 1997, section 5.2.5, and the Introduction to this volume). This emphasis on *active* usage and engagement is, without doubt, an illuminating strand in that approach which would be broadly shared with the perspective in this chapter. Some versions of it arguably take the idea to extremes, as when 'the consumer' is pictured as the liberated single individual choosing among goods on offer (as implied, for instance, in **du Gay, Hall et al.**, 1997, Reading G), but its potential is certainly well demonstrated in, for example, the subtle discussion in Chapter 1 of this volume.

But beyond this overlap the performance perspective and the appropriation and resistance perspective diverge. The picture almost inevitably conveyed by the 'appropriation' and/or 'resistance' terminology is of musicians and their associates as essentially engaged in a kind of struggle to somehow 'resist' or 'appropriate' something generated by larger forces and institutions which are in a sense external to them. I say 'almost inevitably' because it is, of course, true that some analysts have been, as it were, redefining the key term 'consumption' so as to bring it closer to the idea of an active, creative process (see the Introduction to this volume). But however carefully these redefinitions are drawn up, it is almost impossible in my view to divest the term totally of its earlier connotations, still existent in some theoretical writing as well as in popular usage. The resonances linger on. Despite the redefinitions, to me these still convey an implicit picture of consumption and consumers as taking the secondary role, however active; as using and reacting to the productions of others or, at best, of appropriating and fighting back – rather than as actors actively deploying generic artistic conventions to create and enact their own unique performances.

It is perhaps these same lingering resonances around the idea of 'consumption' that lead some commentators to find 'a committed and engaged cultural politics' (Silverstone, 1994b, p. 997) still underlying recent cultural analyses. As Silverstone comments in his review of some recent work in this field:

> Such a politics is grounded, quite literally, in the power of the ordinary; in the capacity of subjects, consumers and readers as members of sub-cultures, or participants in collectivities with shared ethnic, gendered or sexual identities, both individually or collectively, to appropriate and make their own meanings out of the stuff of an imperfectly hegemonic system, and in such appropriation and with varying degrees of con-sciousness, to oppose it.
>
> (ibid., p. 997)

Such a 'politics' may not be shared by all forms of cultural studies (for further comment on the differing viewpoints, see Storey, 1996). Nor would it necessarily be totally contradicted by a performance-focused and collaborative approach – indeed one could feed into the other. But the performance perspective here does present a somewhat different balance from those studies which focus on power and struggle and/or on conflictual models of society, or which extend this (as in earlier Marxist analyses) to a picture of alienating pressures on individuals imposed by the powerful forces of capitalism or the global market – the modern political economy – and the struggles to negate these larger forces and rescue something for ourselves.

To put it in different words (adopting the terms used in Inglis, 1993, pp. xi, 186ff.) the spotlight here is being tilted away from 'power' and towards 'art'. The main focus in this chapter is thus not on concepts such as consumption, hegemony, resistance or appropriation, nor on the relations of power produced and reproduced in our lives. Rather, the focus is on the significance of active collaborating networks of practitioners and cultural conventions which in any given case might or might not suit all the interests of those involved but at any rate constitute the resources which – like language – can facilitate not just constrain or threaten people's pathways.

A somewhat similar point is well put in Gorz's comment on what he calls 'autonomous production':

> The sphere of individual sovereignty is *not based on a mere desire to consume*, nor solely upon relaxation and leisure activities. It is based more profoundly on activities ... which are an end in themselves: communi-

cation, giving, creating and aesthetic enjoyment, the production and reproduction of life, tenderness, the realization of physical, sensuous and intellectual capacities, the creation of non-commodity use-values.

(Gorz, 1982, pp. 80–1, my emphasis; see also Hoggett and Bishop, 1986, p. 122)

The model here then is of an active process through which participants themselves express and perform what they jointly recognize as artistic activities within a given art world and its accepted conventions. Thus I find it illuminating to use less of the vocabulary of 'consumption' or 'power', and more that of 'ritual enactment' and of 'art' – art in the context of recognized conventions and networks, and of collective activities rather than individuals or texts, but artistic creation none the less.

5   In conclusion

This chapter has ended up illustrating a particular perspective that builds partly on Becker's view of art worlds and of art as collective activity, partly on a performance-based rather than a textual approach. This dual perspective – or at least one or the other wing of it – is in one form or another becoming more widespread.

The argument partly began from the problems of analysing music. But the general perspective it has led to could also be applied more widely to other activities in which people jointly participate in some collective event akin to ritual, with its own conventions of enactment – a poetry circle, gardening club, coffee morning, or, of course, the obvious examples of dance and sports performances. Similarly, in considering a dance hall or a football game we can widen our focus from just the 'spectator' role or the 'text' of the game itself to all the participants in the whole event and their collective action. Paul Corrigan explains, for example, how for the semi-delinquent boys he studied in Sunderland:

> The experience of a football match ... represents a challenge to the mere spectator role of the sport and represents a possibility of the group *creation* of action ... – chanting, fighting, singing on the terraces ... There is none of the quiet appreciation of the skills of football or music that might characterize a more intellectually inspired audience. Instead there is involvement and creation of their own kind of action.
>
> (quoted in Cricher et al., 1995, p. 74)

This point about direct and active enactment can be applied more widely. For we experience our cultural activities not solely or even primarily from the viewpoint of 'intellectually inspired' spectatorship, but also as participation in a shared ritual and as creating our own kind of action. And this applies too, to what Bruner has called the:

... little performances of everyday life as well as to those that are not 'art' but are more political or work-oriented, such as demonstrations or meetings. ... The performance, furthermore, does not release pre-existing meaning that lies dormant in the text. Rather, the performance itself is constitutive.

(Turner and Bruner, 1986, p. 11)

The significance lies in that enactment as much as, or more than, in the text.

ACTIVITY 6

An approach in terms of art worlds and performance is not the only possible model for analysing everyday practices. You will certainly wish to scrutinize its weaknesses, not just its strengths. What doubts, limitations or criticisms have occurred to you?

So far I have focused on the insights gained through this perspective. But as with any approach it also has its gaps and limitations. Let me sum these up in a series of questions which you might wish to pursue in reaching your own assessment.

Critics could well ask whether its main spotlight on 'everyday' processes and performances at the local level has not perhaps entailed losing sight of the wider organizational constraints or state controls that also affect people's freedom to organize themselves in art worlds (mentioned, indeed, near the end of Reading A, but not elaborated there). Further, even if the focus on 'performance' as an essential ingredient of humanity and the human self has some meaning for certain everyday practices, can it be extended beyond certain limited art forms in a local setting? Does it apply only to *live* performances of the kind mainly illustrated in this chapter? Is looking to active collaborative networks and performances, or using the vocabulary of 'art', too optimistic and, as it were, humane, missing out the hard questions of power or economic forces? Does the metaphor of 'world' (an 'art world', a 'music world') sound too self-contained or – though this was certainly not intended by Becker – convey the impression of a happy functionalism where everything works to the good?

These are real issues on which you will be reaching your own conclusions. There is certainly no open-and-shut case for this (or any other) approach. Let me just make two brief personal responses on the main perspective outlined in this chapter.

First, I personally find strong merits in analysing people's involvement in society and their investment of the self by drawing on the vocabulary of performance and creative enactment rather than that of the production or handling (whether active or passive) of texts/products. This works better for certain kinds of questions and topics than others, admittedly. But overall the idea of the human being – the self – as *performer* is one that usefully complements the model of humans as essentially *signifying* animals.

And secondly, here as in the previous chapter, I find that both the resonances of the 'consumption' metaphor and a focus on issues of 'power' sometimes obscure questions about the rich diversity of collective activities and enacted arts being actively pursued on our own doorsteps – or by ourselves.

5.1   Over to you ...

Finally, you will, I am sure, make up your own mind on the strengths and weaknesses of this and other approaches to analysing everyday cultural practices, whether judged in general conceptual terms and/or – an equally relevant criterion – in terms of usefulness in analysing cases from your own experience and observation. Whichever approach you focus on, you will be able to do so in the awareness that it is indeed not the only one, and that there are also other, perhaps complementary, perhaps competing, perspectives to consider. There are, it appears, plenty of ways in which to study the 'ordinary', whether in Milton Keynes music-making or in your own everyday practices.

References

ADORNO, T. (1976) *Introduction to the Sociology of Music*, New York, Seabury.

ADORNO, T. (1991) *The Culture Industry: selected essays on mass culture* (ed. Bernstein, J.), London, Routledge.

ADORNO, T. and HORKHEIMER, M. (1979) *The Dialectic of the Enlightenment*, London, Verso.

BAUMAN, R. (1989) 'American folklore studies and social transformation: a performance centred perspective', *Text and Performance Quarterly*, Vol. 9, No. 3, pp. 175–84.

BAUMAN, R. (1992) 'Performance' in Bauman, R. (ed.) *Folklore, Cultural Performances, and Popular Entertainments: a communications-centered handbook*, New York and Oxford, Oxford University Press.

BECKER, H.S. (1951) 'The professional dance musician and his audience', *American Journal of Sociology*, Vol. 66, pp. 32–40.

BECKER, H.S. (1963) *Outsiders: studies in the sociology of deviance,* New York, Free Press.

BECKER, H.S. (1982) *Art Worlds*, Berkeley, CA, University of California Press.

BENSON, S. (1997) 'Body, health and eating disorders' in Woodward, K. (ed.) *Identity and Difference*, London, Sage/The Open University (Book 3 in this series).

BLACKING, J. (1973) *How Musical is Man?* London, Faber.

BLACKING, J. (1981) 'The problem of ethnic perceptions in the semiotics of music' in Steiner, W. (ed.) *The Sign in Music and Literature*, Austin, TX, University of Texas Press.

BOONE, E.H. and MIGNOLO, W.D. (eds) (1994) *Writing Without Words: alternative literacies in Mesopotamia and the Andes*, Durham, NC, and London, Duke University Press.

BOURDIEU, P. (1984) *Distinction*, London, Routledge.

CARRIER, J. and CARRIER, A. (1995) 'Every picture tells a story: visual alternatives to oral tradition in Ponam society' in Finnegan, R. and Orbell, M. (eds) (1995).

CASSEN, C. (1993) *Worlds of Sense: exploring the senses in history and across cultures*, London, Routledge.

CHAMBERS, I. (1990) 'A miniature history of the Walkman', *New Formations*, Vol. 11, pp. 1–4.

COATES, D. (1990) 'Traditions of social thought' in Anderson, J. and Ricci, M. (eds) *Society and Social Sciences: a reader*, Milton Keynes, The Open University.

COHEN, S. (1991) *Rock Culture in Liverpool: popular music in the making*, Oxford, Clarendon Press.

CORRIGAN, P. (1979) *Schooling the Smash Street Kids*, London, Macmillan (extract in Cricher et al. 1995, pp. 71–7).

CRICHER, C., BRAMHAM, P. and TOMLINSON, A. (eds) (1995) *Sociology of Leisure: a reader*, London, Chapman & Hall.

DE CERTEAU, M. (1984) *The Practice of Everyday Life,* Berkeley, CA, University of California Press.

DU GAY, P. (ed.) (1997) *Production of Culture/Cultures of Production*, London, Sage/The Open University (Book 4 in this series).

DU GAY, P., HALL, S., JANES, L., MACKAY, H. and NEGUS, K. (1997) *Doing Cultural Studies: the story of the Sony Walkman*, London, Sage/The Open University (Book 1 in the series).

FINNEGAN, R. (1989) *The Hidden Musicians: music-making in an English town*, Cambridge, Cambridge University Press.

FINNEGAN, R. and ORBELL, M. (eds) (1995) *South Pacific Oral Traditions*, Bloomington and Indianapolis, IN, Indiana University Press.

FRIEDMAN, J. (ed.) (1994) *Consumption and Identity*, Switzerland, Harwood Academic Publishers.

FRITH, S. (1988) *Music for Pleasure*, Cambridge, Polity.

GENDRON, B. (1986) 'Theodor Adorno meets the Cadillacs' in Modelski, T. (ed.) *Studies in Entertainment*, Bloomington and Indianapolis, IN, Indiana University Press.

GILROY, P. (1997) 'Diaspora and detours of identity' in Woodward, K. (ed.) *Identity and Difference*, London, Sage/The Open University (Book 3 in this series).

GLEDHILL, C. (1997) 'Genre and gender: the case of soap opera' in Hall, S. (ed.) (1997).

GORZ, A. (1982) *Farewell to the Working Class*, London, Pluto.

HALL, S. (1997a) 'The work of representation' in Hall, S. (ed.) (1997).

HALL, S. (1997b) 'Introduction' in Hall, S. (ed.) (1997).

HALL S. (ed.) (1997) *Representation: cultural representations and signifying practices*, London, Sage/The Open University (Book 2 in this series).

HOGGETT, P. and BISHOP, J. (1986) *Organizing Around Enthusiasms: patterns of mutual aid in leisure*, London, Comedia.

HUTCHINSON, R. and FEIST, A. (1991) *Amateur Arts in the UK,* London, Policy Studies Institute.

INGLIS, F. (1993) *Cultural Studies*, Oxford and Cambridge, MA, Blackwell.

KEIL, C. and FELD, S. (1994) *Music Grooves*, Chicago, IL, and London, University of Chicago Press.

LAING, D. (1990) 'Making popular music: the consumer as producer' in Tomlinson, A. (ed.) *Consumption, Identity and Style: marketing, meanings and the packaging of pleasure*, London and New York, Routledge.

LASH, S. and FRIEDMAN, J. (eds) (1992) *Modernity and Identity*, Oxford, Blackwell.

LEFEBVRE, H. (1991) *Critique of Everyday Life*, London, Verso.

LIDCHI, H. (1997) 'The poetics and politics of exhibiting other cultures' in Hall, S. (ed.) (1997).

McCLELLAN, M.E. (1995) '" If we could talk with animals": elephants and musical performance during the French Revolution' in Case, S.E., Brett, P. and Foster, S.L. (eds) *Cruising the Performative: interventions into the representation of ethnicity, nationality and sexuality*, Bloomington, IN, Indiana University Press.

MORLEY, D. (1993) 'Active audience theory: pendulums and pitfalls', *Journal of Communication,* Vol. 43, No. 4, pp. 13–19.

NEGUS, K. (1997) 'The production of culture' in du Gay, P. (ed.) (1997).

O'HANLON, M. (1983) 'Handsome is as handsome does: display and betrayal in the Wahgi', *Oceania,* Vol. 53, pp. 317–33.

SCHECHNER, R. (1988) *Performance Theory*, London and New York, Routledge.

SCHECHNER, R. and APPEL, W. (eds) (1990) *By Means of Performance*, Cambridge, Cambridge University Press.

SILVERSTONE, R. (1994a) *Television and Everyday Life*, London, Routledge.

SILVERSTONE, R. (1994b) 'The power of the ordinary: on cultural studies and the sociology of culture', *Sociology*, Vol. 28, No. 4, pp. 991–1001.

STEVENSON, N. (1995) *Understanding Media Cultures: social theory and mass communication,* London, Sage.

STOREY, J. (ed.) (1996) *What is Cultural Studies? A Reader*, London, Arnold.

TURNER, V.W. and BRUNER, E.M. (eds) (1986) *The Anthropology of Experience*, Urbana and Chicago, IL, University of Illinois Press.

WATERMAN, C.A. (1988) 'Asiko, sakara and palmwine: popular music and social identity in inter-war Lagos', *Urban Anthropology*, Vol. 17, pp. 229–58.

WOLFF, J. (1983) *Aesthetics and the Sociology of Art,* London, Allen & Unwin.

READING A:
Howard S. Becker, 'Art worlds and collective activity'

Art as activity

Think of all the activities that must be carried out for any work of art to appear as it finally does. For a symphony orchestra to give a concert, for instance, instruments must have been invented, manufactured, and maintained, a notation must have been devised and music composed using that notation, people must have learned to play the notated notes on the instruments, times and places for rehearsal must have been provided, ads for the concert must have been placed, publicity must have been arranged and tickets sold, and an audience capable of listening to and in some way understanding and responding to the performance must have been recruited. A similar list can be compiled for any of the performing arts. With minor variations (substitute materials for instruments and exhibition for performance), the list applies to the visual and (substituting language and print for materials and publication for exhibition) literary arts.

The list of things that must be done varies, naturally, from one medium to another, but we can provisionally list the kinds of activities that must be performed. To begin, someone must have an idea of what kind of work is to be made and of its specific form. The originators may get that idea long before actually making the work, or the idea may arise in the process of working. The idea may be brilliant and original, profound and moving, or trivial and banal, for all practical purposes indistinguishable from thousands of other ideas produced by others equally untalented or uninterested in what they are doing. Producing the idea may require enormous effort and concentration; it may come as a gift, out of the blue; or it may be produced routinely, by the manipulation of well-known formulas. The way the work is produced bears no necessary relationship to its quality. Every way of producing art works for some people and not for others; every way of producing art produces work of every conceivable grade of quality, however that is defined.

Once conceived, the idea must be executed. Most artistic ideas take some physical form: a film, a painting or sculpture, a book, a dance, a *something* which can be seen, heard, held. Even conceptual art, which purports to consist solely of ideas, takes the form of a typescript, a talk, photographs, or some combination of those.

The means for the execution of some art works seem to be easily and routinely available, so that part of the making of the art work causes no one any special effort or worry. We can, for instance, have books printed or photocopied with relatively little trouble. Other art works require skilled execution. A musical idea in the form of a written score has to be performed, and musical performance requires training, skill, and judgment. Once a play is written, it must be acted, and that requires skill, training, and judgment too. (So, in fact, does printing a book, but we are less aware of that.)

Another crucial activity in the production of art works consists of manufacturing and distributing the materials and equipment most artistic activities require. Musical instruments, paints and canvas, dancers' shoes and costumes, cameras and film – all these have to be made and made available to the people who use them to produce art works.

Making art works takes time, and making the equipment and materials takes time, too. That time has to be diverted from other activities. Artists ordinarily make time and equipment available for themselves by raising money in one way or another and using the money to buy what they need. They usually, though not always, raise money by distributing their works to audiences in return for some form of payment. Of course, some societies, and some art activities, do not operate within a money economy. Instead, a central government agency may allocate resources for art projects. In another kind of society, people who produce art may barter their work for what they need, or may produce work in the time available to them after they have met their other obligations. They may perform their ordinary activities in such a way as to produce what we or they might identify as art, even though the work is not commonly called that, as when women produced quilts for family use. However it is done, work gets distributed and the distribution produces the means with which further resources for making further work can be gathered.

Other activities that we can lump together as 'support' must also take place. These vary with the medium: sweeping up the stage and bringing the coffee, stretching and priming canvases and framing the finished paintings, copy editing and proofreading. They include all sorts of technical activities – manipulating the machinery people use in executing the work – as well as those which merely free executants from normal household chores. Think of support as a residual category, designed to hold whatever the other categories do not make an easy place for.

Someone must respond to the work once it is done, have an emotional or intellectual reaction to it, 'see something in it', appreciate it. The old conundrum – if a tree falls in the forest and no one hears it, did it make a sound? – can be solved here by simple definition: we are interested in the event which consists of a work being made *and* appreciated; for that to happen, the activity of response and appreciation must occur.

Another activity consists of creating and maintaining the rationale according to which all these other activities make sense and are worth doing. Rationales typically take the form, however naïve, of a kind of aesthetic argument, a philosophical justification which identifies what is being made as art, as good art, and explains how art does something that needs to be done for people and society. Every social activity carries with it some such rationale, necessary for those moments when others not engaged in it ask what good it is anyway. Someone always asks such questions, if only the people engaged in the activity themselves. Subsidiary to this is the specific evaluation of individual works to determine whether they meet the standards contained in the more general justification for that class of work or whether, perhaps, the rationale requires revision. Only by this kind of critical review of what has been and is being done can participants in the making of art works decide what to do as they move on to the next work.

Most of these things cannot be done on the spur of the moment. They require some training. People must learn the techniques characteristic of the kind of work they are going to do, whether it be the creation of ideas, execution, some one of the many support activities, or appreciation, response, and criticism. Accordingly, someone must carry on the education and training through which such learning occurs.

Finally, to do all this supposes conditions of civic order such that people engaged in making art can count on a certain stability, can feel that there are some rules to the game they are playing.

[...]

The division of labor

Given that all these things must be done for an art work to occur as it actually does, who will do them? Imagine, as one extreme case, a situation in which one person did everything: made everything, invented everything, had all the ideas, performed or executed the work, experienced and appreciated it, all without the assistance or help of anyone else. We can hardly imagine such a thing, because all the arts we know, like all the human activities we know, involve the cooperation of others.

[...]

Nothing in the technology of any art makes one division of tasks more 'natural' than another, although some divisions are so traditional that we often regard them as given in the nature of the medium. Consider the relations between the composition and performance of music. In conventional symphonic and chamber music in the mid-twentieth century, the two activities occur separately and are seen as two different, highly specialized jobs. That was not always true. Beethoven, like most composers of his time, also performed, both his own music and that of others, as well as conducting and improvising on the piano. Even now, an occasional performer composes, as did the piano virtuosi Rachmaninoff and Paderewski. Composers sometimes perform, often because performance pays a great deal better than composition.

[...]

In jazz, composition is much less important than performance. The standard tunes musicians play (blues and old popular songs) merely furnish the framework for the real creation. When musicians improvise, they use the raw materials of the song, but many players and listeners will not know who actually composed 'Sunny Side of the Street' or 'Exactly Like You'; some of the most important improvisatory frameworks, like blues, have no author at all. One might say that the composer is the player, considering the improvisation the composition.

In rock music, the two activities are, ideally, carried on by the same person. Fully competent performers compose their own music. Indeed, rock groups who play other people's music get tagged with the derogatory label 'copy groups', and a young group comes of age the day it begins to play its own compositions. The activities are separate – performing is not simultaneous with composing, as it is in jazz – but both belong to one person's bundle of tasks [...].

The same variations in the division of tasks can be found in every art. Some art photographers, like Edward Weston, always made their own prints, regarding printing as integral to the making of the picture; others, like Henri Cartier-Bresson, never made their own prints, leaving that to technicians who knew how they wanted it done. Poets writing in the Western tradition do not ordinarily incorporate their own handwriting into the finished product, leaving it to printers to put the material into a readable form; we see autograph copies of their poetry only when we are interested in the revisions they made in their own hand on the manuscript [...] or in a rare case such as that of William Blake, who engraved his own plates, on which poems appeared in his own hand, and printed them himself, so that his hand was part of the work. But in much Oriental poetry the calligraphy is as important as the poem's content (see Figure 1); to have it printed in mechanical type would destroy something crucial. More mundanely, saxophone and clarinet players buy their reeds at the music store, but oboists and bassoonists buy pieces of cane and manufacture their own.

Each kind of person who participates in the making of art works, then, has a specific bundle of tasks to do. Though the allocation of tasks to people is, in an important sense, arbitrary – it could have been done differently and is supported only by the agreement of all or most of the other participants – it is not therefore easy to change. The people involved typically regard the division of tasks as

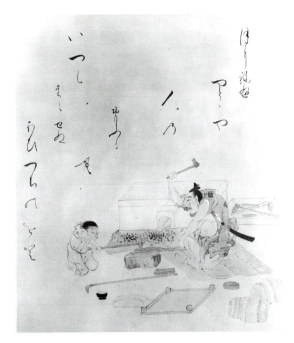

FIGURE 1 Page from a set of Shokunin-e ('depictions of various occupations'), Edo period (1615–1868 AD), Japan. In Western literature, only the poem's words are important, but in much Oriental literature the calligraphy is equally important, and the calligrapher as important an artist as the poet. Ink and wash on paper. Artist, poet, and calligrapher unknown. The poem reads, 'Sounds of hammering continue / Clear moon above / People listening, wonder. ...' (Asian Art Museum of San Francisco, the Avery Brundage Collection.)

quasi-sacred, as 'natural' and inherent in the equipment and the medium. [...]

Every art, then, rests on an extensive division of labor. That is obviously true in the case of the performing arts. Films, concerts, plays and operas cannot be accomplished by lone individuals doing everything necessary by themselves. But do we need all this apparatus of the division of labor to understand painting, which seems a much more solitary occupation? We do. The division of labor does not require that all the people involved in producing the art object be under the same roof, like assembly-line workers, or even that they be alive at the same time. It only requires that the work of making the object or performance rely on that person performing that activity at the appropriate time. Painters thus depend on manufacturers for canvas, stretchers, paint, and brushes; on dealers, collectors, and museum curators for exhibition space and financial support; on critics and aestheticians for the rationale for what they do; on the state for the patronage or even the advantageous tax laws which persuade collectors to buy works and donate them to the public; on members of the public to respond to the work emotionally; and on the other painters, contemporary and past, who created the tradition which makes the backdrop against which their work makes sense [...].

Similarly with poetry, which seems even more solitary than painting. Poets need no equipment, other than what is conventionally available to ordinary members of society, to do their work. Pencils, pens, typewriters, and paper are enough, and, if these are not available, poetry began as an oral tradition and much contemporary folk poetry still exists only in that form [...]. But this appearance of autonomy is likewise superficial. Poets depend on printers and publishers, as painters do on distributors, and use shared traditions for the background against which their work makes sense and for the raw materials with which they work. Even so self-sufficient a poet as Emily Dickinson relied on psalm-tune rhythms an American audience would recognize and respond to.

All art works, then, except for the totally individualistic and therefore unintelligible works of an autistic person, involve some division of labor among a large number of people.

[...]

Conventions

Producing art works requires elaborate cooperation among specialized personnel. How do they arrive at the terms on which they cooperate? They could, of course, decide everything afresh on each occasion. A group of musicians could discuss and agree on which sounds would be used as tonal resources, what instruments might be constructed to make those sounds, how those sounds would be combined to create a musical language, how the language would be used to create works of a particular length requiring a given number of instruments and playable for audiences of a certain size recruited in a certain way. Something like that sometimes happens, for instance, in the creation of a new theatrical group, although in most cases only a small number of the questions to be decided are actually considered anew.

People who cooperate to produce a work of art usually do not decide things afresh. Instead, they rely on earlier agreements now become customary, agreements that have become part of the conventional way of doing things in that art. Artistic conventions cover all the decisions that must be made with respect to works produced, even though a particular convention may be revised

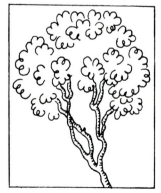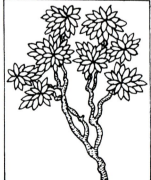

FIGURE 2 Three realistic drawings of a tree. The conventions of visual art make it possible for artists to render familiar objects in a shorthand knowledgeable viewers can read as realistic. These three ways of drawing the same tree (using conventions of the European sixteenth-century, European early twentieth-century, and classical Indian painting) are all easily understood as a tree. (Drawings by Nan Becker.)

for a given work. Conventions dictate the materials to be used, as when musicians agree to base their music on the notes contained in a set of modes, or on the diatonic, pentatonic, or chromatic scales, with their associated harmonies. Conventions dictate the abstractions to be used to convey particular ideas or experiences, as when painters use the laws of perspective to convey the illusion of three dimensions or photographers use black, white, and shades of gray to convey the interplay of light and mass. Conventions dictate the form in which materials and abstractions will be combined, as in music's sonata form or poetry's sonnet. Conventions suggest the appropriate dimensions of a work, the proper length of a performance, the proper size and shape of a painting or sculpture. Conventions regulate the relations between artists and audience, specifying the rights and obligations of both.

[...]

Though standardized, conventions are seldom rigid and unchanging. They do not specify an inviolate set of rules everyone must refer to in settling questions of what to do. Even where the directions seem quite specific, they leave much to be resolved by reference to customary modes of interpretation on the one hand and by negotiation on the other. A tradition of performance practice, often codified in book form, tells performers how to interpret the musical scores or dramatic scripts they perform. Seventeenth century scores, for instance, contained relatively little information; but contemporary books explained how to deal with questions, unanswered in the score, of instrumentation, note values, extemporization, and the realization of embellishments and ornaments. Performers read their music in the light of all these customary styles of interpretation and could thus coordinate their activities [...]. The same thing occurs in the visual arts. Much of the content, symbolism, and coloring of Italian Renaissance religious painting was conventionally given; but a multitude of decisions remained for the artist, so that even within those strict conventions different works could be produced. Adhering to the conventional materials, however, allowed viewers to read much emotion and meaning into the picture. Even where customary interpretations of conventions exist, having become conventions themselves, artists can

agree to do things differently, negotiation making change possible.

Conventions place strong constraints on the artist. They are particularly constraining because they do not exist in isolation, but come in complexly interdependent systems, so that one small change may require a variety of other changes. A system of conventions gets embodied in equipment, materials, training, available facilities and sites, systems of notation, and the like, all of which must be changed if any one component is.

[...]

In general, breaking with existing conventions and their manifestations in social structure and material artifacts increases artists' trouble and decreases the circulation of their work, but at the same time increases their freedom to choose unconventional alternatives and to depart substantially from customary practice. If that is true, we can understand any work as the product of a choice between conventional ease and success and unconventional trouble and lack of recognition.

Art worlds

Art worlds consist of all the people whose activities are necessary to the production of the characteristic works which that world, and perhaps others as well, define as art. Members of art worlds coordinate the activities by which work is produced by referring to a body of conventional understandings embodied in common practice and in frequently used artifacts. The same people often cooperate repeatedly, even routinely, in similar ways to produce similar works, so that we can think of an art world as an established network of cooperative links among participants. If the same people do not actually act together in every instance, their replacements are also familiar with and proficient in the use of those conventions, so that cooperation can proceed without difficulty. Conventions make collective activity simpler and less costly in time, energy, and other resources; but they do not make unconventional work impossible, only more costly and difficult. Change can and does occur whenever someone devises a way to gather the greater resources required or reconceptualizes the work so it does not require what is not available.

Works of art, from this point of view, are not the products of individual makers, 'artists' who possess a rare and special gift. They are, rather, joint products of all the people who cooperate via an art world's characteristic conventions to bring works like that into existence. Artists are some sub-group of the world's participants who, by common agreement, possess a special gift, therefore make a unique and indispensable contribution to the work, and thereby make it art.

[...]

[...] I have given much attention to work not conventionally thought to have artistic value or importance. I have been interested in 'Sunday painters' and quiltmakers as well as in conventionally recognized fine art painters and sculptors, in rock-and-roll musicians as well as in concert players, in the amateurs not good enough to be either as well as in the professionals who are. In doing so, I hope to let the problematic character of both 'artness' and 'worldness' permeate the analysis, and avoid taking too seriously the standards of those who make the conventional definitions of art for a society.

Though art worlds do not have sharp boundaries, they do vary in the degree to which they are independent, operating in relative freedom from interference by other organized groups in their society. Put another way, the people who cooperate in the work being studied may be free to organize their activity in the name of art, as is the case in many contemporary Western societies, whether they make use of that possibility or not. They may, however, find that they must take into account other interests represented by groups organized around other definitions. The state may exercise such control over other areas of society that major participants in the making of art works orient themselves primarily to the concerns of the state apparatus rather than to the concerns of people who define themselves as interested in art. Theocratic societies may organize the making of what we, from the perspective of our society, would recognize as works of art as an adjunct of activity defined in religious terms. In frontier societies subsistence may be so problematic that activities which do not contribute directly to the production of food or other necessities may be seen as unaffordable luxuries, so that work we might

define, from a contemporary vantage point, as art gets done in the name of household necessity. What cannot be justified that way is not done. Before people can organize themselves as a world explicitly justified by making objects or events defined as art, they need sufficient political and economic freedom to do that, and not all societies provide it.

This point needs emphasis, because so many writers on what is ordinarily described as the sociology of art treat art as relatively autonomous, free from the kinds of organizational constraints that surround other forms of collective activity. [...]

Art worlds produce works and also give them aesthetic value. This book does not itself make aesthetic judgments, as the preceding remarks suggest. Instead it treats aesthetic judgments as characteristic phenomena of collective activity. From this point of view, the interaction of all the involved parties produces a shared sense of the worth of what they collectively produce. Their mutual appreciation of the conventions they share, and the support they mutually afford one another, convince them that what they are doing is worth doing. If they act under the definition of 'art', their interaction convinces them that what they produce are valid works of art.

Source: Becker, 1982, pp. 2–5; 7; 9–11; 13–14; 28; 31–2; 34–5; 38–9.

READING B:
Simon Frith, 'Why do songs have words?'

In 1918 the chairman of Chappell and Co., Britain's largest music publishing company, wrote a letter to the novelist Radclyffe Hall. She had complained of receiving no royalties after a song for which she had been the lyricist, 'The Blind Ploughman', 'swept the country'. William Davey replied:

Dear Miss Radclyffe Hall,

I yield to no one in my admiration of your words for 'The Blind Ploughman'. They are a big contributing factor to the success of the song. Unfortunately, we cannot afford to pay royalties to lyric writers. One or two other publishers may but if we were to once introduce the principle, there would be no end to it. Many lyrics are merely a repetition of the same words in a different order and almost always with the same ideas. Hardly any of them, frankly, are worth a royalty, although once in a way they may be. It is difficult to differentiate, however. What I do feel is that you are quite entitled to have an extra payment for these particular words, and I have much pleasure in enclosing you, from Messrs Chappell, a cheque for twenty guineas.

(Dickson, 1975, pp. 45–6)

Davey had commercial reasons for treating lyrics as formula writing, but his argument is common among academics too. In the 1950s and 1960s, for example, the tiny field of the sociology of popular music was dominated by analyses of song words. Sociologists concentrated on songs (rather than singers or audiences) because they could be studied with a familiar cultural research method, content analysis, and as they mostly lacked the ability to distinguish songs in musical terms, content analysts, by default, had to measure trends by reference to lyrics. It was through their words that hit records were taken to make their social mark.

The focus on lyrics did not just reflect musical ignorance. Until the mid-1960s British and American popular music was dominated by Tin Pan Alley. [...] In concentrating on pop's lyrical themes in this period, sociologists were reflecting the way in which the songs were themselves packaged and sold. Most of these songs did, musically, sound the same; most lyrics did seem to follow measurable rules; most songwriters did operate as 'small businessmen engaged in composing, writing or publishing music', rather than as 'creative composers' (Etzkorn, 1966). [...] This simply confirmed what analysts took for granted anyway – that it was possible to read back from lyrics to the social forces that produced them.

Content analysis

The first analyst of pop song words, J.G. Peatman, was influenced by Adorno's high Marxist critique of 'radio music' and so stressed pop's lyrical standardization: all successful pop songs were about romantic love; all could be classified under one of three headings – the 'happy in love' song, the 'frustrated in love' song and the 'novelty song with sex interest' (Peatman, 1942–3).

For Peatman, this narrow range reflected the culture industry's success in keeping people buying the same thing, but subsequent content analysts, writing with a Cold War concern to defend American commercial culture, took pop market choices more seriously. Thus in 1954 H.F. Mooney accepted Peatman's starting point – pop as happy/sad love songs – but argued that they 'reflected, as love songs always do, the deepest currents of thought; for as values change, so change the ideas and practice of love' (Mooney, 1954, p. 226).[... H]is 'reflection theory' of pop lyrics has been shared by most of the more scientific content analysts who followed up his work. American sociologists have used song words, in particular, to chart the rise of a youth culture, with new attitudes to love and sex and fun, and to document the differences between romance in the 1950s and 1960s. [...]

The theoretical assumption here is that the words of pop songs express general social attitudes. But such song-readings depend, in practice, on prior accounts of youth and sexuality. Content analysts are not innocent readers, and there are obvious flaws in their method. For a start, they treat lyrics too simply. The words of all songs are given equal value; their meaning is taken to be transparent; no account is given of their actual performance or their musical setting. This enables us to code lyrics statistically, but it involves a questionable theoretical judgement: content codes refer to what the words describe – situations and states of mind

– but not to how they describe, to their significance as language.

Even more problematically, these analysts tend to equate a song's popularity to public agreement with its message – the argument is that songs reflect the beliefs and values of their listeners. This is to ignore songs' ideological work, the way they play back to people situations or ideas they recognize but which are inflected now with particular moral lessons. The most sophisticated content analysts have, therefore, used lyrics as evidence not of popular culture as such, but of popular cultural confusion. Songs, from this perspective, articulate the problems caused by social change.

[...]

Th[e] interpretation of lyrics as uplift – asserting ideas in order to shape them, describing situations in order to reach them – complicates the concept of 'reflection' but retains the assumption that popular songs are significant because they have a 'real closeness' with their consumers (see Hoggart, 1958, pp. 223–4). The implication now, though, is that this is only true of 'folk' forms; only in country music, blues, soul, and the right strands of rock, can we take lyrics to be the authentic expression of popular experiences and needs. In the mainstream of mass music something else is going on.

Mass culture

Most mass-cultural critiques of pop derive from 1930s Leavisite arguments. Pop songs are criticized for their banality, their feebleness with words, imagery and emotion; the problem is not just that lyrics picture an unreal world, but also that pop ideals are trite.

[...]

For Leavisites, the evil of mass culture is that it corrupts real emotions. [...] Edward Lee, for example, denounces the romantic banality of pop lyrics in terms of their social effects (citing the divorce rate in his disdain for silly love songs) and this argument about the corrupting consequences of the hit parade has been taken up by Marxist critics in their accounts of pop's 'class function' (Lee, 1970, p. 150). Dave Harker, for instance, reads Tin Pan Alley lyrics as straightforward statements of bourgeois ideology (Harker, 1980, p. 48). [...] Love and romance, the central pop themes, are the

'sentimental ideology' of capitalist society. Like Lee, Harker stresses the importance of pop romance for marriage – it is thus that songs work for the reproduction of social relations. Love lyrics do express 'popular' sexual attitudes, but these attitudes are mediated through the processes of cultural control.

[...]

Most critics of mass music assume that there are, nonetheless, alternatives to commercial pap. Hoggart, for example, praises pre-war pop songs by reference to their *genuineness*. [...] For Harker, 'authentic' lyrics express 'authentic' relationships, expose bourgeois conventions with an honest vital language – a language which reflects experience directly, is not ideologically mediated.

[...]

In the 1960s this process was reversed as young musicians and audiences rejected Tin Pan Alley for rhythm and blues – pop's vapidity was replaced by blues 'realism'. The function of rock lyrics became the exposure of false ideology so that, for Harker, Bob Dylan's lyrics ceased to matter (and Dylan himself 'sold out') when they ceased to be true, when (with the release of *John Wesley Harding*) they began to 'sentimentalize the family, legalized sex and the home, in ways wholly supportive of the dominant ideology'. The implication here – an implication embedded deep in rock criticism – is that all songs have to be measured against the principles of lyrical realism. [...]

Realism

As its simplest, the theory of lyrical realism means asserting a direct relationship between a lyric and the social or emotional condition it describes and represents. Folk song studies, for example, work with a historical version of reflection theory: they assume that folk songs are a historical record of popular consciousness. Thus Roy Palmer describes orally transmitted folk songs as 'the real voice of the people who lived in the past', and folk ballads as 'a means of self-expression; this was an art form truly in the idiom of the people'. With the development of industrial capitalism, according to A.L. Lloyd, 'the song-proper becomes the most characteristic lyrical form through which the common people express their fantasies, their codes, their aspirations':

Generally the folk song makers chose to express their longing by transposing the world on to an imaginative plane, not trying to escape from it, but colouring it with fantasy, turning bitter even brutal facts of life into something beautiful, tragic, honourable, so that when singer and listeners return to reality at the end of the song, the environment is not changed but they are better fitted to grapple with it.

(Palmer, 1974, pp. 8, 18; and Lloyd, 1975, pp. 158, 170)

The question is: how does the folk 'consolation' differ from pop 'escapism'? The answer lies in the modes of production involved: folk songs were authentic fantasies because they sprang from the people themselves; they were not commodities. If certain folk images and phrases recur ('lyrical floaters', Lloyd calls them) these are not clichés (like the equivalent floaters in pop songs) but mark, rather, the anonymous, spontaneous, communal process in which folk songs are made. Lloyd continually contrasts the 'reality and truth' of folk lyrics with the 'banal stereotype of lower-class life and limited range of sickly bourgeois fantasies that the by-now powerful entertainment industry offers its audiences to suck on like a sugared rubber teat', but such comparisons rest almost exclusively on an argument about production. (Lloyd, 1975, p. 369)

The problem of this 'sentimental socialist-realist' argument is its circularity [...] The problem, then, is not whether folk songs *did* reflect the real social conditions, but why some such reflections are taken by collectors to be authentic, some not. Whose ideology is reflected in such definitions of folk 'realism'?

Authenticity is a political problem, and the history of folk music is a history of the struggle among folk collectors to claim folk meanings for themselves, as songs are examined for their 'true working-class views', for their expressions of 'organic community', for their signs of nationalism. For a Marxist like Dave Harker, some 'folk' songs are inauthentic because they obviously (from their use of language) were not written or transmitted by working-class people themselves; others are judged inauthentic because of their ideological content, their use not of bourgeois language but bourgeois ideas. Left-wing intellectuals can write authentic

working-class songs (though not working-class themselves) as long as they represent the *real* reality of the working-class.

[...]

The original blues analysts assumed, like folk theorists generally, that the blues could be read as the direct account of the singers' and listeners' lives. [...] The blues, according to Paul Oliver, was 'a genuine form of expression revealing America's gaunt structure without a decorative facade.' [...] Even blues' fancy terms, its rich store of imagery, were derived from everyday life – the blues was a 'tough poetry', a 'rough poetry'. In the words of Francis Newton, blues songs are not poetic 'because the singer wants to express himself or herself in a poetic manner', but because 'he or she wants to say what has to be said as best it can'. The poetic effects 'arise naturally out of the repetitive pattern of ordinary popular speech' (Oliver, 1963, pp. 133–4, 140; Newton, 1961, pp. 145–6)

Linton Kwesi Johnson makes similar points about Jamaican lyrics. Jamaican music, he writes, is the *spiritual expression* of the *historical experience* of the Afro-Jamaican. [...] 'Through music, dreams are unveiled, souls exorcized, tensions canalized, strength realized' (Johnson, 1976, p. 398). [He] notes the ways in which shared religious metaphors of hope and damnation enable Jamaican lyricists to intensify their political comment (and Rastafarian songs draw on the store of religio-political imagery accumulated by Black American spirituals – 'Babylon' as a symbol of slavery and white oppression, for example) (Ames, 1949).

Black songs do not just describe an experience, but symbolize and thus politicize it. For Newton, the lyrical world of the blues was 'tragic and helpless' – 'its fundamental assumption is that men and women must live life as it comes; or if they cannot stand that they must die', Johnson, by contrast, argues that in Jamaican music,

consciously setting out to transform the consciousness of the sufferer, to politicise him culturally through music, song and poetry, the lyricist contributes to the continuing struggle of the oppressed.

(Newton, 1961, p. 150; Johnson, 1976, p. 411)

We are back to the original question in a new form: does 'realism' mean an acceptance of one's lot or struggle against it, the imagination of alternatives?

[...]

Rock 'poetry' opened up possibilities of lyrical banality of which Tin Pan Alley had never even dreamt, but for observing academics it seemed to suggest a new pop seriousness – 'the jingles and vapid love lyrics' had evolved into a genuinely 'mystical vision' (Rosenstone, 1969). This was to suggest a new criterion of lyrical realism – truth-to-personal-experience or truth-to-feeling, a truth measured by the private use of words, the self-conscious use of language. And truth-to-feeling became a measure of the listener too. 'True songs', wrote Paul Nelson, *Rolling Stone*'s Record Editor, are 'songs that hit me straight in the heart.' Alan Lomax had once written that the 'authentic' folk singer had to 'experience the feelings that lie behind his art'. For Nelson the good rock singer made the listener experience those feelings too (Nelson, 1979, p. 120).

Making meaning

[...]

[B]y the end of the 1960s Norman Denzin was arguing that pop audiences only listened to the beat and melody, the *sound* of a record, anyway – the 'meaning of pop' was the sense listeners made of songs for themselves; it could not be read off lyrics as an objective 'social fact' (Denzin, 1969).

This argument was the norm for the sociology of pop and rock in the 1970s. In *The Sociology of Rock*, for example, I ignored lyrical analysis altogether and simply assumed that the meaning of music could be deduced from its users' characteristics. In the USA, empirical audience studies measured pop fans' responses to the words of their favourite songs quantitatively. Robinson and Hirsch concluded from a survey of Michigan high school students that 'the vast majority of teenage listeners are unaware of what the lyrics of the hit protest songs are about', and a follow-up survey of college students suggested that the 'effectiveness' of song messages was limited: the majority of listeners had neither noticed nor understood the words of 'Eve of Destruction' or 'The Universal Soldier', and the minority who did follow the words were not convinced by them (Robinson and Hirsh, 1972, p. 231; Denisoff and Levine, 1972; Frith, 1978).

The implication of this sort of research (which continues to fill the pages of *Popular Music and Society*) is that changes in lyrical content cannot be explained by reference to consumer 'moods'. Instead American sociologists have turned for explanations to changing modes of lyrical production, to what is happening in the record industry, the source of the songs.

[...]

Songs did change the audience ('by gradually creating a self-conscious teen generation'), but the general point is that 'the amount of diversity of sentiments in popular music lyrics correlates directly with the number of independent units producing songs', and more recent research has shown how a tightening of corporate control (in the country music industry) leads to a narrowing range of song forms (Peterson and Berger, 1972, p. 298; see also Ryan and Peterson, 1982).

In this account of pop the banality of Tin Pan Alley words is taken for granted and explained in terms of the organization of their production, but pop is defended from charges of corruption on the grounds that nobody listens to the words anyway. This became one way in which 'authentic' rock was distinguished from its commercial, degenerate versions – real rock lyrics matter because they can be treated as poetry or politics, involve social commentary or truth-to-feeling; bad rock words are just drivel. What most interests me about this position, though, are the questions it begs. Mainstream, commercial pop lyrics – silly love songs – may not 'matter' to their listeners like the best rock words do, but they are not therefore insignificant. Popular music is a song form; words are a reason why people buy records [...] And so the question remains: why and how do song words (banal words, unreal words, routine words) work?

The poetry of pop

In songs, words are the sign of a voice. A song is always a performance and song words are always spoken out, heard in someone's accent. Songs are more like plays than poems; song words work as speech and speech acts, bearing meaning not just semantically, but also as structures of sound that are direct signs of emotion and marks of character. Singers use non-verbal as well as verbal devices to make their points – emphases, sighs, hesitations, changes of tone; lyrics involve pleas, sneers and commands as well as statements and messages and stories (which is why some singers, such as the Beatles and Bob Dylan in Europe in the sixties, can have profound significance for listeners who do not understand a word they are singing).

I do not have the space here to describe how these techniques work in particular songs but from the work that has been done it is possible to draw some general conclusions. Firstly, in analysing song words we must refer to the performing conventions which are used to construct our sense of both the singers and ourselves, as listeners. It is not just what they sing, but the way they sing it, that determines what singers mean to us and how we are placed, as an audience, in relationship to them.

Secondly, in raising questions of identity and audience I am, implicitly, raising questions of genre – different people use different music to experience (or fantasize) different sorts of community; different pop forms (disco, punk, country, rock, etc.) engage their listeners in different narratives of desire. Compare, for example, the different uses of male/ female duets in soul and country music: the former use the voices to intensify feeling, the latter to flatten it. In soul music, realism is marked by singers' inarticulacy – they are overcome by their feelings – and so duets, the interplay of male and female sounds, add a further erotic charge to a love song. In country music, realism is marked by singers' small talk – the recognition of everyday life – and so duets, domestic conversations, are used to add further credibility to the idea that we are eavesdropping on real life (an effect heightened when, as is often the case, the couples *are* lovers or married or divorced).

The immediate critical task for the sociology of popular music is systematic genre analysis – how do words and voices work differently for different types of pop and audience? But there is a third general point to make about all pop songs: they work on ordinary language, and what interests me here is not what is meant by 'ordinary' but what is meant by 'work'. Songs are not just any old speech act – by putting words to music, songwriters give

them a new sort of resonance and power. Lyrics, as Langdon Winner once put it, can 'set words and the world spinning in a perpetual dance' (Winner, 1979).

[...]

Last words

In his study of Buddy Holly, Dave Laing suggests that pop and rock critics need a musical equivalent of the film critics' distinction between *auteurs* and *metteurs en scene*:

> The musical equivalent of the *metteur en scene* is the performer who regards a song as an actor does his part – as something to be expressed, something to get across. His aim is to render the lyric faithfully. The vocal style of the singer is determined almost entirely by the emotional connotations of the words. The approach of the rock *auteur* however, is determined not by the unique features of the song but by his personal style, the ensemble of vocal effects that characterise the whole body of his work.

(Laing, 1971, pp. 58–9)

Ever since rock distinguished itself from pop in the late 1960s, *auteurs* have been regarded as superior to *metteurs* and lyrics have been analysed in terms of *auteur* theory. But Laing's point is that the appeal of rock *auteurs* is that their meaning is *not* organized around their words. The appeal of Buddy Holly's music, for example, 'does not lie in what he says, in the situations his songs portray, but in the exceptional nature of his singing style and its instrumental accompaniment'. My conclusion from this is that song words matter most, as words, when they are *not* part of an *auteur*ial unity, when they are still open to interpretation – not just by their singers, but by their listeners too. [...]

The pleasure of pop is that we can 'feel' tunes, perform them, in imagination, for ourselves. In a culture in which few people make music but everyone makes conversation, access to songs is primarily through their words. If music gives lyrics their linguistic vitality, lyrics give songs their social *use*.

This was, indeed, the conclusion that Donald Horton reached in his 1950s analysis of the lyrical drama of courtship. 'The popular song', he wrote, 'provides a conventional language for use in dating'. The 'dialectic' of love involved in pop songs – the conversational tone, the appeal from one partner to another – was precisely what made them useful for couples negotiating their own path through the stages of a relationship. Most people lacked skill in 'the verbal expression of profound feelings' and so a public impersonal love poetry was 'a useful – indeed a necessary alternative'. The singer became a 'mutual messenger' for young lovers, and pop songs were about emotional possibilities. The singer functioned 'in dramatizing these songs to show the appropriate gestures, tone of voice, emotional expression – in short the stage directions for transforming mere verse into personal expression' (Horton, 1957, p. 577).

Pop love songs do not 'reflect' emotions, then, but give people the romantic terms in which to articulate and so experience their emotions.

References

AMES, R. (1949) 'Protest and irony in Negro folksong', *Science and Society*, Vol. 14.

DENISOFF, R.S. and LEVINE, M. (1972) 'Brainwashing or back-ground noise? The popular protest song' in Denisoff, R.S. and Peterson, R.A. (eds) *The Sounds of Social Change*, Chicago, IL, Rand McNally.

DENZIN, N. (1969) 'Problems in analysing elements of mass culture: notes on the popular song and other artistic productions', *American Journal of Sociology*, Vol. 75.

DICKSON, L. (1975) *Radclyffe Hall at the Well of Loneliness*, London, Collins.

ETZKORN, P. (1966) 'On esthetic standards and reference groups of popular songwriters', *Sociological Inquiry*, Vol. 36, No. 1, pp. 39–47.

FRITH, S. (1978) *The Sociology of Rock*, London, Constable.

HARKER, D. (1980) *One for the Money*, London, Hutchinson.

HOGGART, R. (1958) *The Uses of Literacy*, Harmondsworth, Penguin.

HORTON, D. (1957) 'The dialogue of courtship in popular songs', *American Journal of Sociology*, Vol. 62, p. 577.

JOHNSON, L.K. (1976) 'Jamaican rebel music', *Race and Class*, Vol. 17, p. 398.

LAING, D. (1971) *Buddy Holly*, London, Studio Vista.

LEE, E. (1970) *Music of the People*, London, Barrie and Jenkins.

LLOYD, A.L. (1975) *Folk Song in England*, London, Paladin.

MOONEY, H.F. (1954) 'Song, singers and society, 1890–1954', *American Quarterly*, Vol. 6, p. 226.

NELSON, P. (1979) 'The pretender' in Marcus, G. (ed.) *Stranded*, New York, Alfred Knopf.

NEWTON, F. (1961) *The Jazz Scene*, Harmondsworth, Penguin.

OLIVER, P. (1963) *Meaning of the Blues*, New York, Collier.

PALMER, R. (1974) *A Touch of the Times*, Harmondsworth, Penguin.

PEATMAN, J.G. (1942–3) 'Radio and popular music' in Lazersfeld, P.F. and Stanton, F. (eds) *Radio Research*, New York, Duell, Sloan and Pearce.

PETERSON, R.A. and BERGER, D.G. (1972) 'Three eras in the manufacture of popular music lyrics' in Denisoff, R.S. and Peterson, R.A. (eds) *The Sounds of Social Change*, Chicago, IL, Rand McNally.

ROBINSON, J.P. and HIRSCH, P.M. (1972) 'Teenage responses to rock and roll protest songs' in Denisoff, R.S. and Peterson, R.A. (eds) *The Sounds of Social Change*, Chicago, IL, Rand McNally.

ROSENSTONE, R.R. (1969) '"The times they are a-changing"': the music of protest', *Annals of the American Academy of Political and Social Science*.

RYAN, J. and PETERSON, R.A. (1982) 'The product image: the fate of creativity in country music songwriting', *Sage Annual Review of Communication Research*, Vol. 10.

WINNER, L. (1979) 'Trout mask replica' in Marcus, G. (ed.) *Stranded*, New York, Alfred Knopf.

Source: Frith, 1988, pp. 105–15; 118–23.

'US' AND 'THEM': RE-IMAGINING PLACES, RE-IMAGINING IDENTITIES

Nigel Thrift

CHAPTER FOUR

Contents

1   Introduction: my place or yours?

Place is one of those things that we often think just *is*. It is such an integral part of our being that we often take it for granted: there is always a there there, isn't there?

Of course, it is a truism that all human life is located. We cannot live in a no-where: the proposition makes no sense at all. Even our language presupposes locatedness. For example, the philosopher Michel Serres (Serres and Latour, 1995) has pointed out that the simple prepositions of every language – by, with, toward, from, and so on – all imply a location. But we do not live our lives in a space which is made up of locations which are simply neutral coordinates. We live in *places*. The difference between location and place is that places have meanings for us which cannot be reduced to their location.

Over many years, sometimes over centuries, these places have been saturated with the meanings of the people who have lived in or passed through them. Sometimes these meanings are to be found only in a mundane conversation. Sometimes they may be formalized in a story. And sometimes they can take on a concrete form, as a building or even a memorial signifying that a certain place has a very particular meaning.

Whatever the case, there is a constant struggle over the meanings that are attached to places. And these meanings are not trivial ones, either. It is difficult to dispute that we can all care deeply about certain places. They clearly lie at the core of our identity as part of a sense of belonging to a community of like-minded people, an *us* which can be distinguished from a *them*. Why, otherwise, do we invest so many places with a sacred or a historic significance? Why, otherwise, are some of us willing to lie down in front of bulldozers to protect certain places? Why, otherwise, are some of us even willing to die to defend or to capture a particular place?

To summarize, people mean places. But, in turn, places also mean people. Places form a reservoir of meanings which people can draw upon to tell stories about and thereby define themselves. Thus **place and identity** are inexorably linked.

place and identity

Not surprisingly, many writers have tried to summarize the special qualities of place. They have used words such as 'community', 'region' and 'locality' to try to encapsulate these qualities, to generalize the meaning of places sufficiently to be able to say something general about place. But this task is an increasingly difficult one, because what we mean by place has become increasingly bound up with the growth of the media, the burgeoning of **representations of place**.

representations of place

Thus the book, and subsequently the newspaper and journal, have made it possible for the meanings of places to be transported over great distances, have made it possible for the meanings of places to be, so to speak, pre-circulated and, as a consequence, have made it possible for the meanings of places to be strongly reinforced. Thus peoples' expectations about places have changed. And now, with the advent of media such as radio and television, the degree of pre-treatment that places can receive has become even greater, to the point where some writers have suggested that the meaning of places has become so caught up in their media representations that the place itself becomes increasingly incidental: all that is solid melts into the airwaves. The media representations become the reality of place.

But is this really the case? If one story about place tells of how everything has changed as place has become increasingly 'mediated', another story is that the essential qualities of place remain unchanged, indeed essential to our existence. This 'fundamentalist' story of place identifies **sense of place** as a core human value. To lack a sense of place is 'to be "homeless", indeed, not only in the cultural sense of knowing no permanently sheltering structure but also as being without any effective means of orientation in a complex and confusing world' (Casey, 1993, p. xv).

sense of place

Yet this fundamentalist story links up with the previous one in that it argues that the media are one of the reasons why we are increasingly unable to link up with this sense of place. The result of this increasing 'mediation' is clear at least. Places are turned into mere locations: 'by late modern times, this world had become increasingly placeless, a matter of mere sites instead of fixed places' (Casey, ibid.).

This chapter tries to tread a path between these two stories. It attempts to point to a 'third way' by arguing that, as places have become 'mediated', although some things may be lost, others can be gained. In particular, if our own sense of place has become less sure through the growing power of the media to re-present places, then perhaps the growth of the same media also allows us the opportunity to reach out to other places, and to the people who live in them. In other words, perhaps through redefining our notion of place we can redefine what we mean by 'us' and 'them'.

I want, then, to approach the subject of place as a *moral* problem. That may at first seem a rather odd way of going about things but in fact, the connection between 'moral sentiment' and place has a long intellectual history, one that stretches back to at least the writings of the Ancient Greeks. Put simply, the question that has continually been asked is whether we care less about people the further away they live: does distance in space weaken our feelings of care for others (Ginzburg, 1994)?

The question is perhaps best posed by the famous Scottish writer on morals and economics, Adam Smith. In a book called *The Theory of Moral Sentiments* (1759), Smith tried to produce a theory of ethics based upon the central principle of 'sympathy', a quality which allows us to empathize with and so judge other people's actions. This theory included a clear moral geography; sympathy could only extend so far:

> Let us suppose that the great empire of China, with all its myriads of inhabitants, was suddenly swallowed up by an earthquake, and let us

consider how a man of humanity in Europe, who had no sort of connection with that part of the world, would be affected upon receiving intelligence of this dreadful calamity. He would, I imagine, first of all, express very strongly his sorrow for the misfortune of that unhappy people, he would make many melancholy reflections upon the precariousness of human life, and the vanity of all the labours of man, which could thus be annihilated in a moment. He would too, perhaps, if he was a man of speculation, enter into many reasonings concerning the effects which this disaster might produce upon the commerce of Europe, and the trade and business of the world in general. And when all this fine philosophy was over, when all these humane sentiments had been once finely expressed, he would pursue his business or his pleasure, take his repose or his diversion, with the same ease and tranquillity [*sic*], as if no such accident had happened. The most frivolous disaster which could befal [*sic*] himself would occasion a more real disturbance. If he was to lose his little finger tomorrow, he would not sleep to-night; but, provided he never saw them, he will snore with the most profound security over the ruin of a hundred millions of his brethren, and the destruction of that immense multitude seems plainly an object less interesting to him, than this paltry misfortune of his own.

(Smith, 1976/1759, p. 136)

Now, Smith was writing at a time when it still took 60 hours to travel from Edinburgh to London by stagecoach, and about three weeks to reach North America from Scotland by ship. Other places were therefore a long way away in time. Again, knowledge of other places was patchy and indistinct. For his time, Smith clearly had extensive knowledge of other places – from his own travels in Europe (most especially in France and Switzerland), from his extraordinary web of political and social contacts, from his extensive network of correspondents, from newspapers, and from the contemporary accounts of European travellers recorded in books (Ross, 1995). But, in our terms, this knowledge would now seem both limited and out of date: this was a time before the telegraph or the telephone allowed most 'news' to be what we would regard as new at all.

In this chapter, I want to consider what has happened to how we regard other places and the people within them since Adam Smith's time: do we have more or less 'sympathy'? If there were an earthquake in China now, we would, to begin with, be more likely to know something about the country: we might have been taught about it at school; we might have read regular newspaper reports; we might have visited China on a long-haul holiday; or we might have relatives living there. Then the news of the earthquake would reach us rapidly via the radio or television news. Finally, we would see accounts of the suffering – photographs in the newspaper, film reports on television. As this example shows, there has been an expansion in our geographical knowledge, in our ability to know about other places.

ACTIVITY 1

Figure 4.1 reproduces a newspaper report of a major earthquake in China in 1996 which killed or injured many hundreds of people and made many thousands homeless. Make a list of the main factors that might prompt you to become personally involved in helping the people there. Your connection with China might be a close one: you may have relatives living there or you may have become deeply involved in the country through reading and through visits. On the other hand, your connection might be much more tenuous. What, then, would prompt you to become involved? Perhaps you hold deep moral principles about helping others, or perhaps something in the report might move you. (These reports are rather dry but remember that newspaper and television reports often aim to involve their readers and viewers by 'personalizing the event', for example by focusing on a stricken person or family.)

Make a second list of the main points that would prevent you from becoming personally involved in helping the people struck by the earthquake. For example, you may feel that you are too far away to make a difference or you may feel that what goes on in China is 'none of my business'. Think about why this is.

FIGURE 4.1
Source: *The Guardian*,
5 February 1996

TREMORS HINDER QUAKE RESCUE

Andrew Higgins
Far East Correspondent

Chinese troops searched for survivors in freezing darkness last night after a powerful earthquake killed at least 240 people and left 3,800 seriously injured in a scenic mountain region popular with foreign backpackers.

Worst hit were villages around Lijiang, a town in China's south-western Yunnan province noted for its spectacular scenery, cave art and ancient relics.

The earthquake, measuring 7.0 on the Richter scale, was the deadliest in China since 1988. It struck on Saturday evening as many people were eating dinner and watching television. Tens of thousands lost their homes. About 330,000 people live in the stricken area around Jade Dragon Snow Mountain, which was featured in an acclaimed Channel 4 film.

Scores of aftershocks jolted the region yesterday, hampering rescue efforts and causing more damage.

A number of Chinese tourists were reported injured. One foreign tourist, whose name and nationality were not immediately known, was among those seriously injured, the official Xinhua news agency said. Hotels in Lijiang were evacuated, guests spending the night around bonfires.

Last night Chinese television showed dazed survivors huddled in the dark outside crumpled buildings and rescue workers pumping at the chest of a man pulled from the rubble. Crushed corpses covered with dirt and blood lay in makeshift morgues.

The earthquake is the second large disaster to hit China within a week. Last Wednesday, a huge explosion destroyed a block of flats in Shaoyang city, Hunan, killing more than 100 people.

Xinhua reported that the deputy prime minister, Wu Bangguo, yesterday visited the earthquake zone.

In 1988 China's prime minister, Li

Peng, was criticised for his slow response to an earthquake in the region.

About 2,000 troops of the People's Liberation Army have joined rescue workers. Officials pleaded for donations of blood and medical supplies.

The first offer of aid came from Taiwan, which is eager to defuse tension with its old enemies in Beijing.

Geographical knowledge is one determinant of what Adam Smith called 'sympathy' – that we know something about other places and the people in them. But it is not the only one. We might know all of the minutiae of an earthquake in China but still feel indifferent or even scornful. This is where the stories that we tell about other places are crucial, and for two reasons. First of all, they tell us which places and people we belong to and care about or, to put it another way, which community (or communities) we can claim to be a part of. Second, they tell us whether and how we care about other places and people. These stories about *who belongs where* are the subject of the first section of this chapter.

In the eighteenth and nineteenth centuries the kind of stories told about other places by Europeans were nearly all **Eurocentric**, that is they placed Europe at the centre of the world and other places in a definite moral hierarchy away from this supposed centre. In doing so, Europeans were able to cultivate a sense of their own superiority and others' inferiority. We can see, then, straightaway that these stories were not just about other places but that they also involved the *identity* of Europeans: how Europeans thought about themselves and these places – 'us' – was valorized by these stories. In particular, they were given a sense of belonging to communities that were at the centre of the world and at the forefront of 'progress'. The corollary was that communities in other places – 'them' – were seen as occupying a position on the periphery of the world and some way down the ladder of progress. The next section of the chapter shows how this kind of thinking was an important element in the oppression of one of these 'othered' communities – the Lapps or, more accurately, the Sami of the Nordic countries.

Eurocentrism

In the succeeding section of the chapter, I shall show how recent changes in how we know and what we know, resulting from new forms of transport and communications media, have produced the resources with which it has become possible to tell alternative stories about other places, stories which are much more open to others because they are attempts to think of our sense of place, identity and belonging as a more open and ongoing process. I shall conclude this discussion by looking at the current situation of the Sami to show the ways in which they have been able to re-tell their story so as to produce a sense of place, identity and belonging which gives them the resources to fight for their way of life.

Finally, in the last section of the chapter, I shall return to the nature of places again. I want to demonstrate that the changes I have outlined in the previous section have started to suggest a new notion of place, one which is clearly influenced by the new stories that are now being told. In this new notion, place is still seen as a home in the world, but one that is shared by many others. Instead of a notion of place based on progress, we therefore arrive at a 'progressive sense of place' (Massey, 1994) which, like Adam Smith's geography of 'sympathy', has a strong ethical dimension.

2   Othering places

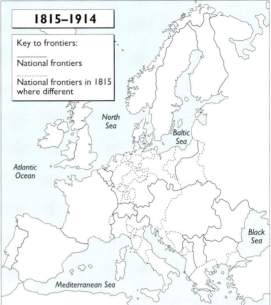

FIGURE 4.2   The changing national map of Europe.

The eighteenth and nineteenth centuries were a time of nation-building in Europe, of the replacement of the old divinely ordained, dynastic realms, such as the Holy Roman Empire, by more broadly-based *nation-states* (see Figure 4.2). But the scale of the change was so great that, living in a world where the nation-state is now the normal political currency, we find it difficult to comprehend just how great it actually was. Trying to convey the size of the shift, the philosopher and anthropologist Ernest Gellner conjured up the idea of two maps of Europe, one from before this period of nation-building and one from after. The 'before' map resembled a picture which is:

> ... [a] riot of diverse points of colour ... such that no clear pattern can be discerned in any detail ... A great diversity and plurality and complexity characterizes all distant parts of the whole: the minute social groups, which are the atoms of which the picture is comprised, have complex and ambiguous and multiple relations to many cultures; some through speech, others through their dominant faith, another still through a variant faith or set of practices, a fourth through administrative loyalty, and so forth.

In contrast, the 'after' map resembles a picture which has very little variety:

> There is very little shading; surfaces are clearly separated from one another, it is generally plain where one begins and another ends, and there is little if any ambiguity or overlap. Shifting from the map to the reality mapped, we see that an overwhelming part of political authority has been concentrated in the hands of one kind of institution, a reasonably large and well-organized state. In general, each such state presides over, monitors, and is identified with, one kind of culture, one style of communication, which prevails within its borders and is dependent for its perpetuation on a centralized educational system...

> (Gellner, 1983, pp. 139–40)

Central to this one kind of culture was the *invention* of a new form of belongingness based in the limited but sovereign territory of the nation-state. The historian Benedict Anderson has called this invention the **imagined community**:

imagined
community

> It is *imagined* because even the members of the smallest nation will never know most of their fellow-members, meet them, or even hear of them, yet in the minds of each lives the image of their communion ... it is imagined as a *community* because regardless of the actual inequality and exploitation that may prevail in each, the nation is always conceived as a deep, horizontal comradeship. Unfortunately it is this fraternity that makes it possible, over the past two centuries, for so many millions of people, not so much to kill, as willingly to die for such limited imaginings.

> (Anderson, 1983, pp. 15–16)

The invention of this new form of community, which was usually depicted as 'the flowering into time of the organic essence of a timeless people' (McLintock, 1995, p. 353) relied on a number of cultural supports. Of these, four were particularly significant. The first was the creation of a national educational system through which, as mentioned above, children learnt the same things – history, geography and so on. The second was the creation or refurbishment of all kinds of traditions – from spectacular ceremonials to 'national' dress – which acted as a crucial link with the nation's newly created or dusted off past. The third was the refiguring of the national space as familial and domestic (and thereby strongly gendered):

> The term nation derives from *natio*: to be born – we speak of nations as 'motherlands' and 'fatherlands'. Foreigners 'adopt' countries that are not their native homes and are naturalized in the national family. We talk of the 'family of nations', of 'homelands' and 'native' lands. In Britain immigration matters are dealt with at the Home Office; in the United States the president and his wife are called the First Family.
>
> (McLintock, 1995, p. 357)

But most important of all, as far as Anderson is concerned, was the invention of print, and especially the first newspapers. These prototypical mass media with their wide circulations gave the new imagined national community the means with which to establish itself in the minds of its participants as an 'us', who could, in turn, be opposed to 'them'.

ACTIVITY 2

Make a list of the main places you connect with being a member of your national culture. Why do you associate them with your national culture? What kinds of people would be 'out of place' in the places you have selected, and why?

Certainly the story of the nation which emerged in the eighteenth and nineteenth centuries – which by its nature is concerned to establish the *difference* between itself and other such imagined communities – was tightly bound up with three more 'othering' stories, each of which was also about the establishment of difference, and each of which added to Europe's sense of a geography of the world with itself at the centre, of Europe's special distinctiveness and, indeed, exclusiveness.

The first of these other 'othering' stories was the story spun by the thinkers of the 'Enlightenment'. From the perspective of Europe, the eighteenth century was, in many ways, a period of hope. New worlds were waiting to be 'known'. Journeys of exploration, and the new cartography they inspired, combined with the rise of science (and especially natural history) to suggest an expanding horizon of knowledge, albeit one seen from only one perspective – that of Europe (Livingstone, 1992).

Furthermore, the media through which the knowledge that was being gathered could be disseminated were all expanding too. Newspapers and journals were increasing in number and circulation; books and encyclopaedias were being published at an unparalleled rate; depictions of other places were becoming more and more common. It is not surprising, then, that these optimistic times were encapsulated in an optimistic cultural movement – the 'Enlightenment' – which began in England in the seventeenth century but reached its apogee in France and Germany in the eighteenth century. Through the application of the power of reason, Enlightenment thinkers wanted to contrast themselves with the darkness of irrationality and superstition that supposedly characterized earlier eras. Thus Immanuel Kant (1724–1804), the last as well as the greatest of the Enlightenment thinkers, wrote that Enlightenment is 'the emergence of man [*sic*] from his self-imposed infancy. Infancy is the inability to use one's reason without the guidance of another. It is self-imposed, when it depends on a deficiency, not of reason, but of the resolve and courage to use it without external guidance.'

It is something of a historical irony that Enlightenment writers, who were chiefly liberal thinkers concerned to establish the importance of a common universal humanity (for example, many of them, including Adam Smith, were fiercely opposed to slavery) should have produced a geography which could be used to suggest the opposite. The Enlightenment had a geography written into its core which depended upon a set of four principles of inclusion which, especially later in history, in the chief era of colonial expansion, were able to be appropriated as principles of exclusion (Hulme and Jordanova, 1990). First of all, this geography emphasized how little was known about most of the rest of the world outside Europe. Then, second, it depended upon a metaphor of *discovery*, of advances into these 'unknown' territories to take what is found there, a metaphor which could be applied not only to the practices of science but also colonialism. Third, it suggested that much greater emphasis needed to be placed on the difference of Europe from the rest of the world. But this is a Europe that is no longer defined as the realm of Christendom but as the continent of secular and rational values surrounded by a sea of irrationality. Fourth, and finally, much greater emphasis was placed on the value of comparative knowledge which not only served to emphasize this difference but also, to a considerable degree, helped to construct it.

In turn this Eurocentric perspective was mapped on to a sense of time through the idea of development or *progress*. Drawing on an increasing archive of comparative work a **model of progress** was constructed. At the base of this model were people who were clearly in a state of nature – for example, Native Americans and Pacific Islanders. These were peoples in their infancy, at the beginning of time. As the nineteenth century wore on, this model became more sophisticated (or cruder, depending on how you look at it), spurred on by the rise of both colonialism and evolutionary theories which conveniently naturalized the survival of the fittest. More complex developmental models were developed which made it possible to look at the world as a 'great map of humankind' in various stages of

model of progress

FIGURE 4.3   A map, dating from 1852, of the world sorted into developmental groups.

development (Marshall and Williams, 1982) (see Figure 4.3). It was not far from these kinds of models to ideas of history as itself being progress, and of certain nations and 'races' as having a historical mission which could be validated by this history. As McLintock (1995, p. 359) puts it: 'the axis of time ... was projected onto the axis of space and history became global.'

These two 'othering' stories about places – the imagined community of the nation and Enlightenment geographies of progress – were not the only two circulating in Smith's time and thereafter. There were two more. One of these was that innovations in transport and communications meant that the world was speeding up and, as it did so, places were being squeezed closer and closer together in time: as a result the world was 'shrinking'. This was already a common theme in the eighteenth century where a number of nervous disorders were thought to be the result of the faster pace of life (Porter, 1993). In the nineteenth century, as Adam Smith's stagecoach was replaced by the train, the telegraph and the telephone, so the theme of the 'annihilation of space by time' became a favourite meditation of many writers (Thrift, 1995). In the twentieth century the idea surfaced yet again: one author even went so far as to calculate the rate (in minutes per year) at which places were converging on one another, a phenomenon which he termed *time–space convergence* (Janelle, 1969). These different variants on the theme of a speeded-up world were nearly always associated with a generalized crisis of identity. From the nervous disorders of the eighteenth century onwards, the acceleration of everyday life was thought likely to lead to volatile, fragmented and spread-out people whose identity was in question because of the shallowness of their lives. Writing in the late nineteenth century the philosopher Nietzsche described the 'tropical tempo' of the modern western world in a way which is typical:

> Sensibility immensely irritable, ... the abundance of disparate impressions greater than ever; cosmopolitanism in foods, literatures, newspapers, forms, tastes, even landscapes. The tempo of this influx *prestissimo*, the impressions erase each other, one intuitively resists taking in anything ... A kind of adaptation to the flood of impressions takes place: men unlearn spontaneous actions, they merely react to stimuli from the outside.

> (Nietzsche, 1983, cited in Prendergast, 1992, p. 5)

But there is one more story about Europe (and the West more generally) which, in a sense, is in contradiction to the previous three. This is that, as Europe accelerates away, it leaves all kinds of good things behind. Places become a shadow of their former selves. They start to lose the vital moral spark which energizes the people who live in them. There is, in other words, a Faustian bargain, to be made: progress but also a kind of damnation. This kind of critique is already found in the late eighteenth century in the emerging 'Romantic' movement. A whole series of writers complain about the loss of moral sentiment represented for them by Nature, a lament which only strengthens through much of the nineteenth century. The Romantic movement laid great emphasis on re-awakening shopworn and jaded feelings through love of nature. Thus they emphasized the imagination and emotions that might be stirred up by Alpine crags and ravines, storms at sea, the sky at night and other manifestations of 'the sublime'. The world seemed to be becoming second-hand, whereas the Romantics wanted to return to these primal experiences and places which could fire up a new kind of human identity, which could 'awaken us to feeling against the too pressing regulative control of an ... order-imposing reason' (Taylor, 1988, p. 301). The geography of this movement is, not surprisingly, one of the wild and remote.

3   The Sami

With these four stories we can see how greater value is given to certain places and people than to others. We shall now apply this approach to the case of the ethnic Lapps or, as they are more properly known, the Sami ('we people'). The Sami are one of a diverse group of 'first peoples' who circle the North Pole (see Figure 4.4). Accurate population figures for the Sami are largely lacking. Much depends on who is defined as Sami and this presents a difficult problem in itself. However, the most recent best estimate is that they number some 70–75,000 people spread through Norway (more than 40,000), Sweden (up to 25,000), Finland (about 6000) and Russia (approximately 2000).

FIGURE 4.4   Locations of the circumpolar peoples.

The Sami have been identified as having existed as a distinctive people in
the Nordic countries over a very considerable period of time. For example, in
AD98 the Roman historian Tacitus wrote of them as a people who lived on
plants and on animals which they hunted (Beach, 1988; Storm, 1987).
Certainly for many thousands of years (the Sami can be historically
identified from about 2000 years BC) the Sami had a subsistence economy
which normally focused on fishing in the spring and summer and on
hunting and berry-picking in the autumn and winter (although with
variations according to location). The Sami territory was split into a
decentralized series of hunting and fishing areas which were collectively
exploited called *sii dâ* or *sita*. In each *sii dâ* there was an elected council
which controlled the use of resources, had juridical authority and supervised
communal life. The *sii dâ* were usually located around a prominent
landscape feature like a fjord or a watercourse and the local Sami population
undertook seasonal migrations within the area in order to fully utilize the
available natural resources.

In other words, the Sami were placed somewhere between what we would,
even now, still recognize as nomadic 'hunter-gatherers' or 'pastoralists'. This
is certainly how the anthropologists of the nineteenth and early twentieth
century classified them. In so doing, they were able to map the Sami into the
Eurocentric classification considered in the previous section, which was
based on a supposed progression from hunter-gatherers, to pastoralists, to
cultivators and so on up to modern urban societies, thereby conveniently
obscuring the fact that 'notions of history, of evolution and of social change,
are themselves the products of history' (Bender and Morris, 1988, p. 4). They
were therefore able to describe the Sami communities as existing on hunting
and gathering to a significant extent, as having hardly changed their way of
life over the millennia, and as having minimal contacts with other peoples
(Bird-David, 1988). In other words, the Sami were understood as: subsisting
in a primordial space which was closer to nature, and thereby more
authentic than those of modern civilizations; attached to unchanging
traditions, and therefore outside modern time-frames; and cut off from the
West's polluting influence, and thereby still able to be regarded as 'pristine'
because 'back in time'. Boosted by Romantic nineteenth-century notions of
the polar North (Steedman, 1995), the Sami, like a number of other such
peoples, therefore acted as an imaginary foil for western societies, rather like
being able to imagine relatives without the inconvenience of having them
come to visit, with all the disappointments such a visit might entail: 'We did
not want to know what they were like after we had decimated, demolished
and destabilized them; we wanted to know what they were like beforehand,
because we wanted to know what *we* were like' (Bender and Morris,
1988, p. 10).

The problem was that the Sami did not fit these stereotypes. So far as their
way of life was concerned, it was a mixture of hunter-gathering and
pastoralism and was not easily assimilated to either category (Ingold, 1976,
1980). So far as an attachment to unchanging traditions went, the Sami had

clearly changed their way of life in quite substantial ways through their history, even moving from mainly settled to mainly migratory ways of life, rather than vice versa. For example, the 'tame' migrating reindeer herds, with which the Sami are now so often associated in popular image, were a development of the sixteenth and seventeenth centuries (Figure 4.5).

FIGURE 4.5
(*Top*) A Sami domestic group, engraved by Schefferus in 1674.
(*Bottom*) A group of Sami in 1913. Nowadays their tent, the 'Lavo', is used only as a 'coffee-break shelter' in bad weather when herding reindeer.

Beforehand, the Sami had relied on hunting wild reindeer and other animals providing fur, sometimes from sedentary locations. Then, so far as having minimal contact with other peoples was concerned, the Sami had clearly been in contact with other peoples over many hundreds of years: other Nordic peoples had traded with them (especially for fur); they had been gradually incorporated into national territories; and their own traditional shamanistic religious practices had been stamped out by Christian missionaries.

Be that as it may, the very depiction of the Sami as nomadic reindeer-hunters from another time was able to be used to justify their control and to 'modernize' them. Their treatment was not as harsh as in some areas of the world (Wolf, 1982), in part because the Sami were able to lay formal title to some of their land, but it was harsh enough. Thus, the Sami languages were not taught in schools and Sami speakers were stigmatized. Their history was discredited or assimilated into national cultures as a romantic accoutrement. Sometimes they were forced to relocate from their land; at other times it was taken into state ownership; non-Sami migrants moved into many of their traditional territories. As a result, Sami culture declined; in particular, language was lost through active discouragement or lack of use. Many younger Sami abandoned their traditional lifestyles and moved southwards to take up jobs: there are now more Sami living in the national capitals of the Nordic countries than in most of the municipalities of Samiland.

4   The old stories continue

Let's now reel forward to the present. For what is remarkable is how often the 'othering' stories I have talked about in section 2 still recur. Let's look at some of the contemporary variations of these stories.

First of all, the grip of nationalism is still very strong, as events such as the conflict in the former Yugoslavia underline only too well (see Figure 4.2 above). It may be arguable how many of the new nation-states which have come into existence over the last few years will survive but, if nothing else, their presence demonstrates the continued durability and power of the idea of belonging to imagined national communities. Indeed, some writers have argued that there is a 'rekindling of national and nationalist sentiments' around the world (for example, Morley and Robins, 1993, p. 6), an argument which is given some credence by the fact that whereas in 1945 the United Nations had 51 members, now it has 185.

Next is the story of the West as the holder of the key to the progress of civilization which still persists, albeit in a more muted form. In particular, the West still tends to be the knower while the rest of the world is the known. This Eurocentric habit of thought is continually reproduced by the enormous media monopolies like Time Warner, Bertelsmann and News Corporation (discussed by **Robins**, 1997) which suck in and process information from around the world and then redistribute it back to the world, but shorn of the participation of its originators and often of any identification with them. Shohat and Stam (1994, p. 23) seem to echo Adam Smith when they accuse institutions like these of 'the refusal of empathy, the withholding of sympathy for people caught up in the struggle for survival within the existing order, the maintenance of a cool sceptical distance in the face of claims of oppression'. But there may be other, more mundane reasons for their Eurocentrism. To begin with, they may present stories about other peoples and places as – precisely – other and therefore worthy of attention (for example, as exotic entertainment) but not care. Then again, these institutions' map of the world is strongly biased to what they perceive as their main (western) audiences' interests. They therefore tend to concentrate on information from certain places to the exclusion of others. For example, Vietnam, a country with a population of 75 million people, is the preserve of only 12 or 14 foreign correspondents all told, in comparison with the thousands of foreign correspondents who cover news from the United States. Finally, it must not be forgotten that these audiences may themselves filter out disturbing or challenging material about other peoples and places, 'distancing' themselves from it by arguing that it is nothing to do with them.

Again, the story of the West as the leading edge of a speeded-up world is still often told. For example, one recent variant of this old story is that the world is now in the grips of another round of what the geographer David Harvey

time–space
compression

calls **time–space compression:**

> ... the processes that so revolutionize the objective qualities of space and time that we are forced to alter ... how we represent the world to ourselves... space appears to shrink to a 'global village' of telecommunications and a spaceship earth of economic and ecological interdependencies ... and as time horizons shorten to the point where the present is all there is ... so we have to learn how to cope with our overwhelming sense of *compression* of our spatial and temporal worlds
>
> (Harvey, 1989, p. 240)

Thus time–space compression – which is discussed by Moores in relation to television audiences in Chapter 5 of this volume and is also central to Mackay's discussion of new information and communication technologies in Chapter 6 – is simultaneously a story of the marked increase in the pace of life brought about by modern transport and telecommunications *and* the upheaval in our experience of space and time that this speed-up brings about as people, images, capital and information all move more and more rapidly around the world. The result is that 'time–space compression ... exerts its toll on our capacity to grapple with the realities unfolding around us' (Harvey, 1989, p. 306), most especially by challenging our sense of identity and our ability to preserve tradition.

The architect Paul Virilio is willing to go further still with this story. For him, Harvey describes only the first effects of speed-up in which physical displacement still presupposes a journey: the individual makes a departure, moves from one location to another, and so arrives. But now, with the 'instant' transmission made possible by electronic technology, a new 'generalized arrival' has occurred, in which the element of a journey across space is lost. The individual can be in two places at once, acting as both a transmitter and a receiver. Thus we have arrived in a historical period in which there is 'a crisis of the temporal dimension of the present':

> One by one, the perceptive faculties of an individual's body are transferred to machines, or instruments that record images, and sound; more recently the transfer is made to receivers, to sensors and to other detectors that can replace absence of tactility over distance. A general use of telecommunications is on the verge of achieving permanent telesurveillance. What is becoming critical here is no longer the concept of three spatial dimensions, but a fourth, temporal dimension – in other words, that of the present itself.
>
> (Virilio, 1993, p. 4)

Finally, the story of places washed of their authentic character still exists. In particular, the essence of places is increasingly seen as under threat (Harvey, 1989; Zukin, 1991): 'the security of actual places' is 'generally threatened' by a rising tide of commodification (Harvey, 1989, p. 68). The rise of the shopping malls is often taken as the most visible sign of the landscape as simply a moment in the circulation of commodities. The landscape is increasingly constructed in the image of the commodities. Worst of all, the landscape itself becomes a commercial package through the growth of a 'heritage industry' which packages the past of places in order to sell them in the present. Thus places increasingly become infected by the condition of **placelessness** (Relph, 1981) which apparently characterizes sites such as   *placelessness* shopping malls: 'We are in the midst of a desert of shops, a wasteland of services, a chaos of commerce. If not nowhere, we are in an extremely shallow somewhere' (Casey, 1993, pp. 268–9).

There are two reactions to this supposedly placeless condition, both of them bearing traces of the longing of nineteenth-century Romanticism for purity. One is to turn to the defence of Nature, because Nature is seen as a pure, wild place in which it is possible to get back in touch with elements of the self which have been defiled by consumption and other aspects of modern life.

The other is to turn to a new technological space – 'cyberspace' – which does much the same job. Cyberspace – discussed at the end of Chapter 6 of this book – can be interpreted as a pure and unsullied space where it is possible to roam freely and produce new meanings for the self at will and without constraint.

5   New stories of places

READING A

Now turn to the Reading by Doreen Massey. Massey, a geographer, is trying to tell stories of places in new ways. This does not mean that she is starry-eyed about what is going on. On the contrary, for her, places are caught up in a complex geometry of social power. As a result, places can be constructed as exclusionary, places can certainly be dangerous and places are always contested. As you read Massey's paper, note how she is trying to tell stories of places in ways which are positive.

In telling these new stories she wants to give people both positive reasons and the communicative resources to construct *their own* stories about places – as we have seen in Chapter 2 – because 'stories are not just practical and symbolic actions: they are also part of the political process' (Plummer, 1995, p. 26).

In this section of the chapter I want to suggest that Massey's article is symptomatic of new thinking about places and identities. The main aim of this thinking is to tell stories which do not come to foregone conclusions about what the world is like but leave endings open; stories which can then be used as reasons to build *new kinds of imagined community* with their own powers over place and space. Note how Massey's story queries the ideas of 'nativity, nationality and migration' (Pollock, 1994, p. 84). She is trying to put into play our ideas of what these terms mean: she wants to question what we mean by terms like 'the local' and 'home'; she wants to question the idea of national identity; and she wants to question the whole notion of origins, of the simple query 'where are you from?' Massey is not so much trying to rid us of these terms as to rework them into what she has called

progressive sense of place

elsewhere a **progressive sense of place** (Massey, 1994), new forms of community which are less exclusive and more open than older forms of attachment such as the imagined national community. But before we can go any further towards articulating what this progressive sense of place might mean, we need to think again about the kind of world we now inhabit since this is, after all, the resources we have to draw on to tell new, less centred kinds of story about place and identity.

It has become something of a cliché to write that the world is undergoing a process of globalization (see **Robins**, 1997). And, quite often, this cliché is attached to others, for example concerning time–space compression or placelessness. But we do not have to adopt these kinds of clichés as a precondition for noting that this is a world in which people are increasingly on the move (see Figure 4.6). We can index this mobility in three ways. First, there is the sheer amount of travel that is undertaken between countries, yet alone within them. The numbers involved are staggering. In the years 1991 and 1992, for example, between 70 and 80 million people were residing outside their countries of origin – about 1.3 per cent of the population on

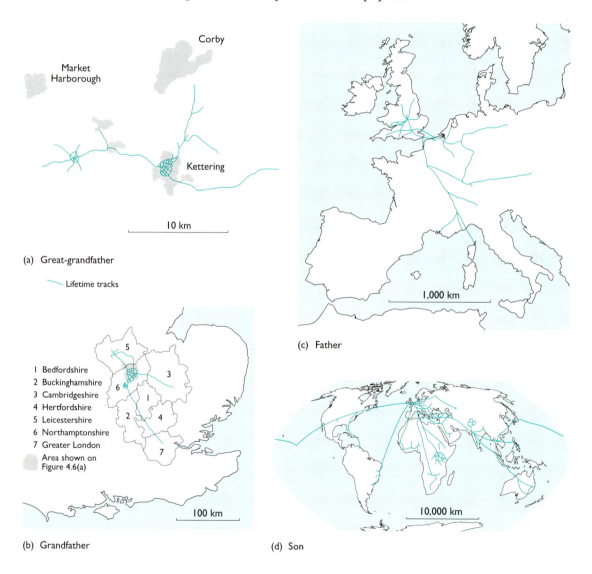

FIGURE 4.6

Increasing travel over four generations of the same family.

Each map shows in simplified manner the lifetime tracks in a widening spatial context.

Earth – including legally admitted immigrants, legally admitted temporary migrants, illegal migrants, asylum-seekers and refugees (Kliot, 1995). Then there are the tourists: on one estimate, every day in the year 2000 about 1.7 million people will be travelling outside their home country, a figure set to increase to 2.5 million every day by the year 2010 (Cater, 1995). Finally, there are travellers more generally. For example, it is estimated that, every day, about 3 million people worldwide take an aeroplane flight (within twenty years this figure is expected to be 6 million). All this travel means that there is a massive fund of personal knowledge about other places.

mediated interaction

mediated quasi-interaction

But this is to ignore the growth of 'mediated' and 'mediated quasi-' interaction (Thompson, 1995). **Mediated interaction** involves media such as the mail, fax, telephones and the like which are still person-to-person but which clearly involve a loss of certain kinds of information. But, there is also **mediated quasi-interaction** which involves books, newspapers, radio, television and so on which transmit information more generally – an explosion of texts, sounds and images.

Such developments, of course, have to be kept in perspective: it is worth remembering, for example, that between a third and a half of the world's population still live more than two hours from a telephone and that 900 million adults are illiterate. But what we can say is that more people have more knowledge of 'other' places than ever before.

ACTIVITY 3

Now think about your own life over the last year. Make a list of all the means by which you have picked up knowledge of other places. What journeys have you made? What 'mediated' and 'mediated quasi-' interactions have you undertaken? Then think back to your childhood. What has changed since then? Do you think you know more or less about other places as a result?

Now recall Daniel Miller's chapter on consumption (Chapter 1 above). Can you think of situations in which your knowledge of the places that consumer goods come from, and how they are produced in those places, has been improved because of the media? For example, can you think of articles that you have read or programmes that you have watched which have alerted you to the links between particular goods and places?

Certainly, in this situation of constant travel and communication, writers in many communities around the world have fixed on the resource of *mobility* as a means of re-imagining themselves, and their own and other communities, in different and more equal ways than could be understood from the old, western stories of nation and progress.

There is an irony here. Precisely because of this unparalleled state of mobility, the desire to belong to a place may never have been greater. Yet, increasingly, how we think of place is connected with mobility. This is not so surprising, perhaps, when writers who are used to a nomadic life live in places where mobility is a constant of everyday life. Thus for a 'voluntary cosmopolitan' (Hannerz, 1992) like Elspeth Probyn, San Diego is:

> ... a very apt place in which to think about belonging. This most southern of Californian cities is a strange place of movements. Across the flight path lies the port, dotted with yachts, criss-crossed with ocean cruisers, the site of cargo ships carrying and going. I navigate San Diego on bike, many trips constantly interrupted by canyons, by signs declaring 'Danger', 'Peligro', 'Naval Property'. I ride along paths enjoying the feeling of self-locomotion, ignoring the refrain of friends who said, 'you're crazy, you can't exist in Southern California without a driver's licence'. Frequently I am stopped, caught in a net of highways, halted before concrete channels of movement, fascinated and appalled by a place that constructs highways as lethal barriers to aliens crossing borders. In fact this is an appropriately strange place in which to consider belonging, a space that crackles with movement as people continually arrive, depart, are thrown out; some try to belong, some take their belonging for granted.
>
> (Probyn, 1995, pp. 1–2)

But what is striking is that this theme of mobility has also been taken up in the writing of communities which are less affluent and therefore less likely to be mobile. Here the 'involuntary cosmopolitanism' which arises from the experience of migration, refugeeism and diaspora seems to have been crucial. For example, Paul Gilroy is keen to emphasize that places are always and everywhere connected by these kinds of interactions between communities, as a means of imagining new kinds of outgoing ethnic identity which are both assertive and tolerant, confident and provisional (see **Gilroy**, 1997).

In the next section, I shall turn to four of the alternative stories that have begun to be told as people try to re-imagine themselves and their own and other communities. They are stories that recognize that, because we live in a world in which many people are on the move, places can no longer be 'the clear supports of our identity' (Morley and Robins, 1993, p. 5) in the same way; instead, perhaps, new stories of mediated places can be told which will also give us some clues to new forms of identity.

These are stories, then, that, unlike the old stories of nations and progress, are much less likely to be the preserve of a privileged set of people and places. Rather, they are more likely to have been generated by people whose identities have been marginalized, whose concerns have too often been scoffed at, or who, in general, feel that they have no voice.

It follows that these alternative stories have a corresponding geography which is more likely to be the geography of the periphery than the core. But this binary geography of periphery and core is complicated by the presence of certain 'world cities' like London, Paris, New York and Los Angeles which act as what Gilroy (1993a) calls 'junction points' or 'crossroads', nodes through which alternative stories can circulate more quickly, bumping up against many cultural worlds at once, and sometimes being changed in the process. Thus, for Gilroy (19931, p. 95), London is 'revealed to be a place where, by virtue of local factors like the informality of racial segregation, the configuration of class relations and the contingency of linguistic convergences, global phenomena such as anti-colonial and emancipationist political formations are still being sustained, reproduced, and amplified.' In previous eras, crossroads cities like London consisted, in large part, of concentrations of commerce fed by airports and telecommunications. These cities therefore act as some of the most important transmitters and generators of stories, including alternative stories like the ones set out below and the *identity experiments* – people's production of hybridized identities – which they help to sustain.

It may be that these alternative stories still have a quite limited circulation; it may be that they are generated in the cities; or generated in the periphery and developed and circulated in the core. But what we can say is that they point towards *new ideas of belonging*, which are, at the same time, less concerned about drawing divides between 'us' and 'them'. In other words, they are trying to invent identities which are more likely to include the element of sympathy and corresponding moral geographies which multiply spaces of tolerance rather than intolerance. Or, as Gilroy (1993b, p. 121) again puts it, 'it ain't where you're from, it's where you're at.'

I have chosen four of these stories: they are meant to replace our sense of belonging and, at the same time, directly challenge the old stories of the nineteenth century.

5.1   Story 1: Intersections

One story that is told is of places as *multiple*, as never the preserve of one cultural group but always of a number of these groups, each with their own traditions and agendas. This story emphasizes places as momentary **points of contact**, sites of 'diplomacy' where people can meet and perhaps start to become reconciled through a mutual reworking of their identities and those of others.

points of contact

Each place is therefore depicted as the point of intersection of the activity spaces of numerous people 'cross-cutting, intersecting, aligning with one another, or existing in relations of paradox or antagonism' (Massey, 1994, p. 3), a whole host of different representatives of different cultures that may be connected for only a moment. In turn, these intersecting activity spaces can stand for all the problems of representing the modern multicultural world in new and often mediated ways: 'at once a metaphor and a speaking position, a place of certainty and burden of humility, sometimes all of these simultaneously, sometimes all of them incommensurably' (Keith and Pile, 1993, p. 23).

A story of this kind is difficult to tell because it is so complex and unsettled. One way is to fix on spaces which clearly show the process of cultural intersection at work; spaces which, as a necessary part of their function, necessitate mixing, and, in particular, spaces of transit such as airports, motorway services, border crossings and shopping malls. Such spaces have been described by anthropologists like Augé (1995) as not really places at all, but rather as empty, uniform and solitary: multiple, certainly, but pointlessly so. But another, more positive, reading might see them as incorporating other, more hopeful, elements: chance meetings and even new beginnings.

READING B

Pico Iyer considers one of these spaces of transit 'where worlds collide' – Los Angeles' chief international airport, LAX – as a symbol of a new multicultural world. He finds a place that is distinctly more ambiguous than either the negative or the positive reading might suggest, a place full of ironies, contradictions and jilted expectations. As you read Iyer's essay, think about whether LAX can be considered to be a place at all. If so, do you consider it to be a good model for a place of mixing? If not, why not? Now read the essay.

5.2   Story 2: More places than ever

Then there is a second story. This is that, just maybe, the world's places are not growing steadily more inauthentic. Rather they must be *recombining* in new ways. As we lose some imaginative resources with which to think places and people, perhaps other such resources open up. Indeed, if we could measure the process, perhaps our experience of place has actually thickened rather than thinned, deepened rather than become more shallow, as the number of places we can know, directly or indirectly, and the number of ways in which we can know them have increased. The other side of the decomposition of place, in other words, is **recombination**.

recombination

One example of this process might be the advent of different forms of artificial light which, in turn, have extended our experience of place into the night. Of course, the night has never been just a blank space in which people slept. All societies have had some activity at night, usually aided by the light from fires, which itself has been a potent source for the imagination over the centuries (Bachelard, 1964/1938). However, for all that, activity in the night was limited by a general lack of light. Thus when

Dr Johnson walked around night-time London in the early eighteenth century, 'we can instantly imagine the scene: the cobbled streets, the stinking rubbish, the tavern signs, the shuttered house-fronts; the moonlight and the dark alleys; the slumbering beggars, the footpaths and the night watch' (Holmes, 1993, p. 35).

This was the 'City of Dreadful Night', still physically present but transformed by danger and lack of light, except for the moon and guttering tapers, into an alternative landscape, peopled by young rakes, the desperate poor and criminals (for a time in the eighteenth century, it was a capital offence to be caught at night out with a blackened face). In turn, the landscape of night stood for many things but especially the unknowable, symbolized by the candle in the window which was knowledge struggling to be born, and the mysterious, symbolized by the shadows cast by what little artificial light existed (Gombrich, 1995).

But over the succeeding centuries all of this changed. As the use of artificial light spread, so urban landscapes began to appear that before had only been figments of the imagination. At first it was the glow of gas light that lit up the city. Then, from the late nineteenth century, it was the gradual spread of electric light. Finally, it was the spread of light attached to mobile objects – cars, aeroplanes, satellites and so on. The night-time city becomes an active landscape which, furthermore, has become actively peopled:

> Now there is a whole after-hours community – everything from evening classes to supermarkets, night clubs, discos and massage parlours, as well as a great array of maintenance people who service and repair the daytime world while its inhabitants sleep. The defence establishment, the financial markets, broadcasting, transport, communications now work on a 24 hour day schedule.
>
> (Alvarez, 1995, p. 20)

The night-time urban landscape is one in which many people work (for example, 14 per cent of the UK workforce is involved in shifts) and in which, for all the real dangers, many people play. Thus what we have also seen is the growth of a specific 'night life'. Night life is hardly a new invention: the Vauxhall pleasure gardens and the theatres of seventeenth-century London were an early manifestation. But night-life has now grown to major proportions: theatres, pubs, night-clubs, shops, cafés, restaurants. Thus Lovatt and O'Connor (1995) can write of a 'twenty-four-hour city' of culture and entertainment (see Figure 4.7).

FIGURE 4.7   Satellite image of the British Isles at night, showing the distribution of city lights.

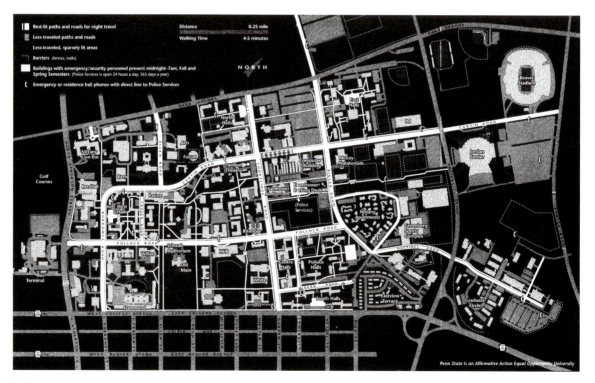

FIGURE 4.8   Penn State University: the Campus Night Map.

The point is that this extension of human activity into the night, resulting from the profusion of artificial light, provides us with *new* imaginative resources (see Figure 4.8). In particular, it has produced a whole set of alternative technologically-induced landscapes that were simply not there before; edited and highlighted landscapes which have now become 'second nature' to us (some, like Nye (1995), have even talked of a 'technological sublime') and which have radically altered our appreciation of many places. For example, for painters at the beginning of the twentieth century, 'the night cityscape was a new visual reality signifying a break in the continuity of lived experience that the painter confronted along with the rest of society' (Nye, 1990, p. 76). Further, as the century went on, so the appreciation of this cityscape at different times of the night began to suffuse into paintings: for example, places in the dusk when lights begin to appear in windows and street-lights are switched on, or places in the deep of night when the glow of powerful electronic light can create a world of intense colours. In other words, painters were able to see *new* places and, in turn, they have helped to make these perceptions into a normal part of the currency of our vision (Zajonc, 1993).

5.3   Story 3: One world?

A third story of places and identities also draws on the knowledge created by mobility, but in this case as the opportunity to imagine the world interdependent whole   as an **interdependent whole** created by the images made available to us by new technologies of vision like satellite photography. These new technologies have allowed us to consider the world as a whole entity, in which all parts relate to all other parts, and in which there is no hiding-place from common problems.

In particular, these kinds of images have been taken up by the burgeoning environmental movement to demonstrate the essential interdependence of the places of the world and of those who live in them which is, at the same time, an account of new forms of ethical 'ecological' identity:

> The ecological self can be viewed as a type of relational self, one which includes the goal of the flourishing of earth others and the earth community among its own primary ends, and hence respects or cares for these others for their own sake. Concepts of care, solidarity and friendship present alternatives to the instrumental mode within existing liberal societies.
>
> (Plumwood, 1993, pp. 154–5)

But a word of warning is in order. For all their potential, the interpretations of these images can remain firmly stuck in the stories of the eighteenth and nineteenth centuries. For example, the geographer Denis Cosgrove (1994) has related how one particular image of Earth – NASA image 22727 taken by one of the three astronauts aboard Apollo 17 in 1972 (see Figure 4.9) – has become a quintessential distillation of the principle of one world. But Cosgrove also shows how what at first seems to be an unproblematic image of wholeness can be read in quite other ways. In particular he suggests that two interpretations have become dominant. One, which he calls 'one-world', reads the images as an expression of the ascendancy of global business and of the technologies that have brought about time–space compression (as in the advertising slogan, 'IBM: solutions for a small planet'). The other interpretation, which he calls 'whole-earth', is an interpretation favoured by some environmentalists which signifies the necessity of planetary stewardship (as in the Greenpeace slogan, 'The Earth: attractive detached residence'). But, for Cosgrove, both interpretations have roots in the kinds of thinking that he is concerned to dispel:

FIGURE 4.9
The classic photograph of Earth taken from the Apollo 17 spacecraft in December 1972, showing Antarctica, Africa and Arabia.

> ... topographically it is iconic. Both interpretations insist on the globality of the image; both are inattentive to the specificity of their cultural and historical assumptions; and, in practice, both obscure local perspectives on the world in their claims to speak for a common humanity ...
>
> Fundamentally, the geographical imaginations that both readings articulate are obdurately Western and ethnocentric.

> (Cosgrove, 1994, pp. 287–8)

5.4   Story 4: New worlds

A fourth and final story of places and identities has come about because of the growth of mediated interaction. Quite clearly, the growth of this form of interaction has redefined the nature of place, in that places are now interconnected in all manner of ways. But this new intensity of interconnection can itself provide a model for thinking about place and

new forms of
publicness

identity as caught up in **new forms of publicness**. Until recently, the impacts of the media tended to be seen in negative terms, as leading, for example, to new forms of surveillance of places and new and highly dependent versions of identity, based on systems for the production and transmission of information over which their audiences had little control. Now, however, partly as a consequence of the growth of research on what audiences are actually doing with media (of the kind documented by Shaun Moores in Chapter 5 in this volume), partly as a consequence of the growth of new media complexes and traditions outside the West (see **Negus**, 1997), partly as the result of new media technologies (like video) which do not require massive capital investments to use, and partly as a result of the growth of new, more interactive forms of media (see Mackay's Chapter 6 in this volume), more positive consequences are likely to be suggested.

Most particularly, the growth of the media has provided new forms of mediated experience, which include images and reports of other and often far-off places and the people in them, which we are able to care about. Sense of community is no longer necessarily linked to a particular locality but is able to spread worldwide. The stirring of this 'global' care – what the sociologist John Thompson (1995) calls the *reinvention of publicness* – is attested to in all kinds of ways, by the money paid into charities when images of suffering in particular places are relayed to us from the television screen, by the growth of organizations that are committed to caring for distant others, from Amnesty to Greenpeace, and even by the growth of 'eco-tourism', based on responsible travel in fragile places:

> As our biographies are opened up by mediated experience, we also find ourselves drawn into issues and social relations which extend well beyond the locales of our day-to-day lives. We find ourselves not only to be observers of distant others and events, but also to be involved with them in some way ... [W]e are called on to form a view about, to take a stand on, even to assume some responsibility for, issues and events which take place in distant parts of an interconnected world.
>
> (Thompson, 1995, p. 233)

READING C

Now turn to the extended Reading by John Thompson. This Reading might be interpreted as a modern reworking of Adam Smith's notion of sympathy. It is a polemical piece which serves to make the point that, in principle at least, sympathy is more and more likely to be able to extend beyond the local as our sense of who and what we can touch by our actions has extended. As you read it, think back to Activity 1 – the earthquake in China. In the light of your reaction to this activity, what do you think about Thompson's arguments? Are they correct? Are they hopelessly optimistic? Or are they simply overgeneralized? (In other words, you may know more about *some* places and you may care about *some* of these places, but only under particular conditions.) What are the reasons for your judgement?

5.5   Some criticisms

These four new stories are not without their critics. These critics usually point to four main problems. First of all, they see these stories as expressing an élite perspective, the hopes and fears of those who are free to be mobile, like tourists, rather than those who are forced into mobility, like refugees (Wolff, 1993). Massey, in Reading A, makes precisely this point. Another criticism might be said to be the way in which these new stories underestimate the importance of bounded spaces like the nation, which are not just oppressive enclosures but are also important sources of identity for many people (Kirby, 1995). For example, what about all those cultural groups which are still striving to become nations? A third criticism is that the kinds of more open identities that these stories are trying to tell may simply prove to be timid, willing to see every viewpoint and champion none (or, even worse, simply simulate the kind of flexible worker that many firms around the world now demand (Martin, 1994)). Finally, critics suggest that the kinds of identities and senses of belonging that are fostered by these stories are simply a more sophisticated version of the kind of liberalism that Adam Smith would have recognized, a liberalism which denies the identities of others by rejecting them as 'hybrid' identities or by transferring the crises of identity and belonging to be found in the West on to other parts of the world: 'your' problems become 'ours' (Friedman, 1995). In other words, these new stories are not accepted always and everywhere: some accuse their teller of simply adopting a more sophisticated Eurocentric perspective. As you might imagine, this is a subject of lively and impassioned debate.

ACTIVITY 4

Which of the four alternative stories of place that I have outlined seems the most credible to you, and why?

In the next section, I shall show how the Sami have had to confront some of the issues raised by these stories as their culture has changed. In particular, the position of particular kinds of places at the centre of their culture has become a more problematic one as the places which the Sami occupy have become increasingly diverse and mediated.

6   The Sami again

By the 1960s anthropologists had begun to question the old accounts of nomadic cultures. In particular, they drew back from the idea of pure hunting and gathering to one of much greater economic diversity and flexibility; they suggested that many nomadic cultures had been continuously in contact with other peoples over many centuries, especially because of trade, and that this contact had become a generic part of their cultures, and they gathered more and more evidence that these cultures were constantly changing (Ingold, Riches and Woodburn, 1988). The description of these cultures as pristine time-capsules was therefore rejected and instead some attempt was made to tell these cultures' stories on their own terms – through 'histories by and for' rather than 'histories of'. In part, this change of tack was a result of the general collapse of the colonial impulse in most parts of the world, and of the evolutionary schemes that had helped to sustain it. But, in part, it was also because these cultures had began to find their own voice and to contest even more vigorously the places they regarded as their own.

For the Sami, this contestation had become particularly necessary since the Sami culture was clearly under threat. However, over the last fifty years or so the Sami have fought back strongly against cultural encroachment and the decline in their culture has at least halted.

Before the 1940s Sami cultural decline was already seen as a problem: a Society for the Promotion of Lappish Culture was set up as early as the 1890s. But in 1945 the discovery of shared Sami concerns led to the setting-up of the all-Sami 'Lappish League' which sought to unify support and assert indigenous needs and aspirations. In 1956 the Nordic Sami Council was founded to promote Sami co-operation and to work to improve the social, cultural, legal and economic status of the Sami. In 1974 a Nordic Sami Institute was founded in Kautokeino, Norway to promote research into Sami traditions, language, values, economic situation and legal rights. In each of the Nordic countries Sami 'parliaments' have been established 'to pursue and secure the rights and improve the economic, and social and educational conditions of the Sami' (Hutchings, 1995, p. x). Most importantly of all, the constitutions of the Nordic States have been altered to recognize the Sami's position as first peoples and to grant them autonomy in matters of languages and culture (most recently, for example, in 1995 in Finland). The Sami have even been able to internationalize their concerns: for example, in 1975 they became members of the World Council of Indigenous Peoples and they also keep in close contact with the United Nations Working Group for Indigenous Populations.

The Sami have been able to use these and other institutional developments to help to build up their culture. They have been able to increase Sami language use through a variety of means so that, currently, about 20,000 people speak Sami in Norway, 10,000 in Sweden, 3000 in Finland and 1000 in Russia. In Norway, Sweden and Finland, Sami children have the right to mother-tongue teaching in state schools and in special Sami schools. As importantly, the Sami language is actively used in the media: there are regular Sami radio programmes and news broadcasts and, periodically, Sami television programmes; there are Sami newspapers and a rapidly growing Sami literature. There are other manifestations of Sami culture such as the numerous Sami artists and designers and even Sami theatre groups (Beach, 1988). Most recently, the Sami have been able to use new media such as video and the Internet to further their cultural causes, with Sami websites in English on the World Wide Web (see Figure 4.10).

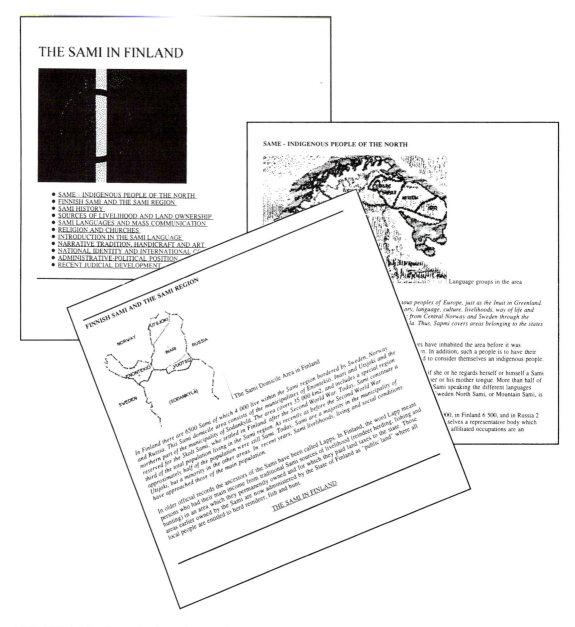

FIGURE 4.10   Examples from Sami web pages.
(http://www.vn.fi/vn/um/finfo/english/saameng.html)

Clearly, the Sami have been able to move towards some degree of cultural autonomy. But other forms of autonomy still elude them and, in turn, the lack of these forms of autonomy is having impacts on the kind of cultural autonomy that is possible. Two of these other forms of autonomy are particularly important. First, there is the matter of rights over the land which is a crucial part of Sami identity. The Sami sometimes have legal claim over their lands. Yet pressure on these lands has still increased, especially but not only because of the increased pressure on reindeer-herding brought about by generalized environmental degradation (including the radiation fallout from the Chernobyl disaster), the loss of land to logging, mining, hydro-electric power, and tourism and recreation, the influence of a plethora of state environmental and other rules concerning the size of reindeer herds (Paine, 1994), as well as the more recent effect of European Union rules and regulations since Sweden and Finland joined the Union. Second, there are rights over livelihood. Reindeer-herding represents a declining proportion of Sami livelihoods: probably only about 10 per cent of Sami are full-time reindeer herders in Norway and Sweden at present (the proportion is somewhat higher in Finland). Increasingly, it has been overtaken by other traditional livelihoods such as fishing and hunting or newer livelihoods such as forestry and, especially, tourism. Tourism has clearly led to problems for the Sami cultures, for example through the use of Sami motifs to construct romantic images of Nordic natural identities, or through the tendency to pointless 'exoticization' (see Figure 4.11). On the other hand, and paradoxically, tourism has also had some beneficial effects. As has been observed by anthropologists in other parts of the world (see, for example, Friedman, 1992, 1995), tourism has sometimes allowed greater cultural identification, for example through the growth of 'traditional' handicrafts, in this case woodwork, bonework, antler work, peltwork and pearl and tin thread embroidery on which many Sami are now economically dependent:

> Hard times means that, like many other reindeer farmers, the Magya are having to supplement their income through tourism. In their backyard they have built a small Sami museum packed with family mementoes, and they hold regular cultural evenings. 'It is difficult these days to make a living just from the reindeer', says Ulla. 'Tourism enables us to make some extra money and gives people a better insight into the Sami life.'

> (Hutchings, 1995, p. xi)

(It is one of the ironies of globalization that the popularity of Sami handicrafts and mementoes for tourists has also led to a flood of cheap imitations from Asia.)

CHRISTMAS IN LAPLAND

*D*ue to our overwhelming success of our holidays to Lapland last year, we have a special programme for this Christmas. You can take the day excursion or stay two nights at the modern Hotel Lapponia. Fly supersonic on Concorde or travel on the luxurious QE2 and Orient-Express. Some holidays include the three superlatives - Concorde, QE2 and the Orient-Express.

You have a choice of airports of departure: Heathrow, Gatwick, Luton,

Manchester, Birmingham, Newcastle, Glasgow or Bristol.

Lapland is magical for both the young and the young at heart. Father Christmas has chosen Lapland to be his natural home. You will visit him at his picturesque Reindeer Farm surrounded by pine trees. Here you can experience a skidoo and reindeer ride. After the Arctic Crossing ceremony you will be presented with a certificate.

Thus we can see that the Sami have fought back against cultural and other forms of encroachment. This has not always been easy. For a start, the Nordic states are committed to strong notions of what constitutes national culture (Lofgren, 1989; Linde-Laursen, 1995). They are also committed to an ideology of equality of all citizens. These states therefore find it difficult to accommodate cultural difference: if all are 'worthy', how can certain groups have more rights than others? (It is one of the ironies of the current situation that the Sami have been able to make certain gains in Sweden in matters like rights to education in Sami, because of legislation relating to immigrants.) Then again, the Sami do not constitute a single culture; such a notion would be deeply

FIGURE 4.11
(*Above and right*) The impact of tourism.

alien to them. There are, for example, three distinct Sami languages and nine dialects within these languages. Sami culture has, in any case, always been decentralized.

In some ways most difficult of all, there is the Sami relation to place. Until quite recently, Sami identity was reliant on practices which were strongly associated with particular places: dialects, specific forms of dress and even local styles of reindeer-herding. Where you belonged was indeed how you belonged. Now these practical links to place are being broken. For example, reindeer-herding has become less and less central to the lives of most Sami: not only are fewer and fewer Sami involved in reindeer-herding but the nature of herding has changed to something more like ranching (Ingold, 1980), involving the use of snowmobiles and even helicopters (see Figure 4.12). For many Sami, especially those living in the cities, their relation to the 'traditional' Sami places now takes the form of brief visits or is mediated by literature, television and so on. In other words, the relation to culturally important places becomes increasingly imagined but not necessarily any less potent.

FIGURE 4.12 Snowmobiles have replaced reindeer for transport, with most families owning at least a couple. Five or six Samis with dogs will herd 5–10,000 reindeer from their summer grazing at the coast to their winter areas using snowmobiles.

ACTIVITY 5

Can you envisage Sami culture surviving without the places it values? Would it be the same culture under these circumstances? Would this matter? Could new places take the place of the old as symbols of Sami culture? Or will the old places simply become mediated but retain their cultural pull?

It is therefore no surprise that there is a considerable debate amongst the Sami about what kinds of identity they want to take on, often associated with controversies over particular cultural 'anchors'. For example, should the Sami become a 'nation'? They have some of the cultural accoutrements. In 1906 a national anthem ('The song of the Sami family') was written which, significantly, ends with the words, 'the land of the Sami to the Sami'. Since 1986 the Sami have had their own flag. Again, in what kinds of ways should the Sami remember themselves? There is currently an outpouring of literature and art on what it is to be Sami. And, what is to be the position of handicrafts, of oral musical forms like the *yoik* (a particular mode of chanting), of the traditional Sami dress (*gapite*), of turf huts, of folk medicine, of shamanism, and so on?

> What can you call 'traditional'? ... Even coffee, came once from outside [the culture], though most people would suppose that it belonged [to the traditional culture]. Older people have said to me that 'before the snowmobile came', their reindeer management was traditional. For them, reindeer were also draft animals. Young people who have grown up with the snowmobile will say that *it* is part of their tradition.
>
> (Dag Elgvin, cited in Paine, 1994, p. 145)

This work of cultural redefinition has required new stories about the places and identities of the Sami, some of which resemble those we examined in section 5. This 'innovative traditionalism' is a means of negotiating a third way between the two options that are usually envisaged for first peoples: that they must remain as they were in the past or become assimilated into a mainstream way of life. This third way is one in which 'traditional forms of cultural expression are developed into distinctive contemporary indigenous cultures with their own creative roots and dynamics' (Bennett and Bundell, 1995, p. 5). In other words, the Sami have to strike a balance: to keep their culture (or, more exactly, cultures), some things must change; to change their culture(s), some things must stay the same.

7   So what is place?

Up until now, I have left the definition of place largely in abeyance. In part, this is because defining exactly what place is turns out to be very difficult. For example, in the past, geographers (who have made the study of place the core of their discipline) have associated place with a set of particular experiences, have made place synonymous with community through notions like 'locality', and have made place a part of larger spatial divisions brought about by major economic and social changes. Most recently, as I noted at the beginning of this chapter, they have tended to assert that place gains its power from the 'maps of meaning' which are laid over a particular site and give it a cultural resonance.

But note how, in all the definitions I have given above, place is assumed to be the result of, or to stand for, something else. Place is always something passive or secondary; it has to be animated by culture. This is a part of what the social anthropologist, Tim Ingold, calls the 'building' perspective in which 'worlds are made before they are lived in'. Ingold sets out to criticize this perspective on place and to try to find another one. For writers like Ingold (1980), Carter (1996) and Thrift (1996) the building perspective harks back to the projects of the eighteenth and nineteenth centuries that we examined in section 2, to Eurocentric dreams of worlds inhabited (or should it be invaded?) by rootless rationalists. For Carter, the end-point of these dreams is clear to see:

> ... colonialism was the consequence: a people without a dreaming, without an attachment to the land, were machines for free movement. They were robots or ghosts, these landless wanderers. Armoured in wonder-working technology, and vulnerable to the agoraphobia all must feel who have no place they can call their own, they proved a fearsome and, as it turned out, irresistible force.
>
> (Carter, 1996, p. 364)

So, says Ingold, if the building perspective is inherently flawed, what then might replace it? Ingold argues for a new sense of place – which he calls the **'dwelling' perspective** – which is neither primary nor secondary, it is simply there as a part of *us*: 'place serves as the condition for all existing things' (Casey, 1993, p. 15) because it is something that we constantly produce, with

'dwelling' perspective

others, as we go along. So, out of the most concrete and localizable details imaginable – campsites and settlement layouts – Ingold derives a general statement about how to think of place as always and everywhere concerning multiple worlds whose inhabitants, whilst they go about their own tasks, are also jointly constructing each other's. This is a sense of place which, in other words, stresses the essential inseparability of being:

> 'We do not dwell because we have built, but we build and have built because we dwell, that is because we are dwellers ... To build is in itself already to dwell ... *Only if we are capable of dwelling, only then can we build*' (Heidegger, 1971, pp. 148, 146, 160, original emphases). I take this to be the founding statement of the dwelling perspective. What it means is that the forms people build, whether in the imagination or on the ground, arise within the current of their involved activity, in the specific relational contexts of their practical engagement with their surroundings. Building, then, cannot be understood as a simple process of transcription of a pre-existing design of the final product on to a raw material substrate. It is true that human beings – perhaps uniquely among animals – have the capacity to envision forms in advance of their implementation, but this envisioning is itself an activity carried on by real people in a real-world environment, rather than by a disembodied intellect moving in the subjective space delimited by the puzzles it sets out to solve. In short, people do not import their ideas, plans or mental representations into the world, since that very world, to borrow a phrase from Merleau-Ponty (1962, p. 24), is the homeland of their thoughts. Only because they already dwell therein can they think the thoughts they do.
>
> (Ingold, 1980, p. 76)

Ingold's dwelling perspective completely overturns the old eighteenth- and nineteenth-century stories we met in section 2. Thus, it argues for an entirely different sense of movement from ours, one which no longer characterizes travel as 'narrowly linear, extra-territorial activity'. Rather, movement becomes something closer in character to that of the Sami, 'a primary condition of human existence' in which 'sedentary nations [are] an eccentricity' (Carter, 1996, p. 365). Its sense of history is no longer a linear one moving along the single frozen axis of progress but is founded in difference and constant circulation. Its sense of time is no longer one of remorseless acceleration along this same axis. And it is therefore able to conceive of places as still rich in all manner of activity, never still but still grounded.

But, for all its fundamental aspirations, you might think about the degree to which this perspective, with its emphasis on place and identity as the *joint* and continually on-going construction of many different kinds of being, is actually *only possible in the kind of world in which we live*. Perhaps Ingold's emphasis on 'ceaseless becoming' only echoes our own current experience of mobility. Perhaps his commitment to a jointly inhabited environment simply mirrors the rise of an ethic of environmental sympathy. And perhaps his reading depends upon the growth of a world of mediated anthropological and geographical knowledges which make it much easier to compare and appreciate life in many places.

Certainly, Ingold seems to be trying to pull off the same trick – a deeper sense of belonging to the world and, at the same time, a more provisional one – which is at the core of much current writing on culture. Like Massey, he is trying to redefine what we mean by 'home' by suggesting that what we regard as home always belongs to many beings at once. By extension, he is also suggesting that we need to redefine what we mean by 'identity' by suggesting that what we regard as identity also always belongs to many beings at once. This non-exclusive and non-exclusionary definition of places and identities returns us once again to Adam Smith's notion of sympathy – but now spread much wider than Smith might have wanted or thought necessary, in an attempt to imagine new kinds of more caring community.

References

ALVAREZ, A. (1995) *Night: an exploration of night life, night language, sleep and dreams*, London, Jonathan Cape.

ANDERSON, B. (1983) *Imagined Communities: reflections on the origin and spread of nationalism*, London, Verso.

AUGÉ, M. (1995) *Non-places: introduction to an anthropology of supermodernity*, London, Verso.

BACHELARD, G. (1964/1938) *The Psychoanalysis of Fire*, (tr. A.C.M. Ross), London, Quartet.

BEACH, H. (1988) *The Sami of Lappland*, London, Worldwatch.

BENDER, B. and MORRIS, B. (1988) 'Twenty years of history, evolution and social change in gatherer-hunter studies' in Ingold, T., Riches, D. and Woodburn, J. (eds) Vol. 1, pp. 4–14.

BENNETT, T. and BLUNDELL, V. (1995) 'First peoples', *Cultural Studies*, Vol. 9, pp. 1–10.

BIRD-DAVID, N. H. (1988) 'Hunters and gatherers and other people – a re-examination' in Ingold, T., Riches, D. and Woodburn, J. (eds) Vol. 2, pp. 17–30.

BRADLEY, D. J. (1988) 'The scope of travel medicine' in Steffen, R. et al. (eds) *Travel Medicine*, Berlin, Springer Verlag, pp. 1–9.

CARTER, P. (1996) *The Lie of the Land*, London, Faber and Faber.

CASEY, E. (1993) *Getting Back Into Place: toward a renewed understanding of the place-world*, Bloomington, IN, Indiana University Press.

CATER, E. (1995) 'Consuming spaces: global tourism' in Allen, J. and Hamnett, C. (eds) *A Shrinking World? Global unevenness and inequality*, Oxford, Oxford University Press/The Open University, pp. 183–232.

COSGROVE, D. (1994) 'Contested global visions: one-world, whole-earth, and the Apollo space photographs', *Annals of the Association of American Geographers*, Vol. 84, pp. 270–94.

DU GAY, P. (ed.) (1997) *Production of Culture/Cultures of Production*, London, Sage/The Open University (Book 4 in this series).

FRIEDMAN, J. (1992) 'Narcissism, roots and post-modernity: the constitution of selfhood in global crisis' in Lash, S. and Friedman, J. (eds) *Modernity and Identity*, Oxford, Blackwell, pp. 331–66.

FRIEDMAN, J. (1995) 'Global system, globalisation and the parameters of modernity' in Featherstone, M., Lash, S. and Robertson, R. (eds) *Global Modernities*, London, Sage, pp. 69–90.

GELLNER, E. (1983) *Nations and Nationalism*, Blackwell, Oxford.

GILROY, P. (1993a) *The Black Atlantic: modernity and double consciousness*, London, Verso.

GILROY, P. (1993b) *Small Acts: thoughts on the politics of black cultures*, London, Serpents Tail.

GILROY, P. (1997) 'Diaspora and the detours of identity' in Woodward, K. (ed.) *Identity and Difference*, London, Sage/The Open University (Book 3 in this series).

GINZBURG, C. (1994) 'Killing a Chinese mandarin: the moral implications of distance', *New Left Review*, No. 298, pp. 107–19.

GOMBRICH, E. H. (1995) *Shadows: the depiction of shadows in Western art*, London, National Gallery Publications.

HANNERZ, U. (1992) *Cultural Complexity: studies in the social organisation of meaning*, New York, Columbia Press.

HARVEY, D. (1989) *The Condition of Postmodernity*, Oxford, Blackwell.

HEIDEGGER, M. (1971) 'Nest and home', *Folia Primatologica*, Vol. 28, pp. 170–87.

HOLMES, R. (1993) *Dr Johnson and Mr Savage*, London, Hodder and Stoughton.

HULME, P. and JORDANOVA, L. (eds) (1990) *The Other Side of the Enlightenment*, London, Routledge.

HUTCHINGS, C. (1995) 'A fighting spirit', *The Geographical Magazine*, October, pp. x–xi.

INGOLD, T. (1976) *The Skolt Lapps Today*, Cambridge, Cambridge University Press.

INGOLD, T. (1980) *Hunters, Pastoralists and Ranchers: reindeer economies and their transformations*, Cambridge, Cambridge University Press.

INGOLD, T., RICHES, D. and WOODBURN, J. (eds) (1988) *Hunters and Gatherers*, Vol. 1: *History, evolution and social change*, Vol. 2: *Property, power and ideology*, Oxford, Berg.

IYER, P. (1995) 'Where worlds collide: in Los Angeles International Airport, the future touches down', *Harper's Magazine*, August, pp. 50–7.

JANELLE, D. G. (1969) 'Spatial reorganisation: a model and concept', *Annals of the Association of American Geographers*, Vol. 72, pp. 8–15.

KEITH, M. and PILE, S. (eds) (1994) *Place and the Politics of Identity*, London, Routledge.

KIRBY, K. (1995) *Indifferent Boundaries: spatial concepts of human subjectivity*, New York, Guilford Press.

KLIOT, N. (1995) 'Global migration and ethnicity: contemporary case-studies' in Johnston, R. J., Taylor, P. J. and Watts M. J. (eds) *Geographies of Global Change: remapping the world in the late twentieth century*, Oxford, Blackwell, pp. 175–190.

LINDE-LAURSEN, A. (1995) 'Small differences – large issues: the making and remaking of a national border', *South Atlantic Quarterly*, Vol. 94, pp. 1123–44.

LIVINGSTONE, D. (1992) *The Geographical Tradition*, Oxford, Blackwell.

LOFGREN, O. (1989) 'The nationalisation of culture', *Ethnologia Europaea*, Vol. 19, pp. 5–23.

LOVATT, A. and O'CONNOR, J. (1995) 'Cities and the night time economy', *Planning Practice and Research*, Vol. 10, No. 2, pp. 16–24.

MARSHALL, P. J. and WILLIAMS, G. (1982) T*he Great Map of Mankind: perceptions of new worlds in the age of enlightenment*, Cambridge, MA, Harvard University Press.

MARTIN, E. (1994) *Flexible Bodies: the role of immunity in American culture from the days of polio to the age of Aids*, Boston, MA, Beacon Press.

MASSEY, D. (1994) *Space, Place and Gender*, Cambridge, Polity Press.

MASSEY, D. (1995) 'Making spaces, or, geography is political too', *Soundings*, Issue 1, pp. 193–208.

MCLINTOCK, A. (1995) *Imperial Leather: race, gender and sexuality in the colonial contest*, Routledge, New York.

MERLEAU-PONTY, M. (1962) *Phenomenology of Perception*, (tr. C. Smith), London, Routledge and Kegan Paul.

MORLEY, D. and ROBINS, K. (1993) 'No place like Heimat: images of home (land) in European culture' in Carter, E., Donald, J. and Squires, J. (eds) *Space and Place: theories of identity and location*, London, Lawrence and Wishart, pp. 3–32.

NEGUS, K. (1997) 'The production of culture' in du Gay, P. (ed.).

NIETZSCHE, F. (1983) *Untimely Meditations*, (tr. R. J. Hollingdale), Cambridge, Cambridge University Press.

NYE, D. (1990) *Electrifying America: social meanings of a new technology*, Cambridge, MA, MIT Press.

NYE, D. (1995) *The Technological Sublime*, Cambridge, MA, MIT Press.

PAINE, R. (1994) *Herds of the Tundra: a portrait of Saami reindeer pastoralism*, Washington, DC, Smithsonian Institution Press.

PLUMMER, K. (1995) *Telling Sexual Stories: power, change and social worlds*, London, Routledge.

PLUMWOOD, V. (1993) *Feminism and the Mastery of Nature*, London, Routledge.

POLLOCK, G. (1994) 'Territories of desire: reconsiderations of an African childhood' in Robertson, G., Mash, M., Tickner, L., Bird, J., Burtis, B. and Putman, J. (eds) *Travellers' Tales: narratives of home and displacement*, London, Routledge, pp. 63–89.

PORTER, R. (1993) 'Baudrillard: history, hysteria and consumption' in Rojek, C. and Turner, B. S. (eds) *Forget Baudrillard*, London, Routledge, pp. 1–21.

PRENDERGAST, C. (1992) *Paris and the Nineteenth Century*, Oxford, Blackwell.

PROBYN, E. (1995) 'Queer belongings' in Grosz, E. and Probyn, E. (eds) *Sexy Bodies: the strange carnalities of feminism*, London, Routledge, pp. 1–18.

RELPH, E. (1981) *Place and Placelessness*, London, Pion.

ROBINS, K. (1997) 'What in the world's going on' in du Gay, P. (ed.).

ROSS, I. S. (1995) *The Life of Adam Smith*, Oxford, Clarendon Press.

SERRES, M. (1995) *Angels: a modern myth*, Paris, Flammarion.

SERRES, M. and LATOUR, B. (1995) *Conversations on Science, Culture and Time*, Ann Arbor, MI, University of Michigan Press.

SHOHAT, E. and STAM, R. (1994) *Unthinking Eurocentrism: multiculturalism and the media*, New York, Routledge.

SMITH, A. (1976/1759) *The Theory of Moral Sentiments*. Oxford, Clarendon Press.

STEEDMAN, C. (1995) 'Maps and polar regions' in Pile, S. and Thrift, N. J. (eds) *Mapping the Subject: geographies of cultural transformation*, London, Routledge, pp. 77–92.

STORM, D. (1987) 'The justified demand of a minority' in Hirsch, L., Liden, H., Mykleburt, D. and Tschudi-Madsen, S. (eds) *Norway: a cultural heritage*, Oslo, Risankiku area Universitats Forlaget, pp. 79–90.

TAYLOR, C. (1988) *Sources of the Self*, Cambridge, Cambridge University Press.

THOMPSON, J. B. (1995) *The Media and Modernity: a social theory of the media*, Cambridge, Polity Press.

THRIFT, N. J. (1995) 'A hyperactive world' in Johnston, R. J., Taylor, P. J. and Watts, M. (eds) *Geographies of Global Change: remapping the world in the late twentieth century*, Oxford, Blackwell, pp. 18–35.

THRIFT, N. J. (1996) *Spatial Formations*, London, Sage.

VIRILIO, P. (1993) 'The third interval: a critical transition' in Conley, V. A. (ed.) *Rethinking Technologies*, Minneapolis, MN, University of Minnesota Press, pp. 3–12.

WOLF, E. (1982) *Europe and the People without History*, Berkeley, CA, University of California Press.

WOLFF, J. (1993) 'On the road again: metaphors of travel in cultural criticism', *Cultural Studies*, No. 7, pp. 224–31.

ZAJONC, A. (1993) *Catching the Light: the entwined history of light and mind*, New York, Bantam.

ZUKIN, S. (1991) *Landscapes of Power: from Detroit to Disney World*, Berkeley, CA, University of California Press.

READING A:
Doreen Massey, 'Making spaces, or, geography is political too'

There is a story – I don't know if it is true or not – about a Native American chief in the middle of the last century. He had been asked by members of his society what had been the biggest mistake of the past generations' leaders. After thinking for a while, he replied 'we failed to control immigration' [King, 1995]. I ponder this story sometimes when I read reports of today's debates in Europe about immigration; when I hear Jean-Marie Le Pen railing against migration into France, or Winston Churchill on the same topic in Britain.

Whatever one's view on international migration, it is difficult to base it on any simple notion of inalienable rights. There are no abstract, generalisable answers to questions of space and place. One might clearly feel sympathy with the Native American chief (or with Australian aborigines or even, at a more local level, with working-class residents of Docklands faced with an invasion of yuppies – but then what of their response to an 'invasion' of people from Bangladesh?). On the other hand, I have no hesitation in my opposition to the views of Jean-Marie Le Pen or Winston Churchill. The point is, of course, that the two attitudes are set within very different power relations, very different geographies of power.

The mobility of the European immigrants to what was, to them, 'the New World' was the mobility of the relatively powerful and, in the case of some of the earliest settlers, that of the conquering invader. In the case of today's Europe, those who would like to enter (or, certainly, the ones against whom the barriers are raised) are international migrants seeking asylum or work; they are in a relatively powerless position and have a million bureaucratic and racist barriers to cross. The relation of the two groups to space is also therefore somewhat different: the one venturing out with a degree of control and confidence; the other more accurately described as escaping [...] Today's potential migrants to Europe would certainly produce effects (there would be cultural and economic influences, and probably social conflict), but they would not completely eradicate the places where they settled

Most crucially of all, we are talking here of two migrations set within very different geographical contexts of uneven development. The early migration to the Americas was outwards from the centres of power and economic development. The pressures for migration today are from the underprivileged parts of the world, as Europe battens down its local hatches to defend its existing advantages against those locked into the wrong side of uneven development.

[...]

Take another pair of examples: this time where the issue revolves more around the question of what might be the 'rights of local people'. In the first case, groups of indigenous people in a coastal region of Honduras are protesting against a development plan which would allow the entry into their area of large-scale commercial development of such industries as logging, coffee production and oil extraction. The local groups argue that this kind of economic development will destroy the forests, create pollution and, through monocultural practices, threaten precisely the small-scale variety of the natural resource base on which their own economy depends. In short, it will, they argue, destroy the place as they know it, and their way of life [see Jess and Massey, 1995].

In much the same period, on another continent, in a First World metropolis, another group of locals is also defending its patch. Here, middle-class people in an expensive suburb (the kind which is defined as 'exclusive') are resisting the building of a community hostel and cheaper housing for rent. Their area is quiet and leafy, and everyone agrees on how to behave within it. That is why they are here: the place and the kind of life they have so carefully constructed over the years go together. An invasion of this place by new and very different people would, so these locals argue... destroy their way of life.

What *are* the rights of 'local people'? The suburban residents clearly want to exclude the entry of people they think of as different. But so do the indigenous groups of the Mosquitia in Honduras: one of the resolutions they have approved is to prohibit the colonisation of the region by non-indigenous peoples, and to relocate existing colonists to other areas. Indeed, who *are* the locals?

Or, more precisely, what does it mean to be 'local'? The wealthy suburbanites claim their status merely on the basis that they are 'already there'. Clearly, they are unlikely to have been the first inhabitants of this place. Even in the immediate past, their leafy roads have been built over land where farmers and farm workers once lived. So is 'local' just a matter of current possession?

The situation in Honduras is not uncomplicated either. Clearly, the indigenous groups have not been there for ever: they came across the Bering Strait some 15,000 years ago. They arrived first, but what does 'indigenous' mean? One of the groups – the Garífuna – derives from a complex and international history, hailing originally from Africa and arriving in the area courtesy of British-run slave trade. Even the group which is usually recognised as 'the most indigenous' is not in any sense composed of purely local influences. The Miskito have certainly lived in the area for centuries, but over those centuries they have absorbed contacts with many other 'external' cultures – from English pirates to Spanish colonisers. Such influences have been absorbed in the past, so why prevent more outside influences now? Moreover, in the past the Miskito themselves have apparently been none-too-respectful of the local rights of others: they seem to have persecuted another group, for instance, pushing them (with British help) into new areas.

Just as with mobility and migration, the 'rights of local people' (whether indigenous peoples, posh residents, or the Isle of Dogs white working class) cannot be elevated into an abstract, generalisable, principle. We are all, somewhere in the past, migrants, and none of us is simply 'local'. Indeed, geography itself may be an important element in establishing our identity, in the sense of defining outsiders *as* outsiders. [...] The designation of the expensive suburb as 'exclusive' really means what it says. The social definition of the place involves an active process of *exclusion*. And in that process the boundaries of the place, and the imagination and building of its 'character', are part and parcel of the definition of who is an insider and who is not; of who is a 'local', and what that term should mean, and who is to be excluded. It is a space of bounded identities; a geography of rejection [see, for example, Sibley, 1992].

The construction of 'the local' is just as much an act of social power as the ability, or inability, to prevent the arrival of new migrants. The social and the spatial are always inextricably entwined.

[...]

From the global to the local

[...]

What treaties such as NAFTA and GATT represent is a potentially massive reorganisation of the world geography of social relations. While multinational companies are freed ever more to roam the globe – their already-existing power forcing down borders and further increasing their power – the local production and trade relations of peasants and small farmers are undermined. More people leave the land and make for the cities. Yet they cannot go to just any city. Free trade does not go so far as that. The US border, and the EU border, still remain closed to such people from outside. And so it is that yet more people arrive in unprepared, polluted, Mexico City.

This is a real, global, spatial reorganisation, but one in which different groups are very differently implicated. Different places (Chiapas, California) and different social groups occupy very different locations in this shifting, global power-geometry. Some barriers are torn down; others are maintained. New spaces are created (of global trade and of new squatter settlements in third world cities); others are destroyed (the spaces of more integrated national economies, and those of small-scale agriculture). Some identities (the hybrid-Mayan cultures of Chiapas) come under threat from such spatial reorganisations; while those who already have more strength within the shifting power-geometry can wall themselves more tightly in. [...]

[...]

A place of their own: geography and the middle class

Power over space and place is, then, a major weapon in the negotiation of today's world. That power may rest on economic muscle, on the loudness of your voice in international fora, on ethnicity or country of origin, on violence, on gender... But whatever it is based on, such power differentiates us. Among other things, in Britain, it is very tied up with social class. Indeed, it is possible to argue – at least for purposes of provoking debate – that spatiality and relation to place (geography) may be significant differentiations between socio-economic groups. It seems, for instance, that in England and Wales if you want to be middle class you may have to move. Certainly, your chances are better if you live in the right place.

Some fascinating recent research shows that, in the 1980s, geographical mobility was an important aspect of gaining access to certain social classes [Fielding, 1995]. In particular, this is true of the middle class (managers, professionals and the petty bourgeoisie). The statistics show that entry into middle-class occupations was often accompanied by movement from one region to another. The quite reasonable inference would be that climbing into these groups may be easier if you are prepared to move house.

There is, moreover, a big difference between these social groups and others. Entry into blue-collar occupations, for instance, shows very little relation to migration between regions. In other words, some groups seem to reproduce themselves in particular places – on the basis of these statistics one might think of working-class communities – while others quite actively gather together from across the country to establish social strata.

Such a picture, and the sharpness of the contrast, can be overdrawn. These statistics refer only to one, recent, decade. The longer historical view shows that now seemingly stable working-class communities were themselves constructed from long migrations of people seeking work: the trek to the coalfields of South Wales and the North East in the 18th-century, the migration of Scots to work the Corby iron, of rural families to the mills of Lancashire and Yorkshire. Moreover, the statistics relate to a decade when the blue-collar working class was in decline, while the managers and professionals of the middle class were growing rapidly in numbers.

One must not, then, generalise beyond the time and place of these particular statistics. But they do catch something important about the social geography of our times. Some classes, or occupational groups, appear to be formed *in situ* far more than are others.

What is more, the mobility of the aspirant middle class is a *particular* mobility: overwhelmingly it consists of movement to the south east of England. As 'the middle class' has grown in size so it has continued to concentrate in the south of the country. Certainly, not all middle-class people live there and, even more surely, not everyone in the south and east is middle class. But this region is its heartland. As middle-class jobs have proliferated, so the geographical distance between them and working-class jobs has been maintained and at times reinforced. This is not something which *has* to happen; it is not somehow a technical necessity of economic efficiency. The middle class putting geographical distance between itself and manual labour is a *social* phenomenon, part of the formation of the middle-class groups themselves. Occupational, social and spatial identities have been constructed together. Much middle-class movement, within regions as well as between them, had had *as its aim* the creation of a geography of difference.

There is, of course, more to 'mobility' than moving house. But in these other areas, too, the middle class seems to score more highly. It is overwhelmingly the middle-class – or, more accurately, it is middle-class *men* – whose jobs take them travelling, whose work-contacts are conducted through international conference calls and the internet. It is middle-class families, on the whole, whose holidays take them further afield; keeping a little ahead, perhaps, of the frontiers of mass tourism. This, moreover, is a mobility of choice, conducted in relative ease and style: quite different from the mobility of the international refugee or the unemployed migrant from Liverpool coming south to find work. Not just the degree of mobility, but also its social meaning and its character as an experience, indeed the way it becomes part of the process of identity-formation, vary hugely between social groups.

But if, for the middle class in this country, the world is increasingly its oyster, the desire for the other side of the coin, for a settled localism, seems equally strong. The mobilities of life are counterposed to, or perhaps even compensated for by, a desire for a place of their own.

I have recently been studying some high-tech scientists, men whose working lives (through the companies they work in, through travel to conferences, through the networks of contacts and debates in which they daily participate) are thoroughly internationalised. And at the end of such globalised days a quite impressive proportion of them go home (should one say 'retreat'?) to a cottage in an 'Olde Worlde' English village whose symbolic essence (if not reality) is stability and localism.

This is, of course, a phenomenon far wider than a handful of scientists. It would be interesting to analyse in the same terms the home-bases of those who work in the City, the prime UK location of untrammelled globalisation. Perhaps the two sides are related. Just as it is often migrants who get most sentimental about 'home', so those whose lives span the globe seem very strongly to want 'a place of their own'. It seems that at least some significant elements of the British middle class today embody in their own lives that tension between the global and the local, between relatively unfettered geographical mobility on the one hand and a commitment to an exclusive localism on the other. (It is, perhaps, a measure of their cultural hegemony that it *their* experience that is taken as the sign of the times. And it is, of course, primarily they who write about it.)

What is more, these are the groups which have the most power to ensure that they *do* have a place of their own. What is at issue here is not just the happenstance congregation of different social groups into distinct geographical locations but the active making of places [...] So often, the power to defend an exclusivist localism is greater for those that are already strong, while the places of others (in Chiapas, in Docklands, or in the lands of the Native American chief) come under threat.

[...]

References

FIELDING, T. (1995) 'Migration and middle-class formation in England and Wales, 1981-91' in Butler, T. and Savage, M. (eds) *Social Change and the Middle Classes*, London, UCL Press.

JESS, P. and MASSEY, D. (1995) 'The contestation of place' in Massey, D. and Jess, P. (eds), pp. 133-74.

KING, R. (1995) 'Migrations, globalization and place' in Massey, D. and Jess, P. (eds), pp. 5-44.

MASSEY, D. and JESS, P. (eds) (1995) *A Place in the World?: Places, Cultures and Globalization*, London, Oxford University Press/The Open University.

SIBLEY, D. (1992) 'Outsiders in society and space' in Anderson, K. and Gale, F. (eds) *Inventing Places: studies in cultural geography*, Cheshire, Melbourne, Longman, pp. 107–22.

Source: Massey, 1995, pp. 193–7, 201, 204–7.

READING B:
Pico Iyer, 'Where worlds collide'

[...]

It is a commonplace nowadays to say that cities look more and more like airports, cross-cultural spaces that are a gathering of tribes and races and variegated tongues; and it has always been true that airports are in many ways like miniature cities, whole, self-sufficient communities, with their own chapels and museums and gymnasiums. Not only have airports coloured our speech (teaching us about being upgraded, bumped, and put on standby, coaching us in the ways of fly-by-night operations, holding patterns, and the Mile High Club); they have also taught us their own rules, their own codes, their own customs. We eat and sleep and shower in airports; we pray and weep and kiss there. Some people stay for days at a time in these perfectly convenient, hermetically sealed, climate-controlled duty-free zones, which offer a kind of caesura from the obligations of daily life.

Airports are also, of course, the new epicentres and paradigms of our dawning post-national age – not just the bus terminals of the global village but the prototypes, in some sense, for our polyglot, multicolored, user-friendly future. And in their very universality – like the mall, the motel, or the McDonald's outlet – they advance the notion of a future in which all the world's a multiculture. If you believe that more and more of the world is a kind of mongrel hybrid in which many cities (Sydney, Toronto, Singapore) are simply suburbs of a single universal order, then Los Angeles's LAX, London's Heathrow, and Hong Kong's Kai Tak are merely stages on some great global Circle Line, shuttling variations on a common global theme. Mass travel has made L.A. contiguous to Seoul and adjacent to São Paulo, and has made all of them now feel a little like bedroom communities for Tokyo.

[...] L.A., legendarily, has more Thais than any city but Bangkok, more Koreans than any city but Seoul, more El Salvadorans than any city outside of San Salvador, more Druze than anywhere but Beirut; it is, at the very least, the easternmost outpost of Asia and the northernmost province of Mexico. When I stopped at a Traveler's Aid desk at LAX recently, I was told I could request help in Khamu, Mien,

Tigrinya, Tajiki, Pashto, Dari, Pangasinan, Pampangan, Waray-Waray, Bambara, Twi, and Bicolano (as well, of course, as French, German, and eleven languages from India). LAX is as clear an image as exists today of the world we are about to enter, and of the world that's entering us.

[...]

Often when I have set off from L.A. to some distant place – Havana, say, or Hanoi, or Pyongyang – I have felt that the multicultural drama on display in LAX, the interaction of exoticism and familiarity, was just as bizarre as anything I would find when I arrived at my foreign destination. [...]

[...]

It is almost too easy to say that LAX is a perfect metaphor for L.A., a flat, spaced-out desert kind of place, highly automative, not deeply hospitable, with little reading matter and no organizing principle [...] Whereas 'SIN' is a famously ironical airline code for Singapore, cathedral of puritanical rectitude, 'LAX' has always seemed perilously well chosen for a city whose main industries were traditionally thought to be laxity and relaxation. LAX is at once a vacuum waiting to be colonized and a joyless theme park – Tomorrowland, Adventureland, and Fantasyland all at once.

The postcards on sale here (made in Korea) dutifully call the airport 'one of the busiest and most beautiful air facilities in the world'. [...]

LAX is, in fact, a surprisingly shabby and hollowed-out kind of place, certainly not adorned with the amenities one might expect of the world's strongest and richest power. When you come out into the Arrivals area in the International Terminal, you will find exactly one tiny snack bar, which serves nine items; of them, five are identified as Cheese Dog, Chili Dog, Chili Cheese Dog, Nachos with Cheese, and Chili Cheese Nachos. There is a large panel on the wall offering rental-car services and hotels, and the newly deplaned American dreamer can choose between the Cadillac Hotel, the Banana Bungalow (which offers a Basketball Court, 'Free Toast', 'Free Bed Sheets', and 'Free Movies and Parties'), and the Backpacker's Paradise (with 'Free Afternoon Tea and Crumpets' and 'Free Evening Party Including Food and Champagne').

Around one in the terminal is a swirl of priests rattling cans, Iranians in suits brandishing pictures of torture victims, and Japanese girls in Goofy hats. 'I'm looking for something called Clearasil', a distinguished-looking Indian man diffidently tells a cashier. 'Clearasil?' shouts the girl. 'For your face?'

Upstairs, in the Terrace Restaurant, passengers are gulping down 'Dutch Chocolate' and 'Japanese Coffee' while students translate back and forth between English and American, explaining that 'soliciting' loses something of its cachet when you go across the Atlantic. [...]

At a bank of phones, a saffron-robed monk gingerly inserts a credit card, while school kids page Jesse Jackson at the nearest 'white courtesy telephone'. One notable feature of the modern airport is that it is wired, with a vengeance: even in a tiny, two-urinal men's room, I found two telephones on offer; LAX bars rent out cellular phones; and in the Arrivals area, as you come out into the land of plenty, you face a bank of forty-six phones of every kind, with screens and buttons and translations, from which newcomers are calling direct to Bangalore or Baghdad. Airports are places for connections of all kinds and *loci classici*, perhaps, for a world ruled by IDD and MCI, DOS and JAL.

Yet for all these grounding reminders of the world outside, everywhere I went in the airport I felt myself in an odd kind of twilight zone of consciousness, that weightless limbo of a world in which people are between lives and between selves, almost sleepwalking, not really sure of who or where they are. Light-headed from the trips they've taken, ears popping and eyes about to do so, under a potent foreign influence, people are at the far edge of themselves in airports, ready to break down or through. You see strangers pouring out their life stories to strangers here, or making new life stories with other strangers. Everything is at once intensified and slightly unreal. One L.A. psychiatrist advises shy women to practise their flirting here, and religious groups circle in the hope of catching unattached souls.

[...]

For many immigrants, in fact, LAX is quietly offering them a view of their own near futures: the woman at the Host Coffee Shop is themselves, in a sense, two years from now, and the man sweeping

up the refuse is the American dream in practice. The staff at the airport seems to be made up almost entirely of recent immigrants: on my very first afternoon there, I was served by a Hoa, an Ephraim, and a Glinda; the wait-people at a coffee shop in Terminal 5 were called Ignacio, Ever, Aura, and Erick. Even at the Airport Sheraton (where the employees all wear nameplates), I was checked in by Viera (from 'Bratislava') and ran into Hasmik and Yovik (from Ethiopia), Faye (from Vietnam), Ingrid (from Guatemala City), Khrystine (from Long Beach, by way of Phnom Penh, I think), and Moe (from West L.A., she said). Many of the bright-eyed dreamers who arrive at LAX so full of hope never actually leave the place.

[...]

In L.A. all of this has an added charge, because unlike many cities, it is not a hub but a terminus: a place where people come to arrive. Thus many of the meetings you witness are between the haves and the hope-to-haves, between those who are affecting a new ease in their new home and those who are here in search of that ease. Both parties, especially if they are un-American by birth, are eager to stress their Americanness or their fitness for America; and both, as they look at each other's made-up self, see themselves either before or after a stay in L.A.'s theatre of transformation. And so they stream in, wearing running shoes or cowboy hats or 49ers jackets, anxious to make a good first impression; and the people who wait for them, under a half-hearted mural of Desertland, are often American enough not to try to look the part. Juan and Esperanza both have ponytails now, and Kimmie is wearing a Harley-Davidson cap backwards and necking with a Japanese guy; the uncle from Delhi arrives to find that Rajiv not only has grown darker but has lost weight, so that he looks more like a peasant from back home than ever.

And the newcomers pour in in astonishing numbers. A typical Sunday evening, in a single hour, sees flights arriving from England, Taiwan, the Philippines, Indonesia, Mexico, Austria, Germany, Spain, Costa Rica, and Guatemala; and each new group colors and transforms the airport: an explosion of tropical shades from Hawaiian Air, a rash of blue blazers and white shirts around the early flight from Tokyo. Red-haired Thais bearing pirated Schwarzenegger videos, lonely Africans in Aerial Assault sneakers, farmers from changeless Confucian cultures peering into the smiles of a Prozac city, children whose parents can't pronounce their names. Many of them are returning, like Odysseus, with the spoils of war: young brides from Luzon, business cards from Shanghai, boxes of macadamia nuts from Oahu. And for many of them the whole wild carnival will feature sights they have never seen before: Japanese look anxiously at the first El Salvadorans they've ever seen, and El Salvadorans ogle sleek girls from Bangkok in thigh-high boots. All of them, moreover, may not be pleased to realize that the America they've dreamed of is, in fact, a land of tacos and pita and pad thai – full, indeed, of the very Third World cultures that other Third Worlders look down upon.

[...] Tibetans who have finally managed to flee their Chinese-occupied homeland arrive at LAX to find Chinese faces everywhere; those who fled the Sandinistas find themselves standing next to Sandinistas fleeing their successors. And all these people from ancient cultures find themselves in a country as amnesiac as the morning, where World War II is just a rumour and the Gulf War a distant memory. Their pasts are escaped, yes, but by the same token they are unlikely to be honoured.

It is dangerously tempting to start formulating socio-economic principles in the midst of LAX: people from rich countries (Germany and Japan, say) travel light, if only because they are sure that they can return any time; those from poor countries come with their whole lives in cardboard boxes imperfectly tied with string. People from poor countries are often met by huge crowds – for them each arrival is a special occasion – and stagger through customs with string bags and Gold Digger apple crates, their addresses hand-written on them in pencil; the Okinawan honeymooners, by contrast, in the colour-coordinated outfits they will change every day, somehow have packed all their needs into a tiny case.

[...]

And as I got ready to leave LAX, I could not help but feel that the Theme Building stands, more and more, for a city left behind by our accelerating planet. LAX, I was coming to realize, was a good deal scruffier than the airports even of Bangkok or Jakarta, more chaotic, more suggestive of Third World lawlessness. And the city around it is no more golden than Seoul, no more sunny than Taipei, and no more laid-back than Moscow. Beverly Hills, after all, is largely speaking Farsi now. Hollywood Boulevard is sleazier than 42nd Street. And Malibu is falling into the sea.

[...]

Nearby, the Soldiers of the Cross of Christ Church stood by the escalators, taking donations, and a man in a dog collar approached another stranger.

I watched the hustlers allowing the spirit to breathe, I heard the Hare Krishna devotees plying their wares, I spotted some Farrakhan flunkies collecting a dollar for a copy of their newspaper, *The Final Call* – redemption and corruption all around us in the air. [...]

Source: Iyer, 1995, pp. 51–7.

READING C:
John Thompson, 'Towards an ethics of global responsibility'

Is there a normative or ethical dimension to the new kind of publicness created by the media? [...]

[...T]he media are one domain, it may seem, from which serious ethical concerns were banished long ago. With the growing commercialization of media institutions, the moral and political ideals held by some of the early media entrepreneurs were increasingly displaced by criteria of efficiency and profitability. Media products themselves – or so the argument goes – became increasingly standardized and stereotypical; they trivialized and sensationalized, they concerned themselves with fleeting events, and they relinquished any capacity they once may have had to transcend the banalities of daily life. And the reception of media products has become just another form of consumption, a source of excitement, entertainment and pleasure. Of course, the reception of media products may have certain distinctive characteristics (require certain skills to decode, give rise to certain kinds of gratification, etc.); but in terms of its ethical significance, it may seem little different from the consumption of refrigerators or potatoes or any other commodity. The rise of the media, or so it seems, was not good news for ethics.

Part of the enduring appeal of Habermas's original account of the transformation of the public sphere is that it offers a sharp critical perspective on what one might describe as the ethical hollowing-out of public life. The emergence of the bourgeois public sphere in eighteenth-century Europe was not just an institutional development: it also had a moral-practical dimension. The bourgeois public sphere was a realization – albeit very partial – of what Habermas sometimes refers to as 'the critical principle of publicity' (or of 'publicness' – *öffentlichkeit*). This is an idea which Habermas traced back to Kant's writings on enlightenment; it is the idea that the personal opinions of private individuals could evolve into a public opinion through a process of rational-critical debate which was open to all and free from domination. Habermas maintained that despite the decline of the bourgeois public sphere, which provided a partial and imperfect realization of this idea, the critical principle of publicity retains its value as a normative ideal, a kind of critical yardstick by means of which the shortcomings of existing institutions can be assessed and the outlines of alternative forms of social organization can be sketched.

[...]

[...] Habermas's proposal is that a norm would be valid or just (*richtig*), or an institution would be legitimate, only if, were the norm or institution to be openly discussed by everyone affected by it under conditions free from constraint, it would elicit their consent; but this requirement seems much too strong, and it is difficult to see how it could be applied with any hope of success to the controversial moral and political issues of our time.

[...T]here is a further problem with Habermas's approach which has hardly been considered by his critics [...] Habermas's conception of the public sphere – whether in the form of the bourgeois public sphere which emerged in the eighteenth century, in the form of his own, philosophically more elaborate model of practical discourse – is a spatial and dialogical conception. It is based on the idea that individuals come together in a shared locale to engage in dialogue with one another, as equal participants in a face-to-face conversation. The problem, however, is that this conception bears little relation to the kinds of action and communication which have become increasingly common in the modern world. Today actions can affect individuals who are widely dispersed in space and time; and the media have created forms of communication which do not involve dialogical conversation in a shared locale. Habermas's model of practical discourse is essentially an extension (albeit a highly elaborate one) of the traditional conception of publicness as co-presence. Hence it is difficult to relate this model to the kinds of action and communication – and to the distinctive type of publicness created by the media – with which we are so familiar today.

[...] In principle it may seem plausible to suggest that an action would be correct or a norm would be just if and only if everyone affected by it, having had the opportunity to discuss it together under conditions free from domination, were willing to assent to it. But what could this possibly mean in practice in a world where many actions and norms affect thousands or even millions of individuals who are widely dispersed in space (and perhaps also in time)? Actions leading to the destruction of the rain forests or the depletion of the ozone layer, for example, are likely to affect populations across the globe and could seriously impair the life conditions of future generations. [...]

Examples of this kind highlight the fact that ways of thinking about moral-practical issues have not kept pace with the developments that have transformed (and continue to transform) our world. [...] Ethics was geared to forms of action whose effective range was small, and to forms of interaction which were essentially face-to-face. The ethical universe was composed of contemporaries, of individuals situated in the here and now, and ethical reflection was a morality of proximity.

Today we can no longer think about moral-practical issues in this way. Today, thanks to the development of technologies and the massive concentration of resources, actions can have consequences that stretch far beyond the immediate locale. The ethical universe can no longer be thought of as a world of co-present contemporaries. The conditions of nearness and contemporaneity no longer hold, and the ethical universe must be enlarged to comprise distant others who, while remote in space and time, may nevertheless be part of an interconnected sequence of actions and their consequences. Moreover, as we have become increasingly aware of the devastating impact of human action on the environment, it has become increasingly doubtful whether the non-human world of nature can be treated simply as the ethically neutral backdrop to human action and interaction. We seem to bear some responsibility for the world of the non-human, even though the inhabitants of this world (as well as the succeeding generations of human beings who will inherit the world) are in no position to press their claims upon us.

We must seek to develop a way of thinking about moral-practical issues which does justice to the new and historically unprecedented circumstances under which these issues arise today. It is a way of thinking that must be based on a recognition of the interconnectedness of the modern world and the fact that spatial and temporal proximity has ceased to be relevant as a measure of ethical significance.

It is a way of thinking that must be based, at least in part, on a sense of responsibility for others – not just the formal sense of responsibility, according to which a responsible individual is one who is accountable for his or her own actions, but a stronger and more substantive sense, according to which individuals bear some responsibility for the well-being of others and share a mutual obligation to treat others with dignity and respect. It is a way of thinking which must recognize that our substantive responsibility extends well beyond the proximate sphere of others with whom we interact in our day-to-day lives; in an increasingly interconnected world, the horizons of responsibility extend increasingly to others who are distant in space and time, as well as to a non-human world of nature whose destiny is increasingly interwoven with our own. And, finally, it is a way of thinking that must take full account of the enormity of the stakes, as the growth of power at the disposal of human beings has reached the point at which the survival of the species and of the planet can no longer be assured.

There can be little doubt that the various media of communication have played, and will continue to play, a crucial role in cultivating some sense of responsibility for our collective fate. They have helped to create a sense of responsibility which is not restricted to localized communities, but which is shared on a much wider scale. They have helped to set in motion a certain 'democratization of responsibility', in the sense that a concern for distant others becomes an increasing part of the daily lives of more and more individuals. It is difficult to watch images of civilians caught up in military conflict or of children dying of malnutrition without feeling that the plight of these individuals is – in some sense and to some degree – a matter for our concern. It is difficult to read reports of animal species threatened with extinction by the activities of poachers without feeling some sense of responsibility – mixed, perhaps, with feelings of sadness and guilt – for their fate. Of course, such feelings do not by themselves constitute a process of moral-practical thinking, but their significance should not be underestimated. They attest to the possibility that the increasing diffusion of information and images through the media may help to stimulate and deepen a sense of responsibility for the non-human world of nature and for the universe of distant others who do not share one's own conditions of life.

It would be naive to suppose that, as a basis for the renewal of moral-practical thinking in the late twentieth century, this incipient sense of responsibility is anything other than precarious. We all know how fragile the sense of responsibility for distant others, how fleeting the pang of conscience, can be; we all know how easy it is, when others are far removed from the circumstances of our daily lives, to turn our attention away from their plight while we concern ourselves with those who benefit from the immediacy of face-to-face interaction. We know how the sheer scale and frequency of the calamities that take place in the world today can threaten to overwhelm us, giving rise to a kind of moral fatigue which can neutralize our capacity to feel compassion. We know how dramatic images can be cynically manipulated and exploited for the purposes of mobilizing sympathy or support on the part of the chasm between a sense of responsibility, on the one hand, and a willingness and capacity to take effective action, on the other. Individuals may feel a deep sense of concern about the plight of distant others or about the destruction of the global environment; but given the enormous complexity of the processes that have produced the crises and predicaments we face today, and given the difficulty of intervening effectively in processes that are in many cases poorly understood, many people may feel reluctant or unable to translate their sense of concern into a determinate course of action.

Precarious, certainly; insignificant, certainly not. The development of communication media has fuelled a growing awareness of the very interconnectedness and interdependency which this development, among others, has helped to create. It has nourished a sense of responsibility, however fragile, for a humanity that is commonly shared and for a world that is collectively inhabited. It is this sense of responsibility which could form part of a new kind of moral-practical reflection which has broken free from the anthropocentric and spatial-temporal limitations of the traditional conception of ethics, a kind of reflection which might stand in some tolerably coherent relation to the realities of an increasingly interconnected world. This is a world, as Jonas

observed, in which our capacity to act at a distance, to set in motion processes that can have far-reaching consequences in space and in time, greatly exceeds our capacity to understand and to judge: the causal reach of our actions constantly outstrips our prescience. Whether we can develop our sense of responsibility into a form of moral-practical reflection which would provide some reasoned guidance for the conduct of human affairs, and whether we can gain sufficient understanding of complex humanly created processes to intervene effectively in them, it is difficult to say. But to attempt to do so might be the best – the only – option we have.

Reference

HABERMAS, J. (1991/1962) *The Structural Transformation of the Public Sphere: an inquiry into a category of bourgeois society*, (tr. T. Burger with F. Lawrence), Cambridge, Polity Press.

JONAS, H. (1984) *The Imperative of Responsibility: in search of an ethic for the technological age*, Chicago, IL, University of Chicago Press.

Source: Thompson, 1995, pp. 258, 259–65.

BROADCASTING AND ITS AUDIENCES

Shaun Moores

CHAPTER FIVE

Contents

1   Introduction: broadcasting as an institution in everyday life

Broadcasting may be thought of as an 'institution' in two different senses of the term. On the one hand, it is an industry for the manufacture of symbolic goods. It has various institutional sites of cultural production that are characterized by particular professional practices and by specific relationships to the state or the market. On the other hand, at the point of cultural consumption where those symbolic goods enter into the social worlds which are inhabited by its audiences, broadcasting can also be understood as 'an institution in everyday life' (Rath, 1985) – as part of the social fabric that goes to make up our routine daily experiences.

This chapter will focus on the latter definition – on broadcasting as an institutionalized feature of cultural consumption. However, in looking at the position which television and radio have come to occupy in the day-to-day lives of viewers and listeners, I want to insist here that we keep the former definition of broadcasting – as an institution of cultural production – firmly in mind. It is important for us to do so because producers, consumers and the communicative forms which pass between them are located on the same integrated 'cultural circuit' (see the diagram in the Introduction to this book).

In the present section, by way of introduction, I consider the distinctive conditions of production and consumption in this cultural circuit – offering a general account of the broadcast media and their audiences that sets the scene for what is to follow later. Section 2 critically examines the industry's own orientation towards its viewing and listening publics, its communicative styles or modes of address and its objectification of 'the audience' as a commodity. Section 3 deals with the significance which broadcasting has in private settings of reception. There, our interest will be in the situated meanings and pleasures that are generated by consumers, and in the social relations of power which operate in routine domestic contexts. Finally, in section 4, there is an exploration of the roles that television and radio play in articulating local cultures and globalizing processes – putting viewers or listeners in close contact with distant events, potentially transforming our senses of self or 'community'. A common theme which runs through this chapter, underpinning each of these important issues, is broadcasting's position within the social arrangements of space and time.

If we are to comprehend the distinctive conditions of production and consumption in broadcast media, and the link between those different points on the cultural circuit, then it is necessary for us to chart their spatial and temporal dimensions – to identify the dynamics of location and 'mediation' which are in play. Images and sounds get produced and consumed in places situated at a distance from one another, yet the moments of transmission and reception in broadcasting are virtually simultaneous. While the place of the studio or outside broadcast is far removed from the dispersed household settings where viewing and listening are ordinarily done, television and radio manage to offer their audiences a feeling of liveness and immediacy, as the organized **flow** of their programme schedules gets intricately woven into the rhythms of our everyday lives.

flow

The spatial separation of producer from consumer, combined with the temporal simultaneity and continuity of transmission and reception, have given rise to an aesthetic or a communicative style that is peculiar to broadcasting. An early attempt to map this aesthetic was Raymond Williams' ground-breaking study of television as technology and as cultural form (Williams, 1974). He showed there how the medium's output and the experience of home viewing are both characterized by what he called 'the fact of flow'. This was first brought to his attention when, as a regular writer of journalistic pieces, he had tried hard to develop an appropriate way of reviewing television content – of finding a subject matter and a method of criticism adequate for the medium:

> Reviewers pick out this play or that feature, this discussion programme or that documentary. I reviewed television once a month over four years, and I know how much more settling, more straightforward, it is to do that ... Yet while that kind of reviewing can be useful, it is always at some distance from what seems to me the central television experience – the fact of flow ... It is indeed very difficult to say anything about this. It would be like trying to describe having read two plays, three newspapers, three or four magazines, on the same day that one has been to a variety show and a lecture and a football match. And yet in another way it is not like that at all, for though the items may be various the television experience has in some important ways unified them.
>
> (Williams, 1974, p. 95)

Building on this discussion, John Ellis (1982) questioned the meaning of the word 'items' towards the end of the passage reproduced here, asking whether Williams had been wrong to hang onto the idea that flows are made up of independent works or discrete programmes: 'he underestimates the complexity of broadcast TV's particular commodity form, which has very little to do with the single text' (ibid., p. 118). Ellis advanced a modified version of the argument which foregrounded **segmentation** and **repetition** as the main features of television output. He suggested the segment should be the basic unit of textual analysis, defining his concept with reference to selected examples – the thirty-second advertising spot, the isolated item or story in a news bulletin, or the short scene from a television drama. In turn, the corresponding concept of repetition was used by Ellis to account for the recursive organization of segments across space and time. He illustrated the widespread application of this principle in broadcasting by pointing to the most common of television formats – series and serials. These are the industry's highly segmented, standardized products which return at the same place in the schedule day after day, week after week. In the case of a

segmentation, repetition

continuous serial or soap opera, the fiction may be stretched over years or even decades, creating a strong sense of its own past and future (Geraghty, 1981). (See Christine **Gledhill**, 1997, on the narrative form of soap opera.)

Just as Williams' notion of flow was designed to account for the domestic experience of viewing as well as the aesthetics of television programming, so Ellis's arguments about the segmented and repetitive nature of the medium's output were tied to a series of reflections on the household context of reception. He described the television set itself as 'another domestic object, often the place where family photos are put – the direction of the glance towards the personalities on the TV screen being supplemented by the presence of "loved ones" immediately above' (Ellis, 1982, p. 113). Broadcasting, unlike cinema, is 'intimate' and familiar – part of the furniture of ordinary daily life in private homes rather than a site of spectacular public entertainment. For that reason, its symbolic products are tailored to meet the requirements of consumers who are routinely present, yet typically 'distracted'. According to Ellis, this means television tends to be much more of a sound-based medium than does cinema – constructing a 'regime of the glance' as opposed to the voyeuristic gaze of the film spectator at large-screen images in a darkened auditorium.

Of course, television makes available to its viewers a specific sort of 'look' at various happenings which take place in the world beyond the living-room, but its modes of address and presentation are once again shaped by the profoundly domestic character or 'feel' of broadcasting:

> Broadcast TV creates a community of address in which viewer and TV institution ... look at the world that exists beyond them both. So TV is a relay, a kind of scanning apparatus that offers to present the world beyond the familiar and the familial, but to present it in a familiar and familial guise ... TV assumes that it has certain kinds of viewers ... that it speaks for them and looks for them. Interviewers base their questions on 'what the viewers at home want to know', drama bases itself on the notion of the family.
>
> (Ellis, 1982, pp. 163–5)

Perhaps the classic instance of that general process which Ellis described is television news presentation. In this genre of broadcast output, viewers are invited to 'travel' – electronically at least – to distant corners of the globe, witnessing what can often be quite disturbing events. However, the direct and seemingly personal address of the newsreader might best be seen as an attempt to reassure domestic consumers who are watching from their own local settings. The newsreader is a regular 'visitor' in the living-room, 'bringing it all back home' to audiences (Figure 5.1).

FIGURE 5.1   Bringing it all back home: the newsreader's style combines authority with familiarity.

First and foremost, the issues raised by my example are experiential ones. They have to do with the role of television in mediating social subjectivity – in articulating private and public, or 'the local' and 'the global', in particular ways. Any consideration of broadcasting as an institution in everyday life must take these experiential issues very seriously indeed. They are closely bound up with what Anthony Giddens (1990) refers to as 'a phenomenology of modernity', with the project of understanding how it feels to live day-to-day in late-modern society. Television news is involved here in a dramatic reordering of traditional time–space relations and has the potential to change previous patterns of familiarity and estrangement (see below, sections 2.1 and 4.1).

Secondly, though, Ellis's remarks concerning the look which television constructs for its viewers also lead us to ask crucial questions about the ideological power of the broadcast media. He asserted that a complicity is continually being created between institution and audience. This bond, so the argument goes, is forged by addressing the viewer at home as 'you' – and by assuming a shared 'we' position from where several 'theys' may then be identified. A cultural distinction between insiders and outsiders is thereby produced – between social groups or constituencies which are placed either as the subjects or the objects of television's look. The main difficulty with his otherwise sharp observations lies in the fact that not all audience members will necessarily take up their designated place within this ideological hailing and framing. As John Corner (1995, p. 19) puts it in a recent commentary: 'Ellis's qualities as an alert critic of the medium ... fall victim to a familiar problem, that of extrapolating too freely from an analysis of a text's form to predictions about its social effects.'

Over the past twenty years, many researchers in the field of media and cultural studies have sought to avoid the problem which Corner identifies by investigating empirically the interpretative interactions between television and its audiences. The initial aim of this type of research was to plot the varied 'decodings' of audio-visual signs made by different audience groupings – to gauge the varying distances that the readings depart from those preferred meanings which get 'encoded' in texts at the point of production. (I will be discussing the encoding/decoding model more fully in section 3.1 below.) Such distances are primarily social and semiotic but they rely upon spatio-temporal divisions too. For sociologist John Thompson (1988), a critical theory of ideology and mass communication has to try to incorporate each of these dimensions. So it is partly as a consequence of their 'extended availability' in space and time that broadcasting's symbolic goods are open to **differential interpretations** at the moment of reception and everyday use:

differential interpretations

> A distinctive characteristic of mass communication concerns ... the fact that the messages are potentially available to an extended audience which is altogether different from the interlocutors of a face-to-face interaction ... But the term 'mass' may be misleading ... For this term connotes not only a large quantity but also an indefinite shape, an inert, undifferentiated heap. However, the messages transmitted by the mass media are received by specific individuals in definite social-historical contexts. These individuals ... actively interpret and make sense of these messages and relate them to other aspects of their lives. This ongoing appropriation of media messages is an inherently critical and socially differentiated process ... there are systematic variations in their appropriation of media messages, variations which are linked to socially structured differences within the audience.
>
> (Thompson, 1988, pp. 365–6)

For instance, when watching television coverage of an industrial dispute you might make sense of and respond to it in different ways depending upon a combination of factors which are to do with your class position, social values or political allegiances. Similarly, soap operas may be enjoyed and appreciated by some viewers yet despised and denigrated by others – chiefly because of variations in the age, gender or cultural competence of audience members. This is not to propose any crude 'sociological reductionism' where positions within the social structure are automatically assumed to determine patterns of meaning and taste. Nevertheless, the capacity to actively interpret and gain pleasure from broadcast output is inevitably constrained to some extent by our cultural backgrounds and belief systems. Knowledges and competencies are unevenly distributed.

Thompson is rightly cautious about using the word 'mass' to describe communications between the producers and consumers of broadcast messages, but there could also be a question-mark over our continued and taken-for-granted use of the term 'audience'. The plural, **audiences**, is preferable – denoting several groups divided either by their reception of various media and genres, or else by their social and cultural location – although a further conceptual difficulty still remains. Tracing the origins of this word, Janice Radway (1988, pp. 359–60) finds that it once referred exclusively to an individual act of hearing in face-to-face verbal interaction. Only much later was it employed as a collective label for the absent receivers of electronically mediated communication.

She points out how these two situations are far from being equivalent. In the former, the producer and receiver of sound are co-present: they share a physical locale. If a valid comparison can be made with the theatre audience, where people are gathered together in one place to give their attention to a stage performance, the parallel with watching television or listening to the radio is less clear. Here, as I stated at the outset, consumption practices are geographically dispersed across a multitude of settings and frequently in competition with other domestic practices as a result of their embedding in day-to-day life. It therefore becomes harder to specify exactly where broadcasting's audiences begin and end. The boundaries of 'audiencehood' are inherently unstable. Radway's discussion certainly does invite us to be suspicious of any efforts to treat the audience unproblematically as a singular, stable entity. In the following section, we shall see how similar doubts concerning the status of television audiences as calculable objects have led to a critique of the industry's perspective on domestic consumption being launched by scholars in the field of media and cultural studies.

Before bringing this introduction to a close, though, I want to highlight an additional feature of the analytical model which Thompson has attempted to build. As well as advocating that we explore the significance of media messages as they are routinely appropriated and interpreted, he encourages us to consider 'the significance of the activity of reception' (Thompson, 1988, p. 378) in its own right. His proposal owed much to the evolving research agenda of David Morley (1980, 1986), whose empirical work on television audiences had spanned both these areas of critical inquiry. So, after investigating the varied responses of viewing groups to selected segments from a popular current affairs programme, Morley proceeded to carry out further research on household contexts of consumption. 'My own interests are now focused on the "how" of television watching', he declared:

> This is to say that I ... prioritize the understanding of the process of television viewing (the activity itself) over the understanding of particular responses to particular types of programme material ... It is for this reason that ... the decision was taken to interview families ... in their own homes – so as to get a better understanding of the ways in which television is watched in its 'natural' domestic context ... I would wish to argue that this is the necessary framework within which we must place our understanding of the particularity of individual responses to different types of programming.
>
> (Morley, 1986, p. 41)

With this shift, his previous concerns with the ideological power of the text and the meanings made by its readers were articulated to new interests in the interpersonal dynamics and 'cultural politics' of the viewing situation – a shift of focus which proved to be absolutely crucial for the study of broadcasting as an institution in everyday life (see below, section 3).

ACTIVITY I

Before reading on, you should first reflect on your own experiences as a consumer of television and radio. Where, when and with whom do you routinely view and listen? How are you addressed by the broadcast media? What kind of responses do you have to those styles of presentation? Does broadcasting ever give you feelings of belonging – to a national culture or to another collectivity of some sort? (See Christine **Gledhill**'s (1997) notes on media fictions and everyday life for further discussion of these ideas.)

2   Ways of addressing and knowing 'the audience'

Ever since the early years of radio, broadcasters have faced the twin problems of how to address and gather knowledge about their dispersed and distant audiences. In the day-to-day production of programmes and the organization of schedules, they were constantly having to ask themselves what was an appropriate way of speaking to their listeners at particular times and in particular domestic places. They were also in the position of knowing very little about the habits or size of their new listening publics. In the intervening period, radio and, later, television have gradually come to develop their own distinctive 'voices' or communicative styles for addressing the consumer in the private sphere, and have found specific ways of inquiring into audience behaviour – most notably through the manufacture of 'ratings' figures. In this part of the chapter, we look historically and critically at these key features of the industry's relationship to its audiences – its orientations towards viewers and listeners in the home environment. You will notice that while most of the examples I draw on refer to British television and radio, there are references to literature on broadcast output and ratings research in the United States when it is deemed relevant to the issues being discussed.

2.1   Intimacy at a distance

We have already touched on John Ellis's (1982) important assertions about the 'domesticity' of television as a medium of communication – the familiar and intimate place of the technology and its symbolic forms in our daily lives – and in order to push those insights further now, it is necessary for us to turn to some of the work done by historian and theorist of British public service broadcasting, Paddy Scannell (1989, 1991). Tracing the emergence of what he chooses to call 'the communicative ethos of broadcasting', Scannell (1989, p. 152) remarks on the tendency of television and radio to employ increasingly 'relaxed ... and spontaneous **modes of address** and forms of talk'. Across a spread of programme types, from studio talk formats through to popular game-shows, he detects the adoption of interactive styles which have traditionally been associated with more private interpersonal encounters – producing a universe of discourse that is designed to be experienced by audiences as ordinary, accessible or sociable.

modes of address

Of course, this feat was not accomplished overnight. Much of the talk to be heard on BBC radio in the pre- and immediate post-war era was marked by a certain degree of awkwardness or 'communicative unease'. An initially authoritarian mode of address, which was combined with a rather paternalist attitude towards the listener, only gave way later to 'a more populist and democratic manner and style' (Scannell, 1991, p. 10). The key to this change was a realization that existing forms of public communication – such as the sermon, the lecture or the stage performance – were wholly inappropriate as models for the routine fare of broadcasting because of the space which separates producers from consumers in mediated interaction, and because of the private nature of reception contexts:

> It was recognized that broadcast output, though articulated in the public domain as public discourse, was received within the sphere of privacy, as an optional leisure resource. Within this sphere ... people did not expect to be talked down to, lectured or 'got at'. They expected to be spoken to in a familiar, friendly and informal manner as if they were equals on the same footing as the speaker. The voices of radio and television ... are heard in the context of household activities and other household voices, as part of the general social arrangements of households and their members. It is this that powerfully drives the communicative style and manner of broadcasting to approximate to the norms not of public forms of talk, but to those of ordinary, informal conversation ... this is overwhelmingly the preferred communicative style of interaction between people in the routine contexts of day-to-day life and especially in the places where they live.
>
> (Scannell, 1991, pp. 3–4)

Although Scannell's chief concern as a historian of public service broadcasting is with the gradual emergence of this communicative ethos in BBC output, it is no accident that the key moment of transformation which he points to – from the late 1950s through into the 1960s – was also the period of ITV's arrival on the media landscape. The confident 'populist tone' of independent commercial television was undoubtedly a significant factor in shifting the style towards a more sociable manner of broadcasting in Britain.

Indeed, on the other side of the Atlantic where television had established itself earlier, a number of the now common characteristics of broadcasting's address to audiences was already assuming a recognizable shape before the mid-1950s. Perhaps the most striking and distinctive of these was the direct address to camera in which television show hosts or presenters spoke to consumers at home in an apparently personal and familiar way – what two American researchers, Donald Horton and Richard Wohl (1956), termed **para-social interaction**. This is the phrase they coined for that routine, taken-for-granted, yet quite remarkable encounter between small-screen personalities and domestic viewers – a serial interaction which takes place at a distance between public performers and their unknown audiences, but which 'simulates' many aspects of regular face-to-face conversation amongst friends or acquaintances. Despite the physical space that separates them, performers and viewers are brought together in live time, so that some of the immediacy of physical co-presence may be captured in circumstances of absence. As Horton and Wohl (1956, p. 215) observed, the television host often 'faces the spectator, uses the mode of direct address, talks as if ... conversing personally or privately'. Referring to popular American programmes of the day such as *The Steve Allen Show*, they believed an illusory yet deeply felt 'bond of intimacy' was being formed in which loyal fans or devotees got to 'know' the personality.

para-social interaction

READING A

You should now turn to Reading A, 'Mass communication and para-social interaction' by Donald Horton and Richard Wohl. As you read, ask yourself if, over forty years later, their observations are still applicable to the role of television personalities in contemporary media culture.

Not having monitored the actual responses of viewers to this direct mode of address, Horton and Wohl might be in danger of assuming too much here about audience identifications and pleasures. There are clearly questions concerning social patterns of identification that they failed to answer satisfactorily – questions to do with which viewing publics appreciate or dislike a particular 'persona' and screen performance. However, their analysis of para-social interaction and 'para-sociability' contains extremely valuable insights into the developing presentational forms of television.

John Langer (1981) picked up one of the main threads of their analysis in his article on television's **personality system**, where he examined the cultural roles played by 'those individuals constituted more or less exclusively for and by television, who make regular appearances as newsreaders, moderators, hosts, compères or characters' (p. 351). His comparison reveals a sharp contrast between these figures and the representatives of the cinematic star system, providing further evidence of broadcasting's distinctive quotidian qualities:

personality system

> Whereas the star system operates from the realms of the spectacular, the inaccessible, the imaginary, presenting the cinematic universe as 'larger than life', the personality system is cultivated ... as 'part of life', whereas the star system always has the ability to place distance between itself and its audiences through its insistence on 'the exceptional', the personality

system works directly to construct and foreground intimacy and immedi
acy; whereas contact with stars is unrelentingly sporadic and uncertain,
contact with television personalities has regularity and predictability;
whereas stars are always playing 'parts' emphasizing their identity as
'stars' as much – perhaps even more than – the characters they play,
television personalities 'play' themselves ... personalities are distinguished
... for their typicality, their 'will to ordinariness'.

(Langer, 1981, pp. 354–5)

Nowhere is this 'will to ordinariness' more evident than in the presentation
of a 1990s' daytime magazine such as *This Morning*. Transmitted on ITV
between mid-morning and lunchtime each day during the week, the show
has a highly segmented format with studio guests, phone-ins and various
lifestyle features. Note that the programme title itself conveys a strong sense
of immediacy – the 'here and now' of live television – which is central to the
communicative ethos of broadcasting. The husband-and-wife team who
present *This Morning* are known and informally addressed by guests and
phone-in callers as 'Richard and Judy' (Figure 5.2). Viewers are also expected
to be on friendly, first-name terms with the personalities hosting the show.

FIGURE 5.2   A simulation of domesticity: Judy Finnigan and Richard
Madeley host *This Morning*.

This Morning actively constructs a simulation of domesticity by having the
studio set furnished in the manner of a family living-room. The two
presenters and their guests sit in armchairs beside a coffee table. To reinforce
this relaxed household atmosphere, their celebrity guests are thanked for
'dropping in' or invited to 'visit again'. At certain pivotal moments in the
magazine show, the personalities' para-social relationship with audiences
has to be established and regularly re-established. The initial encounters at
the start of each broadcast, the points at which viewers are returned to the

studio after some kind of break or video insert, along with closing farewells at the finish – all offer an opportunity for the hosts to talk directly to camera in a casual fashion. The typical greetings and partings uttered by Richard and Judy – 'morning to you', 'hiya', 'bye' and 'see you tomorrow' – reflect a far wider process of change in late-modern culture that Norman Fairclough (1994) calls a *conversationalization of public discourse*. A key characteristic of this cultural trend is what he refers to as **synthetic personalization**, the simulation of a personal relation between a spoken or written text and an audience (ibid., p. 260).

synthetic personalization

Other instances of synthetic personalization and 'performed sincerity' in broadcasting can be found in a long tradition of programmes which could best be described as 'people shows'. This is because they involve different sorts of face-to-face interaction between a television or radio personality and ordinary members of the general public – who also appear momentarily as personalities in front of the camera or microphone – as well as para-social interaction with dispersed domestic audiences. I have in mind Wilfred Pickles presenting *Have a Go!* on BBC radio in the 1950s, and contemporary figures such as Cilla Black on *Blind Date* or Michael Barrymore in *My Kind of People* on ITV in the 1990s (see Figure 5.3). Each of these personalities made their name in broadcasting, not through being extraordinary or special but precisely by seeming to viewers to be familiar, homely and down-to-earth. In chat shows and studio discussions, too, there have been similar television performers whose own names often provided the programme's title – *Wogan, Kilroy!, Esther, Vanessa* and so on. All have presented themselves to viewers as men or women 'of the people', asking common-sense questions on 'our' behalf. From the United States, meanwhile, come programmes which have helped to shape and define those popular genres of studio talk – *Donahue, The Oprah Winfrey Show* and *Ricki Lake*.

FIGURE 5.3 Woman of the people: Cilla Black shares a joke with her contestants on *Blind Date*.

2.2   Behind the ratings

This long search to find suitable modes of address and forms of talk was accompanied by a parallel quest on the part of broadcasting organizations to devise particular ways of researching and 'knowing' their audiences. By the mid-1930s the BBC had set up a Listener Research Department to help to improve the quality of its service to the public – although its precise aims and methods of inquiry were, according to David Chaney (1987, p. 272), rather ill-defined at the outset: 'Not only was the relevance of research accepted only cautiously ... but those concerned were not consistent about what they hoped to do or what ... could be accomplished.'

No such doubts were in evidence when listener research took off in the United States. From the end of the 1920s onwards, ratings figures compiled by market research agencies became the industry's primary measure of performance in the context of a commercial broadcasting system where it was necessary to demonstrate the existence of an audience to potential advertisers or sponsors. As Dallas Smythe (1981) once put it in a provocative and memorable phrase, broadcasting which operates under market conditions is in the business of 'delivering audiences to advertisers'. To ensure its economic survival and prosperity, the industry must fill the spots within or between radio and television programmes. Following that logic, programmes themselves are merely the 'bait' to attract consumers to the advertisements. While symbolic goods manufactured by commercial broadcasters are commodities of a sort, it is ultimately the sale of the audience commodity **audience commodity** which is crucial in financial terms.

On both sides of the Atlantic now, principles of **audience measurement** are audience measurement central to the kind of research conducted and commissioned on the industry's behalf – either by agencies such as Nielsen in America or by the Broadcasters' Audience Research Board (BARB) in Britain, a body jointly funded by the BBC and the various commercial television companies. Despite the continued use of qualitative scales such as viewer 'appreciation indices', it is quantitative data on audience size that currently dominates industry thinking. However, this specific way of thinking and constructing knowledge about television viewing has recently been subjected to a radical critique which comes from outside the institutional framework of broadcasting – notably in the writings of media and cultural studies academic, Ien Ang (1991, 1992). She recognizes that the ratings are institutionally enabling, a necessary 'fiction' for the broadcasters, but also believes them to be epistemologically limited. In other words, they can serve a useful economic function for the industry and yet simultaneously misrepresent everyday activities of television consumption. (See **du Gay, Hall et al.**, 1997, for further discussion of the limits of quantitative methods in explaining consumer practices.)

READING B

You should now turn to Reading B, 'In search of the audience commodity' by Ien Ang. As you read, consider carefully her challenging argument that the audience commodity has no objective existence outside of ratings research – and is therefore produced in those very practices of audience measurement.

The inevitably partial story which Ang tells here, in her work on institutional audience research, is of an industry's on-going desire to convert the 'elusive' occurrence of real people watching television into a known, objectified category. This narrative features an increasingly desperate quest to come up with the perfect technical fix, a 'panoptic' measurement technology that might be able to monitor viewers' movements in front of the screen at every moment of the day or night – thereby revealing the exact size and demographic shape of a television audience to broadcasters and advertisers.

Initially, the technique of audience measurement was quite simple – a questionnaire survey carried out by brief telephone or street interviews. Later, ratings figures were calculated on the basis of data gathered from electronic 'set meters' and diary entries in a chosen 'panel' of households. These panels were samples which had been designed to represent the viewing population as a whole. Their programme choices were supposedly generalizable – resulting in the claim that a given number of people, counted in their millions, watched a particular television broadcast. The set meter gave an accurate statement of when the television was switched on, off or channels were changed. It told researchers which channel was being received in the panel home. A diary served as a supplementary source of data, with the household members being asked to keep a written record of their personal viewing habits.

More recently, though, ratings researchers have acknowledged some of the problems associated with these old-established methods and procedures. Diaries depended upon viewers in the panel homes filling them in conscientiously, and knowing whether a set is switched on is not the same thing as knowing whether anyone is actually looking at the screen. As we know from our own experiences of daily domestic life, 'watching television' is not always a clear-cut activity. Instead, it is frequently done in combination with a range of other tasks – such as reading the newspaper, holding a conversation or eating a meal – so that television has to compete for space and time in the household context. The response of those whose job it is to measure audiences has not been to register the full complexity of situated viewing practices by turning to more qualitative methods of investigation. Rather they continue undaunted in their efforts to transform the complex into the concrete and the calculable, producing a plausible fiction for sale to advertisers.

Faced with the vagaries of domestic consumption, and with viewers who are regularly 'zapping' around multi-channel broadcasting systems or else 'zipping' through video-recorded material, industry or market researchers in both Britain and the United States have now developed an audience measurement technology called the 'people meter'. Designed to monitor individual viewing habits within the panel home, it combines the previous functions of set meter and diary in an integrated electronic gadget:

> When a viewer begins to watch a programme, (s)he must press a numbered button on a portable keypad, which looks like the well-known remote control device. When a viewer stops watching, the button must be pressed again. A monitor attached to the television set lights up regularly to remind the viewer of the button-pushing task. Every member of a sample family has her or his own individual button, while there are also some extra buttons for guests.
>
> (Ang, 1992, p. 137)

Doubts about the co-operation of consumers in using the gadget remain, however, and this has led to the piloting of a further innovation – known as a 'passive people meter'. Here, the necessity for a human hand to intervene is apparently eliminated altogether. The passive people meter is a camera-like, 'image recognition' device fitted to the television set. It is capable of recording precisely which faces in the living room are directed towards the screen. Of course, it cannot tell us what sense viewers might be making of what they see and do, but it does promise finally to realize the dreams of ratings agencies for a panoptic system of audience **surveillance**.

surveillance

'Surveillance' may seem far too strong a term in this particular context, with all the connotations of discipline and control that it carries – yet Ang uses it with exactly those connotations in mind. She comprehends this sort of quantitative research on television viewing as an attempt by the industry to impose a degree of order on what is an increasingly undisciplined and elusive set of cultural practices. The audience for broadcasting is understood as an object which is constituted by the ratings rather than as pre-given entity. Within the terms of her critique, there is no such thing as the television audience – at least not in any coherent, homogeneous form – although she stops short of arguing there is nothing outside of institutional categories, retaining a crucial place in her analysis for 'the social world of actual audiences' (Ang, 1991, p. 13).

That world is the realm of day-to-day life and of household cultures of consumption. It does not lend itself to being measured because it exists as a dispersed domain of lived experiences and cultural meanings – not as a calculable object. For this reason, in order for us to get 'behind the ratings'

(Morley, 1990) to explore these experiences and meanings, we have to adopt different methods with very different purposes:

> The kind of research that needs doing would involve identifying and investigating ... the differences hidden behind the catch-all category of 'watching television'. We all watch television ... but with how much attention and with what degree of commitment, in relation to which types of programmes and occasions? ... Research needs to investigate the complex ways in which television is embedded in a ... range of everyday practices.
>
> (Morley, 1990, p. 8)

In the next section of the chapter, I consider several examples of work in media and cultural studies which has attempted to answer the sort of questions posed in the passage above. As you read on, you will notice that researchers working in this field have adopted what can be described as an **ethnographic approach** to the social world of actual audiences – usually involving conversational interviews with consumers and observations of their routine reception contexts. So, whereas ratings agencies seek to construct a profitable audience commodity through techniques of measurement, reception ethnographers are trying instead to produce rich and detailed accounts of broadcast media consumption which are sensitive to the dynamics of interpretation, taste and power – sensitive, in other words, to the qualitative aspects of reception or 'the politics of the living-room'.

ethnographic approach

3   The social relations of viewing and listening

As we turn our critical attention now to the social relations of viewing and listening in broadcast communication, let us start by restating a couple of interrelated points that were made in the introduction when I was commenting on John Thompson's social theory of the media (Thompson, 1988, 1994). Firstly, media messages have an extended availability in space and time – this is one of the reasons why they are open to being differentially received and appropriated – and, for Thompson (1994, p. 44), the process of appropriation is structured yet selective and creative: 'individuals draw on the resources available to them in order to ... make sense of the symbolic material transmitted by the media'. Secondly, he noted that there are two dimensions to an act of cultural consumption – the meanings and pleasures which are generated in semiotic encounters between a 'text' and a 'reader', and the significance that reception practices themselves have in everyday locations. Each of those important points is taken up and developed further in this section, with reference to selected examples from the literature.

3.1   Interpretation and taste

encoding, decoding

An early attempt in media and cultural studies to conceptualize the interpretation of broadcast messages by distant audiences was Stuart Hall's model of **encoding** and **decoding** in the television discourse (Hall, 1973). His model was designed to deal principally with the ideological dimensions of broadcasting. It drew partly on existing theories of meaning production in semiotics, but also on accounts of social structure and cultural reproduction from the sociological tradition. He sought to explain, on the one hand, how television texts are constructed so as to 'prefer' a particular dominant reading of social events. This is not the result of a conscious bias of the broadcasters, more a taken-for-granted set of assumptions about how the world is to be represented. On the other hand, Hall wanted to account for the engagement of actual readers with the encoded representations which are offered to them by television. His contention was that the varied class positions and cultural knowledges of viewers and listeners are likely to generate differential responses to and interpretations of broadcast texts. Depending on what it is they bring with them to the message, their readings will vary. (Hugh Mackay – in Chapter 6 of this volume – will be deploying the concepts of encoding and decoding, although Mackay's concern there is with the meanings of technologies rather than with interpretations of the texts that are transmitted by a communications technology such as television.) Hall tentatively identified three hypothetical positions from which the decodings of a television text might be made – 'dominant', 'negotiated' and 'oppositional'. In short, the first involves an acceptance of the preferred reading, the second allows a limited challenge to it on matters of local detail, while the third entails a wholesale rejection of the dominant definitions on offer, often accompanied by an effort to provide alternative ones.

David Morley (1980) was later to adopt and adapt this conceptual framework in an empirical research project that set out to analyse the decodings of a television news magazine which were made by groups consisting of managers, students, apprentices or trade unionists. In all, Morley conducted interviews with twenty-nine such groups before using Hall's categories as a way of classifying their differential interpretations of recorded extracts from the programme. For instance, he found management groups, schoolboys and apprentices to inhabit the dominant decoding position and to accept the text's preferred meaning. Negotiated readings were made by teacher-training and university arts students. Trade union groups, depending on their members' roles as either full-time officials or shop stewards, produced versions of a negotiated or oppositional decoding. Meanwhile, the black FE college students interviewed in his study were constructing oppositional readings of another kind altogether – not so much contesting the programme's preferred view of the world as 'refusing' to engage with current affairs coverage that had little relevance to them. Ultimately, though, Morley was constrained by the categories he inherited from Hall. They lacked the subtlety required to cope with certain contradictions which had arisen in an analysis of the group responses. So, for example, bank managers who occupied a dominant decoding position were nevertheless dismissive of the populist style in which events and issues were presented. The reverse was also the case for groups of trade unionists: while some respondents were willing to endorse the programme's presentational style, the shop stewards forcefully rejected what was perceived to be its right-wing political sympathies and its failure to tackle fundamental questions about class and economics. There are evident difficulties in trying to hold onto both of those dimensions of decoding at once. What the interviewees said, or did not say, to the researcher was only partly concerned with distances taken from a preferred reading – the stances they adopted in relation to specific ideological propositions or framings; the responses of the bank managers or trade unionists clearly had just as much to do with patterns of taste and preference. Indeed, it may have been a little premature to ask how the text is interpreted when several of Morley's research subjects did not routinely watch the early evening programme that he was inviting them to discuss.

This led him to propose, in his critical postscript to the project (Morley, 1981), a more 'genre-based' model of media consumption which could focus its attention on the 'salience' of particular types of text for particular sorts of reader – and on the **cultural competencies** necessary for viewers and listeners to be able to understand and enjoy various genres of broadcast output. It would, he stated, 'involve us in dealing more with the relevance/ irrelevance and comprehension/incomprehension dimensions of decoding rather than being directly concerned with the acceptance or rejection of substantive ideological themes' (ibid., p. 10).

> cultural competencies

A consequence of this modified approach was that pleasure and displeasure were to be investigated as complex social accomplishments. In other words, our likes and dislikes are not just to be approached as a matter of personal taste; rather they are related to our position in the social structure. It was recognized that enjoyment of a given television or radio programme requires an articulation of certain generic forms and preoccupations with those unevenly distributed stocks of 'cultural capital' (Bourdieu, 1984) which different audiences or taste publics possess. Much of the subsequent research on decoding went on to examine issues of gender and genre – choosing to look, for instance, at women's engagements with soap opera. (Again, see **Gledhill**, 1997, on gendered competencies.) Carried out in the main by feminist researchers in media and cultural studies, this work was often motivated by a political desire to 'rescue' previously denigrated feminine pleasures and to demonstrate the highly skilled and discriminating nature of fans' preferences. Writing in a journal known for its championing of avant-garde 'art-house' cinema, Charlotte Brunsdon (1981) suggested somewhat controversially that the competent soap-opera viewer deserves to be treated as seriously as the film buff:

> Just as a Godard film requires the possession of certain forms of cultural capital on the part of its audience ... an extra-textual familiarity with ...

artistic, linguistic, political and cinematic discourses – so too does soap opera ... It is the culturally constructed skills of femininity – sensitivity, perception, intuition and the necessary privileging of the concerns of personal life – which are both called on and practised in the genre.

(Brunsdon, 1981, p. 36)

Ethnographies which try to re-evaluate positively the pleasures of popular television – producing what Brunsdon was later to call a 'redemptive reading' – can run the risk of celebrating subordinated experiences uncritically. The dangers of 'going native' here are great. Equally great, though, is the importance of mapping gendered distinctions in media consumption. It enabled feminist critics to open up a politics of cultural taste and value, shaking the foundations of established aesthetic judgement and giving an authentic voice to viewing communities that had been mocked or silenced in the past. Dorothy Hobson's (1982) work on the now defunct serial, *Crossroads*, is a good case in point. She visited the homes of female fans, watching an episode of the programme and getting into discussion with them about the characters and storylines. Her research revealed an intriguing mix of feelings amongst these women about their favourite programme. They were able to talk at considerable length about what it was they enjoyed, but were also deeply conscious of the low status which their pleasures had in the wider cultural economy – leading many to be either apologetic or defensive. So some seemed to accept, with reluctance, the dismissive judgements of *Crossroads* being made by husbands or television critics – yet others were well aware they had a rich stock of feminine skills at their disposal. This awareness is neatly expressed in the following extract from the interview transcripts: 'Men ... think it's just stupid and unrealistic because they are not brought up to accept emotional situations ... They don't like it 'cos it's sometimes sentimental ... I don't know any men who watch it' (Hobson, 1982, p. 109).

Of course, we must be careful not to reduce cultural distinctions of this kind to an essential biological difference between the sexes. Feminist theorists in media and cultural studies have been keen to stress that **gendered identifications** with different genres of broadcast output are always socially constructed and historically contingent. The list of skills which Brunsdon presents us with above – sensitivity, perception, intuition and a privileging of 'the personal' – is not a catalogue of 'natural' female attributes but a recognition that, under present cultural circumstances, many women have made a heavy investment in the sphere of 'emotionally significant ... interaction' (Brunsdon, 1981, p. 34). It would be possible for a biological male to occupy the same imaginative realm. In practice, given current masculine discourses and subjectivities, men rarely do. Instead, the masculine 'world' of television is more typically populated by news, current affairs, sport and 'realist' fiction (Morley, 1986).

gendered
identifications

FIGURE 5.4 Rita Fairclough and Mavis Wilton in *Coronation Street.*
Emotionally significant interaction: what makes soap opera pleasurable
for viewers?

> ### ACTIVITY 2
>
> You should pause at this point and make a note of those types of
> television and radio programme which you most like or dislike. What is
> it about them that gives you such feelings of pleasure or displeasure?
> Which cultural knowledges and competencies are required in order to
> appreciate the genres you enjoy? How are these knowledges and
> competencies related to your social position – in terms of gender, but
> perhaps in terms of class, generation or ethnicity too? Have you ever
> experienced any embarrassment with regard to your tastes and
> preferences?

It is interesting that men should dismiss classic soap opera on occasion as
'unrealistic' because women who enjoy the genre will frequently say they
like it precisely for its 'true to life' qualities. This was what Ien Ang (1985)
found when she analysed letters which were sent to her by Dutch followers
of the globally distributed American serial, *Dallas*. Many of the
correspondents indicated that their enjoyment of the programme was derived
in large measure from its relevance to everyday experience. For example, 'I
like watching it ... because ... it's really ordinary daily problems more than
anything that occur in it and that you recognize ... the characters reflect the
daily life of a family' (Ang, 1985, p. 43).

Bearing in mind the obvious imbalance between the Ewings' extravagant
lifestyle at Southfork and the day-to-day domestic conditions of television
viewers in Holland, we might be surprised initially – as Ang was – to find
Dallas being understood in quite this way. She faced the predicament of how
to account for the puzzling claims of her letter-writers, who were responding
to fictional representations produced on the other side of the Atlantic. Her

emotional realism
solution was to introduce the concept of **emotional realism**. She saw that the correspondents were empathizing with the characters and situations in what is basically a family tragedy. A powerful emotional resonance rendered the fiction real and pleasurable for them.

As melodrama, *Dallas* embodies what Ang named the 'tragic structure of feeling'. Whereas British and Australian soap operas are sometimes ridiculed for their lack of dramatic action, critics of American serials like this one usually accuse them of the exact opposite – of overplaying sensational incident. In the life of the Ewing family, then, there is a literally unbelievable procession of major events and crises – but the deliberate purpose of these exaggerated plot-lines is to heighten emotional tension. Dismissing the programme as 'overdone' is to miss the point completely. It strives to stir the passions with its continual round of remarkable happenings. Whether or not audiences are duly stirred depends on the dispositions which are brought to the text by its readers:

> The tragic structure of feeling, which is inscribed in the meaning-structure of *Dallas*, will not automatically and obviously agree with the meanings viewers apply ... That will only happen if they are sensitive to it. In other words, the tragic structure of feeling ... will only make sense if one can ... project oneself onto, i.e. recognize, a 'melodramatic imagination'. Viewers must therefore have a certain ... orientation to understand and evaluate *Dallas* in a melodramatic way.
>
> (Ang, 1985, p. 79)

Ang suggests this melodramatic imagination is a predominantly feminine recognition. She notes that it emerges out of a willingness to face 'life's torments' from a particular emotional standpoint. It results in a vicarious identification with characters such as Sue Ellen or Miss Ellie – a wife driven to drink by a scheming husband and a mother who carries the worries of the whole family on her shoulders – both seen as 'really human' by several of the women who wrote letters to the researcher.

However, popular programmes like *Dallas* have obviously not gone out to a wholly female audience. Ang acknowledged that there must be pleasures in the text which are on offer to men as well. Speculating about possible masculine readings, she wondered whether their enjoyment might have come more from a recognition of 'the business relations and problems, the cowboy elements, and the power and wealth represented' (Ang, 1985, p. 118). Her suspicion was that male viewers are unlikely to have the same orientation towards the tragic structure of feeling. In a survey of prime-time soaps, Geraghty (1991) traces the growing trend of introducing narrative features into the continuous serial which are familiar from other genres. To widen the appeal of their programmes, producers are bringing in a broader range of male characters – developing plot-lines reminiscent of crime series or else working with sports themes. *Brookside* and *EastEnders* may be read as examples of this 'defeminization' process. (See **Gledhill**'s (1997) conclusion, especially her notes on 'Soap opera: a woman's form no more?' in section 6.1. Also see Daniel Miller's discussion of how a US serial is appropriated by viewers in Trinidad, in Chapter 1 of this volume.)

3.2   Power in domestic cultures

While the literature on interpretation and taste which I discuss above has encouraged us to examine social constructions of meaning and pleasure in media consumption, we now need to consider further the significance that reception practices themselves have in our everyday lives – the 'how' of viewing and listening in domestic cultures. This means investigating the household uses of television and radio as technologies, asking about their status as objects in the home alongside their role as providers of broadcast output. It will also be necessary for us to think about how communication technologies become embedded in the interpersonal dynamics and power relations of life in **the private sphere**.

the private sphere

One of the difficulties which we face in doing this is that broadcasting is so much a taken-for-granted part of modern domestic experience, an institution in everyday life, that it is not easy to distance ourselves enough to explore its significance in routine situations. A way around the problem is to chart the historical formation of broadcasting's relationship with the home, and my own oral history research on the entry and incorporation of early radio into household contexts in the 1920s and '30s was an attempt to begin this mapping (Moores, 1988). What I found when talking to elderly people about their memories of 'the box on the dresser' was evidence of living-room wars being fought out between men and women over the initial arrival of the gadget in domestic geographies and routines. Masculine discourses constituted radio sets as 'toys for the boys', as objects for technical experimentation, whereas a typical feminine response was to treat the technology as a troublesome intruder. Only later did women come to welcome the wireless, as changes were made to the form of the listening apparatus, and broadcasters started to address their audience as 'the family' – seeking to construct the cosy pleasures of the hearth. (See Hugh Mackay's account of my work on early radio in section 5.1 of Chapter 6 of this volume.)

Nevertheless, despite popular images which still depict a harmonious family audience gathered around the television set, it would appear from recent ethnographic research on viewing practices that the realities of household life are often less cosy and idyllic. For instance, Hermann Bausinger (1984) observed how turning on the television can signify very different things depending on the context of the act and the intentions of the person who is switching it on. In certain circumstances, it might mean 'I want to watch this', but at other times it could equally be signalling 'I would like to hear and see nothing'. James Lull (1990, p. 36) has referred to similar sorts of mundane activity as tactics of affiliation and avoidance. His typology of the social uses of television in the home is extremely valuable in highlighting numerous **relational uses** to which the technology is put by its consumers – and, here, he is arguing that television may either serve as a basis for a shared occasion or an excuse for not communicating with fellow family members at all. You will probably be able to recognize this distinction from your own past or present experiences of day-to-day domestic living.

relational uses

Lull is interested, too, in how families select television programmes to watch. This is potentially an indicator of **power relations** within a household – especially if there are clashes of taste and preference. Reporting on research during the 1980s in the United States, he concludes:

power relations

> The locus of control in the programme selection process can be explained primarily by family position ... In this study, observational and survey data converged to demonstrate convincingly that fathers had more perceived and actual control of the selection of television programmes than any other individual in the family. Mothers were the least influential family members in this regard.

> (Lull, 1990, p. 93)

The same conclusions were reached independently by Morley (1986, 1988) in Britain following conversational interviews which he taped at the homes of eighteen families from south London. A limitation of his previous decoding study had been its failure to situate viewers' interpretations of television in the 'natural' settings of domestic life, and this follow-up research was designed to explore precisely that – to track down the medium's meanings at the site of reception. So the purpose of Morley's conversations with consumers was to supply qualitative data for an analysis of television reception as a routine 'social event'. Looking at the interview transcripts, he saw a consistency of response around gender-related themes – starting with the question of power and control over programme choice.

READING C

You should now turn to Reading C, 'The framework of family viewing in Great Britain', by David Morley. As you read, ask yourself to what extent the data presented in this extract reflect and resonate with the circumstances of watching television in your home.

Morley admitted there were also some limitations to this follow-up study. It focused exclusively on traditional 'nuclear' family units in which both parents lived together with their dependent children. In addition, all were white, lower middle- or working-class households located in a specific urban area. This led the researcher to be quite cautious about the generalizability of his findings, claiming them 'to be representative, at most, of viewing patterns within one type of household, drawn from one particular ethnic and geographic context and from a relatively narrow range of class positions' (Morley, 1986, p. 11). However, gender is also a significant variable in the vast majority of domestic cultures – even if the gender dynamics of other household types may differ.

With the benefit of hindsight, we can now add a further qualification to those listed by Morley – the historical specificity of his findings. Back in the mid-1980s when he carried out that research, it was far more common for a household to have a single television set around which struggles for control of family viewing would take place. Today, though, many of us will live in homes where there is multiple set ownership and where other screens – such as personal computers or video games – compete with television for our attention. The home is becoming a 'cellular' media environment, with the consumption and use of communication technologies taking increasingly fragmented and individualized forms. Even so, power relations in domestic settings remain a pressing issue. There are questions about who gets to watch the main set in the living-room and who makes do with a smaller screen in the bedroom or kitchen.

On a final note in this section, I invite you to consider whether Morley's investigation is centrally concerned with broadcasting after all, or whether his work here takes us in the direction of a broader sociology of the family. Television viewing certainly gives him a good 'way in' to the private domain, a convenient point of departure, but maybe we could conclude that the emphasis he puts on processes of domestic interaction and on divisions of labour and leisure transcends any narrow interest in media audiences. If our objective is to comprehend television's 'embedding' in everyday household life (Silverstone, 1990), then the boundaries of 'reception studies' – like the boundaries of audiencehood itself – become increasingly unstable. In fact, there are several striking parallels between the stories told by Morley's interviewees and remarks made by women in an ethnography of family food consumption carried out by Charles and Kerr (1988).

Just as in Morley's sample, which features homes where men had the symbolic power to control programme choice, so Charles and Kerr found that the content of meals in households they visited was usually determined by the husbands' tastes. The wives' culinary preferences were often less conservative – they were willing to try out new flavours and 'foreign' dishes – but the men's demands for so-called 'proper meals' limited what could be served up. As you listen to the voices of the women below, compare them with those quoted in the reading by Morley:

> 'My husband is very traditional-minded about food ... so I tend to stick to the same thing most weeks – I rarely buy anything just for myself ... I'd like to eat all sorts of foods, foreign foods, but I don't bother ... I forgo it.'

> 'If I cook something that's got a whiff of herbs in it he'll put his knife and fork down and say, "I'm sorry but I'm not eating it." ... He usually waits until ... I've prepared something a bit out of the ordinary, and he'll leave it. I'm not happy but there again I'll not make a scene. I'm not one for rowing.'

'I cook what I know he will like ... I mean I won't try things knowing he won't like them. Things like pasta, I know he won't eat that, so I don't cook it.'

(Charles and Kerr, 1988, pp. 70–2)

Gendered relationships to the two domestic technologies involved – a television remote-control device and a kitchen cooker – are obviously different. Men dominate use of the former yet they delegate responsibility for operating the latter to women. But still the same basic dynamic is revealed in each of these separate research projects. Where there is a clash of tastes, it is masculine preferences which tend to prevail – while the women feel that their place as wife and mother requires them to exercise a degree of 'self-denial'.

guilty pleasures

The exceptions to this general rule in Morley's study were particular instances where women took the opportunity to indulge in the **guilty pleasures** of solo viewing, managing to escape temporarily from their ongoing duties as wives and mothers by watching a film on video or a favourite television serial when the rest of the family were out of the house: 'If I'm here alone, I try to get something a bit mushy and then I sit ... and have a cry ... I enjoy that ... I get one of those love stories if he's not in ... Yes, it's on his nights out. It doesn't happen very often' (Morley, 1986, p. 160). In parallel, Charles and Kerr (1988, p. 71) discovered an example of what we might call the guilty pleasures of a 'solo serving': 'I have a passion for spaghetti and butter, that kind of thing, which nobody else in the family likes, so occasionally I do that ... when I'm on my own.'

4   Senses of identity and formations of 'community'

If my comparison between television viewing and food consumption helps us to see how broadcasting's audiences are caught up in a contextual web of domestic relations, we must remember what it is that distinguishes media technologies from other objects in the household setting. Through sound and image, broadcasting serves to connect the private sphere of the home with various public worlds beyond the front door, mediating our senses of personal and collective identity. Television and radio provide us with routine access to flows of communication and information which can then be appropriated in what Anthony Giddens (1991) names the *reflexive project of the self*. Broadcasting also brings us into intimate contact with events in far away locations and makes available different identifications with its 'territories of transmission' at a regional, national or trans-national level. In this last section of the chapter, we will be searching for ways of explaining those changing connections between the local and the global – exploring the consequences for formations of self and community.

4.1   The mediation of experience

Although he has little to say in specific terms about broadcasting as an institution in everyday life, Giddens (1990, 1991) offers an account of modern institutions and ways of living which deals precisely with the shifting relations between local cultures and globalizing processes. His social theory of modernity seeks to explain how the small details of personal experience and self-identity are now inextricably bound up with large-scale institutional and technological transformations, so that one of the main aims of his work is to try to understand how it feels to live in the modern age – to comprehend what could well be described as the 'subjective side' of social change. He demonstrates a deep concern, then, with experiential or phenomenological issues – yet he insists on approaching them with reference to broader historical questions about the distinctive character of contemporary society.

The starting-point for his discussion of experience and self-identity in conditions of late-modernity is an argument which has to do with 'the separation of time and space'. He asserts that in the transition from traditional to modern society, social relationships have increasingly been 'lifted' out of situated locales and 'stretched' across often vast geographical distances – resulting in a **disembedding** of social systems. For people who lived in pre-modern cultures, the experience of time had tended to be linked to a sense of place. 'When' was closely associated with 'where', and with regular natural occurrences such as the cycle of the seasons. Modernity, in contrast, is characterized by 'empty time' – uniformly measured by the mechanical clock and standardized over space with the adoption of worldwide time-zoning and a common calendar. In turn, this gives rise to a corresponding 'emptying of space' – its dislocation or 'tearing' from the particularities of place:

disembedding

> 'Place' is best conceptualized by means of the idea of locale, which refers to the physical settings of social activity ... In pre-modern societies, space and place largely coincide, since the spatial dimensions of social life are, for most of the population, and in most respects, dominated by 'presence' – by localized activities. The advent of modernity increasingly tears space away from place by fostering relations between 'absent' others, locationally distant from any given situation of face-to-face interaction.
>
> (Giddens, 1990, p. 18)

In addition, not only are relations with others no longer confined to a bounded locale, but daily life is touched to a much greater extent by forces or happenings from afar. Places become 'phantasmagoric'; they are 'thoroughly penetrated by ... influences quite distant from them' (ibid., p. 19).

Giddens accounts for this lifting and stretching of social relations by pointing to key disembedding mechanisms. For instance, he examines the role of a 'symbolic token' like money. In its fully developed form as information on a computer screen rather than as bank-notes or coins, it functions as a means of removing financial transactions from specific contexts of exchange – and on the international money markets, such a transaction may be made between two traders located on opposite sides of the globe. Similarly, he does acknowledge the part played by television, radio and other media in redefining what Joshua Meyrowitz (1985) has

situational geography

called the **situational geography** of social life: 'With ... mass communication, particularly electronic communication, the interpenetration of self-development and social systems, up to and including global systems, becomes ever more pronounced' (Giddens, 1991, p. 4). Our experiences are no longer place-bound in quite the same way as they once were prior to the arrival of modern electronic media in the twentieth century. Many of the materials which we draw upon in order to construct senses of personal identity are mediated.

This is certainly not to suggest that local experience and face-to-face interaction have ceased to be important in the formation of the modern self. Despite the potential for access to global networks of communication and information, there is still a powerful 'compulsion of proximity' (Boden and Molotch, 1994) in contemporary culture. It is also the case that those immediate contacts which we develop with family, friends and colleagues continue to shape our senses of who we are and our subjective outlooks on the world. Rather, the task here for media and cultural theory is to think through the nature of the articulation between local and mediated experience in the day-to-day routines and biographies of social subjects.

John Thompson (1995) expresses exactly what is at stake when he writes about the changing 'interaction mix' of modern life, and the fashioning of self and experience in technologically mediated cultural environments:

> Living in a mediated world involves a continuous interweaving of different forms of experience. For most individuals, as they move along the time–space paths of their daily lives, lived experience continues to exert a powerful influence ... we think of ourselves and our life trajectories primarily in relation to the others whom, and the events which, we encounter ... in the practical contexts of our daily lives. However ... while lived experience remains fundamental, it is increasingly supplemented by, and ... displaced by, mediated experience, which assumes a greater and greater role in the process of self-formation. Individuals increasingly draw on mediated experience to inform and refashion the project of the self.
>
> (Thompson, 1995, p. 233)

His notion of the self as a symbolic 'project' is borrowed from Giddens' social theory, and it requires some explanation since you may not have come across that conception of subjectivity before. For Giddens, self-identity has to do with the capacity 'to keep a particular narrative going' – individuals make use of those symbolic resources which are to hand as they struggle to maintain an ongoing 'story' about the self. For example, he contends that the serial form in broadcasting can provide its viewers with 'a feeling of coherent narrative which is a reassuring balance to difficulties in sustaining the **narrative of the self** in actual social situations' (Giddens, 1991, p. 199). More generally, though, the argument is that we each act as our own 'unofficial biographer' – trying to produce a meaningful story with a past, present and future. The specific kinds of story being told will inevitably differ, as there is only a limited range of 'scripts' available to us in our different cultural circumstances, but the wider principles of autobiographical narration are common in the late modern era. (You should refer back to Ruth Finnegan's valuable remarks on 'storying the self' in Chapter 2 above.)

narrative of the self

ACTIVITY 3

You should pause again at this point and consider the conception of selfhood which is summarized above. How convincing do you find the proposition that identity is a narrative construction? Do you ever tell yourself stories about who you are and where your life is heading? What forms do these narratives take, and what purposes do you think they serve? Are any of the biographical storylines which you use recognizable from your experiences of mediated culture – and of television and radio programmes in particular?

A further significant feature of self-formation, according to Giddens and Thompson, is the highly 'reflexive' nature of that project. Narrating personal identity requires us constantly to monitor our routine activities and to reflect on various lifestyle options. Indeed, modernity is characterized by a distinctive type of **institutional reflexivity** – where the knowledge produced about social life becomes a constitutive element in its organization and transformation. For instance, we might consider how information circulated in the public domain concerning global ecological issues can impact on the local purchasing decisions of private individuals who revise their day-to-day practices in the light of this flow of communication. The same goes for knowledge or advice – distributed via the broadcast media – about health matters or else how to cope with moral dilemmas and emotional problems. These television and radio discourses are selectively and reflexively appropriated by viewers and listeners as they monitor their lifestyles or interpersonal relationships.

institutional reflexivity

4.2   Electronic landscapes

So far in this final section I have concentrated on the making of personal rather than collective identities – although the theorists whose work we have looked at clearly see the self as a social product which is fashioned at the interface between private lives and public cultures. I now want us to focus on formations of modern community in greater detail. Many aspects of the analysis presented above are still relevant here – especially those insights offered by Giddens into the 'emptying' of space and time, and the disembedding of social systems. Whereas pre-modern communities were chiefly organized around a fixed place or location, mediated experience has meant that contemporary community is increasingly stretched across spatial distances, yet held together in conditions of temporal simultaneity. The institution and technologies of broadcasting are therefore central to our changing senses of collective identity.

Communities might best be understood as 'fictional realities'. They appear to have an objective existence, but are actually products of the imagination. In his book on the origin and spread of nationalism, historian Benedict Anderson (1983) has adopted this line of argument, referring to nations themselves as **imagined communities**. (See also Nigel Thrift's discussion of Anderson in section 2 of Chapter 4 in this volume.) A short passage in Anderson's book which is of particular interest to us concerns the symbolic function of media consumption in the 'fictioning' of nationhood. He comments on the ritual act of reading the newspaper, taking it to be a sign of the individual consumer's participation in an 'extraordinary mass ceremony':

imagined
communities

> The significance of this mass ceremony ... is paradoxical. It is performed in silent privacy, in the lair of the skull. Yet each communicant is well aware that the ceremony he [sic] performs is being replicated simultaneously by thousands (or millions) of others of whose existence he is confident ... Furthermore, this ceremony is incessantly repeated at daily or half-daily intervals throughout the calendar. What more vivid figure for the ... historically clocked, imagined community can be envisioned? At the same time, the newspaper reader, observing exact replicas of his own paper being consumed ... is continually reassured that the imagined world is rooted in everyday life ... creating that remarkable confidence of community in anonymity which is the hallmark of modern nations.
>
> (Anderson, 1983, p. 35)

The same sort of confidence of community in anonymity was available to audiences for public service broadcasting in Britain with the arrival of radio and, later, television (Scannell and Cardiff, 1991). In fact, the experience of simultaneous reception that Anderson describes was probably heightened with the coming of the broadcast media. Programmes were heard or seen 'live' by absent millions who were dispersed in their domestic settings. So, from the privacy of their homes, listeners or viewers could now tune into a common schedule of broadcast output – including national news bulletins and coverage of major state and sporting occasions. They were thereby invited to identify with a wider 'general public', to imagine themselves as members of a national community which then became reproduced through broadcasting day in day out, week in week out, and year in year out. Although it was a public institution of the modern age, the BBC gradually 'invented' its own traditions, establishing its own calendar of events. One such occasion was the monarch's Christmas Day message, first instituted back in the 1930s yet accepted soon afterwards as a taken-for-granted part of the festive period. This event involved the head of state speaking directly and intimately to the British people, addressing them both individually and collectively as national subjects.

Today, however, that traditional feeling of confidence in the existence of the nation as a shared community is not so readily available from broadcasting. Of course, the BBC continues to provide its viewers and listeners with common access to a schedule of national programming, but by the 1990s several factors have contributed to a shift in the imaginative geography of community and in broadcasting's 'electronic landscapes' (Morley and Robins, 1995). (Think back to Nigel Thrift's arguments in Chapter 4 about changing senses of identity and belonging.) Alongside more general changes in the organization of modern institutions – the scale of trade and commerce, or the expanding geographical 'reach' of telecommunication and transportation networks – we are witnessing a trend towards the 'trans-nationalization' or **globalization** of media and audiences. The 'deregulation'   globalization of broadcasting and the introduction of new technologies for cable and satellite transmission have led to greater competition between television companies. A good example of this is the battle between satellite and terrestrial broadcasters over the right to cover major sporting events – in which a multinational company run by an Australian tycoon is currently seeking to prise previously sacrosanct occasions like the English FA Cup Final from the BBC's grasp. Indeed, policies of deregulation have led to a marked decline in the influence of national public service broadcasting within Western European countries:

> The political and social concerns of the public service era ... with national culture and identity ... have come to be regarded as factors inhibiting the development of new media markets ... Driven now by the logic of profit and competition, the overriding objective of the new media corporations is to get their product to the largest number of consumers. There is ... an expansionist tendency at work, pushing ceaselessly towards the construction of enlarged audio-visual spaces and markets. The imperative is to break down the old frontiers of national communities ... Audio-visual geographies are thus becoming detached from the symbolic spaces of national culture ... The new media order is set to become a global order.
>
> (Morley and Robins, 1995, p. 11)

In these changed economic circumstances, a crucial question is how viewers in the local context are responding to global shifts. As David Morley and Kevin Robins (1995, p. 64) have stressed, any discussion of the impact of new television technologies and **territories of transmission** 'needs to be   territories of grounded in the analysis of ... everyday practices and domestic rituals'. It is   transmission necessary, then, for us to enter the private sphere of the home – in order to ask what difference the altered 'menu' of cultural resources offered by a technology like satellite television is making to patterns of identification.

My own qualitative research into the consumption of satellite television in three residential areas of a South Wales city (Moores, 1996) can be seen as a modest attempt to answer that difficult question, along with several others which are to do with the dynamics of daily life in particular urban places. The work is based on interviews and observations carried out in household and neighbourhood settings, where I sought to investigate the articulation of local and mediated experience – situating the technology within social contexts of reception and use.

> READING D
>
> You should now turn to Reading D, 'Satellite television and everyday life', by Shaun Moores. As you read, consider how discourses of innovation and conservation here are mapped onto divisions of gender and generation in domestic life – and the ways in which they help to shape senses of personal or collective identity.

It should be emphasized that my analysis of the two families discussed in this extract refuses to link technological change directly with cultural transformation. The arrival of a television technology and its programme services does not translate automatically into new identifications. Instead, I am calling for a more cautious approach in which we identify connections between broadcasting's **spaces of identity** and the existing social subjectivities of consumers. Expressions of 'Europeanness' – and orientations towards 'Britishness' or 'Americanness' – must be explained in those specific terms.

spaces of identity

Our model of collective identities and imagined communities must remain flexible enough to cope with contradictions too. For instance, I interviewed a middle-class couple who regularly watched CNN and ABC news broadcasts on satellite television in an effort to sustain a sense of trans-Atlantic reach that they had developed through travel to the United States: 'We're Americophiles ... we like to know what's going on over there – and the satellite keeps you up to date as it happens' (Moores, 1996, p. 55). Despite their declared interest in all things American, though, this couple tell me they feel fervently Welsh 'when it comes to rugby matches' screened on terrestrial stations. Meanwhile, when travelling abroad in Europe, they are anxious about being labelled as British 'because of the lager louts and the Crimplene frocks', and are pleased to be mistaken for Germans as the husband is a competent German speaker; yet their views on some political issues are surprisingly close to those of the 'Eurosceptics' in Britain. Evidently, the same individuals in different contexts can associate themselves with quite varied formations of community.

In conclusion, I would encourage you to reflect on your own cultural identifications and associations with the idea of community – taking into consideration the various channels of access which television and radio now give you to electronic landscapes. Think carefully about the types of 'journey' that you are being invited to make from the confines of your domestic environment, and also about your participation with others in everyday rituals or 'ceremonies' of the kind described earlier by Anderson. You might want to pay particular attention to any contradictory elements in your sense of collective identity.

References

ANDERSON, B. (1983) *Imagined Communities: reflections on the origin and spread of nationalism*, London, Verso.

ANG, I. (1985) *Watching 'Dallas': soap opera and the melodramatic imagination*, London, Methuen.

ANG, I. (1991) *Desperately Seeking the Audience*, London, Routledge.

ANG, I. (1992) 'Living room wars: new technologies, audience measurement and the tactics of television consumption' in Silverstone, R. and Hirsch, E. (eds) *Consuming Technologies: media and information in domestic spaces*, pp. 131–45, London, Routledge.

BAUSINGER, H. (1984) 'Media, technology and daily life', *Media, Culture and Society*, Vol. 6, No. 4, pp. 343–51.

BODEN, D. and MOLOTCH, H. (1994) 'The compulsion of proximity' in Friedland, R. and Boden, D. (eds) *NowHere: space, time and modernity*, pp. 257–86, Berkeley, CA, University of California Press.

BOURDIEU, P. (1984) *Distinction: a social critique of the judgement of taste*, London, Routledge and Kegan Paul.

BRUNSDON, C. (1981) '*Crossroads*: notes on soap opera', *Screen*, Vol. 22, No. 4, pp. 32–7.

CHANEY, D. (1987) 'Audience research and the BBC in the 1930s: a mass medium comes into being' in Curran, J., Smith, A. and Wingate, P. (eds) *Impacts and Influences: essays on media power in the twentieth century*, pp. 259–77, London, Methuen.

CHARLES, N. and KERR, M. (1988) *Women, Food and Families*, Manchester, Manchester University Press.

CORNER, J. (1995) *Television Form and Public Address*, London, Edward Arnold.

DU GAY, P., HALL, S., JANES, L., MACKAY, H. and NEGUS, K. (1997) *Doing Cultural Studies: the story of the Sony Walkman*, London, Sage/The Open University (Book 1 in this series).

ELLIS, J. (1982) *Visible Fictions: cinema, television, video*, London, Routledge and Kegan Paul.

FAIRCLOUGH, N. (1994) 'Conversationalization of public discourse and the authority of the consumer' in Keat, R., Whiteley, N. and Abercrombie, N. (eds) *The Authority of the Consumer*, pp. 253–68, London, Routledge.

GERAGHTY, C. (1981) 'The continuous serial: a definition' in Dyer, R., Geraghty, C., Jordan, M., Lovell, T., Paterson, R. and Stewart, J., *Coronation Street*, pp. 9–26, London, British Film Institute.

GERAGHTY, C. (1991) *Women and Soap Opera: a study of prime-time soaps*, Cambridge, Polity.

GIDDENS, A. (1990) *The Consequences of Modernity*, Cambridge, Polity.

GIDDENS, A. (1991) *Modernity and Self-identity: self and society in the late modern age*, Cambridge, Polity.

GLEDHILL, C. (1997) 'Genre and gender: the case of soap opera' in Hall, S. (ed.) *Representation: cultural representations and signifying practices*, London, Sage/The Open University (Book 2 in this series).

HALL, S. (1973) 'Encoding and decoding in the television discourse', Stencilled Paper, Centre for Contemporary Cultural Studies, University of Birmingham.

HOBSON, D. (1982) *'Crossroads': the drama of a soap opera*, London, Methuen.

HORTON, D. and WOHL, R. (1956) 'Mass communication and para-social interaction: observations on intimacy at a distance', *Psychiatry*, Vol. 19, No. 3, pp. 215–29.

LANGER, J. (1981) 'Television's "personality system"', *Media, Culture and Society*, Vol. 3, No. 4, pp. 351–65.

LULL, J. (1990) *Inside Family Viewing: ethnographic research on television's audiences*, London, Routledge.

MEYROWITZ, J. (1985) *No Sense of Place: the impact of electronic media on social behavior*, New York, Oxford University Press.

MOORES, S. (1988) '"The box on the dresser": memories of early radio and everyday life', *Media, Culture and Society*, Vol. 10, No. 1, pp. 23–40.

MOORES, S. (1996) *Satellite Television and Everyday Life: articulating technology*, Acamedia Research Monograph 18, Luton, John Libbey Media/University of Luton Press.

MORLEY, D. (1980) *The 'Nationwide' Audience: structure and decoding*, London, British Film Institute.

MORLEY, D. (1981) 'The "Nationwide" Audience: a critical postscript', *Screen Education*, No. 39, pp. 3–14.

MORLEY, D. (1986) *Family Television: cultural power and domestic leisure*, London, Comedia.

MORLEY, D. (1988) 'Domestic relations: the framework of family viewing in Great Britain' in Lull, J. (ed.) *World Families Watch Television*, pp. 22–48, Newbury Park, CA, Sage.

MORLEY, D. (1990) 'Behind the ratings' in Willis, J. and Wollen, T. (eds) *The Neglected Audience*, pp. 5–14, London, British Film Institute.

MORLEY, D. and ROBINS, K. (1995) *Spaces of Identity: global media, electronic landscapes and cultural boundaries*, London, Routledge.

RADWAY, J. (1988) 'Reception study: ethnography and the problems of dispersed audiences and nomadic subjects', *Cultural Studies*, Vol. 2, No. 3, pp. 359–76.

RATH, C. (1985) 'The invisible network: television as an institution in everyday life' in Drummond, P. and Paterson, R. (eds) *Television in Transition: papers from the First International Television Studies Conference*, pp. 199–204, London, British Film Institute.

SCANNELL, P. (1989) 'Public Service Broadcasting and modern public life', *Media, Culture and Society*, Vol. 11, No. 2, pp. 135–66.

SCANNELL, P. (1991) 'Introduction: the relevance of talk' in Scannell, P. (ed.) *Broadcast Talk*, pp. 1–13, London, Sage.

SCANNELL, P. and CARDIFF, D. (1991) *A Social History of British Broadcasting, Vol. 1: 1922–1939: Serving the Nation*, Oxford, Blackwell.

SILVERSTONE, R. (1990) 'Television and everyday life: towards an anthropology of the television audience' in Ferguson, M. (ed.) *Public Communication – The New Imperatives: future directions for media research*, pp. 173–89, London, Sage.

SMYTHE, D. (1981) *Dependency Road: communications, capitalism, consciousness and Canada*, Norwood, NJ, Ablex.

THOMPSON, J. (1988) 'Mass communication and modern culture: contribution to a critical theory of ideology', *Sociology*, Vol. 22, No. 3, pp. 359–83.

THOMPSON, J. (1994) 'Social theory and the media' in Crowley, D. and Mitchell, D. (eds) *Communication Theory Today*, pp. 27–49, Cambridge, Polity.

THOMPSON, J. (1995) *The Media and Modernity: a social theory of the media*, Cambridge, Polity.

WILLIAMS, R. (1974) *Television: technology and cultural form*, London, Fontana.

READING A:
Donald Horton and Richard Wohl, 'Mass communication and para-social interaction'

One of the striking characteristics of the new mass media [...] is that they give the illusion of face-to-face relationship with the performer. The conditions of response to the performer are analogous to those in a primary group [...] We propose to call this seeming face-to-face relationship between spectator and performer a *para-social relationship*.

In television, especially, the image which is presented makes available nuances of appearance and gesture to which ordinary social perception is attentive and to which interaction is cued. Sometimes the 'actor' [...] is seen engaged with others; but often he [*sic*] faces the spectator, uses the mode of direct address, talks as if he were conversing personally and privately. The audience, for its part, responds with something more than mere running observation; it is, as it were, subtly insinuated into the program's action and internal social relationships and, by dint of this kind of staging, is ambiguously transformed into a group which observes and participates in the show by turns [...] This simulacrum of conversational give and take may be called *para-social interaction*. [...]

[...]

Radio and television [...] are [...] extending the para-social relationship now to leading people of the world of affairs [...], sometimes even to puppets anthropomorphically transformed into 'personalities' [...] But of particular interest is the creation by these media of a new type of performer: quiz-masters, announcers, 'interviewers' in a new 'show-business' world – in brief, a special category of 'personalities' whose existence is a function of the media themselves. These 'personalities', usually, are not prominent in any of the social spheres beyond the media. They exist for their audiences only in the para-social relation. Lacking an appropriate name for these performers, we shall call them *personae*.

The role of the persona

The persona is the typical and indigenous figure of the social scene presented by radio and television [...] The spectacular fact about such personae is that they can claim and achieve an intimacy with what are literally crowds of strangers, and this intimacy, even if it is an imitation and a shadow of what is ordinarily meant by that word, is extremely influential with, and satisfying for, the great numbers who willingly receive it and share in it. They 'know' such a persona in somewhat the same way they know their chosen friends: through direct observation and interpretation of his appearance, his gestures and voice, his conversation and conduct in a variety of situations. Indeed, those who make up his audience are invited, by designed informality, to make precisely these evaluations – to consider that they are involved in a face-to-face exchange rather than in passive observation. When the television camera pans down on a performer, the illusion is strong that he is enhancing the presumed intimacy by literally coming closer. But the persona's image, while partial, contrived, and penetrated by illusion, is no fantasy or dream: his performance is an objectively perceptible action in which the viewer is implicated imaginatively, but which he does not imagine.

The persona offers, above all, a continuing relationship. His appearance is a regular and dependable event, to be counted on, planned for, and integrated into the routines of daily life. His devotees 'live with him' and share the small episodes of his public life – and to some extent even of his private life away from the show. Indeed, their continued association with him acquires a history, and the accumulation of shared past experiences gives additional meaning to the present performance. This bond is symbolized by allusions that lack meaning for the casual observer and appear occult to the outsider. In time, the devotee – the 'fan' – comes to believe that he 'knows' the persona more intimately and profoundly than others do, that he 'understands' his character and appreciates his values and motives. [...]

[...]

The bond of intimacy

It is an unvarying characteristic of these 'personality' programs that the greatest pains are taken by the persona to create an illusion of intimacy [...] There are several principal strategies for achieving this. [...]

Most characteristic is the attempt of the persona to duplicate the gestures, conversational style, and milieu of an informal face-to-face gathering [...] The persona tries to maintain a flow of small talk which gives the impression that he is responding to and sustaining the contributions of an invisible interlocutor. [...]

In addition to creating an appropriate tone and patter, the persona tries as far as possible to eradicate, or at least to blur, the line which divides him and his show, as a formal performance, from the audience both in the studio and at home. The most usual way of achieving this ambiguity is for the persona to treat his supporting cast as a group of close intimates. Thus all the members of the cast will be addressed by their first names, or by special nicknames, to emphasize intimacy. [...]

Furthermore, the persona may try to step out of the particular format of his show and literally blend with the audience. Most usually, the persona leaves the stage and mingles with the studio audience in a question-and-answer exchange. In some few cases, and particularly on the Steve Allen show, this device has been carried a step further. Thus Allen has managed to blend even with the home audience by the manoeuvre of training a television camera on the street outside the studio and, in effect, suspending his own show and converting all the world outside into a stage. Allen, his supporting cast, and the audience, both at home and in the studio, watch together what transpires on the street – the persona and his spectators symbolically united as one big audience. In this way, Allen erases for the moment the line which separates persona and spectator [...] All these devices are indulged in not only to lure the attention of the audience, and to create the easy impression that there is a kind of participation open to them in the program itself, but also to highlight the chief values stressed in such personality shows. These are sociability, easy affability, friendship, and close contact – briefly, all the values associated with free access to and easy participation in pleasant social interaction in primary groups. [...]

Source: Horton and Wohl, 1956, pp. 215–18.

READING B:
Ien Ang, 'In search of the audience commodity'

A short consideration of the corporate structure of American commercial broadcasting will make us comprehend more fully why the practice of audience measurement has acquired the central role it has been occupying almost from its inception. In economic terms, production for profit is the sole objective of the commercial broadcasting industry [...] To finance the whole system, the networks are dependent on advertisers as sponsors. The idea of advertising is principally based upon the assumption that it is possible to enlarge sales of products through communication. It is the prospect of fusing selling and communicating that induces interest on the part of advertisers to make use of television or radio to disseminate their promotional messages. Therefore, a system has emerged in which advertisers buy air time from the broadcasters, either fifteen- or thirty- or sixty-second spots, to be inserted in programmes that are furnished by the networks.

Important in this transaction is the need advertisers feel to have some kind of guarantee that they haven't spent their money for nothing. They need to be reassured that their messages actually reach those for whom they are intended: the potential consumers of the products advertised. Here, the audience enters the story. Advertisers see the audience as potential consumers, and thus it is the audience's attention that advertisers want to attract. From this perspective, then, what advertisers buy from the networks is not time but audience: commercial television is based on the principle that the networks 'deliver audiences to advertisers' [...] But how does one know that the exchange is a fair one? If 'chunks of audience' are the commodities that the networks sell to the advertisers, some measure has to be set to determine the price the latter must pay to the former.

At this point the idea of audience measurement acquires its relevance. Audience measurement bears an economical meaning in so far as it produces the necessary standard through which advertising rates can be set. That standard is fixed according to the number of people who watch the programmes in which the commercials appear [...]

The ratings firms occupy a key position in this corporate transaction, because it is their product, the ratings information, that forms the basis for the agreed-upon standard by which advertisers and networks buy and sell the audience commodity. [...]

However, ratings are not only products with an economic exchange value. In fact, they could only become saleable products in the first place because they contain a certain productivity, a certain use value. In Meehan's words [1984, p. 222], what ratings do is provide the industry with 'an official description of the audience', that becomes the foundation upon which the economic negotiations of the industry are effectuated. The permanent institutional uncertainty about the audience which is inherent to the broadcasting situation makes an official description necessary: in the commercial context of mutual dependency between networks and advertisers, that uncertainty is a catastrophic condition – a condition that would be lethal for the industry if it would not be surmounted. After all, the selling and buying of the audience commodity can only take place if and when one can define the object of the transaction. Uncertainty about the audience must therefore be combated at all costs. It must be converted into a situation in which there is at least agreement among the parties involved about what they are referring to when they speak about the audience commodity. [...]

[...]

Ratings then deliver the very currency of the industry's economic transactions. But that currency does not exist in material form: the audience commodity is not a material object that can be readily exchanged such as a car or a pack of cigarettes. Therefore, an instrument is needed to object-ify the audience, as it were, and this is exactly the specific productivity of audience measurement. And while this practice originated in the commercial necessities of radio broadcasting, it is in the area of television that the production of ratings has become a truly prominent industry in itself. It is the specific achievement of audience measurement that it converts an elusive occurrence – the real occurrence of people actually using television in their everyday lives – into a hard substance, a calculable object, an object suitable for transaction.

This process of object-ification is established and maintained through the procedures of audience measurement as a discursive practice. Audience measurement is not just an innocent way of quantifying television's reach. The very act of 'head counting', which is the most basic operation of ratings production, is a very specific discursive intervention that results in moulding 'television audience' into a quantifiable aggregate object. Ratings discourse transforms the audience from a notion that loosely represents an unknown and unseen reality [...] into a known and knowable taxonomic category, a discrete entity that can be empirically described in numerical terms. The audience commodity is thus a symbolic object which is constructed by, and is not pre-existent to the discursive procedures of audience measurement. It is this symbolic object – 'television audience' as it is constructed in and through ratings discourse – that is the target of the television industry's practices, advertisers and broadcasters alike.

[...]

It is through ratings discourse that the social world of actual audiences is incorporated in the complex system of production and exchange that keeps the industry going. The system performs a double objectification of actual audiences: by turning 'television audience' into an object of knowledge, ratings discourse simultaneously enables the making of 'television audience' as an object of economic exchange. This makes audience measurement a clear instance of what Foucault [1980] has called a technology of power, in which the wish to exert control over people is connected to and articulated in the institutionalized production of knowledge about them.

[...]

But [...] since the days of its original conception, the practice of audience measurement has encountered many real and perceived imperfections. These imperfections have created tensions within the industry, which have not only led to continuing competition between ratings firms, but also, often enough, to skirmishes between advertisers and networks over the right measurement standards. Given the enormous financial consequences of every variation in the outcome of the measurements, such concern is not at all surprising. In fact, the desire to have a better and better measurement service in industry circles has spurred the development of ever more sophisticated measurement procedures, which are hoped to deliver more accurate, detailed and useful official descriptions of 'television audience'. The growing emphasis on demographic information, for example, was a direct consequence of the advertisers' wish to advertise their products to specific market segments [...] rather than to the general 'mass audience'.

References

FOUCAULT, M. (1980) *Power/Knowledge: selected interviews and other writings, 1972–1977*, Brighton, Harvester Press.

MEEHAN, E. (1984) 'Ratings and the institutional approach: a third answer to the commodity question', *Critical Studies in Mass Communication*, Vol. 1, No. 2, pp. 216–25.

Source: Ang, 1991, pp. 53–4, 56–7.

READING C:
David Morley, 'The framework of family viewing in Great Britain'

As will be seen, men and women offer clearly contrasting accounts of their viewing habits in terms of their differential power to choose what they view, [...] their viewing styles, and their choice of particular viewing material. However, I am not suggesting that these empirical differences are attributes of their essential biological characteristics as men and women. Rather, I am trying to argue that these differences are the effects of the particular social roles that these men and women occupy within the home. [...]

[...] The dominant model of gender relations within this society (and certainly within that subsection of it represented in my sample) is one in which the home is primarily defined for men as a site of leisure – by distinction from the 'industrial time' of their employment outside the home – while the home is primarily defined for women as a site of work, whether or not they also work outside the home. This simply means that, in investigating television viewing in the home, one is by definition investigating something that men are better placed to do wholeheartedly, and that women seem only to be able to do distractedly and guiltily, because of their continuing sense of domestic responsibility. [...]

When considering the empirical findings that follow, care must be taken to hold in view this structuring of the domestic environment by gender relations as the backdrop against which these particular patterns of viewing behavior have developed. [...]

[...]

Power and control over program choice

Masculine power is evident in a number of the families as the ultimate determinant on occasions of conflict over viewing choices ('We discuss what we all want to watch and the biggest wins. That's me, I'm the biggest.'). It is even more apparent in the case of those families that have a remote control device. None of the women in any of the families uses the remote control device regularly. A number of them complain that their husbands use the device obsessively, channel-flicking across programs when their wives are trying to watch something else. Characteristically, the remote control device is the symbolic possession of the father (or of the son, in the father's absence) that sits 'on the arm of Daddy's chair' and is used almost exclusively by him. It is a highly visible symbol of condensed power relations:

> *Daughter:* Dad keeps both of the automatic controls – one on each side of his chair.

> *Woman:* Well, I don't get much chance, because he sits there with the automatic control beside him and that's it. I get annoyed because I can be watching a program and he's flicking channels to see if a program on the other side is finished so he can record something. [...]

> *Woman:* No, not really, I don't get a chance to use the automatic control. I leave that down to him. It is aggravating, because I can be watching something and all of a sudden he turns it over to get the football result.

> *Daughter:* The control's always next to Dad's chair. It doesn't come away when Dad's here. It stays right there.

Interestingly, the main exceptions to this overall pattern are those families in which the man is unemployed while his wife is working. In these cases it is slightly more common for the man to be expected to let other family members watch what they want to when it is broadcast, while he videotapes what he would like to see in order to watch that later at night or the following day. His timetable of commitments is more flexible than those of the working members of the family. Here we begin to see the way in which the position of power held by most of the men in the sample (and which their wives concede) is based not simply on the biological fact of being men but rather on a social definition of masculinity of which employment (that is, the 'breadwinner' role) is a necessary and constituent part. When that condition is not met, the pattern of power relations within the home can change noticeably.

[...]

Styles of viewing

One major finding is the consistency of the distinction made between the characteristic ways in which men and women describe their viewing activity. Essentially, men state a clear preference for viewing attentively, in silence, without interruption 'in order not to miss anything'. Moreover, they display puzzlement at the way their wives and daughters watch television. The women describe viewing as a fundamentally social activity, involving ongoing conversation, and usually the performance of at least one other domestic activity (ironing, etc.) at the same time. Indeed, many women feel that to just watch television without doing anything else at the same time would be an indefensible waste of time, given their sense of domestic obligations [...] The women note that their husbands are always 'on at them' to shut up, and the men can't really understand how their wives can follow the programs if they are doing something else at the same time:

> [...]
>
> *Man:* I can't concentrate if there's anyone talking while I'm watching. But they can, they can watch and just talk at the same time. We just watch it, take it all in. If you talk, you've missed the bit that's really worth watching [...] We listen to every bit of it [...] My attitude is sort of 'go in the other room if you want to talk'.
>
> *Man:* It really amazes me that this lot [his wife and daughters] can talk and do things and still pick up what's going on. To my mind it's not very good if you can do that.
>
> [...]
>
> *Woman:* I knit because I think I am wasting my time just watching. I know what's going on, so I only have to glance up. I always knit when I watch.
>
> [...]
>
> *Woman:* There is always something else, like ironing. I can watch anything while I'm doing the ironing. I've always done the ironing and knitting and that ... You've got things to do, you know, and you can't keep watching television. You think, 'Oh my God, I should have done this or that.'

Brunsdon [1986] offers a useful way of understanding the behavior reported here. As she argues, it is not that women have no desire to watch television attentively, but rather that their domestic position makes it almost impossible for them to do so unless all other members of the household are 'out of the way' [...] Again, we see that these distinctive viewing styles are [...] characteristics of the domestic roles of masculinity and femininity.

[...]

'Solo' viewing and guilty pleasures

A number of the women in the sample explain that their greatest pleasure is to be able to watch 'a nice weepie' or their favorite serial when the rest of the family isn't there. Only then do they feel free enough of their domestic responsibilities to 'indulge' themselves in the kind of attentive viewing in which their husbands routinely engage [...] The point is expressed most clearly by the woman who explains that she particularly enjoys watching early morning television at the weekends because these are the only occasions when her husband and sons 'sleep in', providing a chance to watch television attentively without keeping half an eye on the needs of others.

Several of these women will arrange to view a video with other women friends during the afternoon. It is the classically feminine way of dealing with conflict – in this case, over program choice – by avoiding it, and 're-scheduling' the program (often with someone's help in relation to the video) to a point where it can be watched more pleasurably:

> *Woman:* That's one thing we don't have on when he's here, we don't have the game programs on because he hates them. If we women are here on our own, I love it [...] if I'm here alone. I try to get something a bit mushy and then I sit here and have a cry, if I'm here on my own. It's not often, but I enjoy that.
>
> *Woman:* If I get a good film on now, I'll tape it and keep it, especially if it's a weepie [...] If I'm tired, I'll put that on – especially in the

winter – and it's nice then, 'cause you sit there and there's no one around.

Woman: If he's taped something for me [...] I come down and watch it very early about 6.00 or 6.30 Sunday morning [...] I love Saturday morning breakfast television. I'm on my own, because no one gets up till late. I come down and really enjoy that program.

[...]

What is at issue here is the guilt that most of these women feel about their own pleasures. They are, on the whole, prepared to concede that the dramas and soap operas they like are 'silly' or 'badly acted' or inconsequential. They accept the terms of a masculine hegemony that defines their preferences as having low status. Having accepted these terms, they then find it hard to argue for their preferences in a conflict because, by definition, what their husbands want to watch is more prestigious. [...]

Reference

BRUNSDON, C. (1986) 'Women watching TV', Paper presented to Women and the Electronic Mass Media Conference, Copenhagen, Denmark.

Source: Morley, 1988, pp. 34–8, 41–2.

READING D:
Shaun Moores, 'Satellite television and everyday life'

The households discussed [below] are located in a city suburb which [...] has strong connotations of 'heritage' [...] Estate agents refer to the 'authentic' historical character of this area, and while some of the road names echo those of English stately homes, others recall famous military battles overseas [...] In these circumstances, the arrival of a new communications technology – with its futuristic dish on open display – results in a curious collision of aesthetic and cultural codes. Charlotte Brunsdon [1991], in her review of newspaper reports on controversies over the siting of aerials, noted that tensions tend to surface when the objects are installed on old buildings considered to have architectural merit. Discourses of 'innovation' and 'conservation' confront each other head on, exerting pressure in opposite directions, and it is precisely this contradiction between senses of the modern and the traditional which runs through much of my subsequent commentary. Such a conflict, I will argue, is not confined to antagonisms at the level of the residential area. It can get 'gridded', in complex and shifting ways, onto social divisions of gender and generation in domestic life, and may also help to constitute our broader feelings of collective identity.

The Gibsons

Let me start to unpack my introductory remarks by looking in more detail at some of the homes in this neighbourhood. For instance, the Gibsons[1] – whose aerial is a rarely seen Cambridge model – live in an old house that once belonged to a well known family of solicitors in the city. There is a striking divergence of tastes and competences here between Mr Gibson and his nineteen-year-old son. So the father takes great pleasure in talking about the 'character' and heritage value of the building they own. He is currently restoring an original antique fireplace, which he discovered hidden behind a plasterboard wall, and has plans to strip and varnish a built-in wooden dresser in the back dining room. As we shall see, Mr Gibson is extremely anxious about the dish's appearance on their housefront. It was his son, Tony, who wanted a satellite receiver.

[...]

At the top of the house, separated from the main living area by a narrow staircase and landing, is Tony's room. He is intensely proud of this space and the objects arranged inside it – regarding the attic as a place into which he can retreat, and as a symbol of independence from the rest of his family. Showing me round the room, Tony explains:

> I'm the only one who knows how to use any of my electrical equipment. Nobody else comes in my room – I think of it as my space. ... Up here, I can watch anything I want, read, sleep, think about life, listen to music. ... As soon as I go into my room, it's like I'm on another planet.

Gathered around his television set, there is a remarkable entourage of technical hardware and software – as well as an array of decorative images and artefacts. Two video recorders, a hi-fi system and the satellite receiver are all stacked on shelves underneath the TV. They have been wired together, too, so that the sound comes out of four Dolby Surround speakers mounted on brackets in each corner of the room. According to Mr Gibson, 'it's like a disco in there [...] if he turned the volume up any more, it'd blow the whole roof off'. Tony has moved his bed to a central point between these sources of sound, and five different remote control devices rest on top of the Bart Simpson duvet cover [...] The walls are covered with posters of sports cars, while neat piles of video tapes and compact discs lie on the floor. His viewing preferences are for science fiction and horror – recording several films off the Sky Movies channel – and he collects tapes about the making of films, notably those concerned with stunts and special effects.

It is possible, I believe, to read these assembled goods as signs of a struggle to fashion some limited degree of autonomy in the face of parental authority. He does not have a home of his own, still relying on parents for accommodation, but Tony's job [...] enables him to save up and purchase things – items that are treasured precisely because they provide a statement of personal identity. Of course, that identity takes shape under conditions not entirely of his own choosing. He is, as the

structuralists might say, constituted as a subject only as a consequence of being subjected to and positioned within the 'symbolic order' of culture. Tony inhabits a specifically masculine world of gadgets, fast cars and sci-fi fantasies – a world of meaning which he shares, incidentally, with his friends and fellow male workers.

However, [...] my suggestion would be that we apply a more 'negotiated' theory of subjectivity and power to Tony's situation – one that recognises a measure of human agency, and understands the contradictions of social reproduction and resistance. For this teenager in this immediate context, then, satellite television is part of a 'constellation' of technologies and practices which supplies the cultural resources to express difference and establish competence. It is important for us to appreciate his 'symbolic creativity' in circumstances of material and ideological constraint. Tellingly, his father confesses complete incompetence when it comes to operating the machinery in Tony's bedroom: 'He knows where everything is, but I don't [...] I remember glancing over at it – the electronics and wiring – and just one look was enough for me.'

Mr Gibson's interest in restoring antique furnishings and fittings has grown considerably over the period since satellite TV entered their home. This heightened investment in 'the old' is presumably a direct response to his son's passion for 'the new' [...] Tony makes a partial bid for independence. His father, meanwhile, defines a clearly contrasting field of knowledge and skills. [...]

The story of how their external aerial got selected [...] is a revealing account of conflict and compromise. In this instance, installing the satellite dish was very much a public enactment of private tensions. It was also going to be a potential cause of embarrassment for Mr Gibson, given the 'tone' of the neighbourhood that they live in. Realising the technical impracticalities of siting at the rear of the house – as dishes must be aligned at a particular angle to the sky in order to pick up satellite transmissions – Tony had to enter into a protracted debate with his father about the aesthetics of display.

His father's comments on the circular Amstrad Fidelity dishes – the most common model currently on the market – are decidedly uncomplimentary. Mr Gibson calls them 'frying pans', and says:

> They look completely out of place on houses like this, old houses with character [...] I didn't want an unsightly thing hovering up there. If it was just a prefabricated sort of house, then sure, I wouldn't mind – but as we've got bay windows and all the stonework at the front, I wasn't going to have something that wouldn't blend in [...] wouldn't retain the character of the area.

After consulting one of the consumer guide magazines which were available from the local newsagents, Tony eventually managed to convince him of the Cambridge system's unobtrusive qualities. The name itself connotes a higher status commodity, offering distant associations of 'education' and heritage, and its aerial is a rectangular stone-coloured block with a circular hollow 'carved' into it – rather than the usual white or black mesh disc design. Even Mr Gibson admits that 'it's compact and looks neater on the side of houses [...] there's many a person'll pass and not notice you've got it'. [...]

[...]

My final remarks on the Gibsons provide a convenient link with the next household portrait which I sketch – and they concern this family's identifications, through television, with larger national or transnational communities. It might be argued that small-scale ethnographic research of the sort I have been doing is an inappropriate means of investigating the construction of collective identities. Much of the existing work on this theme in cultural studies has taken public representations and narratives as a starting point for analysis, rather than trying to explore the sentiments of actual social subjects in the private domain. However, [...] conversational interviews with families can be of the utmost relevance for examining discourses of community as they are articulated 'on the ground' in routine domestic contexts.

Talk about TV – both in its terrestrial and satellite varieties – may deliver [...] insights into processes of collective identification. For example, in the case of the Gibsons there is an interesting distinction which is made between different image spaces or 'territories of transmission'. Tony's positive feelings about the Astra broadcasts – he tunes into continental stations like RTL Plus or Pro 7, as well as the Sky channels and MTV Europe – are intimately related to his dismissal of established terrestrial programming as traditional, boring and old fashioned. In fact, it is interesting that he labels this negatively as 'British television'. [His parents] use precisely the same label themselves, but here its value is completely reversed. They prefer to watch BBC or ITV in the living room downstairs.

The Harveys

For the Harveys, a family living nearby, there are further interesting connections being forged between everyday experience and the new 'spaces of identity' made available by satellite TV. Dave and Liz Harvey are in their late twenties and have three children [...] They moved to South Wales from the Midlands region of England, where he had studied for a polytechnic degree in electronic engineering. She works as a housewife and Mr Harvey is now self-employed – having given up a salaried job to start his own small business designing and manufacturing computer robotics equipment for export. This married couple perceive the satellite technology to be offering them an expanded range of viewing choices – although Dave gets to exercise that choice more than Liz – and, significantly, he speaks about the 'larger feel' created by a type of television transmission which transcends the boundaries of narrowly British broadcasting.

Whilst the first of these perceptions is what we might reasonably expect to hear from satellite TV consumers, since the technology has been marketed in terms of increased 'freedom' of choice for its viewers, the second is less predictable. Mr Harvey explains that:

> When I'm watching Sky – because it's from a European satellite – and when I'm looking at some of the other continental stations that are available, I very much get the sense of being a European. A lot of the channels are an hour ahead, they're on European time. If you're just channel-hopping, which is a bit of a sport for me – buzzing round eight or nine stations to see what's going on – you do get the feeling of not being restricted in the good old British way. It's

quite something when you can sit down in your own front room and watch what's on in another country.

[...] The opposition he constructs here between restriction and mobility is mapped onto another distinction in which 'Britishness' and 'Europeanness' are contrasted – 'not being restricted in the good old British way'. Even if his viewing pleasures do take the form of 'channel grazing', a kind of armchair 'televisual tourism', it remains the case that satellite TV is helping him travel to new places and to reimagine the boundaries of community. Of course, the image spaces produced by a communications technology cannot reshape national subjectivities on their own. Only when those audio-visual territories are articulated with existing situations and discourses can a fiction like Europe come to be realised by particular groups of people.

So Mr Harvey, who manufactures hi-tech goods for the export market, already identifies strongly with a transnational business community. The fact that his parents have bought a retirement home in Spain also contributes to Dave's recognition of himself as 'a European'. Their villa is now a regular destination for family holidays abroad. Mrs Harvey, too, finds that the idea of Europe has a certain limited salience. When her younger sister – a university arts student – came to visit with a boyfriend from France, they were able to show them a few French language programmes on satellite television. Some of these circumstances are obviously unique to the Harvey household – while others, such as the commercial and cultural significance of a single European market, have much wider 'currency'. What we need to specify, though, are precisely those interdiscursive moments at which private lives and public worlds meet and mesh together. Any transformation of collective identities will inevitably be uneven in its development and will necessarily be grounded in quotidian practices.

The theme of 'modern versus traditional' runs just as powerfully through pursuits and disputes in the Harveys' home as it did through the Gibsons'. In this family, it is the father who is a self-confessed 'gadgeteer'. From the stage he began playing around with lightbulbs and circuits as a teenager, Dave has always been enthusiastic about electronics. He can

be located within what Leslie Haddon [1988] has called 'hobbyist' culture – a predominantly masculine sphere of social activity where consumers are concerned to experiment with all the latest innovations in information and communications technology. Their house currently contains three computers – one of which he assembled himself out of IBM parts – two VCRs and two TVs, in addition to the satellite system and a CD player. An interest in electronic music has also resulted in plans to buy a synthesiser. Liz, however, is extremely conscious of the fact that 'people do take the mickey out of us ... we're constantly tripping over monitors and things'. Her feelings towards these gadgets are distinctly more ambivalent than those of her husband. Indeed, she is clearly frustrated by the fact that money spent on his 'toys' is money which goes unspent on her preferred pastime of collecting antique furniture.

[...]

Meanwhile, Mrs Harvey's mother and father have taken exception to the satellite aerial which is mounted on the house exterior. It has even been the source of arguments between daughter and parents when they visit. 'My mum thinks it's rather vulgar', Liz explains. 'She says to me, "You really shouldn't have that thing on the front of such a lovely Edwardian home".' There could be no more emphatic statement of the conflict involving discourses of innovation and conservation. Comparing the perceived ugliness of a [...] dish with the assumed beauty of period architecture, Liz's mother forms a critical judgement on the basis of certain moral and aesthetic values which privilege 'past' over 'present'.

We have seen how the juxtaposition of traditional and modern codes is at the root of [...] frictions in this family. Mrs Harvey's desire for pieces of antique furniture is opposed to Dave's fascination with electronic gadgets [...] As for the disagreement between Liz and her parents over the dish on the front wall, she chooses temporarily to side with her husband – reluctantly identifying with the modern because she is forced onto the defensive by their unfavourable comments. In these different situations, she must skilfully negotiate the contradictions of her gendered and generational subject positions as they are related to particular senses of old and new.

Both Mr and Mrs Harvey tell me they are amused by her parents' remarks on the satellite dish – and yet there are strong indications that they, too, are anxious over its appearance. So Dave sees it, in part, as a symbol of technological progress – a sign of them being 'ahead of the times' – but worries simultaneously about the connotations this object may have for others, in view of the traditional character of their neighbourhood. He admits that if they were to put the property on the housing market in the near future, he would seriously consider taking the aerial down 'if it proved detrimental to the sale of the house'. As Liz confesses, 'most of the people we know do actually think it's a bit vulgar'. Also, a local city councillor has been distributing leaflets to residents in the district – asking for people's opinions on the spread of dishes – and that kind of public consultation could have added to their discomfort.

This extract from my interview with the Harveys clearly demonstrates the anxieties they have concerning the positioning and visual impact of the aerial, which Dave installed himself, on the housefront:

> *Liz*: We did try to put the dish round the back, didn't we? [...] Still, I don't think it's as bad – as noticeable – on our house as it is on some where there's just a straight row of houses in a line. Then it can look awful.

> *Dave*: Yes. If it was out at the end of the bay, it'd be apparently obvious from all directions – whereas at the moment you can actually come down the road and not realise it's there.

It is interesting to compare the sentiments expressed here with the opinions which were voiced by Mr Gibson. He believed aerials on modern 'prefabricated' buildings to be less of an eyesore than those on traditional Edwardian structures. Mrs Harvey disagrees – but only because she thinks bay fronts help hide them better. What Liz and Dave share with Mr Gibson is a wish for the thing to be made 'invisible'.

Note

1   I have changed the names of all household members referred to in my study.

References

BRUNSDON, C. (1991) 'Satellite dishes and the landscapes of taste', *New Formations*, No. 15, pp. 23–42.

HADDON, L. (1988) 'The home computer: the making of a consumer electronic', *Science as Culture*, No. 2, pp. 7–51.

Source: Moores, 1996, pp. 36–44.

CONSUMING COMMUNICATION TECHNOLOGIES AT HOME

Hugh Mackay

Contents

1   Introduction

information and
communication
technologies (ICTs)

In this chapter we shall examine the consumption of new **information and communication technologies (ICTs)** in the home. We shall explore the *active* nature of consumption practices and how these, far from being determined by production, are crucial in shaping technology. As with earlier chapters, our concern is with both creativity and constraint, and with situated, everyday practices. In examining the significance of the consumption of technology for everyday lives and routines, we shall draw mainly on qualitative and ethnographic accounts, but also on quantitative data, examining patterns of ICT ownership and usage.

ICTs are no different from other artefacts in that, as we have seen in Chapter 1 in this volume, they are material for the construction – even constitution – of our identities. So ICTs, like other artefacts, are important in terms of ownership and display. But they have a *particular* significance as a form of consumption because of their role in mediating boundaries between private and public: ICTs both *isolate* us (in our private homes or with our personal stereos) and, at the same time, *connect* us (with the world beyond our doorsteps or localities), mediating our knowledge and understanding of the outside world and playing a part in linking us in communities.

At the same time as exploring the consumption of ICTs, I hope to dispel any ideas you may have about technology not being an issue for those with an interest in culture! This chapter introduces and applies some key ideas and concepts from studies of technology as culture, to equip you with an understanding of the consumption of ICTs at home. In so doing, it will provide you with an understanding of the technologization of contemporary culture more broadly. You will be introduced to some key analytical concepts, and to case studies of domestic leisure technologies, many of which will be familiar to you. It will give you the opportunity to reflect critically on some of your everyday routines and practices, and to challenge taken-for-granted assumptions about technology. Crucially, the chapter will apply and extend our understanding of processes of cultural consumption.

The chapter has six objectives. After reading it, you should be able to:

- Understand, evaluate and apply key debates about the relationship of technology to culture, including notions of technological determinism and the social shaping of technology.

- 'Read' the technology 'text' and understand the crucial role of consumption in shaping technology.

- Evaluate, or deconstruct, the discourse surrounding new technologies.

- Understand and research how media technologies are used and made sense of in everyday life, as an example of cultural consumption.

- Be familiar with patterns of ownership and usage of some familiar ICTs in the home and able to analyse data on these.

- Understand the role of ICTs in mediating the boundary between private and public, in linking the global and the local, and in shaping and constructing communities.

Section 2 sets the scene by introducing both 'technology' and 'the home'. Section 3 defines 'technology', explains its social nature, and introduces the key concepts of 'technological determinism' and the 'social shaping' of technology. In section 4 we will explore how we can understand technology as text, and will apply to technology a set of concepts developed for the study of culture, using the history of computer games as one example. In section 5 we will review studies of new ICTs in the home, and explore how technologies and everyday life are transformed as new technologies are 'domesticated'. A key issue is the gendering of technology and we shall be using the gendered nature of telephone usage to illustrate this point. An ethnographic portrait will be used to summarize section 5, in which the meanings and uses of a range of ICTs in one family are explored in depth. In section 6 we move on to explore the ways in which ICTs link us with the world beyond our homes and communities, and will examine the role of technology in mediating these boundaries; our main example there is the Internet, the global computer network.

2   Consumption, technology and the home

First, you may wonder why the focus on technology – and why on the home? Well, we live in a world in which we are surrounded by discussions and representations of new information and communications technologies as the key to the future – holding out the promise of alleviating the drudgery of work, of overcoming the problems of large classes and demoralized teachers, of allowing access to up-to-date global information and news, and of providing ever new forms of entertainment and leisure. In films and novels, policy documents and political discourse, we find technology invoked in visions of the future. Following President Clinton and Vice President Gore, we now have Tony Blair proclaiming the 'information superhighway' to be 'a revolution as profound as that brought about by the invention of the printing press' (cited in Webster, 1996, p. 17). Through new distance-learning technologies, digital libraries, electronic voting, e-mail, video-conferencing, on-line chat, video-on-demand and teleshopping, we are invited to increase our knowledge, enhance our pleasure, increase our personal fulfilment, re-establish our lost communities and achieve our liberation. Even more, through virtual reality we are told that we can float free of time and place, free of our bodies and our identities, as we roam cyberspace.

On the one hand, it is easy to dismiss such rhetoric as hollow, misguided or naive. To many of us, such claims seem far-fetched, implausible or just banal. The spirit of the Enlightenment with its notion of progress through science and technology, for so long central to western modernization, has lost some of its hold; many no longer see technology as the harbinger or the symbol of progress, and reject the notions that higher-tech is better or that progress is to be equated with technological developments. On the contrary, the claim by science of context-free truths about nature, and the positivism of its experimental methods, have been undermined by the relativist critique of objectivity – the argument that truth depends on context and is culturally constructed, rather than inherent in the natural world. Similarly, technology has come to be associated by many with risk and uncertainty, as our faith in progress through technology has been shattered by Hiroshima and Bhopal, Chernobyl and Challenger, not to mention the growing concern over global warming and sustainable development.

Despite this sea change, our culture becomes ever more dominated by and reliant on increasingly sophisticated technologies. Technology, in short, has become a powerful material and symbolic force in contemporary culture. It is pivotal in processes of transformation, which is perhaps one reason for the rhetoric which surrounds so much discussion of new technology, and for the ambitious claims which are so often made for its potential. For decades it was argued that television would lead to illiteracy; in the 1960s there were predictions of holidays on the moon; and very few of us yet shop by computer, despite the predictions of the 1980s. But at the same time as threatening our very existence, technology amplifies human capacity and enables an ease and standard of living hitherto unprecedented. Many of us therefore feel ambivalent towards technology – wary of the claims made for it, but interested in seeing what's new, what we can do with it and how it can improve our lives. And whatever our reservations about the hyperbole, it is clear that some technologies have been crucially implicated in social change – the atomic bomb and television, for example.

The effects of a technology, however, are not determined by its production, its physical form or its capability. Rather than being built into the technology, these depend on how they are consumed, and this consumption takes place *in context*. So this chapter is based on the premise that in order to understand the media, and technology, we have to understand the workings of households, since the context mediates any possible direct 'effects' which might be attributed to the technology.

And what has the *home* to do with technology? However we look at it, or measure it, for people in the developed world the home has become increasingly saturated with such technologies – the television, the telephone, the video-cassette recorder, home computers, computer games and CD-ROM players. Imagine your everyday routines and activities for a day – let alone a week – without them. This influx of leisure technologies into the home is an obvious physical manifestation of the 'withdrawal to interior space' discussed by the cultural theorist Jacques Donzelot (1980). The sociologists Ray Pahl (1984) and Jonathan Gershuny (1983) are among those who have argued that the family has shifted from being a unit of production to one of consumption. This idea has been criticized (notably by Ann Oakley, 1974) for conveniently forgetting the fact that for most *women* the home is a site of work, but there can be little doubt that leisure-time spent in the home has increased – 80 per cent of leisure time is spent in the home according to one estimate (Tomlinson, 1990). The home-focused nature of consumption (discussed in Chapter 1 of this volume) represents an important part of the broader retreat to the confines of one's home and garden. And with new ICTs a greater range of experiences, services and pleasures can be enjoyed on the screen instead of on the street: 'The pleasures, horrors and uncertainties of physical human contact with other people or places can be translated through technological systems into experiences which can be enjoyed vicariously' (Furlong, 1995, p. 170). Tomlinson argues that the development of the home as an autonomous, self-sufficient and self-contained unit constitutes a form of **privatization**; it is a process of atomization, in which there is a shifting emphasis on consumption, consumer power and cultural tastes, and a retreat from the public realm of the community. In this vein it might be argued that the information highway, like motor highways, promises to bring us closer but actually serves our sense of separateness.

privatization

Leisure technology is thus a key element of the privatization which Raymond Williams (1983) discusses. Williams argues that, although the emergence of the television is celebrated by many as a *technological* breakthrough, it is better understood as the product of two related, long-running social trends: **mobilization**, the break-up of communities and the shift from the country to the city with the onset of industrialization; and *privatization*, the increasing preference (which followed this mobilization) for privatized rather than public or collective, leisure. By 'privatization' Williams refers not to some sort of *isolation*, but (in conjunction with the inextricably linked 'mobilization') to a key tendency in urban industrial society for homes to be physically and socially more distant, and, as Daniel Miller has argued in Chapter 1, to be the focus of consumption. So the home isn't privatized in the sense of being impervious or impermeable, but in that it is the place where we can feel secure and from where we can enjoy contact with the world beyond. Peter Saunders has pointed out that:

mobilization

> ... privatism and home-centredness have long *coexisted* with collectivism and working-class organization. Emphasis on the importance of the home does not necessarily result in withdrawal from collective life outside the home, for it is possible for people to participate fully in both spheres of life.

(Saunders, 1990, p. 283)

ACTIVITY 1

You should consider whether you are inclined to position yourself with Tomlinson or with Saunders on this point. The home has grown as the focus of both consumption and of our leisure activities. Has this meant that our lives are becoming more privatized in the sense that we are becoming less engaged in public or community activities? Or do the ever-increasing luxuries of the home enhance the haven to which we can retreat after our active engagement in such outside activities?

Whatever your answer, the boundaries of the home aren't breached only when *we* come in or out. Rather like broadcasting in Moores' account (in Chapter 5 of this volume), ICTs are implicated in mediating its boundaries. As we proceed, you will be able to judge for yourself whether you see this process as progressive and democratic, or as involving our withdrawal from community and civil society.

3   Technology and social relations

Many of us think of technology as hard, physical and asocial – perhaps even as something which is antithetical to the social, or incompatible with an interest in matters cultural. One consequence of this common understanding, I think, is that many of us are happy to leave technology to technologists. If we see technology as *culture*, then we are less likely to approach technology in such a passive way. In this section I shall outline, then evaluate, the dominant orthodoxy for understanding the relationship between technology and society – technological determinism. Countering this orthodoxy, I shall outline and evaluate the main *sociological* approach to technology, the 'social shaping of technology' thesis; this is concerned with how technologies do not just arrive, but are shaped by the social circumstances from which they emerge. Finally, a cultural studies approach (see, for example, **du Gay, Hall et al.**, 1997) to technology is presented as extending the 'social shaping' approach.

3.1   What do we mean by 'technology'?

First of all, let us try to establish what we mean by 'technology'. Many of us associate technology with machines, with tangible, physical artefacts. For some of us the image is the car engine, a factory assembly-line, gears and cogs, or electronic circuits. Sociologists of technology, Donald Mackenzie and Judy Wajcman (1985), argue that this is the first of three 'layers of meaning' of a technology – the *physical artefact*. A technology, it is commonly argued, is an artefact which is designed or used to achieve some human purpose. They argue that an artefact *does* nothing without some *surrounding human activity* – steelworks without its workers cannot make steel, and a Walkman is useless until it is switched on. More than this, there is a third layer of meaning to any technology: the systematic *human knowledge*, or know-how, which went into its design (or its maintenance or the design of the next generation of the technology). Mackenzie and Wajcman thus argue that any technology involves the physical artefact, the surrounding human activity, and the human knowledge which lies behind it; and that technology has to be considered at all of these three levels.

Clearly such a definition points us to the profoundly and inherently **social nature of technology**: technologies are not simply isolated, physical entities. Others, notably the cultural theorist Michel Foucault, might not dissent from this definition, but would stress the notion of *technique* more than the artefactual nature of technology – technology as a way of doing something, which may or may not involve artefacts. Either approach, however, is very far removed from popular understandings of the relationship between technology and culture (which I sketched in section 2).

social nature of technology

3.2   Technological determinism

Mackenzie and Wajcman (1985, p. 4) argue that 'the single most influential theory of the relationship between technology and society' is **technological determinism**. According to technological determinism, the nature of our culture is determined by the prevailing technology. You will be familiar with such expressions as 'the stone age', 'the steam age' or, perhaps, 'the silicon age'. Each of these assumes that the prevailing technology – stone, steam or silicon chips – *determines* the prevailing form of social organization – hunter-gatherer society, the dark Satanic mills and slums of the Industrial Revolution, or the Information Society into which, some say, we are now moving. According to technological determinism, technology is something which develops *outside* society, following some sort of trajectory of its own making. Technologies, as they arrive, have an impact on society. To a technological determinist 'the IT revolution' is a technical matter – the key issues are processor speeds (MIPS), chip storage capacity (megabytes) and the like. According to such an approach, the future is conceived in terms of developments in bits, bytes and MIPS. A 'hard' form of technological determinism asserts that technology is *the key* motor of social change and of the shape of society.

technological determinism

> ### READING A
>
> You should turn to the Reading by Donald Mackenzie and Judy Wajcman at the end of this chapter, in which they outline the meaning and implications of technological determinism, and argue against both technological determinism and the 'effects tradition'.

3.3   The social shaping of technology: the home computer

As Mackenzie and Wajcman argue, sociologists should quickly reject the argument of technological determinism because it ignores the social processes surrounding the technology. The theory is important not so much for any theoretical sophistication but because it is how many of us commonly see technology. It is an approach which positions us in a profoundly passive relationship vis-à-vis technology: the technology is going to develop anyway, so all that we or our culture can do is perhaps to mitigate the worst excesses of the inevitable. (I hope that as you develop your understanding of technology and culture in this chapter you will develop a more active approach to technology.) We shall start by exploring how the form of one technology – the home computer – was far from inevitable or merely a technical matter. On the contrary, we shall see how its forms, uses and meanings were culturally contingent.

Now that home computers are reasonably commonplace, and a prominent feature of consumer electronics sales outlets, it may seem strange to reflect that at the outset (as late as 1980) there was no *one* (nor even a dominant) conception of what the home computer would be. Let's recap the history. Quite unusually for a consumer electronic, the home computer was a product not of corporate capitalism and organizations like Sony, but of the counterculture of California. It was here that the technological developments were made, the industry and many of its household names (such as Apple) were created, and the very nature of home computing was established. The home computer emerged from the culture of enthusiasts – hobbyists and hackers. These enthusiasts emerged from the male DIY/hi-fi culture, and were motivated not by corporate profit but by a concern to change the world and to empower ordinary people.

self-referential

In the UK Clive Sinclair later played a pivotal role. Aided by the government's IT awareness campaign and the discourse surrounding IT, Sinclair benefited from, and contributed to, a fervour that created millions of sales – of a device which was entirely **self-referential** (Haddon, 1988a): his early computers (notably the ZX80) could *do* roughly nothing – they had neither screen nor printer – but were desired on a massive scale, and at a far from insignificant price, to explore the machine, to learn about computing – for no particular specified end. The computer boom of the early 1980s involved buying micros not for what they could do but because ownership symbolized participation in the emerging (if ill-defined) computer or information society.

This early (self-referential) computer was itself transformed around the mid-1980s by two factors. First, the emergence of the discourse of IT in education, in which parents were exhorted by manufacturers to buy a computer if they cared about their child's education or future. Second, and largely coterminously, was the rapid growth of home computer games. Although a vast industry, its image was not helpful to manufacturers, who were stressing the utilitarian value of their product for enhancing educational attainment (and this despite the absence of any proven value of the technology to education). Thus the shift from hobbyist to games machine was not without its tensions. The explosion of software producers and magazines played a key role in the development of the discourse of home computing. Home computer games, as we shall see later, had their own, rather different, antecedents – in the form of arcade games and arcade culture; their entry to the home cannot be understood without a grasp of this origin, as it shaped both popular perceptions (the dangers of 'addiction', and an association with the 'aimlessness' of youth culture) and texts (the game formats).

Only much later, with the arrival of the Amstrad PCW8256 – the Morris Minor of computing – came the **instrumental** home computer, the computer which was intended to do a productive job. Nowadays business machines are sold as home computers, and much of the home computer market has become a segment of the business machine market. The home computer market has fragmented: digital music has arrived, and constitutes one of its niches; whilst games have *either* transferred to dedicated consoles (some attached to the television screen) *or* have become CD-ROM based, often multimedia, and running on general-purpose machines. Most recently, these machines have been sold with not just CD-ROM drives and modems (to allow external connections via the telephone system) but also television receivers (for which some are made in black cases, like televisions), as the home computer vies with the television to be the new hearth for home entertainment.

instrumental

In summary, the shift from a hobbyist machine, to a business machine, to a consumer good was the outcome of a complex set of processes whereby the very nature of the technology was **contested and transformed**. Like the Walkman, the home computer shows us that the form of the technology is not inevitable, (pre-)determined or immutable. The technology is cultural – not simply in that it exists in a cultural context, that technological artefacts are surrounded by culture, but is cultural through and through, in its design, its meaning, its use and thus its very form. As the media theorist Bill Keen has said of the video, it 'arrived, like most technologies, through a complex process of negotiation and struggle between different agencies, with many false starts and abandoned or neglected options' (1987, p. 9).

contested and transformed

In contrast with technological determinism, the **social shaping of technology** approach (Mackenzie and Wajcman, eds, 1985) focuses our attention on actors – engineers, managers, consumers – and the networks in which they are implicated. The argument of the social shaping of technology school is that technologies, in their very form, embody the culture from which they arose. Cultures give rise to technologies and they, in turn, embody key elements of that culture. The Walkman as a whole illustrates this vividly, but so do its various components: many of the bits and pieces *inside* the Walkman – miniaturized circuits, for example – are the product of US Department of Defense research and development priorities and procurement practices in the era of the Cold War (**du Gay, Hall et al.**, 1997). Without the Cold War, the development of these technologies would not have been a priority of the social formation; other technologies, say for education or health, might have been a greater priority. Clearly, this is quite the opposite of technological determinism: technology, in this view, is seen as being shaped by culture, rather than culture shaped by technology.

social shaping of technology

3.4   The constraining capacity of the physical

In debunking the notion of technological determinism, we must take care not to ignore the powerful constraining capacity of the physical technology. However much technologies are social in their origins, once they arrive, technologies restrict what is possible, and thus exercise some degree of determination. And, in the process of design, new technologies are constrained by the material: although a profoundly cultural activity, design is inextricably linked to the capacity of the material. Plastics, for example, have become incredibly widespread, initially as a cheaper alternative to wood or metal, and they have had a tremendous influence on product design – think of all of the domestic products which have been transformed or developed through their plastic casings. The form of the Walkman, enabling the privatized consumption of music while on the move, could only go so far – it still needed power to drive the motor to turn the tape, and hence space for a battery, for example. In other words, whatever the priorities of the social formation, there is always a degree of material constraint, a degree of technological determinism. So I would argue that we should reject more extreme forms of social determinism as much as technological determinism.

4   Technology as text

It is a short step from debunking technological determinism and establishing the essence of the 'social shaping of technology' approach to understanding the notion of 'technology as text'. You will be familiar with the notions of television discourse being a text, and of texts being inscribed with 'preferred readings' (Moores in Chapter 5 of this volume; see also **Hall**, 1997). The same approach can be employed to the very hardware of television or any other ICT.

4.1   The encoding and decoding of artefacts

encoding, decoding

Technologies, like other texts are **encoded** – in a physical sense in their design, and symbolically in their styling and marketing – and are **decoded** – that is, read by their consumers. At both ends, symbolic 'work' is being done; and this is where cultural studies extends sociologists' 'social shaping of technology' approaches to technology. Our notion of the 'cultural circuit' forces us to consider symmetrically the realms of consumption and production, and to take account of the complex (not unilinear or one-way) linkages between the two. And a cultural studies approach alerts us to the *symbolic* (as opposed to simply functional) significance of technologies. Finally, the encoding/decoding model, as we shall see, has the merit of allowing some capacity of determination to the technology. I shall use the example of the personal computer to explain this notion of the encoding of a technology

Tracy Kidder (1982) has written a fascinating account of a small team of men who were involved in designing and building a microcomputer. In *The Soul of a New Machine* he portrays how the group worked compulsively, around the clock, living on Coca Cola and junk food, and with no life beyond work. Their culture was profoundly gendered (women are almost entirely absent from the story except as the wife alone at home) and their verbal interaction is replete with military and sexual metaphors. Through their work on the machine they are bound together, as men and as technologists, as they strive to beat any rival company in the race to build the latest and best machine. Kiddor's work shows us how gender is involved not just in the construction of the machine, but in its very design: the physical form which the computer takes cannot be separated from the values and culture of those behind it. Even the structure of the organization producing the computer is explained as playing a part in the encoding process: DEC is a rival company, racing to complete its machine, the VAX. One night a member of the Eagle's team gets into DEC's building to check out their machine, to see whether it is a serious rival:

> Looking into the VAX, West had imagined he saw a diagram of DEC's corporate organization. He felt that VAX was too complicated. He didn't like, for instance, the system by which various parts of the machine communicated with one another; for his taste, there was too much protocol involved. He decided that VAX embodied flaws in DEC's corporate organization. The machine expressed that phenomenally successful company's cautious bureaucratic style ... With VAX, DEC was trying to minimize the risk.
>
> (Kidder, 1982, p. 36)

In this example we see the encoding of both an organizational culture and of designers' masculinity, or masculine values, in the computer. In a similar way, cultural histories of technologies can provide us with an understanding of the encoding of the physical design of other technologies.

In the design process **preferred readings** are thus encoded – in technologies as other texts, be they advertisements, television programmes or news stories (as we saw in **Hall**, 1997, and in Chapter 5 of this volume). By a 'preferred reading' Hall (1980) means a reading towards which the text directs its readers. This is not to say that this is how the text will be read; there are always possibilities of alternative, negotiated or oppositional readings. There are differing 'relations of equivalence', Hall argues, between the encoding and decoding moments, for two reasons. First, any text is, to some extent, polysemic. This means that it can, potentially, generate a range of possible meanings. At the same time, 'Polysemy must not, however, be confused with pluralism ... there exists a pattern of "preferred readings"' (Hall, 1980, p. 134). In applying this to technology, we can say that technologies vary in their degree of openness or closedness, in the degree to which they can be used for purposes which differ from the intentions of their designers. A

preferred readings

microcomputer, for example, is an extremely 'open' device: it can be used for entertainment, education, business or warfare; a mortar bomb, on the other hand, cannot be used for much other than its intended purpose. With technology, we have to consider this at the levels of soft as well as hardware: the Walkman can only play tapes, but these can be for music (and, within that, they can be of any variety of music), Open University course materials, poetry, a heritage tour or whatever. Nonetheless, even with the extremely open microcomputer, users remain constrained; there is some degree of technological determinism, and a powerful 'preferred reading'.

The second cause of the disjuncture between encoding and decoding is the possibility of an aberrant decoding since decoding is shaped by the reader's '... general framework of cultural references ... his [*sic*] ideological, ethical, religious standpoints ... his psychological attitude, his tastes, his value systems, etc.' (Eco, 1972, p. 115).

So, despite the work of cultural intermediaries in design, advertising and marketing, there is space for creative (albeit circumscribed) consumption, **resistance and transformation**. It is important, of course, as was argued in the Introduction to this Book, not to overrate the power involved in such transformative 'work'. As Ien Ang argues about television: 'audiences may be active, in myriad ways, in using and interpreting media ... it would be utterly out of perspective to cheerfully equate "active" with "powerful"' (1990, p. 247).

resistance and
transformation

4.2   Power and contest

Clearly, consumers have the power to buy, or not buy, a given technology. But to approach the power of the consumer in only this way is to ignore the active role of consumers in shaping technology. In contrast with approaches to cultural consumption which see it as a passive activity, the consumption of ICTs in households seems an *active* process, in which meanings and uses are contested: uses, forms and meanings are the outcome (and focus) of power and contest – as the technologies and their protagonists battle to win a place in our everyday lives and routines.

In these processes of struggle, alternative uses for technologies may emerge. Among these **aberrant or oppositional decodings** are possibilities for the progressive appropriation of new technologies. Williams (1983) refers to possibilities for local television and the regeneration of communities through cable television (in contrast with the pessimism about cable television of 'mass culture critique' theorists); the camcorder not only serves the interests of hardware manufacturers such as Sony and of software producers, but also allows for the filming of the LA police assault on Rodney King – providing powerful evidence of police treatment of black people in that city; the fax serves businesses well, but was also invaluable for the students in Tiannamen Square in communicating their version of events to the outside world; and the Internet, developed with multiple switching nodes in order to

aberrant or
oppositional
decodings

ensure its effectiveness in the context of a nuclear strike, now enables participatory, global communication while defying centralized control.

The transformation of technologies by consumers can be taken much further than such 'countercultural' uses – especially at the moment of arrival. Williams, in *Television: technology and cultural form* (1974), explains how the moment of the arrival of a new technology is a crucial and exciting one, a time of contest. When new technologies arrive, they do so within the context – the organizations, professional practices, media forms and regulatory regimes – of existing media. Neither software nor uses are built in to the technology; particularly at the time of its arrival these are shaped, negotiated and contested. I shall illustrate this through the example of the telephone.

Like new ICTs today, the emergence of the telephone was accompanied by the development of new bodies of knowledge, new occupations, new terminology and new metaphors. Quite remarkably similar to today's discussion of the Internet – which we explore in section 6 below – there were prophesies of utopias, claims about decentralization, freedom and community, and concerns about family life, boundaries between private and public, and use of the technology by the criminal element (Marvin, 1988). Important in these discussions, of course, were the bodies with vested interests – notably the telephone companies, which had to convince people that they needed the telephone, so sought to teach consumers how and what to use it for. There are two remarkable aspects to the uses which emerged.

First, at the turn of the century there were in fact two conceptions of the most fruitful use of electronic voice transmission – broadcasting and conversation. However, the former was dropped fairly early on, and was not to become common practice for a further half-century. According to the sociologist Ithiel de Sola Pool (1977), this was for two interlinked reasons: the visions of developers for such a system, which encouraged them to solve the technical problems which obscured its realization; and society's choice. In the early days, the telephone, in both the USA and Britain, was used for the transmission and reception of religious services ('to bring God to the home of the sick and invalid' (Martin, 1991, p. 136)), concerts (Queen Victoria was amongst the subscribers who had a connection to the Opera House in Covent Garden and the Theatre Royal in Drury Lane), political rallies, sporting events and even for regular news and information broadcasting. At the end of the nineteenth century Telefon Hormondo in Budapest began 'broadcasting' by telephone – demonstrating that transmitting regular news and entertainment to large audiences existed well before the advent of twentieth-century broadcasting. As late as 1921 an internal Bell Telephone memorandum projected the future of broadcasting simply in terms of the transmission of important occasions, such as Armistice Day or presidential inauguration ceremonies (Marvin, 1988). Over an extended period telephone exchanges filled the role of local radio or newspapers as the focal point for the distribution of news.

'proper' use

Second, **'proper' use** of the telephone in these early days was for business or, in the home, for household management – such as ordering goods and services. For decades telephone companies discouraged women's conversations on the telephone – which were seen as 'abuse' of the technology. It took from about 1880 until well in to the 1920s before the telephone began to be promoted as suitable for sociability, as opposed to practical, economic matters. The sociologist Claude Fischer (1991, p. 111) argues that the sociable use of the telephone was seen in the early years as frivolous, trivial and unnecessary because of 'the cultural "mind set" of the telephone men'. By this she is referring to the roots of telephony and telephone personnel in telegraphy and the practices surrounding the telegraph; for decades, the uses of the telephone replicated the functional, factual and gendered prior use of the telegraph. What is remarkable is that it took so long for telephone companies to realize that conversation on the telephone could be good for business. Today the tables have turned and BT advertisements ask 'Why can't men be more like women?' Other advertisements refer to 'the simple joys of talking'; and to the value of *men chatting* on the telephone, and of talking to maintain family relationships. Whilst this may seem an obvious marketing strategy, it is very far removed from the purposes which it had been envisaged that the technology would fufil.

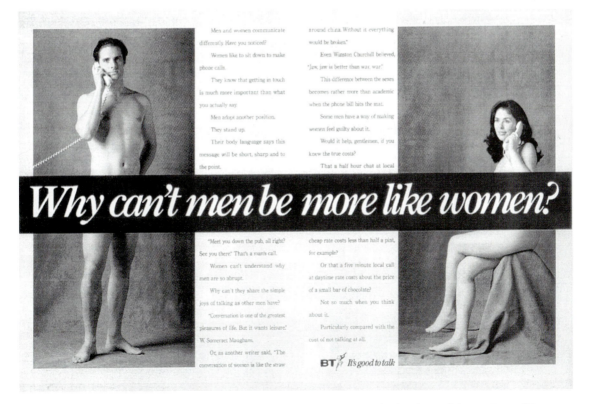

FIGURE 6.1   British Telecom advertisement: one of a campaign with the slogan 'It's good to talk'.

The example of the telephone shows us that new technologies are not simply invented to meet some human need, and then taken up – or not, as in the case of Sinclair's C5 tricycle and so many other 'inventions'. In contrast to the pessimism of the Frankfurt School, in which consumers are seen as the passive recipients of the products of corporate capitalism, the outcome of technological development often differs from any early vision. The sociologist of technology David Noble refers to the **'double life'** of a technology:

'double life'

> Close inspection of technological development reveals that technology leads a double life, one which conforms to the intentions of designers and interests of power and another which contradicts them – proceeding behind the backs of their architects to yield unintended consequences and unanticipated possibilities.
>
> (Noble, 1984, pp. 324–5)

Clearly this resembles Hall's encoding/decoding model which we have discussed. So our domestic technology – what it is used for and what it means to us – is far from a narrow technical matter. Rather than being built into hardware, technologies are shaped, in a very real way, by local everyday lives and routines in households. Rather than secondary, our notion of the cultural circuit shows that the processes involved are not one-way, and that consumption plays a key role in informing technology (re)design – through market research and consumer feedback (see **du Gay, Hall et al.**, 1997, and **Negus**, 1997). Consumers, rather than simply recipients of innovations, can thus be seen as playing a key role in the innovation process.

4.3   Shifting meanings/emerging technologies

By now you should be getting the idea that technologies are not simply functional, but, like other artefacts, carry meanings: think of the Volkswagen Beetle or the Walkman, for example. And these meanings, of course, are inseparable from representational practices.

ACTIVITY 2

Consider the home computer: how is it represented, what associations do you construct around it and what does it mean?

My response to these questions would be to say that it is commonly represented in ways which stress its 'revolutionary' nature, its associations with the burgeoning social order, its small size ('laptop', 'hand held', 'palmtop', 'micro'), its high power, its 'intelligence', its ease of use, and its interactivity – all pretty positive associations. The computer has become a key symbol of modernity and the future – some have argued that it should be seen as *the* symbol of the late modern era, in the same way as the steam engine symbolized the Industrial Revolution.

Nor are these meanings fixed. The meanings of technologies have shifted dramatically as they have become more commonplace and diffused through our culture – which is happening fast: the two most popular Christmas presents at the time of writing are mobile telephones and multimedia computers. Computers are no longer associated exclusively with men and hackers, as feminists espouse their networking capabilities and cybercafés open in provincial cities. Although the male hacker culture lives on, computing has become an important part of youth subculture, and associated with fashion and pleasure.

So the cultural shaping of technology is not confined to function, to the uses to which a technology is put; the same flexibility applies to the meanings, symbolic significance the **symbolic significance**, of the technology. Two examples will illustrate the symbolic nature of a technology: the first, the mobile telephone, is concerned with the *shifting* meaning of a technology over time; the other refers to a symbolic significance which varies with *locales.*

First is the case of the mobile (cellular) telephone (Wood, 1993). You may hate it, you may love it, but my experience is that it is a technology which arouses strong feelings – the British public seemed delighted when Nigel Lawson imposed a tax on it. It is an interesting technology to me because, like the Walkman, it transgresses the public–private boundary: it is a technology for conducting private conversations but in public space. As with the Walkman, this private use in public can easily generate antagonism. In the early 1990s mobile phones were the preserve of the business elite – and a powerful status symbol. To use a phone in public it has to be displayed – despite the hunched shoulders of some users to avoid this. So, more than just a symbol, it's a very public symbol, carried prominently and hard to use discreetly. To be contactable anywhere, anytime may now seem straightforward, even meaningless. In the early 1990s it was an expensive luxury, the preserve of an elite – almost entirely male, in well-paid employment, important and powerful. With the mobile phone, one could mark oneself out in this way; the rest of us continued to use payphones.

HELLO JULIE
WHAT HAPPENED
IN EASTENDERS?

... For the sake of good relations within the performing arts, remember to switch off during the show.

After a while we found mobile phones being used by more ordinary people – social workers, plumbers, van-drivers and housewives. At this moment that fundamental division between white- and blue-collar work – access to a telephone – was changed. The mobile phone very rapidly moved down the social scale; and, as it did so, exclusivity came to be redefined – in terms of *in*accessibility or privacy. So the meanings of the technology, rather than being fixed, are emergent and situated.

The second example is that of computer games – a far from trivial phenomenon. Over a decade ago the industry was worth three times

Hollywood and twice the pop music industry: the revenue from Pac-Man exceeded the cinema box office success *Star Wars* (Haddon, 1988b). Games are an interesting technology because they have been a key raw material of male youth subculture through the 1980s and 1990s. Perhaps 80 per cent of games players are teenagers, 80 per cent of these are male, and with an overrepresentation of the working classes (Haddon, 1988a, b).

Some argue that computer games increase hand–eye co-ordination and teach computer literacy, and can relieve stress and tension. The dominant discourse concerning arcade games, however, is moral outrage. As spaces in which adolescents gather, not under the control of the home, school or workplace, they are condemned by politicians and the media as breeding-grounds for petty crime, vandalism and hooliganism, for encouraging truancy from school, for wasting time and money, for their addictive nature and for their violent content. Ferdinand Marcos, when President of the Philippines, ordered 3,000 coin-operated games to be dismantled, smashed or surrendered to the police within 15 days, after civic groups had referred to them as 'devilish contraptions' that 'wreak havoc on the morals and discipline of our youth' (Toles, 1985, p. 210). Nearer home, a Labour MP promoted the Control of Space Invaders (and other Electronic Games) Bill in 1981.

The first computer games were developed in the NASA-funded Artificial Intelligence (AI) laboratories at MIT, by computer scientists who were using their (real-time) programming skills to explore the capabilities of their machines. In this milieu, the fount of hacker culture, their powerful computers were treated as toys, on which to play chess and, later, the first computer-based games. The content of these early games – with an emphasis on battles and shooting – can be seen as reflecting the tastes of these male programmers. Games were then run on microcomputers, as that product emerged, and later moved to the arcade. Leslie Haddon, a cultural theorist who researches new technologies, explains how amusement park owners adopted electronic games to add respectability to their operations, to shed their sleazy image and make themselves places for modern, clean, family entertainment. In the arcades there was already another form of electronic game – pinball. Haddon argues that the values, rules and rituals surrounding pinball were transferred to the new video games: the public display of skill, and rules about waiting for a game and single players, for example. His research suggests that, far from being an isolated or isolating activity, playing computer games is a collective activity, and the focus of talk and interaction. He found that computer games stimulate a network for boys to transact with one another through a subculture of computer talk.

The very same games were then supplied, in the next leg of the journey of the computer game, to the home. (Atari's *Pong* was the first significant release for the home market.) In the home the text and narrative were identical to the arcade, but the context (and surrounding social activity) profoundly different: computers at home were, by definition, exempt from the moral panic surrounding arcade culture. Rather, they enjoyed the status of educational technologies. Manufacturers, in their attempts to penetrate the home market, were reluctant to stress the games-playing capacity and usage of their machines, preferring to emphasize the educational implications of the product. The meanings and uses of computer games have thus varied enormously, depending on the context of consumption.

Both the mobile telephone and computer games illustrate the centrality of their *symbolic significance*, and how this meaning, rather than being fixed, depends on the spatial and temporal context of consumption.

4.4   Summary of sections 2, 3 and 4

We have covered considerable ground so far in this chapter, introducing and applying some key concepts for making sense of technology. We started, in section 2, by introducing the importance of technology and its relevance to 'the home'. In section 3 we defined technology in a way which takes us beyond the common, everyday understanding of the artefactual. We discussed technological determinism, the orthodox way in which the relationship between technology and society is conceived. We then developed the notion that, to the contrary, technologies are socially shaped – but we also retained some notion of the constraining nature of the hardware. Section 4 went on to apply notions of encoding and decoding, to see technology as text, addressing questions of power and contest in the processes; and we discussed the symbolic significance of technology. Technologies can thus be used in a variety of ways, with different effects. In the next section of the chapter we shall look at some of these ways, and will examine the context of technology consumption, the household, in more detail – to see how it is that technologies are shaped in households, and households are shaped by technologies.

5   Communications technologies and everyday life in households

To understand the consumption of technologies in households, we have to understand the practices of everyday life there – how new technologies are implicated in household routines and activities. This is a far from insignificant matter; it is not something which simply follows (good) design and marketing, but is crucial to shaping technology. In the **'domestication' of technologies** there are implications for the subjectivities of those involved: identity and a sense of self are inextricably bound up in the consumption of technologies in the household – and, through such consumption, technologies are shaped. Although the success or failure of an innovation is commonly conceived in technical terms, consumption by households, as we shall see, is quite as important as the lab bench or policy regulation in shaping technology

'domestication' of technologies

When new technologies arrive in households their uses, meanings and forms are not predetermined nor fixed. Encoded in particular ways, with preferred readings or uses, they *may* be used, and carry meanings, as intended by their designers. But they may, alternatively, be rejected or modified through their use in households. There are several important issues which arise from this and I shall be unpacking and illustrating these in this section. As well as having to win a place in the home, a new technology itself contributes to domestic routines and practices; these are disrupted and modified by the entry into the home of a technology. We shall be exploring how new technologies have to slot in with the texture and rhythms of everyday life in households, and how new technologies have to capture time and space in households.

In this process, technologies engage with the internal dynamics of the organization of domestic space. So whilst there is 'negotiation' by the consumer of the text (see **Gledhill**, 1997, and Chapter 5 in this volume), with ICTs in the home (in particular) we have to add the negotiation between members of households: consumption patterns and everyday practices in households are themselves the outcome of complex domestic politics – of power relations between household members. The ways in which we lead our lives in households are negotiated – in relation to domestic power relations, and in terms of gender and generational differences in particular. The significance and usage of ICTs in the home are similarly negotiated.

The acquisition of technologies, and the uses to which they are put, depend on a complex set of factors relating to the cultural dispositions and competencies of households and their members. These factors, at one level, appear as varied as households, and we shall be examining the idiosyncratic ways in which one household works with (and against) its ICTs. These consumer practices, however, are patterned in various ways – notably in terms of gender, class, generation and geography; we shall be examining some of these patternings in relation to the home computer.

In sum, our concern is with the significance of the consumption of ICTs for people's domestic lives, and for household and family relationships; with how ICTs are implicated in shifting individual and family identities, and in the relationship between household members' private and public worlds; and with how the technology (as well as the household) is transformed in the process of domestication and incorporation.

Before going any further, let's clarify briefly what we mean by 'the home', 'the household' and 'the family'. Our *home* is the place to which we return, and a symbol of freedom, choice, security and comfort: we might see our ideal home as a private utopia. Within the home, we live in *households* (made up of *families* or other social units) – economic and cultural units which, as Daniel Miller has argued in Chapter 1 of this volume, are the key units of consumption, and the environment in which meanings and pleasures are constructed. With the recent shift in sociology to a focus on consumption, the household has become more important as a field of study.

It is in terms of households that we both define the private and engage with the public. The *domestic* is a looser term, encompassing elements of the home, the household and the family and invoking (and conferring?), in the dominant orthodoxy, notions of belonging, security and identity. All of these – the home, the family and the domestic – are, of course, culturally constructed and historically specific.

5.1   The arrival of new technologies in the home

How can we see households as shaping technology? Let's start with the moment of the *arrival* of a new technology. When this happens, as we have said, its uses, meanings and form are not predetermined and fixed; rather, they are fluid, and have to contend with the rhythms and texture of everyday life in households; new technologies have to *capture time and space* in the home.

ACTIVITY 3

Think of the ICTs which you have in your home. Choose *one* of these and note what it means to you. Think back to when it was bought. Why was it bought? Who made the decision to purchase? How did you choose which model, or brand, to purchase? Who decided where to keep it? Did it look right? Was it an intrusion? Who learnt to use it first?

Hopefully, if only at a preliminary level, you have taken your thinking about a technology in your home beyond the utilitarian (for example, that you have a telephone to make telephone calls) and you have begun to problematize some of its taken-for-granted characteristics.

Shaun Moores (1988) has undertaken oral history research on the entry of early radio to the home (in the inter-war years) and has reported on its gradual incorporation into household life (mentioned in Chapter 5 in this volume). Quoting his interviewees in their own words, he discusses how broadcasting entered the private sphere in the shape of a 'miraculous toy' – which the men of the household often built from kits, and which they enjoyed experimenting with. The equipment, however – unlike today's radios – was obtrusive and in many ways unsuitable for the domestic sphere: lengths of wire often had to be spread around a room to act as an aerial, and early sets had heavy batteries which sometimes leaked acid, corroding the furniture or carpets. Listening generally involved the (male) head of the household donning headphones and adjusting the crystal, while other members could only watch – having to keep quiet so that the crackly signal could be heard by the one listener. The transformation of this miraculous toy

capturing of time and space

... proved pivotal to radio's **capturing of time and space** in the household. Three interrelated shifts began to take place during the 1930s ... First the technological and aesthetic form of the receiving apparatus changed dramatically, turning it into a fashionable piece of living-room furniture.

Second was the formation of radio discourses that symbolically constructed their audience as 'the family', and which sought to interpellate mothers as monitors of domestic life. Finally, broadcasters increasingly ordered programmes into 'routinized' schedules that revolved around the imagined daily activities of the housewife.

(Moores, 1993, p. 80)

Let's unpack each of these three ways in which the radio 'captured time and space'. The first point – the changing form of the radio – included modifications to make the technology more suitable for family listening. Moores' respondents reported holding out the headphone so that a partner could hear a broadcast, improvisation such as adding a pudding basin to amplify the sound and, later, the addition of loudspeakers. As well, wirelesses came to be designed as attractive pieces of furniture, signalling dignified harmony. (The manufacture of home computers with television receivers and in black is similar – shifting their associations from the world of the office to that of leisure, and enabling them to fit unobtrusively into living-rooms.) In the process of domesticating the wireless in these ways, the home itself became transformed – becoming more attractive as a locus of leisure. Moores' respondents referred to the pleasures of enjoying music in the home, hitherto not possible, and to a father transferring his beer-drinking from the pub to the home.

The second change which enabled the radio to capture time and space in the home was the development of radio discourse to construct the audience as 'the family'. The very titles of programmes such as *Housewives' Choice, Listen with Mother* and *Children's Hour* suggest this process. The modes of address of these programmes were premised on, and reinforced, dominant domestic relations, identities and moralities. Broadcasting addressed the family, be it shows for entertainment or childminding while mothers cooked the evening meal.

The third point that Moores makes is that radio developed its scheduling in such a way that it slotted into households' temporal regimes. Strange as it may seem retrospectively, early radio left periods of silence between programmes; it also broadcast the same programme at different times each day or week. Gradually, scheduling became more predictable (and continuous): 'Radio began to weave itself skilfully into the repetitive rhythms of quotidian culture' (ibid., p. 85).

The arrival of television in the 1950s has been researched by the media theorist Tim O'Sullivan (1991), also using oral history methods. O'Sullivan found that, like the radio, it was men who had made the decision to purchase – perhaps unsurprisingly given their control of household budgets for major purchases and the associations between masculinity and technology. Like new technology today, 'The act of getting a television generally seems to be remembered above all as a sign of progress, a visible sign of joining, or at least not being left out of "the new"' (O'Sullivan, 1991,

p. 166). O'Sullivan reports rearrangements of domestic layout and the routinization of viewing.

Another media researcher, Lynn Spigel (1992), has explored the *discourses* surrounding the entry of television to the home, particularly in women's magazines. She shows that these were ambivalent about the arrival of television, because of its potential to distract housewives from housework. In their advice, these magazines contributed to the development of cultural rules for watching television, in ways which ensured that it supported family life.

With the mobile telephone, too, at the time of writing, we can see the active construction of the user – in this case by a service-providing organization. Cellnet has actually produced a booklet for new owners, offering tips on *how* to use the technology, in an attempt to make it more congenial:

> ... we all know that it's bad form to take a call from the bookmaker while the MD is droning on about the latest marketing push.

> Similarly, only the terminally inept will choose to interrupt an important 'So, where-do-we-go-from-here?' conversation with a soon-to-be ex-partner by lunging for the mobile in order to confirm tonight's take-away curry, or checking the score on the day's football match. Between these extremes, however, the user faces the more subtle dilemma. Should you use the phone in the street? Where should you use it? Should you use your mobile when you are visiting someone else's office or conducting a meeting? And when should you switch it on or off?

> ... the owner of the phone who wishes to use it considerately and thoughtfully will be negotiating relatively uncharted territory.

(Cellnet, no date)

...it's bad form to take a call from the bookmaker while the MD is droning on about the latest marketing push.

These examples show us that, although today commonplace in the home, at the time of their arrival new technologies are disruptive to family life. Their uses and success are far from assured: rather than fitting in naturally, they have to be domesticated, made to fit the spatial and temporal rhythms of households; and, in these processes, they become adapted and modified.

5.2   The gendering of technology: the telephone

Both the radio and television show us that any understanding of ICTs in the home has to take on board the **politics of domestic life** – the structured relations between young and old, and between men and women. So it is not surprising that gender is central to understanding the take-up, uses and meanings of technologies. Ann Gray (1987) has explored women's uses of the VCR. Following Cynthia Cockburn's (1985) research technique, she asked her interviewees to code their domestic activities and technologies on a pink–blue scale, to delineate their gender specificity:

politics of domestic life

> This produces almost uniformly pink irons and blue electric drills, with many interesting mixtures along the spectrum. The washing machine, for example, is most usually pink on the outside, but the motor is almost always blue ... we must break down the VCR into its different modes in our colour-coding. The 'record', 'rewind' and 'play' modes are usually lilac, but the timer switch is nearly always blue, with women having to depend on their male partners or their children to set the timer for them. The blueness of the timer is exceeded only by the deep indigo of the remote control switch which in all cases is held by the man.
>
> (Gray, 1987, p. 42)

Clearly these technologies acquire gendered meanings in their circulation and appropriation; but, more than that – as we saw with the example of the VAX computer – the technology is far from neutral when it leaves the factory in the first place. At the very least, it is likely to *embody* dominant assumptions about power in households and the role of men and women in relation to particular household activities and technologies. Cockburn (1985) has argued that the exclusion of women from technology – which shows little sign of abatement – is far from the case historically: she argues that women became excluded from technology with the onset of the Industrial Revolution, with the separation of home from work, and the sexual division of labour which is a part of that. Today women remain marginalized from technology – in design, in education and in the language and professional practices of engineers. She sees technology as 'the material of male power', rather than as neutral though perhaps biased by the power interests which deploy it. Others are more optimistic (or naive?), celebrating the appropriation of cyberspace as a space for feminist activity. Sadie Plant (1996, p. 170), for example, argues that: 'There is more to cyberspace than meets the male gaze ... women are accessing the circuits on which they were once exchange ... discovering their own post-humanity.'

Work on television audiences (Morley, 1986; Hobson, 1982), too, shows a strong gender dimension, as is shown in Chapter 5: viewing patterns are gender-distinctive in the amount and style of viewing, programme preferences, control of viewing choice and experiences of viewing. Morley (1986) has provided a fascinating account of the gendered nature of the television remote control – the 'zapper' – which is the focus of friction and contest in family life; and Lull (1988) has explored the masculinity of the VCR. We shall explore the gendering of a technology by focusing on the telephone – a technology which has had a far-reaching influence on our daily lives, but which we commonly experience as transparent, and which has been little researched by scholars in cultural, communication and media theory.

The telephone is used by men and women for different purposes and in different ways. Several commentators (de Sola Pool, 1977; Marvin, 1988; Rakow, 1992) have referred to the telephone as reducing women's isolation. Specifically, Lana Rakow points to the telephone as a technology which both causes and alleviates the loneliness and isolation of housewives.

Rakow's work is based on an ethnographic study in the Midwest of the USA. She argues that women's relationship to the telephone is complex but distinctive. On the one hand, the telephone has opened up new possibilities for women's talk and women's relationships. For many women, the telephone serves as a lifeline, in a context in which housework is an isolated activity, especially for farmers' wives; and the telephone can relieve women of the need to travel and shop. At the same time, the telephone itself probably contributed to the processes of dispersal which brought about the isolation of women in the first place – the development of the suburb, and patterns of social organization:

> If the telephone was indeed implicated in the development of suburbs, the separation of homes and business, and the decline of neighbourhoods, it was also implicated in the physical separation of women's private sphere and men's public sphere and the isolation of the home and of individual women in them. That is, the telephone may have been implicated in creating the very conditions from which it was praised for having rescued women.
>
> (Rakow, 1992, p. 203)

So the telephone shrinks time and space, and ameliorates (though doesn't overcome) the problems caused by dispersion. Rakow's argument is that the telephone has contributed to possibilities for women but has also maintained and constructed gender differences and hierarchies – with (for example) women more likely to be the recipients of malicious calls (Stanley and Wise, 1979) and less likely to be listed in telephone directories.

Ann Moyal (1992) has identified a distinct pattern of telephone usage by women – often referred to (perjoratively) as 'chatter'. Moyal administered a questionnaire in Australia to a sample of 200 women and followed this with semi-structured interviews with a range of women in a diversity of social situations – in terms of (non)employment, urban/rural location, age and ethnicity. Like Rakow, her concern was to explore the feminine culture of the telephone, and to gather the experience, attitudes and voices of women. From the outset, she explains, telephone companies saw (women's) gossip as *misuse* of the technology. Moyal asked interviewees to distinguish between 'instrumental' and 'intrinsic' telephone calls. Instrumental calls are defined as appointment and arrangement-making, purchasing and seeking information; whilst intrinsic calls are for personal exchange and communication. She found that women make an average of four instrumental calls a week, and twenty-four intrinsic calls, which were longer in duration and many of which were long-distance.

Moyal then relates this pattern of telephone usage to key elements of Australian culture. Families, she argues, are deep-rooted, and family relationships are sustained by telephone contact between female family members. The other main form of intrinsic call is networking with close friends. Here, again, the telephone was seen as central to maintaining relationships, providing support and care and, in some cases, alleviating boredom and loneliness. Interestingly, her interviewees reported that they talk *more* freely and intimately on the telephone than face-to-face. Moyal concludes that – in contrast with the common and pejorative view of women's telephone usage – the telephone is a crucial technology in holding together families and communities.

5.3   Families and technologies

We have seen how, when they arrive, new technologies have to capture time and space in the home. Although the place of ICTs in our homes, and the purposes and context of their use may appear to us natural, obvious or inevitable, these are, to the contrary, the outcome of struggle – both between actors and the technologies, and between household members – as the work of domesticating (and transforming) the technology takes place. Household members work with each other and the technology to convert it to their desired ends. Obviously, one crucial element of household interaction is gender, and we have explored the gendering of one important domestic technology. Let us now broaden our concern by addressing more fully how the internal dynamics and values of the household shape technologies – how consumption is shaped by the **material and symbolic resources of households**. These inform everyday lives and routines, both within the home and in terms of the household's links with the outside world.

material and symbolic resources of households

ACTIVITY 4

Think back to the leisure technology in your home on which you based the last Activity, and note your answers to the following questions:

1   Who uses it, when, and what for?

2   Is it used as you anticipated originally?

3   What pleasures does it offer you and others?

4   Have you been disappointed with it?

5   Have you changed how you see it?

6   Does its use tie in with other technologies?

7   In what context is it used?

8   Who controls its use, or decides when or how it is used?

Since the late 1980s researchers have explored ethnographically the consumption of ICTs in the everyday life of households. Best known perhaps is the work of Roger Silverstone, Eric Hirsch and David Morley (1992) who have been involved in a project which gathered in-depth qualitative data on twenty households, from which they have produced detailed, descriptive accounts of the interrelationship between a household's 'moral economy' and its consumption of ICTs, in an attempt to explore the links between social and technological change in the everyday, domestic, world. They gathered data from participant observation in four households, and in sixteen households they made seven visits over eight months; in addition, respondents kept time-use diaries, made diagrams of the location of kin and friends, and made maps of the location in their home of technologies. Unsurprisingly, such qualitative exploration of a few households in considerable depth yields some fascinating data about the use and significance of technology in everyday life. From this study we are provided with some rich accounts of situated consumption practices, and we are shown how family values, domestic relationships and everyday routines interact with the technology.

READING B

You should now read the ethnographic portrait of the first family by Roger Silverstone and David Morley from their paper 'Families and their technologies: two ethnographic portraits'. As you read their account you should note in particular:

1   the headings under which they organize their ethnographic account; and

2   the strengths and limitations of this ethnographic family portrait.

The great strength of this Reading for me is that it brings the subject to life, making us only too aware that we are talking about everyday life. By going into people's homes and interviewing them, Silverstone and Morley generate a wealth and richness of data about how people experience and interpret their technologies, and the significance these hold for their everyday lives. The detail is both plausible and fascinating. But what are the limitations? Let me raise three.

First, as Ruth Furlong argues, I think that they tend to over-emphasize the boundedness of the home. Clearly, any study has to have its boundaries, but it seems to me altogether too neat to draw a boundary around the context of consumption which is coterminous with the boundary of the home. The outcome is that the home is presented as somewhere safe and secure, from which the world beyond can be safely explored. Leaving aside the problem that the home is (for many people) an extremely *dangerous* place (in terms of accidents and domestic violence), let me make three points: first, plenty of children nowadays have parents who are separated, and many of these move (with varying degrees of independence) between two parental homes; clearly the meaning of 'home' in such a situation is complex. Second, the emphasis on domestic relations and interactions tends to relegate the significance of peers and friends in people's lives and identities. There's an interesting crowd of youths whom I often see on the common on my way home who almost live in their cars – with friends and a sound system. The car constitutes something of a mobile home – and is appreciated, I imagine, precisely because it is out of sight and sound of the family home. Finally, the focus on the home seems to me to make an artificial divide in leisure activities. Hanging around, going to the cinema, to football or a concert or a friend's house are alternative leisure activities – which are somehow missed by focusing on the home and its leisure technologies; the use of these is embedded in broader leisure culture as well as in the domestic.

Second is the question of 'ethnography'. For me, this means research which is based on an extended period of *in situ* fieldwork, and an approach which is concerned with eliciting actors' understandings of their everyday lives and with how these activities and interactions take place naturally. But in practice this 'naturalism' is rather problematic: ethnography is a representational practice; and ethnography is generally 'reflexive', in that the researcher brings to bear categories or concerns of their own to enable them to organize and make sense of their data, and to tell their story. Silverstone and Morley, in fact, readily acknowledge that they analyse their respondents' lives in terms of the categories in which they as researchers are interested. It seems to me that a real concern with how actors use and make sense of technologies in their everyday lives would have to be rooted more in actors' own sense-making, in the traditions of symbolic interactionism or ethnomethodology.

The final point I should like to raise is the descriptive nature of the account – which is, at the same time, its strength and its weakness. It's what brings this family to life; and a series of such accounts, emphasizing the situatedness and contingent nature of the use of technologies in the everyday life of households, provides us with a wealth of empirical data. But it fails to address any *patternings* which lie behind the specificities of the setting. There is a danger that we end up with a pluralist approach to households and power, in which structured patterns are lost in the thick, ever-contingent description. Behind this diversity, are there any patterns which can be identified in how ICTs in the home are used and understood – patternings in terms of class, gender, generation, ethnicity or geography? Despite the value of Silverstone and Morley's qualitative research, we need to complement it with quantitative data on patterns of ownership and use of ICTs.

READING C

You should now read the extract from an article by Hughie Mackay on the pattern of ownership of home computers.

You should make notes on the differences – of class, gender, generation or geography – in patterns of ownership and use of the home computer. You should also note how these patternings have changed over time.

This sort of quantitative data usefully complements the in-depth qualitative work of Silverstone and Morley, and leaves us with an idea of ways in which consumption patterns are *structured* – in terms of class and other factors. Whilst ethnographic work gives us a rich, qualitative account, this quantitative data provides a broader (if less deep) picture. Because it uses a much larger sample, we can gain an understanding of what is typical, and of the range and nature of deviations from this: we can generalize from the data with greater confidence and, by gathering the same data from a similar sample, we can generate a longitudinal picture which gives us an understanding of trends.

5.4   Summary

In this section we have explored in-depth the cultural consumption in households of ICTs. Far from being a straightforward process of acceptance or rejection, we have seen that it is one which both depends on and shapes domestic relations – involving negotiation and contest between household members, and with the technology. We have examined some underlying patternings – of gender and generation – to these consumption practices. In these processes of negotiation and contest we have seen how technologies and households are transformed. To conclude the chapter, let us return to the outside world and examine the ways in which ICTs mediate the links between households and the public world – and thus how domestic consumption practices link us with the world beyond, rather than isolate us from it.

6   Emerging ICTs, shifting boundaries

In this final section we shall be exploring how ICTs play a crucial role not just *within* the home, but in **connecting** us to the world beyond, mediating the local and the global, bringing the global home and contributing to our construction of community. We shall refer to ways in which the consumption of new ICTs shrinks time and space, and to their implications for identity and community in the contemporary era. In Chapter 5 Shaun Moores examined these issues in relation to broadcasting; in this section we shall be looking at new ICTs and, specifically, the Internet.

First, let's introduce briefly these new ICTs, the context of their arrival and their consumption. The global media corporations are experiencing organizational integration (discussed in **du Gay, Hall et al.**, 1997): Sega has bought a Hollywood studio, where it is making its own movies as well as computer animations for its interactive games; Sony, JVC and Matsushita, known traditionally as hardware manufacturers, have interests in film production; and the synthesized music which accompanies Super Mario and other computer games has been in the pop music charts. Nevertheless, as Kevin **Robins** (1997) argues, one must not forget that there is also the opposite process at work – of vertical *dis*integration, for example the outsourcing of television production to small producers to reduce costs, enhance creativity and increase flexibility. Such organizational *dis*integration, however, still tends to leave *power* in the hands of the major players (Storper and Christopherson, 1987). At the same time the media world is no longer one of isolated technologies: with digitization, convergence, competition, choice and interactivity we are seeing media synergy. And the software and activities which have for some time been associated with television are now being delivered and consumed using other media technologies. The telephone can be used for video-on-demand, the interactive transmission of film to the home; the Internet can be used for telephone calls and video-conferencing; games can be played on PCs or the television screen; and CD players can be connected to the television (for games or PhotoCD), the PC or the stereo; and with many of these developments we are witnessing the emergence of new media forms.

So it is not simply the case that one technology *displaces* another – that we watch less television and take up video-on-demand, for example, or that playing computer games replaces television viewing. New media alter the function, significance and effects of earlier media; new technologies become absorbed, or integrated, with the old, and in the process themselves become transformed. In changing the old, new ICTs break down a number of conventional categories and boundaries: spatial and temporal boundaries of human interaction and communication are altered; new linguistic terms and conceptual systems are developed; the computer industry comes to overlap heavily with broadcasting, film, print and publishing industries; and new organizations and professional practices emerge. Broadcasting and other

<aside>connecting</aside>

media are increasingly directed at niche audiences (as segmented markets replace the *mass* media); locales of leisure – and the very nature of leisure activity – are changing; and the very boundaries between play and reality are broken down (with computer games and virtual reality). In all this, there are implications for the power and control of the consumer; and the relationship between producers and consumers is transformed. The implications of these new technologies are only beginning to emerge; as they mature, we can expect to see the development of new organizations, new practices, systems of regulation, and new media forms.

With new ICTs we are witnessing the extension of the long-term trend towards increasingly instantaneous communication. At the same time we are experiencing the **loss of simultaneity**: in the shift from broadcasting to niche markets and multiple choice (of cable, satellite, digital television and the Internet) we are seeing a move away from the simultaneity of mass consumption which characterized earlier broadcasting, and from broadcasting having to fit with the temporal rhythms of the home. A range of technologies have been developed to facilitate this process: with the VCR for time-shifting television (recording it for later viewing), telephone-answering machines, e-mail, video-on-demand and the Internet, we are able to control *when* we transmit or receive our messages and we are thereby losing the common simultaneity of reception which has been associated with broadcasting.

loss of simultaneity

This is the context in which the Internet has arrived. The Internet is a global communications network which has developed in recent years from an obscure web of computer networks used by a small elite of scientists, academics and hobbyists to an incredibly fast-growing new media technology. Recent reports suggest that there are connected to the Internet some 12.9 million host computers, with an estimated ten users per host (Kehoe, 1995); in the UK there are several hundred thousand subscribers to Compuserve, the largest Internet access provider in the UK. The Internet covers a host of uses: the World Wide Web (WWW) (which allows access to web sites around the world, as well as various other Internet facilities), e-mail (the electronic transmission of (normally) text messages), Inter Relay Chat (IRC) channels (on which individuals can type and transmit one-to-one messages in real time), Avatars and MUDs (multi user dungeons or domains – virtual worlds and games where you can play your selected character or persona), long-distance telephone calls, video- and audio-conferencing, mailing lists (which send to subscribers material on a given subject), file transfer and accessing other computers, bulletin boards (BBSs), newsgroups (covering thousands of topics, on each of which contributions are made), and electronic publishing (on-line versions of print journals). With each, transmission is nearly instantaneous, and between them they deal with sound, text, data and moving images, all in 'real time'. The Internet is largely free from state interference, governed by informal self-regulation and a libertarian ethos. Despite challenges by nation-states and commercial interests, at the time of writing there is little indication of success at regulation or marketization.

So what are the implications of the emergence of reasonably large-scale, popular, usage of the Internet? I shall make a couple of points briefly, and will discuss at greater length its implications for our notions of community. First, new CTs change ideas of distance – making some groups more accessible and, perhaps, others less so; they redefine our **sense of place**. But with the Internet space becomes not just shrunk but almost abolished – in that it becomes virtual. **Cyberspace** (a term coined by William Gibson in his sci-fi novel *Neuromancer* – and already showing signs of becoming less fashionable than it was) is interesting because it is notional space. A network of virtual sites is being superimposed on the world of physical places: people can now talk of 'meeting', in a communicative sense, yet the interaction is placeless – where connection takes place is not at any specific or known location. You can't say 'where' it is, and you can find things you want without knowing 'where' they are. You don't 'go to' a place, but you 'log in' to it from where you are. Space is no longer just physical or material. As an aside, it is interesting that, by contrast, metaphors of the net are, for the most part, spatial ('information superhighway', 'cyberspace').

Second, the Internet is acclaimed for offering new possibilities for experimenting with identities (Turkle, 1996). On the Internet, and particularly on Usenet, messages can be posted anonymously and psuedo-anonymously. Anonymity creates opportunities to invest in alternative versions of oneself and to engage in untried forms of interaction. Sadie Plant is a feminist who extols the virtues of **mutable identities**, claiming that 'off the shelf identity is an exciting new adventure' (1993, p. 16). Whereas social relations are based conventionally on largely fixed identities, on MUDs personalities can be more fragmented, and there is the possibility of constructing multiple identities.

The issue which we shall examine in greater depth is the capacity of the Internet to enable new forms of assembly and **community**. Howard Rheingold, a leader of the Californian counterculture, is perhaps the staunchest advocate of the capacity of the Internet to (re)establish community:

> People in virtual communities use words on screen to exchange pleasantries and argue, engage in intellectual discourse, conduct commerce, exchange knowledge, share emotional support, make plans, brainstorm, gossip, feud, fall in love, find friends and lose them, play games, flirt, create a little high art and a lot of idle talk. People in virtual communities do just about everything people do in real life, but we leave our bodies behind ... To the millions who have been drawn into it, the richness and vitality of computer-liked cultures is attractive, even addictive ... Virtual communities are social aggregations that emerge from the Net when enough people carry on [computer-mediated] public discussions long enough, with sufficient human feeling, to form webs of

sense of place

cyberspace

mutable identities

community

personal relationships in cyberspace ... these new media attract colonies of enthusiasts because CMC enables people to do things with each other in new ways, and to do altogether new kinds of things – just as telegraphs, telephones, and televisions did.

(Rheingold, 1994, pp. 3, 5–6)

Rheingold roots his argument firmly in the decayed state of modern community life, referring to the disintegration of traditional communities and the demise of public spaces: 'one of the explanations for this phenomenon is the hunger for community that grows in the breasts of people around the world as more and more informal public spaces disappear from our real lives' (ibid., p. 6). So Rheingold represents a technological variant of a long-standing theme – the decline of community. The technology, we are told, offers the utopia of interactivity, and can bridge the gaps caused by social separation and difference. To Rheingold, the net is the ultimate flowering of community, where individuals choose the community to which they belong: there is no longer any need to *create a new* place, merely to choose from the menu of those available. Steven Jones (1995) argues that this is a community like communities in the arts, communities of common *interest* rather than common location – and which are seen by participants as communities. In the net, argues Rheingold, we have 'access to a tool that could bring conviviality and understanding into our lives and might help revitalize the public sphere' (1994, p. 14).

The *public sphere* is a term developed by Jurgen Habermas (1989) (and you may recall the notion from Reading C of Chapter 4 above). It is the domain where public opinion can be formed, and is open to all. It is the place where people come together to form a public – dealing with matters of general interest and developing 'public opinion'. Free association, free assembly and freedom of expression are crucial if people are to govern themselves, and thus the public sphere is coterminous with democracy. According to Habermas, the public sphere has been replaced by a media which is *not* a forum for public opinion, by politicians working in soundbites, and by 'public relations'. With the Internet, however, Rheingold argues that we have the possibility of an *agora*, or forum, a revitalized public sphere.

So what are we to make of these claims? To begin, it seems pretty incontrovertible that with new ICTs we are seeing more and more distant flows of information – an exacerbation of a fairly established trend towards the shrinking of time and space. More than that, we are witnessing the development of new conceptions of 'presence' and (non)place. Physical place, however – despite the rhetoric of the protagonists of virtual reality – still exists (for most us!). More than this, a sense of place (as we have seen in Chapter 4 of this volume) remains central to identity in the contemporary era. Protagonists of the liberating capacity of the Internet in relation to identities have been criticized for suggesting that identities can be free-floating. Kevin Robins (1996) has argued that, whatever the seductions of the virtual world, they (and we) are still a part of the *real* world. It is quite remarkable how discussions of the Internet largely fail to engage with discussions of problems in contemporary culture – widening gaps of income and wealth, violence and crime, and the collapsing fabric of cities. It is extremely rarely that links are made with prevailing social movements and political activities, or institutions of civil society – which lends support to arguments that such interaction on the Internet is best seen as a technologically mediated leisure activity, rather than something more fundamental.

Communities on the Internet beg consideration of the relationship between on-line communities and communities as the term is commonly understood. The invocation of the term 'community' is perhaps unsurprising since, although it is a term with many meanings (Williams, 1976), all of these are positive. Most of them are about how an unchanging, bounded, harmonious and mythical state which, regrettably, is seen as in decline. But in discussion of communities on the Internet we find little reference to *conflict* – all too common in the real world (Robins, 1996) and acknowledged in sociological studies of communities (Bell and Newby, 1971). To the contrary, there is an implicit assumption that connection (or communication) automatically makes for shared meanings and community; further, that, almost by dint of being electronic, these new communities are democratic or egalitarian. Given the centrality of boundaries to communities (Cohen, 1982), it is ironic that the key to new communities is claimed to be the *breaking down* of boundaries. Crucially, however, we must remember that community – as commonly understood – is about very much more than shared interests, involving (normally) a shared history and everyday life.

So my argument here is that whilst we are seeing new forms of association on the Internet, these are better seen as continuities of the sorts of non-geographically based communities – of those with common interests – that have existed for a long time. One lesson we can learn from the telephone is that most telephone usage is about reinforcing existing face-to-face links, rather than establishing new ones. And the WELL (Whole Earth 'Lectronic Link), the focus of Rheingold's passion, is also a face-to-face, physically-based community (in Los Angeles): 'The WELL felt like an authentic community to me from the start because it was grounded in my everyday physical world' (Rheingold, 1994, p. 2).

Nor is involvement in the Internet that egalitarian or universal. Despite the rhetoric of openness, most of the world's population remains excluded – given the requirement for electricity, a computer and a telephone connection. And, although it can be argued that access is becoming more egalitarian – following the trajectories of earlier ICTs – users are probably about 75 per cent male, and the major usage is accessing pornography. The predominance of the English language, and the cost and charge structure of most countries' telephone systems also contribute to exclusion.

7   Conclusion

One thing which is quite clear is that most of the claims which are made about new technologies involve a pretty heavy dose of technological determinism. Technologies have probably *never* – and certainly never so quickly – had such dramatic cultural effects as are routinely claimed in relation to new ICTs today. Radio, television, colour television and the VCR all achieved high levels of household penetration; but that is no reason why new communications technologies – videodiscs, high definition television (HDTV), digital television or home computers – will do the same. Fragmentation may be replacing mass ownership, and it may well be that the technologies have to be transformed to become mass consumer goods. In this sense, the Internet – which by the time you read this may have been replaced by another technological fix for the problems of the late-modern era – is merely the latest in a long line of technologies for which similar claims have been made – virtual reality, multimedia, artificial intelligence and the information society. Despite the rhetoric of speed-up and implosion, we are left with powerful cultural continuities.

And, indeed, history would suggest that we treat these developments with caution. So many of the claims made for the Internet today are replicating debates which occurred at the time of the arrival of both electricity and the telephone: the technology then as now is invoked as a way of talking about an idealized vision of the future. Despite their exclusive ownership and usage, today's new technologies are presented as harbingers of utopia – just as claims were made that electricity would make society more democratic (Marvin, 1988).

Having said that, it is clear that the era of television as the hearth of the household has been replaced – by multiple television sets in households, VCR time-shifting of broadcasting, and of new ICTs including the Internet. The consumption of broadcasting, in the tradition of Lord Reith, first Director General of the BBC, in some ways united us as members of a community and nation. But with the Internet, cable and satellite television we are experiencing dispersal and fragmentation and even a shift from notions of the *mass* media (for further discussion of this issue, see **Thompson**, ed., 1997). With several hundred television channels, a range of on-line newspapers from which you can compile your own 'paper' of your chosen subjects or commentators, and publishing on the Internet, choice is vast (in some ways), and consumption patterns can become more varied, both reflecting and shaping social patternings, strengthening or weakening patterns of association and contributing to the fragmentation of communities and nations. New ICTs such as the Internet (or the camcorder) challenge the authority of the producer, democratize production capability, and empower consumers – again, showing us the inextricable links between production and consumption. Nor are these matters of interest only to students of culture: the consumption of ICTs is crucial to understanding innovation, diffusion and the take-up of these artefacts and products. The complex processes of technological development, organizational change and media regulation (see again **Thompson**, ed., 1997) are very much shaped by our everyday lives, domestic routines and consumption practices.

In the chapters of this book we have provided a series of case studies of consumption practices. In these we have drawn on a range of concepts and theories from debates on consumption. Specifically, it has been argued in each chapter for a balance between creativity and constraint; each has drawn out the interrelationship of consumption and production; and each has been examining some specific practices of everyday life. This focus on everyday life has drawn us to the ethnographic method; and also to the context of consumption – the home; and to place, or locality – which, as Nigel Thrift argues in Chapter 4 of this volume, remains so central to contemporary identities.

References

ANG, I. (1990) 'Culture and communication: towards an ethnographic critique of media consumption in the transnational media system', *European Journal of Communication*, Vol. 5, Nos 2/3, pp. 239–60.

BELL, C. and NEWBY, H. (1971) *Community Studies*, London, Allen and Unwin.

CELLNET (no date) *Mobile Manners: a guide to mobile etiquette in the '90s*, London, Cellnet.

COCKBURN, C. (1985) *Machinery of Dominance: women, men and technical know-how*, London, Pluto.

COHEN, A. P. (1982) *Belonging: identity and social organization in British rural cultures*, Manchester, Manchester University Press.

DONZELOT, J. (1980) *The Policing of Families*, London, Hutchinson.

DU GAY, P., HALL, S., JANES, L. MACKAY, H. and NEGUS, K. (1997) *Doing Cultural Studies: the story of the Sony Walkman*, London, Sage/The Open University (Book 1 in this series).

DU GAY, P. (ed.) (1997) *Production of Culture/Cultures of Production*, London, Sage/The Open University (Book 4 in this series).

ECO, U. (1972) 'Towards a semiotic inquiry into the television message', Working Papers in Cultural Studies No. 3, pp. 103–121, Birmingham, Centre for Contemporary Cultural Studies, University of Birmingham.

FISCHER, C. (1991) '"Touch someone": the telephone industry discovers sociability' in Lafollette, M. and Stine, J. (eds) *Technology and Choice: readings from technology and culture*, Chicago, IL, University of Chicago Press.

FURLONG, R. (1995) 'There's no place like home' in Lister, M. (ed.) *The Photographic Image in Digital Culture*, London, Routledge.

GERSHUNY, J. (1983) *Social Innovation and the Division of Labour*, Oxford, Oxford University Press.

GLEDHILL, C. (1997) 'Genre and gender: the case of soap opera' in Hall, S. (ed.).

GRAY, A. (1987) 'Behind closed doors: video recorders in the home' in Baehr, H. and Dyer, G. (eds) *Boxed In: women and television*, London, Pandora.

HABERMAS, J. (1989) *The Structural Transformation of the Public Sphere: an inquiry into a category of bourgeois society*, Cambridge, Polity (originally published in German, 1962).

HADDON, L. (1988a) 'The roots and early history of the British home computer market: origins of the masculine micro', PhD thesis, Imperial College, University of London.

HADDON, L. (1988b) 'Electronic and computer games: the history of an interactive medium', *Screen*, Vol. 29, No. 2, pp. 52–73.

HALL, S. (1980) 'Encoding/decoding' in Hall, S., Hobson, D., Lowe, A. and Willis, P. (eds) *Culture, Media, Language*, London, Hutchinson. (First published as 'Encoding and decoding in television discourse', Stencilled Paper 7, Centre for Contemporary Cultural Studies, University of Birmingham, 1973.)

HALL, S. (1997) 'The work of representation' in Hall, S. (ed.).

HALL, S. (ed.) (1997) *Representation: cultural representations and signifying practices*, London, Sage/The Open University (Book 2 in this series).

HOBSON, D. (1982) *'Crossroads': the drama of a soap opera*, London, Methuen.

JONES, S. G. (1995) 'Community in the Information Age' in Jones, S. G. (ed.) *Cybersociety: computer-mediated communication and community*, London, Sage.

KEEN, B. (1987) '"Play it again Sony": the double life of home video', *Science as Culture*, No. 1, pp. 7–42.

KEHOE, L. (1995) 'So how big is cyberspace?', *Financial Times,* 20 February.

KIDDER, T. (1982) *The Soul of a New Machine*, Harmondsworth, Penguin.

LULL, J. (ed.) (1988) *World Families Watch Television*, London, Sage.

MACKAY, H. (1995) 'Patterns of ownership of IT devices in the home' in Heap, N., Thomas, R., Einon, G., Mason, R. and Mackay, H. (eds) *Information Technology and Society*, London, Sage.

MACKENZIE, D. and WAJCMAN, J. (eds) (1985) *The Social Shaping of Technology*, Milton Keynes, Open University Press.

MARTIN, M. (1991) *"Hello Central?" Gender, technology and culture in the formation of telephone systems*, Montreal, McGill-Queen's University Press.

MARVIN, C. (1988) *When Old Technologies Were New: thinking about communications in the late nineteenth century*, Oxford, Oxford University Press.

MOORES, S. (1988) '"The box on the dresser": memories of early radio and everyday life', *Media, Culture and Society*, Vol. 10, No. 1, pp. 23–40.

MOORES, S. (1993) *Interpreting Audiences: the ethnography of media consumption*, London, Sage.

MORLEY, D. (1986) *Family Television: culture, power and domestic leisure*, London, Comedia.

MOYAL, A. (1992) 'The feminine culture of the telephone: people, patterns and policy', *Prometheus*, Vol. 7, No. 1, pp. 5–31.

NEGUS, K. (1997) 'The production of culturo' in du Gay, P. (ed.)

NOBLE, D. (1984) *Forces of Production*, New York, Alfred A. Knopf.

OAKLEY, A. (1974) *The Sociology of Housework*, London, Martin Robertson.

O'SULLIVAN, T. (1991) 'Television memories and cultures of viewing' in Corner, J. (ed.) *Popular Television in Britain: studies in cultural history*, London, BFI.

PAHL, R. (1984) *Divisions of Labour*, Oxford, Blackwell.

PLANT, S. (1993) 'Beyond the screens: film, cyberpunk and cyberfeminism', *Variant*, No. 14, pp. 12–17.

PLANT, S. (1996) 'On the matrix: cyberfeminist simulations' in Shields, R. (ed.) *Cultures of Internet: virtual spaces, real histories, living bodies*, London, Sage.

RAKOW, L. (1992) *Gender on the Line: women, the telephone and community life*, Urbana, IL, University of Illinois Press.

RHEINGOLD, H. (1994) *The Virtual Community*, London, Secker and Warburg.

ROBINS, K. (1996) 'Cyberspace and the world we live in' in *Into the Image: culture and politics in the field of vision*, London, Routledge.

ROBINS, K. (1997) 'What in the world's going on?' in du Gay, P. (ed.).

SAUNDERS, P. (1990) *A Nation of Home Owners*, London, Unwin Hyman.

SILVERSTONE, R. and MORLEY, D. (1990) 'Families and their technologies: two ethnographic portraits' in Putnam, T. and Newton, C. (eds) *Household Choices*, London, Futures Publications.

SILVERSTONE, R., HIRSCH, E. and MORLEY, D. (1992) 'Information and communication technologies and the moral economy of the household' in Silverstone, R. and Hirsch, E. (eds) *Consuming Technologies: media and information in domestic spaces*, London, Routledge.

SOLA POOL, I. DE (ed.) (1977) *The Social Impact of the Telephone*, Cambridge, MA, The MIT Press.

SPIGEL, L. (1992) *Make Room for TV: television and the family ideal in post-war America*, Chicago, IL, University of Chicago Press.

STANLEY, L. and WISE, S. (1979) 'Feminist research, feminist consciousness and experiences of sexism', *Women's Studies International Quarterly*, Vol. 2, pp. 359–74.

STORPER, M. and CHRISTOPHERSON, C. (1987) 'Flexible specialization and regional industrial agglomeration: the case of the US motion picture industry', *Annals of the Association of American Geographers*, Vol. 77, pp. 104–17.

THOMPSON, K. (ed.) (1997) *Media and Cultural Regulation*, London, Sage/The Open University (Book 6 in this series).

TOLES, T. (1985) 'Video games and American military ideology' in Mosco, V. and Wasko, J. (eds) *The Critical Communications Review, Volume 3: Popular Culture and Media Events*, New Jersey, Ablex.

TOMLINSON, A. (1990) 'Home fixtures: doing-it-yourself in a privatized world' in Tomlinson, A. (ed.) *Consumption, Identity and Style: marketing, meanings and the packaging of pleasure*, London, Routledge.

TURKLE, S. (1996) *Life on the Screen: identity in the Age of the Internet*, London, Weidenfeld and Nicolson.

WEBSTER, F. (1996) 'The Information Age: what's the big idea?', *Renewal*, Vol. 4, No. 1, pp. 15–22.

WILLIAMS, R. (1974) *Television: technology and cultural form*, London, Fontana.

WILLIAMS, R. (1976) *Keywords: a vocabulary of culture and society*, London, Fontana.

WILLIAMS, R. (1983) 'Culture and technology' in *Towards 2000*, London, Chatto and Windus.

WOOD, J. (1993) *Cellphones on the Clapham Omnibus: the lead-up to a cellular mass market*, SPRU CICT Report 11, Falmer, University of Sussex.

READING A:
Donald Mackenzie and Judy Wajcman, 'The social shaping of technology'

Introductory essay

[...] Technological change seems to have its own logic which we may perhaps protest about or even try to block, but which we appear to be unable to alter fundamentally.

When we turn to what social scientists have written about technology, we find a dominant approach that does little to share this way of looking at things. Social scientists have tended to concentrate on the 'effects' of technology, on the 'impact' of technological change on society. This is a perfectly valid concern, but it leaves a prior, and perhaps more important, question unasked and therefore unanswered. What has shaped the technology that is having 'effects'? What has caused and is causing the technological changes whose 'impact' we are experiencing?

[... W]e are interested in the *social* factors that shape technological change. To what extent, and how, does the kind of society we live in affect the kind of technology we produce? What role does society play in how the refrigerator got its hum, in why the light bulb is the way it is, in why nuclear missiles are designed the way they are?

[...]

Such a shift of focus is not without consequence. If our thinking centres on the effect of technology on society, then we will tend to pose questions like, 'How can society best adapt to changing technology?' We will take technological change as a given, as an independent factor, and think through our social actions as a range of (more or less) passive responses. If, alternatively, we focus on the effect of society on technology, then technology ceases to be an independent factor. Our technology becomes, like our economy or our political system, an aspect of the way we live socially. It becomes something whose changes are part of wider changes in the way we live. It even becomes something whose changes we might think of consciously shaping – though we must warn right at the beginning that to say that technology is socially shaped is not to say that it can necessarily be

altered easily. To draw an analogy, political systems clearly are shaped by the wider societies they are part of, but changing them is no simple business, no straightforward consequence of an individual or collective decision to try to change them.

[...]

Technological determinism

The single most influential theory of the relationship between technology and society is 'technological determinism'. This is the theory that technology is indeed an independent factor, and that changes in technology cause social changes. In its strongest version, the theory claims that change in technology is the most important cause of change in society.

According to technological determinism, technology impinges on society from outside of society. There is a parallel with nineteenth-century theories of 'climatic determinism', where it was said that the climate (an independent factor, over which societies had no influence) shaped the nature of society. Sometimes technological change may be seen as outside of society, in the same way as the weather is, as when a 'backward' society is affected by the superior technology of a more 'advanced' one with which it has come into contact. At other times, technology may be seen as outside society only metaphorically. The technologists who produce new technology are in this view indeed members of society, but their activity is in an important sense *independent* of their membership of society. In the most common version of technological determinism, these technologists are seen as 'applying science', as working out the practical implications of new scientific discoveries, and those scientific discoveries are seen simply as new, more accurate insights into natural reality. Scientists discover, technologists follow the logic of those discoveries in turning them into new techniques and new devices, and these techniques and devices are then introduced into society and have (often unpredicted) 'effects' – that is the most widespread account of how technology comes to be an independent factor.

So the first part of technological determinism is that technical change is in some sense *autonomous*, 'outside' of society, literally or metaphorically. The second part is that technical change *causes* social change. Sometimes the social changes referred to can be quite particular. Thus Ogburn and Nimkoff (1964, pp. 571–5) quote a list of no fewer than 150 suggested social effects of the radio in the United States, such as 'regional differences in culture become less pronounced'. The more dramatic versions of technological determinism, however, are those that see the entire form of a society as being conditioned by technology.

Some more futuristic commentators, such as Large (1980), claim this of the microchip. The microelectronic revolution, they claim, is *causing* a new form of society to emerge [...] It is the changes in technology that are bringing about the new 'leisure society', or 'post-industrial society'. Our human role is at best to choose the most civilised variant of this technologically determined new society.

Technological determinism is not always futuristic. It has also been employed as an historical theory, explaining why past forms of society came into being and passed away. While it would be an over-simplification to present his theory as a straightforward technological determinism, historian Lynn White's account of the coming about of feudal society reveals how a technologically determinist history can be constructed. By 'feudalism' he means a 'society dominated by an aristocracy of warriors endowed with land' (White, 1978, p. 38). He attributes the coming about of this society in Western Europe to the invention, and diffusion westwards, of the stirrup. Prior to the stirrup, fighting on horseback was limited by the risk of falling off. Swipe too vigorously with a sword, or lunge with a spear, and horse-borne warriors could find themselves lying ignominiously in the dust. Because the stirrup offered riders a much more secure position on the horse, it 'effectively welded horse and rider into a single fighting unit capable of a violence without precedent' (ibid., 2). But the 'mounted shock combat' it made possible was an expensive as well as an effective way of doing battle. It required intensive training, armour and war horses. It could be sustained only by a re-organisation of society designed specifically to support an élite of mounted warriors able and equipped to fight in this 'new and highly specialized way' (ibid., p. 30).

Does technology have 'effects'?

The example of the stirrup and feudalism, however, shows us the problems of the second aspect of technological determinism, the claim that technological change causes social change. Leaving aside issues of archaeological and historical evidence [...] we can immediately note a grave difficulty in seeing the stirrup as *the* cause of feudalism. White himself identifies it (1978, p. 28): 'a new device merely opens a door; it does not compel one to enter'. The device itself does not force societies to adopt it. We know of plenty of instances where technologies later judged useful or essential were not taken up, or at least were strongly resisted [...] *The characteristics of a society play a major part in deciding which technologies are adopted.* Once we admit this – and it is hard to see how it can justifiably be denied – technology begins to look rather less like a genuinely *independent* factor.

Even more damaging to a simple technological determinism is the fact that *the same technology can have very different 'effects' in different situations.* Amongst the Franks, the stirrup 'caused' feudalism. But it had no such effect in, say, Anglo-Saxon England prior to the Norman Conquest. There is nothing essentially mysterious about this. To explain why the creation of a feudal system was attempted, and to explain why it was possible, inevitably requires reference to a wider set of social conditions than military technology alone – the decline in European trade, which made land the only reliable source of wealth; the possibility (under some circumstances and not others) of seizing land for redistribution to feudal knights; and so on. Since these other conditions are not necessarily the same everywhere, it is not surprising that the stirrup did not everywhere have the same 'effects'. Indeed, it becomes difficult to see why technology should be singled out for special attention, rather than be treated as one condition amongst many others.

So the idea of technology having straightforward social 'effects' is altogether too simple. Assessing the effects on society of a given technology is an intensely difficult and problematic exercise, despite the apparent clarity of the question and the frequent desire of research sponsors to know its answer. Take one pressing example – the effect of the microchip on employment. It is relatively easy to guess what proportion of existing jobs could be automated away by present or prospective computer technology. But that is *not* the effect of the microchip on employment precisely because the question cannot justifiably be approached in isolation like this. To know the microchip's effect on employment levels, one needs to know the different rates at which it will be adopted in different locations, the likely siting and nature of the industries producing computer technology, the indirect economic effects of the creation and destruction of jobs, the likely role of trade union action and government policy, the interaction of all of these developments in one country with what goes on in other countries, the growth or decline, and changing patterns, of the world economy [...] In other words, answering the question of the effects on society of a particular technology requires one to have a good theory of how that society works. The simplicity of the question is misleading. Answering it properly will often require an understanding of the *overall* dynamics of a society, and it is thus one of the most difficult, rather than one of the easiest, questions to answer.

It would be terribly mistaken, however, to jump from the conclusion that technology's effects are not simple to the conclusion that technology has *no* effects [... Langdon Winner's] is one of the most thoughtful attempts to undermine the notion that technologies are in themselves inherently neutral – that all that matters is the way societies choose to use them. Technologies, he argues, can be inherently political. This is so, he says, in two senses. Technologies can be designed, consciously or unconsciously, to open certain social options and close others. Thus New York builder Robert Moses designed road systems to facilitate the travel of certain types of people and to hinder that of others. Secondly, he argues that not only are certain design features of technologies inherently political, but some technologies in their entirety are political. Even if it is mistaken to see technologies as *requiring* particular patterns of social relations to go along with them, some technologies are, in given social circumstances, *more compatible* with some social relations than with others. Hence, argues Winner, basing energy supply around a nuclear technology that requires plutonium may enhance pressure for stronger state surveillance to prevent

the theft of plutonium, and help erode traditional civil liberties.

Furthermore, the adoption of particular technologies is of long-term as well as immediate significance: technologies cannot always be traded in at will. Road and rail systems remain – and influence patterns of housing and industrial development – long after their designers are dead. A national electricity grid is a massive embodied investment that no society would lightly scrap – yet a national grid may well cause bias towards huge, centralised energy sources such as nuclear power rather than small-scale, local sources of solar or wind power. Adoption of nuclear energy now will leave generations to come in need of technologies for nuclear waste management, even if they have themselves abandoned nuclear power. Marx once wrote (Marx, 1968, p. 97) that people 'make their own history, but they do not make it just as they please; they do not make it under circumstances chosen by themselves, but under circumstances directly encountered, given and transmitted from the past'. Amongst the circumstances transmitted from the past is, often significantly, the technological legacy of previous generations.

References

LARGE, P. (1980) *The Micro Revolution*, London, Fontana.

MARX, K. (1968) 'The Eighteenth Brumaire of Louis Bonaparte', in Marx, K. and Engels, F., *Selected Works in One Volume*, London, Lawrence and Wishart.

OGBURN, W. F. and NIMKOFF, M. F. (1964) *A Handbook of Sociology*, London, Routledge and Kegan Paul.

WHITE, L. JR (1978) *Medieval Technology and Social Change*, New York, Oxford University Press. (First published in 1962.)

WINNER, L. (1977) *Autonomous Technology: technics out-of-control as a theme in political thought*, Cambridge, MA, The MIT Press.

Source: MacKenzie and Wajcman, 1985, pp. 2–3, 4–7.

READING B:
Roger Silverstone and David Morley, 'Families and their technologies: an ethnographic portrait'

The husband is 48 and the wife 46; they have 2 children, a boy aged 15 and a girl of 12. The husband is a self-employed consultant in the market research field; the wife works part-time as a sandwich maker and cleaner in the cafeteria in a local school. They own a small house in a slightly down-market area of suburban London. Both husband and wife left school at 15. Both vote Conservative.

They have three televisions: the one with the remote control is in their sitting room; the others are in the children's bedrooms. They have two computers: the son has a Sinclair in his room, and the father has an Amstrad with a printer which he uses for work in the front room; this is now converted into his office. There is video in the sitting room, and an electric cooker, a refrigerator, an electric kettle, a toaster, a radio and a microwave (as well as the wife's clock) in the kitchen. There is a washing machine and a spin drier in the utility room. The wife has an electric iron and a hair crimper. There are two phones: one in the sitting-room, one in the office. The son has a hi-fi system and a Walkman, as well as his computer and his computer games in his room, and the daughter also has a hi-fi, a radio and an under-used Walkman. They have a car which both husband and wife use.

[...]

[... T]he family is not well off and lacks the financial resources to engage in many forms of consumption. Thus, for instance, the children are encouraged to ensure that they mainly receive rather than make phone calls to their friends and the wife has put up on the wall a list of the cost per minute of calling the people they most often do phone. However it is not only a matter of money. The father in particular also expresses moral disapproval of various forms of consumption; and the controls exercised over telephone communication also relate to certain family rules about the boundaries and privacy of the household.

[...]

Boundaries: external and internal

In this family there is a stress on the importance of boundaries and control. Perhaps by way of compensation for his sense of lack of control over the outside world, the father, in particular, is very concerned to regulate the functions of communicative technologies in breaking the boundary between the private and public spheres. While there seemed to be a low level of integration (for the adults) in the neighbourhood at large, there was a high level of integration within the family (both in terms of visible expressions of closeness, and a low level of gender based separation in the parents' social life). The family displayed a common pattern, in which the effective family unit (for leisure purposes such as watching television) was mother and father and daughter, based in the sitting room, while the teenage son separated off – spending his time with his own technologies in his bedroom. However the degree of differentiation/separation between the son and the rest of the family was weaker than in some of the other families studied.

The family's concern with regulating the cost of phone calls has already been noted. However, while some part of the parents' anxieties are, no doubt economic, broader issues concerning their ability to control and supervise their children do also seem to arise in this connection. The parents are proud of the fact that their daughter, on the whole, receives calls from, rather than makes calls to her friends, and she asks permission before making a call out herself. However, they are deeply concerned about the stories they have read of teenagers using British Telecom's 'party lines', and running up huge bills for their parents to pay. They worry about leaving their children alone in the house for this reason and are anxious that the introduction of teleshopping facilities will exacerbate these temptations for their children. Similarly, they are concerned by the prospect of deregulated satellite broadcasting bringing pornographic or violent programming within their children's grasp: '(They) have sets in their rooms and (we) can't know what they're watching all the time.' So deregulation is not only a concern at the level of the disruption of national boundaries by transnational broadcasters – for this family at least it is a question of the fear of family boundaries being transgressed.

Their parents concern to regulate their children's use of information and communication technologies is powerfully symbolised by the 'umbilical' character of the electricity supply in this house: the only power point upstairs is in the parent's bedroom, from which wires are run into the children's rooms – and the children's electricity supply can thus be controlled directly by the parents. This, naturally, is a source of some tension, certainly for the son, since part of the attraction of watching television in his room is his sense of this as a relatively unpoliced/unsupervised activity.

The parents explain that they feel that they do need to 'supervise' their daughter's use of the phone, as noted earlier, but again this is perhaps not only an economic issue. It is also a question of parental resentment of their daughter's incoming calls, as an intrusion into their domestic privacy – as events threatening a potentially fragile boundary, which they feel some need to reinforce. Thus, the daughter explains that her father doesn't like her friends ringing her so much:

> Because lots of people go too far ... some of my friends do funny phone calls ... They ... dial your number and when you answer they start laughing ... they do raspberries down the phone and my Dad doesn't like it.

Unlike the majority of the families studied, where it is the wife who uses the phone most, as a psychic life-line to alleviate her sense of isolation, the pattern is different in this family. Here the wife feels less need to use the phone in this way for her own purposes, as she goes out to work herself. In fact she principally uses the phone as the medium for discharging what she sees as her familial obligations of keeping in touch both with her and her husband's kin. Even this has been a source of some tension: the list of telephone costs on the wall arose as a result of an occasion when her husband felt she spent 'too long' on the phone when speaking to his sister.

In this family it is the husband who uses the phone most, for business purposes, as he works from home. He insists, however, on a strictly limited

definition of the phone – as a 'tool' for necessary contact 'passing information back and forth'. And even then, he mistrusts the phone 'because it's so much easier to lie over the phone than it is face to face.' Beyond that, he regards it as 'an intrusion, it gets in the way ... the phone rings when you don't want it to ring.' For this man the maintenance of internal boundaries is also important. Thus he explains that he 'wouldn't have a telephone in the bedroom ... unless someone was ill'.

Technology and control

[...]

[...] To some large extent [the husband] blames his own current economic difficulties on technology, given that he sees his own cultural capital as having been devalued and replaced by computerised information systems in the company for which he worked. Thus his present position of insecure freelance employment has had powerful consequences on the family in two senses. Not only has it simply reduced their overall standard of living – technology has also been constructed within this family's mythology as an inherently problematic and contradictory force.

He distinguishes strongly between the (positive) potential of technology and it's [sic] regressive uses. Indeed he has a distinct interest in communications technologies in themselves. So, not only has he mastered the operational use of his home computer (which he needs for his work) but he literally experiments with the family's microwave (putting different things in for different periods of time to 'see what happens to them'). However the computer is an object of great ambivalence for him: while he has mastered it for his own purposes he cannot communicate his mastery to other professionals in the field. He has a 'one-sided' form of mastery of technology in which he has not learnt to externalise his knowledge and skills by acquiring the appropriate professional vocabulary and thus has trouble gaining external recognition of his abilities.

[...]

[...] He is very concerned about the ways in which technology 'has now taken over', and has dehumanised skills of various sorts, destroyed crafts and skills by its 'mechanical or logical' methods, 'once it's all been taken away from people and put in machines'. This, for him, is perhaps best symbolised by the telephone answering machine. He will not leave messages on these machines, because it seems unnatural and improper to him that he should have to 'talk to the stupid machine ... I don't like that robot type of thing ... it's too impersonal.'

This man frequently expresses a distinctly fearful attitude towards the possibility of large organisations manipulating technology to take advantage of the individual in the same way. In a general sense, he is fearful of the potential of information and communication technologies for disembedding information from a human context. This fear of a 'loss of control' concerns him greatly. So, he refuses to have a PIN number because of the danger of someone else using it and leaving him responsible for the bill. He is deeply anxious about the possibility of errors in British Telecom's 'System X' leading to the family being wrongly billed for phone calls they haven't made. He is anxious about the misuse of personal data by the police and other agencies, 'Well it's on computers, so [sic – RS/DM] sooner or later it's going to be misused' – an attitude which is meshed in with a fundamental view of the incompetent and corrupt nature of most large institutions. He is basically concerned that with 'the electronic thing, nothing's really secure any more' and is fearful of computer hackers because 'there's always somebody who will find a way of getting through' and thus 'they' may, in his worst fears, end up being able to know 'exactly what is in your head'.

[...]

The organisation of familial domains: space, gender, generation

[... I]t is clear that, within the home, the mother has responsibilities for a clear set of concerns. Thus, by way of dealing with their precarious financial position, she keeps the family finances in a set of books. It is she who knows all the names, ages and birthdays of her and her husband's kin and she who takes responsibility for managing kin relations – principally via the telephone. Indeed this is the principle [sic] significance of the phone for her – as a way of conveying and receiving 'family news' and as a way of keeping tabs on her children (she

requires them to phone her to let her know what they are doing, if they are out late or otherwise have departed from their normal routines).

On the whole, she displays a fairly passive and accommodative attitude to their household information and communication technologies [...] When her son is playing loud music in his room, her response is to 'want to disappear somewhere where you couldn't hear it'. Even her sense of her own pleasure in watching television ('I like all the soaps of course, though I know, deep down it's a lot of drivel') is expressed not only guiltily but also passively. Thus, what she likes about television is 'it makes me sit down and relax ... I stop thinking about what I've got to do, the next job.' She does, of course, have her own domain, the kitchen, and there the radio is tuned to Capital – which is her preferred station. Thus, within her own domain she can exercise a degree of choice. However, she does not only have her own physical domain, she also has her own organisation of time. In the kitchen she has her 'private clock', which she keeps 15–20 minutes fast 'so I'm always early and ... can have some time for myself.'

[... T]he son spends most of his time in his own room, utilising the collection of technologies which he has bought (with money earned from his Saturday job) and installed there (a pattern which is replicated in several of our families).

His mother refers to his room as 'his womb' and it certainly seems to function as a significant retreat for him. Here he can stay up late watching TV (and possibly watching his preferred form of 'action movies', of which his parents disapprove). In the room he has a computer, a hi-fi, a TV and he is saving for a video. He and his friends are very interested in technology. He spends school lunch times at a friend's house playing video games. They often visit consumer electronic shops just to see 'what's new', they read consumer electronic catalogues like magazines, and will go to W.H. Smiths just to browse through the computer magazines. The son is heavily dependent on technology to offer him a sense of 'something going on', preferably in the form of music (or, as his mother puts it, 'noise'). He says that he 'can't work without it ... I like music, I don't like sitting and being dull. If I'm in my bedroom and it's all quiet, it feels like school and it depresses me.'

He wears his Walkman whenever he leaves the house and takes it to school. He remarks that his classmates 'reckon my Walkman is my life-support system.' He says that he does 'feel lost without it ... it just feels like I'm not all there ... As soon as I run out of batteries I'm down the shop, even if I've only got a pound left.' The other technology on which he is quite dependent is his Swatch: 'If my watch broke down I wouldn't know what to do ... my other watch kept breaking, It was hopeless – I had to find people (at school) who had watches to walk around with ...'

Despite their contradictory attitudes towards technology the parents encourage their children's acquisition of information and communication technologies – both for rather undefined educational purposes and as training in budgeting/saving. This works well with their son, but fails with their daughter. Her brother would be willing to give her his old equipment, as hand-me-downs when he upgrades his systems, but his father insists that she should save up and buy them from him. However the daughter, along with many teenage girls, is more interested in buying clothes and other such 'frivolous' things. Indeed, her very investment in femininity is at odds with the attitudes that would be required to engage more seriously with ICT (cf. McRobbie and Garber, 1976; Turkle, 1988). In fact the daughter is both much less dependent on technology than her brother ('I plug in less than he does') and less concerned to differentiate herself from her parents by demarcating her own private space within the house.

Gendered technologies and technological competence/confidence

The contrasts in attitudes towards different technologies displayed by the mother and the son in the family are perhaps the most revealing. The boy is positively disdainful of computers – as mere tools which he feels well able to master:

> A computer's dumb, isn't it ... you've got to tell it what to do ... it doesn't know what to do until you load something in to it ... say you programmed it to wash dishes, and then put it in front of a car ... it would wash an area the size of a dish ... or just look at it and say ... that's not the object I've been told to wash.

Given this attitude, he has no particular fear of 'technical breakdowns' – 'I just do things as I do them, and if it goes wrong, it goes wrong' – which doesn't bother him, given his basic confidence in his ability to 'figure it out'. On the other hand, the son cannot operate the washing machine, and is frightened of 'touching the cooker', although he will now use the microwave because 'it's safer ... because it's a closed unit.'

Conversely, his mother, while being the only member of the household who can operate the washing machine, cannot operate the video and is positively frightened of the computer. She has a very basic fear of uncontrollable technological muddles, with 'everything all wrong, twisted around; what do I do, where do I go?' She explains that she's 'not confident' with the computer 'it makes me feel uneasy, I'm afraid that if I touch a button I shouldn't, everything will go haywire ... if I touch one button it will all go wrong, that's the way I feel.' She is quite uninterested in the computer: 'it does completely nothing for me. The only time I use it is if (her husband) wants me to do something ...'

[...]

Technological inheritances

Within families, of course there are many forms of gender-based learning. Thus [...] the son's desire for the 'real thrill' of riding a motorbike is perhaps not unrelated to his father's claim that a cut-throat razor is really 'the only way to shave.' However, beyond this level of quite banal and predictable (though nonetheless powerful) form of learning of the appropriate forms and symbols of gender identity, we can also identify some interesting processes, when we look at the technological inheritance of attitudes and competences from father to son, within this family.

We have already noted the son's easy confidence with his ability to 'figure out' technologies. The further point is that, in this, he takes a very much more 'adventurous' attitude than does his father. Indeed, he is quite (humorously) scornful of his father's 'logical' approach – 'you'd read the manual', he says, when asked by his father what he would do when confronted with an unknown machine or problem. For him, on the contrary it is a matter of pride to 'figure it out' for himself without reference to any 'manual'. His attitude is that:

> you've got to work around ... and just try to work it out, without reading the instructions ... press the buttons and work it out from there ... work them out by using them ... I never read the instructions ... I'd rather figure it out for myself.

In one sense, this can be seen as an advance in confidence in relation to technology in the part of this young man, as compared with his father. But inheritances are complex equations, and his seeming bravado takes on another meaning if we note also that he 'hates reading' and is 'not very good at spelling' – which means that using the manual (or indeed the dictionary) is not, in fact, an easy option for him. Which perhaps takes us back to the disjunction between his father's practical/operational skill and his own lack of communicative/linguistic skills. Perhaps this young man has inherited not only a certain interest in, and operational ability, with technology, but much more precisely a rather narrow and specifically limited operational form of technological competence.

References

MCROBBIE, A. and GARBER, J. (1976) 'Girls and subcultures' in Clare, J. et al. (eds) *Resistance through Rituals*, London, Hutchinson.

TURKLE, S. (1988) 'Computational reticence: why women fear the intimate machine' in Kramarae, C. (ed.) *Technology and Women's Voices*, London, Routledge.

Source: Silverstone and Morley, 1990, pp. 74–9.

READING C:
Hugh Mackay: 'Patterns of ownership of IT devices in the home: the home computer'

The home computer arrived at about the same time as the VCR; but has subsequently achieved a far lower penetration. [...]

The market grew faster during the period 1985–88, after which sales for educational purposes declined (it became apparent that they were used mainly for games playing) and sales shifted to more upmarket, business style, PCs. Falling prices contributed crucially to this shift, as a business machine became available at a price affordable to most households. The shift of games from general purpose machines to dedicated consoles (see below) further slowed the growth, whilst developing use of Midi, for music, has led to an increased demand. The home computer market can be seen in terms of three key segments.

Together, these lead to an ownership level of 19.1%, or 34%, depending on whose data one is using (Tables 6C.1 and 6C.2).

Mintel (1994a) come up with rather higher figures than 'Family Spending' (Table 6C.3); most recently, Mintel reported a 30% ownership level in 1993 (Mintel 1994b). Mintel's figures also show considerable trading up as a proportion of sales: of 2.5m sales in 1991, 2.4m were replacements or additions, and only 0.2m first purchases.

Behind these overall figures lie sharp distinctions between social classes (Tables 6C.4 and 6C.5) and age groups (Table 6C.5). Whereas the economically inactive have a 7% level of ownership of a home computer, the professional class has a 52% level. Regarding age, ownership is highest in the 15–19 year old age bracket, then the 35–44 bracket, with other age bands roughly the same except for a rapid drop of ownership level in those age 55+. Regarding regional differences, Harlech and TSW television areas have the highest ownership levels and the Granada area the lowest. The differences between men and women are greater than with television or VCR ownership.

The future market depends on a number of factors: first, the recovery from the recession. The home computer is becoming a part of the broader brown (i.e. leisure, as opposed to white, utility) goods industry. Second, it depends on demography: whilst the number of 5–14 year-olds will grow up to the end of the millennium, the number of 15–24 year-olds will decline. The growth of 'empty nesters' – adults aged 45+ whose children have left home – is likely to be important; they may take up computing for a hobby, or purchase computers for their grandchildren. Third, prices affect levels of consumption – and they have been falling quite dramatically. Apple Computers is reported reckoning that 7m US families can afford to purchase a home computer but have not, so far, done so (Kehoe, 1992a). As global sales of computers are falling, the home becomes an increasingly important target market (Kehoe, 1992b). Fourth, the market is stimulated by a new generation or model of hardware, new processors, for example, render older machines obsolete. Finally, the uses to which home computers are put will affect the size of the market. For example, the home computer *could* become the focus of the centre of home leisure/entertainment technologies, interfacing with the telephone system (e.g. for working at home, banking, shopping and film watching), CD players (for holiday snaps as well as interactive multimedia applications – for education and entertainment), infrastructure controls, etc. [...]

Turning to use, there are three main reasons for ownership: first, to play games, which remains the key to the market, though with declining importance. Second is the business role, which has declined due to the recession; homeworking levels depend on a broad range of external factors. Third is the computer education of children, which parents have become less committed to as the use of computers by children has been shown to be for games.

Similar data which uses respondents' age in addition shows that the games motive is strongest for the youngest consumers, showing that it is the main motivation of children and young adults to have a home computer. The educational motive is strongest among the 25–44 age group – in other words, parents views' differ from those of children. The main users of computers for business purposes are ABs and those aged 20–24.

References

KEHOE, L. (1992a) 'Technology: computers on the home front – technically speaking', *Financial Times,* 22 September, p. 11.

KEHOE, L. (1992b) 'International company news: first global decline in sales of computers', *Financial Times,* 21 January, p. 4.

MINTEL (1994a) *On Line* (on line marketing database).

MINTEL (1994b) 'British lifestyles', reported in *The Guardian,* 1 February 1994.

Source: Mackay, 1995.

TABLE 6C.1 Segmentation of home computer market, by volume and value, 1989–91

	1989		1990		1991		% change by volume
	(000)	£m	000	£m	000	£m	1989–91
Games-based machines	270	28	220	27	181	20	–33
Home computers	362	157	527	226	545	215	+51
Business computers	118	115	153	147	149	125	+26
Total	750	300	900	400	875	360	+17

Source: Mintel, 1994a.

TABLE 6C.2   Availability in households of home computer

	%
1985	12.6
1986	15.1
1987	16.6
1988	16.9
1989	16.6
1990	16.8
1991	18.1
1992	19.1

Source: *Annual Abstract of Statistics*, 1993, Table 15.4: Family Spending 1992.

TABLE 6C.3   Number of adults with home computer, 1985–91 (year ending March)
(Base: approx 25,000 adults)

	% of adults	Installed base (000)	Net addition to base (000)
1985	14.7	6,351	–
1988	28.7	12,878	+6,527
1989	29.7	13,400	+522
1990	30.0	13,559	+159
1991	30.4	13,731	+172

Source: TGI, BMRB 1985–91 cited by Mintel, 1994a.

TABLE 6C.4   Households with home computer: by socio-economic group of head, 1992

	%
Professional	52
Employers and managers	41
Other non-manual	33
Skilled manual	27
Unskilled manual	21
All economically active	33
Economically inactive	7
All heads of household	23

Source: General Household Survey, cited in *Social Trends*, 1994.

TABLE 6C.5   Home computer owners, demographic detail, April 1992
(Base: 1,121 adults)

		Owner (%)
All		32
Gender	Men	37
	Women	27
Age	15–19	59
	20–24	32
	25–34	34
	35–44	54
	45–54	35
	55–64	13
	65+	6
Socio-economic group	AB	44
	C1	35
	C2	30
	D	30
	E	17
TV areas	London/TVS	33
	Anglia/Central	30
	Harlech/TSW	38
	Yorkshire/Tyne Tees	32
	Granada	26
	Scotland	30
Family status	Children	55
	No children	19

Source: BMRB cited by Mintel, 1994a.

TABLE 6C.6 Percentage of households with home computer, 1992

All households	19.1

Household weekly income		Household composition	
Under £60	4.7	Households with:	
£60 and under £80	3.4	One adult	
£80 and under £100	6.5	Retired, mainly dependent on state pension	0.4
£100 and under £130	8.3	Other retired	1.8
£130 and under £160	8.8	Non-retired	10.8
£160 and under £200	12.5	One adult, one child	16.4
£200 and under £240	14.7	One adult, two or more children	29.7
£240 and under £280	17.8	One man, one woman	
£280 and under £320	16.3	Retired, mainly dependent on state pension	–
£320 and under £370	22.4	Other retired	4.8
£370 and under £420	23.3	Non-retired	16.1
£420 and under £470	26.1	One man, one woman, one child	29.2
£470 and under £540	29.1	One man, one woman, two children	43.7
£540 and under £640	34.6	One man, one woman, three children	45.5
£640 and under £800	36.9	Two adults, four or more children	40.7
£800 and more	43.9	Three adults, one or more children	38.4

Tenure of dwelling			
Rented unfurnished	10.6	Rented furnished	19.7
Local authority	10.0	Rent free	15.4
Housing association	12.2	Owner occupied	22.9
Other	12.4		

Source: Family Spending 1992,

TABLE 6C.7 The main use for a home computer, 1985–92 (percentage) (Base: approx. 1,000 adults)

	1985	1987	1990	1992
To play computer games	57	64	16	34
For children to learn computing	31	18	46	31
For business purposes	6	11	21	15
For adults to learn computing	19	10	6	4
For managing family finances	1	4	5	3
Other reasons	8	7	2	3
Don't know	15	2	7	10

Source: BMRB/Mintel, Market Intelligence, August 1992, p. 21.

Acknowledgements

Grateful acknowledgement is made to the following sources for permission to reproduce material in this book:

Cover

(Upper image): Elizabeth Whiting Associates; *(lower image)* Barbara Smith.

Chapter 1

Text

Reading A: Gullestad, M. (1992) *The Art of Social Relations*, Scandinavian University Press; *Reading B:* Drakulic, S. *(1992) How We Survived Communism and Even Laughed*, W. W. Norton and Co Inc; *Reading C:* Gillespie, M. (1995) *Television, Ethnicity and Cultural Change*, Routledge; *Reading D:* Wilk, R. (1995) 'Learning to be local in Belize: global systems of common difference', in Miller, D. (ed.) *Worlds Apart: modernity through the prism of the local*, Routledge; *Reading E:* George, S. and Sabelli, F. (1994) *Faith and Credit: the World Bank's secular empire*, pp. 61–62, 64, 65, 72, Penguin Books, Copyright © Susan George and Fabrizio Sabelli, 1994. Reproduced by permission of Penguin Books Ltd. Also by permission of Boulder Press, Colorado.

Figures

Figures 1.1, 1.2, 1.3, 1.4, 1.5: courtesy of Daniel Miller.

Chapter 2

Reading A: Bruner, J. (1987) 'Life as narrative', *Social Research*, Vol. 54, New School for Social Research.

Chapter 3

Text

Reading A: Becker, H. S. (1982) *Art Worlds*, University of California Press. Copyright © 1982 The Regents of the University of California; *Reading B:* Frith, S. (1988) *Music for Pleasure: Essays in the Sociology of Pop*, Polity Press.

Figures

Figure 3.2: Ian Fraser; *Figure 3.4:* Vivien Bayley; *Reading A: Figure 1:* Asian Art Museum of San Francisco, the Avery Brundage Collection; *Figure 2:* Drawings by Nan Becker.

Chapter 4

Text

Reading A: Massey, D. (1995) 'Making spaces or, geography is political too', *Soundings*, No. 1, Autumn 1995, Lawrence and Wishart Ltd; *Reading B:* Iyer, P., 'Where worlds collide', Copyright © 1995 by *Harper's Magazine*. All rights reserved. Reproduced from the August issue by special permission; *Reading C:* Thompson, J. (1995) *The Media and Modernity: a social theory of the media*, Blackwell Publishers Ltd. Reprinted from *The Media and Modernity: a social theory of the media* by John B. Thompson with the permission of the publishers Stanford University Press. © 1995 by John B. Thompson.

Figures

Figure 4.1: Higgins, A. (1996) 'Tremors hinder quake rescue', *The Guardian*, 5 February 1996, © The Guardian; *Figure 4.4:* Ingold, T. (1980) *Hunters, Pastoralists and Ranchers: reindeer economies and their transformations*, Cambridge University Press; *Figure 4.5 (top):* J. Schefferus, *The History of Lapland, wherein are shewed the original, manners, habits, etc. of that people*, Oxford, 1674; *Figure 4.5 (bottom):* © NTB (AS Norsk Telegrambyrå); *Figure 4.6:* Bradley, D. J. (1988) 'The scope of travel medicine', in Steffen, R. et al. (eds) *Travel Medicine*, pp. 2–3, Springer-Verlag GmbH & Co. KG; *Figure 4.7:* NRSC Ltd/Science Photo Library; *Figure 4.8:* Penn State University; *Figure 4.9:* NASA/Science Photo Library; *Figure 4.10:* web pages written for Finfo (Finland Information), the Information Service Unit of the Department for Press and Cultural Affairs at the Ministry for Foreign Affairs of Finland © 1997; *Figure 4.11:* (above) Superlative Travel, (right) Reproduced from *Geographical Magazine*, March 1996; *Figure 4.12:* © NTB (AS Norsk Telegrambyrå).

Chapter 5

Text

Reading A: The William Alanson White Psychiatric Foundation, Inc for 'Mass communication and para-social interaction', by Donald Horton and Richard Wohl from *Psychiatry*, Vol. 19, (1956), pp. 215–29, reprinted by special permission of and © renewed 1984 by The William Alanson White Psychiatric Foundation, Inc; *Reading B:* Ang, I. (1991) *Desperately Seeking the Audience*, Routledge, © 1991 Ien Ang; *Reading C:* Morley, D. (1988) 'The framework of family viewing in Great Britain', in Lull, J. (ed) *World Families Watch TV*, pp. 34–8, 41–2, copyright © 1988 by Sage Publications, Inc. Reprinted by permission of Sage Publications, Inc; *Reading D:* Moores, S. (1996) *Satellite Television and Everyday Life: articulating technology*, John Libbey Media at the University of Luton Press.

Figures

Figure 5.1: ITN; *Figure 5.2:* Granada Television Ltd; *Figure 5.3:* London Weekend Television; *Figure 5.4:* Granada Television Ltd. With thanks to Barbara Knox and Thelma Barlow.

Chapter 6

Text

Reading A: MacKenzie, D. and Wajcman, J. (1985) *The Social Shaping of Technology*, Open University Press; *Reading B:* Silverstone, R. and Morley, D. 'Families and their technologies: two ethnographic portraits', in Putnam, T. and Newton, C. (eds) *Household Choices*, © Middlesex Polytechnic and Futures Publications Limited; *Reading C:* Mackay, H. (1995) 'Patterns of ownership of IT devices in the home: the home computer', in Heap, N. et al. (eds) *Information, Technology and Society*, Sage Publications Ltd.

Figures

Figure 6.1: BT Corporate Picture Library. ND Comtec Integrated Publishing Systems.

Cartoons

pp. 275, 281: David Haldane/Telecom Securicor Cellular Radio Limited.

Every effort has been made to trace all copyright owners, but if any have been inadvertently overlooked, the publishers will be pleased to make the necessary arrangements at the first opportunity.

Index